The
STRUGGLE FOR LAND
and the
FATE OF THE FORESTS

The
STRUGGLE FOR LAND
and the
FATE OF THE FORESTS

Edited by

Marcus Colchester & Larry Lohmann

The World Rainforest Movement

———

The Ecologist

———

Zed Books

Sections of this report may be reproduced in magazines and newspapers provided that acknowledgement is made to the authors and the World Rainforest Movement.
This book has been produced with the assistance of Novib, Oxfam (UK) and the International Development Research Centre of Canada. Special thanks are due to Nicholas Hildyard of *The Ecologist* and Dorothy Jackson of the World Rainforest Movement for their tireless editorial assistance.

Second impression, 1995.

Published by the World Rainforest Movement, 228 Macalister Road,10400 Penang, Malaysia, with *The Ecologist*, Agriculture House, Bath Road, Sturminster Newton, Dorset, DT10 1DU, England and Zed Books Ltd, 7 Cynthia Street, London N1 9JF, England and 165 First Avenue, Atlantic Highlands, New Jersey 07716, USA, in 1993.
Printed by Jutaprint, 54 Kajang Road, 10150 Penang, Malaysia.
Copyright World Rainforest Movement 1993
Cover: Andrew Corbett
Photo: Max Fulcher/Still Pictures
ISBN Pb 1 85649 140 4   ISBN Hb 1 85649 139 0

CONTENTS

PART THREE: CONCLUSIONS

ACRONYMS

ALRO	Agricultural Land Reform Office, Thailand
ANGOC	Asian NGO Coalition for Agrarian Reform and Rural Development
ASS	Anti-Slavery Society (now Anti-Slavery International)
CACIF	Guatemalan Chamber of Commerce
CCCIL	*Collected Commentary and Cases on Indonesian Law*
CDPV	Centro de Documentacao e Pesquisa Vergueiro, Sao Paulo
CEDI	Centro Ecumenico de Documentacao e Informacao, Sao Paulo
CEG	Conferencia Episcopal de Guatemala
CERJ	Runujel Junan Council of Ethnic Communities
CIA	Central Intelligence Agency, USA
CIDA	Canadian International Development Agency
CNS	Conselho Nacional dos Seringueiros, Brazil
CSE	Centre for Science and Environment, India
CPT	Comissao Pastoral da Terra, Brazil
CPT	Communist Party of Thailand
CUC	Comite de Unidad Campesina, Guatemala
DIGEBOS	Directiva General de Bosques
DTE	Down to Earth (International Campaign for Ecological Justice in Indonesia)
DUPs	Directly unproductive profit-seeking activities
EC	European Community
EEC	European Economic Community
EMB	Environmental Management Board, Philippines
EMBRAPA	Brazilian Ministry of Agriculture
EPOCA	Environmental Programme for Central America
FAO	Food and Agriculture Organisation of the United Nations

FDN	Fundacion Defensores de la Naturaleza, Guatemala
FYDEP	Empresa Nacional del Fomento y Desarollo Economico del Peten, Guatemala
GDP	Gross Domestic Product
GTZ	Gesellschaft fur Technische Zusammenarbeit
IAN	Instituto Agrario Nacional
ICATA	Instituto de Ciencias Ambientales y Tecnologia Agricola, Guatemala
ICIHI	Independent Commission on International Humanitarian Issues
ILO	International Labour Organisation
INCRA	Institute of Agrarian Reform, Brazil
INPE	Brazilian Institute for Space Studies
INSAN	Institute of Social Analysis
INTA	Guatemalan Government Agrarian Transformation Institute
IPEA	Brazilian Institute of Economic Analysis
ITTO	International Tropical Timber Organisation
IUCN	International Union for the Conservation of Nature and Natural Resources
IWGIA	International Work Group for Indigenous Affairs
KMP	Kilusang Magbubukid ng Pilipinas (Peasants' Federation of the Philippines)
MPR	Mouvement Populaire de la Revolution, Zaire
MST	Movimento dos Trabalhadores Rurais Sem Terra, Brazil
NGO	Non-Governmental Organisation
NRF	National Reserve Forests, Thailand
PAFG	Plan de Accion Forestal para Guatemala
PANAMIN	Presidential Assistant for National Minorities
PER	Project for Ecological Recovery, Thailand
RFD	Royal Forest Department, Thailand
RIC	Rainforest Information Centre, Australia
SAM	Sahabat Alam Malaysia
SKEPHI	Indonesian Network on Forest Conservation
STRs	Sindicatos dos Trabalhadores Rurais

SUDAM	Superintendency of Amazonia
SWDC	State Watershed Development Cell, Bangalore
TABAK	Indigenous Peoples' Support Group (Philippines)
TAPOL	Indonesian Human Rights Campaign
TFAP	Tropical Forestry Action Plan
UDR	Union of Democratic Ruralists ("The Ranchers' Union"), Brazil
UFCO	United Fruit Company
UN	United Nations
UNDP	United Nations Development Programme
UNEP	United Nations Environment Programme
UNICEF	United Nations Childrens Fund
USAID	United States Agency for International Development
UNRISD	United Nations Research Institute for Social Development
UNCED	United Nations Conference on Environment and Development
WCARRD	World Conference on Agrarian Reform and Rural Development
WCED	World Commission on Environment and Development
WOLA	Washington Office on Latin America
WRI	World Resources Institute
WRM	World Rainforest Movement

PART ONE:

INTRODUCING THE ISSUES

COLONIZING THE RAINFORESTS: THE AGENTS AND CAUSES OF DEFORESTATION

MARCUS COLCHESTER

Historical patterns of development that have led to skewed land distribution underlie many of the problems forestry faces today. Thus, any discussion of solutions to tropical deforestation should address this issue. Strong political commitment by national governments to pursue land reform policies that would lead to more equitable land ownership would, in the short term, do more to relieve pressure on forest lands than any other single policy intervention or any conceivable level of investment in forest resource development.

John Spears and Edward Ayensu
The Global Possible, 1984

RATES OF FOREST LOSS

The world's tropical forests are disappearing faster than ever. Every succeeding study shows a startling acceleration of the process. For many years the baseline figures accepted for rates of deforestation were those prepared by the Food and Agriculture Organization (FAO) in 1980. The study demonstrated that, globally, deforestation was proceeding at some 114,000 square kilometres per year (FAO 1980).

More recent studies show that forest loss is speeding up. According to Norman Myers, in a study completed for Friends of the Earth, some 142,000 square kilometres of tropical forests were destroyed in 1989, and a further 200,000 square kilometres were seriously degraded. Myers estimated that forest loss had increased by 90% since 1979, while the three countries which account for half the world's tropical forests, Brazil, Zaire and Indonesia, also accounted for nearly half the annual loss (Myers 1989). Interim results from a new study being carried out by FAO, which is due out in 1992, place the global rate even higher, at some 170,000 square kilometres per year (FAO 1990). According to the FAO, rates of forest loss have increased by 54% over the past decade. A study by the World Resources Institute suggests that the total figure could be higher still, as much as 204,000 square kilometres annually (WRI 1990).

Regionally, deforestation has speeded up even further. In Central Africa, in the Caribbean and in South-East Asia rates of forest loss have surged ahead even of this dismaying global average increase (WRI 1992:285). At the same time, areas that three years ago had seemed likely to remain forested for longer — like Papua New Guinea, Western Amazonia, Guyana and the Zaire basin — are now facing a massive acceleration of logging and road-building (Marshall 1990; Monbiot 1991; Colchester 1991; Witte this volume; *BBC Wildlife* May 1992).

All these estimates have been subject to criticism: definitions of deforestation vary; data are imprecise and open to different interpretations; rates of forest loss fluctuate in any one country, sometimes massively, from one year to the next. Yet, while the data may be disputed, the overall trend is unmistakable: the area of the planet under tropical forests is rapidly decreasing. Many tropical countries face the almost complete elimination of natural forest cover by the end of the century. Few countries will have any substantial tracts of moist tropical forest left by the middle of the next century, if present trends continue.

UNDERLYING CAUSES

Why this massive loss of forests? If studies have disagreed about the rates of deforestation, they have found even less agreement about exactly why it is happening. This is not so much because the immediate causes of deforestation have been hard to determine

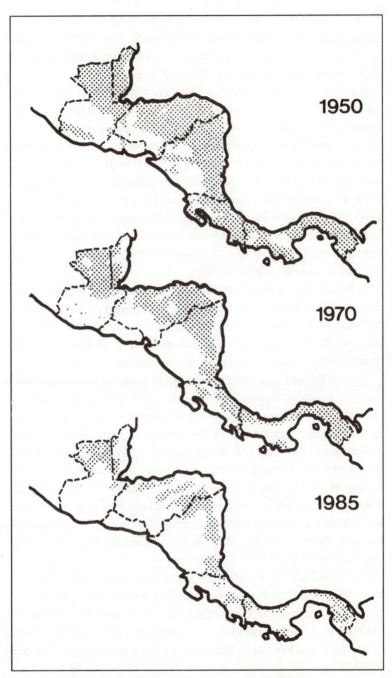

Legend: *Deforestation in Central America 1950 – 1985*
from Leonard 1987

and assess. On the contrary, the proximate causes are clear. Forests are being lost principally through clearance for agriculture — and, in the drier areas, for fuelwood — while the main cause of degradation has been uncontrolled logging.

But if the immediate causes of forest loss have become clear, the underlying forces are the subject of much dispute. On the one hand, many of the international development agencies and inter-governmental bodies have stressed that deforestation results from overpopulation and under-development. Poverty is seen as the main cause of forest loss to which the main remedies are surely obvious — more development and less people (FAO 1985; Shiva 1987). On the other hand, many non-governmental organizations lay the blame for deforestation on transnational companies, development agencies and the excessive consumption of Northern industrial nations (WRM 1990).

In fact, as this study attempts to demonstrate, both explanations are partially correct — it is both wealth and poverty which underlie deforestation and it is in the inequitable structures which link the two that the roots of forest loss can be located. Deforestation, in other words, is an expression of social injustice.

Vested interests, however, have fought long and hard to disguise these unpalatable truths. The fact that it is impoverished farmers who are the principal and direct agents of forest loss, as they move in ever greater numbers into the forests, has encouraged many government officials to blame them directly for deforestation and divert attention from the forces that deprive them of land and other means of subsistence. On the other hand many developers have simultaneously argued that such colonization is both inevitable and necessary. Forests, they say, have to be cleared for agriculture because there exists no other means of feeding the burgeoning populations of third world countries.

The Food and Agriculture Organization, which subscribes to this view, estimates that some 83 million hectares of new agricultural land will need to be brought into production by the year to 2000 to meet third world food needs. According to the FAO, "most of this land will have to be transferred from tropical forests" (FAO 1988:26).

The argument that tropical forests have to be cleared for "national development", both in order to overcome poverty and accommodate population increase, pervades the policies of most third world countries. Yet we should pause before we uncritically accept the assumption. Is it true that there is insufficient land outside the forests to provide for the needs of the rural poor? Why indeed are so many of the rural poor outside the forests without land? Is population increase the cause of poverty or vice versa? If further forest colonization is deemed inevitable are we accepting that rural agriculture outside the forests is inherently unsustainable and out of control? Does forest colonization appreciably alleviate population pressure? Does it promote development? Does it justify the social and environmental costs? Who, indeed, is to make such judgements?

Few national governments have found it politically expedient to answer these questions or even ask them. Rather they have pressed ahead with programmes of forest conversion in the name of progress heedless of the consequences. In Indonesia, for example, the country with the second greatest extent of tropical forests in the world, vanishing at the rate of some 1.2 million hectares a year, no fewer than 305,370 square kilometres — 16 per cent of all the country's forests — are already classified as "Conversion Forests" and are slated for clearance (Collins et al. 1991:143). This figure is soon to be revised upwards, due to the recent policy commitment of the Indonesian government to promote vast plantations of tree-crops for pulp and paper production (DTE 1991).

Massive transfers of population into tropical forests are thus occurring right through the tropical forest belt. In many countries these flows are actively promoted, and even subsidized, by government policies and international agencies. Planned land settlement in tropical forests has been promoted in countries such as Paraguay, Bolivia, Peru, Ecuador, Colombia and, to a minor extent, Venezuela (Stearman 1983; Schmink and Wood 1983; Corry 1984; Colchester 1985b; Hicks et al. 1990). In Brazil, the colonization of the Amazon has been especially strongly promoted (Davis 1976; Bourne 1978; Moran 1983; Branford and Glock 1985) (and see Monbiot this volume). Similar colonization efforts have been undertaken in Panama, Costa Rica, Nicaragua, Honduras and Guatemala (Jones 1990). In Mexico, too, there has been extensive, planned settlement of tropical forests (UNRISD 1990).

A very similar programme was also promoted by the Mengistu regime in Ethiopia, threatening to destroy the last of the country's forest cover, already down to only 3% of the land area (Colchester and Luling 1986; Survival International 1991). Planned colonization of forested areas has also been undertaken by governments in Bangladesh (Survival International 1984; ASS 1984; Mey 1984), Malaysia and Vietnam (Collins et al. 1991), Indonesia (Colchester 1986c) and the Philippines (Leonen this volume).

Drawing the line between planned and unplanned settlement is very tricky. In Indonesia, for example, the World Bank estimates that for every colonist resettled under the official Transmigration programme, two more move into the forests due to its "draw effect". In the statistics these figure as "spontaneous" migrants (World Bank 1988a). Yet a recent study carried out for the Indonesian government notes that these "spontaneous" transmigrants (*transmigran swakarsa*) are "explicitly encouraged by the Ministry of Transmigration". Transmigration, the same study shows, is the single greatest cause of forest loss in Indonesia *directly* causing an average annual loss of 200,000 hectares per year since 1974 (Dick 1991).

Even where such explicit support for forest settlement cannot be documented, "laissez-faire" government attitudes are a major part of the problem. In West Africa, where "spontaneous" colonization has been the main cause of forest loss, many of these population movements may have been "unplanned", in the sense that the decision to move into the forests has been made by individuals and families without government's express authorization or encouragement, but usually the movements are far from unforeseen or unnoticed. Moreover, much of this movement has been directly facilitated by planned infrastructural developments. Road-building in Brazilian Amazonia may have been primarily initiated to promote colonization — to open up, in the words of the government slogan, a "land without men for men without land" — but in many other tropical forest countries roads have been constructed to gain access to timber, hydro-electric power and minerals.

ROADS TO DESTRUCTION

In Ecuador, for example, roads have been constructed by the oil companies, thereby opening the forests to a wave of settlement by landless poor from the highlands, and giving the country the highest rate of deforestation in South America. In Guyana, the southern penetration road, which now links south Guyana to Brazil, even though it is not yet linked to the Guyanese capital, has been constructed with Brazilian government finance by a Brazilian mining company (Colchester 1991). In Indonesia, forest colonization by "spontaneous" settlers has been greatly facilitated by logging roads (Dick 1991).

In Côte d'Ivoire, it is logging roads, followed by settlement, that have been the main cause of forest loss. So clear is this correlation between logging and colonization that Norman Myers has calculated that for every cubic metre of harvested timber, approximately 1/5 hectare of forest is destroyed by farmers who press in close behind the logger (Lamprecht 1989:102). The irony is that the less intensive the logging the more damaging it can be in terms of the area of forest opened to settlement. Africa, in particular, has suffered from this problem, where the high transport costs have meant that interior logging is often limited to only the most valuable timber species (Rietbergen 1989). Extraction rates of just one trunk per hectare are common in West Africa, for example (Martin 1991:185). As Claude Martin puts it:

> Very selective exploitation is synonymous with very extensive exploitation and a low yield per area quickens the pace at which further rainforest is opened up. Since the massive trunks can only be transported out of the forest over logging routes and feeder tracks, even selectively logged areas must be criss-crossed with a network of access roads. At least 10 kilometres of road must be allowed for every ten square kilometres of rainforest. And they are the beginning of the end. Logging roads are the real reason why 90% of slash-and-burn activities by immigrant farmers is concentrated in exploited areas. (Martin 1991:189)

7

So prevalent is this problem indeed that Robert Repetto of the World Resources Institute ranks commercial logging as the top agent of deforestation. Globally, states Robert Goodland of the World Bank "settlement along logging roads and peasant agriculture may be the main causes of tropical moist deforestation" (Goodland et al. 1990:4). According to the World Bank's latest report on "Environment and Development", some 60% of tropical forest loss is due to agricultural settlement, while a further 20% results from logging, though "its impact is larger (as) it establishes access, encouraging farmers and ranchers to follow" (World Bank 1992b:20-21).

CROSS-BORDER MIGRATION

Nor are these population movements restricted by national frontiers. Impoverished people, displaced by landlessness and war, have been flooding out of Bangladesh into Assam, after it was opened up for tea plantations, for well over a century (Tucker 1988). Filipino migrants make up nearly a third of the population of Sabah, while landless Indonesians are snapping up the low paid jobs in the palm oil plantations established in areas of "conversion forest" in Sarawak and Peninsular Malaysia.

Settlers from Mexico, El Salvador, Honduras and Nicaragua have added their numbers to the tide of colonists flowing into the Peten in Guatemala. Displaced peasants from southern Brazil have been spilling across the border into eastern Paraguay since the 1960s, clearing the forests that are the traditional homelands of Mbya Indians. Now they face a reverse displacement as World Bank-funded agricultural development programmes have led Paraguayan absentee landlords to assert their land claims and mechanize agriculture on what had become peasant holdings. Of the estimated 300,000 Brazilian peasants in Paraguay, about half have had to move back to Brazil, where, despised as "Braziguayans", they face desperate conditions and worsening rural violence (CIMI 1992). Other landless Brazilians have flooded across the borders into French Guyana, Guyana, Venezuela, Peru and Bolivia.

Colombian settlers and gold panners are streaming north into the forest lands of the Kuna and Embera Indians of the Panamanian isthmus.

In West Africa, cross-border migration has occurred on so extensive a scale that it defies statistical analysis. Political and economic turmoil has provoked massive migrations between Côte d'Ivoire, Ghana, Togo, Benin and Nigeria. Moreover, the collapse of agriculture in the Sahelian zone has caused a steady southward flow of dispossessed farmers. In Côte d'Ivoire this southward migration of settlers from Mali and Burkina Faso was most marked between 1966 and 1980. The migrants, moving into the forests along logging roads, caused populations in forest areas to increase by 600% between 1972 and 1980, from 1.3 to 7.7 people per square kilometre. The colonists not only overwhelmed the traditional inhabitants but were also totally unfamiliar with forest agriculture. The result has been irreversible and massive deforestation (Martin 1991:184-5).

Cross-border migration is an increasing problem in Central Africa also, the exodus of Rwandans into Zaire, for example, being a major factor in the accelerating deforestation there (see Witte this volume).

THE NEED FOR STRUCTURAL CHANGE

Population increase has exacerbated this crisis and no one denies that one of the main reasons that these people feel obliged to move is because of their poverty. But underlying this mass movement of impoverished people into the forests lie much more deep-seated social and economic problems. This book has been written because of our conviction that unless these underlying issues are addressed, a solution to the problem of tropical deforestation will not be found.

Norman Myers has said:

> There is strong reason to believe that the present deforestation rate will continue to accelerate for the foreseeable future unless vigorous measures are taken with due urgency to tackle the main causes of deforestation, viz. the commercial logger, the cattle rancher and

the small-scale farmer. The third appears to account for much more deforestation than the other two combined, while being far less 'blameworthy'. In his main manifestation as the shifted (displaced) cultivator, the small-scale farmer is subject to a host of forces — population pressures, pervasive poverty, maldistribution of traditional farmlands, inequitable land tenure systems, inadequate attention to subsistence agriculture, adverse trade and aid patterns, and international debt — that he is little able to comprehend, let alone control. Thus he reflects a failure of development strategies overall, and his problem can be confronted only by a major restructuring of policies on the part of the governments and international agencies involved. (Myers 1989:2)

In a similar vein the Washington-based World Resources Institute has concluded that "one of the primary forces pushing landless migrants into the forests is the inequitable distribution of agricultural land . . . land reform policies, therefore, are one of the most potent tools governments possess to stabilize forest use" (WRI 1992: 122).

The connection was long ago pointed out by Jack Westoby:

There is no technical fix which can save the tropical forests. The main instruments of forest destruction are the disinherited of tropical forest countries: peasant farmers, shifting cultivators, rural landless. But these are the agents not the causes. Their pressure on the forest is steadily increasing as a consequence of policies bent on preserving a highly skewed distribution of private property in land and other resources. This pressure will inevitably increase, until there is more equal access to land and other resources. This is not a sufficient condition for saving the tropical forests, but it is a necessary condition. (Westoby 1987:311)

This collection of papers is designed, then, to explore more fully the relationship between the linked issues of rural poverty and landlessness, land tenure and tropical deforestation. It is designed to bring the issue of agrarian reform back into the international debate and focus attention above all on the problems of the rural poor who lack land or secure rights to their land.

The need to refocus attention on the issue is all the more urgent because the international development community, having accepted the need for land reform over two decades ago, has since shied away from addressing it; this despite the fact that the total numbers of rural people living in absolute poverty and without adequate land continues to rise.

According to an FAO study of 90 developing countries, the numbers of mini-land holders and landless people continues to rise world-wide, being projected to rise from 167 million in 1980 to 220 million by the year 2000 (El-Ghonemy 1990:4). Meanwhile, the number of people in developing countries below the poverty line rose from 1.15 billion in 1986 (UNDP 1990) to 1.2 billion in 1990 (UNDP 1992). From 1980 to 1989, 61% of the rural population in the 38 countries with the highest under-five mortality rates lived below the absolute poverty level (UNICEF 1992).

As the studies in this book also clearly demonstrate, the links between the rural poor and the fate of the forests are not simple ones. Migration into the forests, whether planned or "spontaneous", is only one part of the picture. Within the forest zone itself disruptions of traditional systems of tenure have caused major social and environmental problems, while settlers are far from the only forest invaders. Just as skewed land distribution outside the forests has been a major cause of landlessness and rural migration, so this pattern of inequity replicates itself inside the forests. What fertile lands are released by forest clearance are soon taken over by the richer farmers. Vast areas of land, cleared in order to secure title, are held by speculators and as a hedge against inflation. State enterprises and private companies are gaining control of huge chunks of previously forested lands for plantations, of both food crops and tree monocrops.

LANDLESSNESS AND THE COLLAPSE OF THIRD WORLD AGRICULTURE

The core of this book consists of seven chapters, which examine these themes in some detail in six specific countries — Brazil, Guatemala, Zaire, Thailand, Indonesia and the Philippines. The countries, which were purposefully chosen to illustrate the complexity of the problem and the diversity of situations that exist, nevertheless hammer home one common point. At issue in all these countries is the central question of who has rights to own and control the land.

What the studies also make clear is that inequitable patterns of

11

land use and ownership in the tropics have been exaggerated by the incorporation of the third world into the global market. For many countries the pattern was set by brutal colonial interventions in the agrarian economies of the third world, which undermined indigenous systems of land ownership and land management. Whether in Latin America, Africa or Asia, the common intention of the colonials was to turn previously self-sufficient economies into zones of agricultural production for export.

Since independence, the pattern has not changed. The new élites of independent countries have done little to reverse unjust patterns of land use and tenure or their dependence on Northern markets. On the contrary, the pressure of the market, mediated through local rulers has reached deeper and deeper into third world farming systems creating ever greater instability, poverty and environmental degradation, while securing the power of wealthy land-owning élites.

Since the 1950s, international funding agencies like the World Bank and the FAO have played a key role in promoting this market-orientated agricultural model. Global trade flows in agricultural produce have increased almost exponentially over the last century with an ever greater variety of agricultural products entering the world market.

THE DEMAND FROM THE NORTH

Northern consumerism has created an ever greater demand for the products of the South. As this study makes clear, this has led to a far more diverse range of pressures on the forests than campaigns against hamburgers and tropical timber may have suggested. Direct forest clearance is carried out for a very wide range of other products that stand on our supermarket shelves — from bananas, pineapples and oranges to cloves and tobacco. Our pigs are fed on cassava grown in once-forested areas of Thailand, margarines and soaps are made from palm oil from vast plantations in Malaysia, condoms are made from rubber from estates in Indonesia and, increasingly, paper and rayon products are manufactured from wood pulp from huge softwood tree-plantations that are spreading like a sea across the third world.

This book shows too that even where the products of cash-cropping that we demand are not produced in forest zones, they are often linked to the loss of forests. The vast coffee estates and sugar plantations of Guatemala deprive the Indian peasantry of lands on which to live, obliging them to push high up into the vulnerable hill forests to cut their meagre cornfields or migrate to the tropical forest frontier of the Peten. Protein-rich soya feed for European cattle comes from vast mechanized agribusinesses that have taken over peasant lands in southern Brazil, causing of wave of emigration into the forests of Amazonia and neighbouring Paraguay.

International markets in foodstuffs may undermine third world agrarian systems in far more subtle ways than these (Barry 1987; Barraclough 1991). For example, the incorporation of Mexico into the North American Free Trade Zone has frightening implications for the 11 million Indian peasants and smallholders who grow maize for local consumption on traditional communal (*ejido*) lands. Unable to compete with cheap maize imports from the USA, almost a whole class of people is now faced with the prospect of penury, which planners see as the inevitable cost of gaining access to the lucrative markets to the North. In the long term, the thinking goes, these people will find alternative employment in the blossoming industrialization process that free trade will bring. And in the short term?

The distorting demands of urban populations on third world agrarian systems come also from the cities in the South. In Africa, as Lloyd Timberlake (1988) has shown so lucidly, price fixing to ensure cheap grains in urban centres has been one of the main pressures undermining the viability of dryland farming systems. In the Philippines, the ancestral domains of upland tribal peoples are being "developed" with the help of funding from the European Community to produce potatoes to sell as french fries in fast food stores in Manila. The relentless commercialization of world agri-culture is undermining the livelihoods of rural people all across the third world. Denied real choice, the forested lands on the frontiers provide the only alternative to the squalor of urban shanty towns.

Some of these connections are hinted at in the chapters that follow; others are to be developed in a planned companion volume to this work, which will also set out more clearly the connections between trade, pricing, debt and investment policies, third world agriculture and deforestation.

THE RESPONSE FROM THE TOP

As Larry Lohmann points out in the following chapter, the main response of those in power has been to hide these unpalatable truths behind a "developmentspeak" that disguises social injustice and the politics of vested interests in an anodyne language of "poverty alleviation", "underdevelopment" and "overpopulation". Yet the fact that rural development programmes have hurt the poor and thus the environment has been too obvious for international agencies to ignore completely.

Since the 1970s most international agencies have committed themselves in one way or another to agrarian reforms and "equity with growth", but these commitments have proved almost worthless. Even where national land reform initiatives have been pursued this has more often than not been with the intention of "modernizing" agriculture by promoting capital-intensive farming and freer land markets — the concerns of the poor have been secondary considerations at best (Powelson and Stock 1990).

RESISTANCE AND REFORM

Peasant movements that have resisted the takeover of their lands have been as varied as the cultures and political economies in which they have grown up. In some areas, resistance to imposed agrarian change is part of a long tradition memorialized in indigenous and peasant cultures. In many other parts, the turmoil of colonialism and modernization have shattered traditional institutions and customs, forcing rural peoples to formulate new visions around which to rally. Only on the basis of these social movements can effective rural transformation be achieved.

For a dismal reality that the authors have had to confront is that agrarian reforms in the third world have, in large part, failed. They have failed to achieve their targets, they have failed to alleviate rural poverty, they have failed to secure peasant tenure, they have failed to effect adequate redistribution of land, they have failed to stem the rising tide of landlessness and, above all, they have failed to respond to the needs and demands of the peasants themselves. New models of agrarian reform which give the initiative to local peoples are the solution, the achievement of which requires a devolution of power not only from the first world to the third, but also within the third world itself.

AGAINST THE MYTHS

LARRY LOHMANN

This book argues that farmers invade tropical forests mainly because they and their communities become incorporated into expanding market and state systems which deprive them of power and rights over land.

This conclusion has always been unwelcome to governments, aid agencies and large companies. It implies that by their very nature they create more problems and conflicts than they can solve. Thus they have consistently cast about for a vocabulary in which the conclusion cannot be easily expressed.

Such a vocabulary is readily available. It consists of terms such as *overpopulation*, *poverty*, *ignorance*, *underdevelopment*, *lack of political will*, *poor management*, *lack of technology*, *policy failure*, *lack of economic opportunities* and *unsustainability*.

Cobbled together from many different technical fields over the past 50 years, this vocabulary has been invaluable in helping modern institutions defuse the crises resulting from the growth of their power. Preventing anyone from pointing the finger at modern market and state systems as destroyers of livelihood, it suppresses any suggestion that there are real conflicts of interest between different social groups and institutions. Whenever problems arise, it can be dipped into for analyses that imply that bureaucracies and the market economy hold all the answers.

Northern powers met the breakdown of colonialism, for example, by categorizing the ex-colonies as "underdeveloped" in order to demonstrate that they still needed "expert advice" to show the way to "economic growth". When industrialization and export agriculture created destitution and deep rural-urban divisions, similarly, the same experts suggested that peasants' "lack of technology and opportunities to participate in the modern economy" were at fault and could be remedied by "rural development", education, and state promotion of agribusiness and export manufacturing zones.

Today, crises are increasingly seen as ecological. True to form, however, most experts do not examine modern institutions' role in eroding the cultural norms which prevented these crises in the past. Rather, they blame ordinary people's "poverty" and "ignorance of ecological limits" while assuming once again that these failed institutions will provide solutions. In particular, they cast about for a way of instituting a management regime which balances "population" and "resources" in an "optimal" way.

It should not be surprising that this vocabulary fails to illuminate what is happening to ordinary people and their forests. It is, after all, not the vocabulary ordinary people use to explain what is happening to them but rather a vocabulary professionals in large institutions use to justify their own work. Nevertheless, because these experts hold much power — in government, education and the media — the vocabulary has come to dominate debate on tropical forests in the North and among many élites in the South, just as it dominates debate on pollution, energy, fisheries and many other topics. Mention the "tropical forests crisis" to UN officials, timber dealers, taxi drivers or *New York Times* readers and they will tell you it is due to "overpopulation", "underdevelopment" and "primitive slash-and-burn agriculture". Asked about solutions, they will point to technical rather than political measures — to "family planning" rather than land reform, to economic growth and resource management rather than limits on Northern consumption, to education and technological progress rather than campaigns to prevent the World Bank and transnational corporations from decimating peasant societies.

Thus, before laying out the main thesis of this book, it is important to suggest why this vocabulary fails to explain tropical deforestation.

"POPULATION": THE POLITICAL ECONOMY OF A CONCEPT

"Population" as a manipulable statistical entity was invented in the nineteenth century, when scientists began to make predictions about "populations" of beans, stars and mosquitoes. Later, this abstract, impersonal usage began to be applied to people, and by the later twentieth century had invaded newspapers to become a part of the "common sense" of educated people (Duden 1992).

The word "overpopulation" which subsequently emerged provided "scientific"-sounding justification for élites' actions against groups which, in their judgment, had "too many" members. The word's appeal for the powerful has several dimensions. First, it implies that humans, like beans or mosquitoes, can be regarded as if they had a single, enduring type of social organization with neither history nor luxury-consuming classes. This suggests that deforestation can be addressed without evaluating consumption patterns or social and political relations, simply by bringing a fixed social system into line with a similarly fixed, "external" nature. Élites are both exempted from criticism and flattered as those who must predict, control and manage social action on a global scale. Second, by raising the spectre of unmanageable multitudes of future poor, the word "overpopulation" draws attention away from the powerful, overconsuming policymakers of the present. Third, by allowing human beings to be pictured as manipulable statistical entities, it masks the indecency of rulers' attempts to dictate to other people the details of their intimate lives. Finally, and crucially, the term is particularly attractive to male élites in that it cloaks the suppression, mutilation, infection, repression, poisoning, death and disempowerment of women by such modern fertility-controlling techniques as sterilization, IUDs, injectable contraceptives, implants, and now anti-pregnancy "vaccines" (*The Ecologist* 1992). In so far as the word "overpopulation" suggests that procreativity is to be mastered through technical means, it implicitly discourages addressing issues of male dominance.

To maximize its usefulness to élites, "overpopulation" has to be assigned an uncontroversial meaning which it is the prerogative of technical expertise to define. This is not easy. Which groups have "too many" people, and how many are "too many"? Distressingly for élites, the answer is always relative to the interests and assumptions of the group doing the counting. Malthusians felt it was the urban unemployed, whom they had helped to create through expropriation, bankruptcies, rural famines and increasing productivity in factories, who were getting to be too many (Meillassoux 1981: 107). The capitalists Marx wrote about were worried about a surplus of producers, while development economists have often felt that there is a surplus of subsistence farmers who do not produce for the market. In South-East Asia, ruling élites whose forebears had worried there were too *few* people (since scarce labour was the main limitation to rulers' power) quite suddenly joined the ranks of those concerned about "overpopulation" when, following the onset of the development era, they discovered that increasing numbers threatened rather than boosted their interests (Chaiyon 1990). For the foreign and domestic companies who have usurped 40% of Kenya's arable land to grow coffee, tea and sisal for export, "overpopulation" occurs when peasants outside the plantation sector begin to covet its land for their own subsistence. In India a "population explosion" has been posited by leaders to justify their failures in "developing" the country as well as their brutal suppression of those who threaten their interests. For Northerners concerned about access to Southern resources needed to maintain their extravagant lifestyles, "overpopulation" is primarily a characteristic of dark-skinned societies who pose a "radical challenge to the international order" (Bondestam and Bergstrom 1980). For many Southerners, it is a characteristic of Northern overconsumers. For nature-lovers, one person of any society may be too many for certain areas. For biologists, "too many people" may mean simply "too many for the group to be able to survive".

Attempting to get rid of this awkward plethora of possible senses of "overpopulation" in favour of a single "objective" one under their control, élites often appeal to the concept of "human carrying capacity", which dictates how many people can survive or flourish at particular consumption and technology levels on a particular area of land. If "carrying capacity" is exceeded, the reasoning goes, then population can be said to be "objectively" excessive relative to land, consumption and technology.

It is not as easy as all that, however, to remove the concept of "overpopulation" from the realm of moral criticism and debate. Outsiders' claims that a given area of land has a certain "carrying capacity" are open to criticism in three different ways. First, the number of people who can live on a piece of land depends largely on their culture, which determines both their needs and their agriculture. The nature and success of their farming systems cannot easily be predicted in advance on the model of outsiders' cultures. Second, the fact that the question of consumption and technology levels must be raised in any discussion of "carrying capacity" means that the normative issues of what sort of society or economy people desire cannot be evaded when talking of "overpopulation". Third, a given land area's "carrying capacity" will depend largely on what happens outside its borders: upstream deforestation, global commodity price fluctuations, greenhouse gas emissions, acid rain and so forth. Local inhabitants will always be justified in pointing out that their land could support a great many more people if damaging external influences were curbed, and on this ground to call into question the presumption of those partly responsible for such influences in suggesting "proper" local population levels. This latter problem might be evaded, of course, by an attempt to determine *global* carrying capacity. However, this is usually acknowledged to be technically far-fetched even if the world's peoples could be induced to accept uniform global consumption levels and technology. And it would of course leave wide open the question of which local "populations" would have to be "adjusted" to meet the purported "global" requirements.

LACK OF EXPLANATORY POWER

One response to such arguments is that, while "overpopulation" cannot be precisely or "objectively" defined, there are at least unambiguous statistical correlations between "population" and deforestation on a national scale. On close examination, however, even this assertion turns out to be false. As Jack Westoby, former head of forestry at FAO, writes,

> There is no simple relationship between the extent of the forests and the size and distribution of the human population. Instances can be found in which large numbers of people live in harmony with their forests, and others where forests are devastated although few people are present. (Westoby 1989: 137)

Malaysia, for example, although it has only a tenth as many people as neighbouring Indonesia, has cleared fully 40 per cent as much forest as Indonesia has done. While less than 0.2 hectare of India's original forest cover has been converted per current inhabitant, the corresponding figure is six times higher for both Côte d'Ivoire and Colombia (Myers 1989; World Bank 1992b). Japan, with a "population" density of 327 persons per square kilometre, retains closed forests over 63 per cent of its land area, while Cuba, with a "population" density less than a third that of Japan and a similarly extensive original forest endowment, has less than 2 per cent forest cover remaining (World Resources Institute 1992). Central America, with under 30 million people and a "population" density of only 57 persons per square kilometre, has cleared 410,000 square kilometres of forests, or 82 per cent of its original forest cover, while France, covering the same land area with double the number of people, has cleared less. And those who would explain the destruction of half a million square kilometres of Brazilian Amazonian forests between 1975 and 1988 in Malthusian terms:

> overlook the inconvenient fact that although the Amazon forms over 60 per cent of Brazilian national territory, less than 10 per cent of Brazil's population lives there . . . more than half the population within the Amazon region lives in cities. Only six million or so people live in rural zones, of whom two to three million dwell in the forest itself. (Hecht and Cockburn 1990: 97)

If "population" and "population" density are poorly correlated with extent of forests, "population" increase is, similarly, poorly correlated with rate of deforestation. Vietnam, Peru and Papua New Guinea are each clearing forests at a rate of 3,500 square kilometres per year, but annual "population increase" is running at 1,400,000 in Vietnam, 450,000 in Peru and only 90,000 in Papua New Guinea (Myers 1989; WRI 1992). Costa Rica and Cameroon are clearing their forests faster than Guatemala and Zaire, respectively, in spite of having lower "population" growth rates (WRI 1991; Myers 1989). Thailand's rate of forest encroachment, similarly, has varied less closely with the rate of population increase than with changes in political climate, villagers' security, road and dam-building, and logging concessions. In the Sahel, environmental degradation is actually correlated with *de*population (David and Myers 1991).

"It is not so much the number of human beings that has the crucial impact," Westoby explains, "as the way in which human society is organized" (Westoby 1989: vii-viii). The periods of most rapid deforestation in the past "have not necessarily been at the times when population was most rapidly expanding. They have occurred when the exploitation of subordinate groups (as well as of resources) has intensified" (Westoby 1989: 45).

Forests first became subject to overexploitation with the emergence of hierarchical societies whose top strata strove to expand their wealth and power. This process was accelerated greatly by new forms of social organization and administration introduced by imperial powers. The forests of England and Wales, for instance, "suffered their sharpest reduction in serving Roman imperialism" (Westoby 1989: 49). In the Mediterranean as well, "the periods of most rapid deforestation coincided with the pressing new need to feed growing empires and support the consequent build-up in the categories of non-food producers" (Westoby 1989: 165). Following the 16th century spread of European sugar plantations across the Atlantic, it was export-oriented agriculture, not "too many children", which played the key role in deforesting the tropics of the New World. In Asia, European merchant enterprise backed by European nation-states took over and expanded trade, siphoning off agrarian surplus normally taken by local potentates. When the machinery of administrative control required more profits, taxes were instituted which required a money economy. Domestic agriculture was switched from subsistence to cash crops, displacing or otherwise putting pressure on rural people to clear more land. Direct colonial exploitation for timber for ships, railways or trade was also important, especially in India (Shiva 1987: 24-25, 31-34; Pereira and Seabrook 1990: 4-9).

Today military and technocratic governments carry forward this tradition, promoting forest destruction not "to meet the needs of a growing population" but rather to line the pockets and secure the power of a few. The halving of Central America's forest area between 1950 and 1990, for example, is due not to a "population explosion" but to the concentration of land in the hands of a limited number of rich ranchers and landowners raising bananas, cotton, coffee and cattle. Peasants have been used as land-clearers only to be pushed into the hills, where they displace others and are forced to cut yet more forest. Elsewhere, transnational corporations such as Finland's Jaakko Pöyry Oy, the US's Scott Paper, and Japan's Marubeni often supervise forest plunder, with additional destruction resulting from expropriative cattle-raising, road, hydro-electric and industrial projects (SKEPHI 1990; Hecht and Cockburn 1989; Moore Lappé and Collins 1986; Nectoux and Kuroda 1989; Lohmann 1991).

Schemes to displace people to sparsely-settled areas of Indonesia and Brazil, meanwhile, have been not a response to "population pressure", but in fact attempts to evade agrarian reform in areas coveted or dominated by the rich or to assure political and military domination of outlying territories (Westoby 1989: 162; *The Ecologist* 1986).

Such schemes have often actually prevented careful stewardship of forests. Peasants on Java and Bali, which are supposedly the "overpopulated" islands of Indonesia, still practise "complex and highly successful agroforestry systems which enable them to obtain high yields continuously from surprisingly small parcels of land" (Westoby 1989: 137), whereas farmers uprooted to unfamiliar lands of Irian Jaya or Sumatra are often unable to find ways of supporting themselves. In the Amazon,

> most land cleared of forest produces little in the way of food and often was not cleared for that purpose. Migration into the region has much more to do with structural changes in the region of emigration than with population growth. Thus, decline in access to land, as it occurred in [North-Eastern Brazil], stimulated emigration. In the

case of migrants from the South, the expansion of mechanized agriculture and the flooding of enormous areas of agricultural land forced small farmers out of their holdings. Finally, threat of violence and lack of employment have also expelled farmers from their holdings. Since more than half of all agriculturalists in Brazil rely on wage labour as well as cropping for their income, activities like mechanization which reduce rural employment are often as disastrous to peasants as brute expulsion from their lands. (Hecht and Cockburn 1990: 97)

Even in countries which have a high "population" growth rate and a high forest colonization rate, it is more plausible to argue that both stem from the same causes — small farmers' lack or loss of power over land and means of livelihood — than to argue that the "population" growth rate causes colonization. There is much evidence that colonization and fertility increase are both ways of coping with expropriation and increased economic insecurity among the rural oppressed (Moore Lappé and Collins 1986; Moore Lappé and Schurman 1990: 135).

Many, especially marginalized women, view children as their sole source of power and means of survival in old age. Children's labour can augment meagre family income by freeing adults and elder siblings to earn outside income, or by bringing in money directly. Children's earnings also provide insurance against risk of property loss for many rural families for whom a bad crop year or unexpected expense can spell catastrophe. Large families make especially good sense in contexts in which local areas have been integrated into national economies but personal networks continue to be the main guarantors of social security. Here it is desirable to have as many family members engaged in as wide a range of livelihoods in as many towns and cities as possible. As development cuts into women's power relative to men and their control over their own fertility declines, pressures for large families can increase further (Wichterich 1988). In short, "to attribute tropical deforestation to population pressure is to argue that spots cause measles", since the two are "joint manifestations of exploitative social relations . . . The tropical forest cannot be saved by distributing IUDs and condoms" (Westoby 1989: 45, 161).

In at least two important senses, it is at least as plausible to claim that deforestation causes "overpopulation" (which in turn exacerbates colonization) as to hold the reverse. First, as corporate and state enclosure and destruction of forest cause reductions in soil fertility, water availability and climatic stability, the result may be loss of security and migration, increasing the need for children. Second, when people are induced to migrate away from regions where their presence interferes with the interests of more powerful groups to areas like Thailand's uplands or Indonesia's outer islands, they often find themselves on infertile land at the mercy of the market, cut off from cultural supports which would minimize the land area needed for subsistence. Transmigrants in Indonesia, for example, have a higher birth rate than is prevalent in rural Java (*The Ecologist* 1986). Deforestation in such areas in turn uproots other groups, who must then also encroach on forests, displacing still others. Each displaced group will appear to ruling groups to be "overpopulating" the area to which it has been forced to migrate.

Throughout the history of deforestation, the "populations" with the greatest negative impact on forests, both direct and indirect, have tended to be distant élites, not people who are accustomed to living in or close to particular forests. The bulk of the trees removed from tropical forests go for urban or foreign use. Northern consumers, of course, take a much bigger bite out of forest resources than even their urban counterparts in the South. The "population" of India, for example would have to expand to 34 *billion* before it could match the US's paper consumption (Pereira and Seabrook 1990: 84). The advertising sections of a single issue of the Sunday *New York Times*, meanwhile, contain enough paper to print all the school books in Cameroon (Bondestam and Bergstrom 1980: 71). Yet it is typically countries like India and Cameroon that are charged with "overpopulation".

Admitting all this, many observers nevertheless insist that "population control", cloaked as family planning, should at least be regarded as a minimum precondition for checking forest destruction, on the uncontroversial ground that human numbers cannot increase indefinitely. "No matter what your cause, it's a lost cause if we don't come to grips with overpopulation," warns one organization (Population Institute n.d.).

However, it does not follow from the fact that growth in human numbers cannot continue indefinitely that state-backed attempts to limit "population growth" are either an effective or a necessary background to other efforts to save the forests. While there is no solid evidence that "population control" projects have ever succeeded in their stated objective, there is abundant evidence that they have both increased people's insecurity and provoked resistance from women whom they have disempowered and brutalized (*The Ecologist* 1992; Moore Lappé and Schurman 1989; Wichterich 1988). As Tariq Banuri and Frédérique Apffel-Marglin put it, a focus on population as *the* problem is a "political stance which, though ineffective in eliminating the problem, is quite effective in justifying unnecessarily deleterious practices" (Banuri and Apffel-Marglin 1993). Far from being a "neutral prerequisite" for conservation of forests, "population control" tends to undermine precisely the social groups and cultures which defend them.

THE UNDERDEVELOPMENT EXPLANATION

Since the 1980s, another explanation of forest colonization has often been paired with the "overpopulation" explanation. This is the claim that the landless are invading the forests because they are "poor" (and, often, "ignorant").

By this is meant not only that forest colonizers are often desperate and exploited, but also that their desperation results from the fact that they, and their society, *lack development*. It is implied, in other words, not only that forest colonizers are poor but also that (i) their poverty is not the *result* of development and that (ii) it is *remediable* by development. It follows from this analysis that more development — in particular economic expansion — will cure this poverty and relieve the pressures on the forest. "Deforestation or development in the Third World?" has thus become a typical symposium title, and Western leaders frequently refer to deprived practitioners of "undeveloped slash-and-burn agriculture" as prime culprits for forest loss.

Like the concept of "population explosion", the concept of "poverty (or ignorance) as underdevelopment" is designed to serve the interests of political and economic élites, especially in the North. It enables Northern interests to blame deforestation on faraway peasant groups rather than companies or agencies closer to home, and to suggest that the solution lies in Northern wisdom and capital.

To appreciate fully the meaning and attractions of the "poverty-as-underdevelopment" idea, it is necessary to glance at its half-century history. Before 1940, world powers saw little need to conceptualize "poverty" as "underdevelopment". If the immature, ignorant, effeminate, unscientific natives of the South could be improved at all, it would be through the civilizing mission which accompanied colonial plunder and deforestation. After the Second World War, former colonies demanded more respect. At the same time, the "national security" requirements of the *pax Americana* necessitated a more far-reaching global economic mobilization than had even been possible under colonialism. The broad cultural standards which had previously been used to measure colonizers against colonized accordingly had to be replaced with a specifically economic yardstick. Placed against it, the majority of the world's peoples became *economically backward* rather than culturally inferior.

The battle against "poverty" rather than the "improvement" of customs and religions thus became the North's excuse for intervention and expropriation. The same societies which came to view Christian proselytizers or colonial armies in Asia and Africa as a relic of a racist past dispatched hundreds of economic advisers to retool and "correct" the "backward" economies of the third world to "ensure prosperity for all". Former colonial possessions were "freed" only to take their assigned places in a single world economic race led by the US.

To underscore the importance of this race, Northern agencies tried to collapse as many important characteristics of Southern societies as possible into the single omnibus category of "poverty". Traditional frugal, self-sufficient, or risk-minimizing lifestyles were run together with the destitution caused by colonialism, the modern market, military incursion, or natural disasters. Traditional common property regimes, similarly, were confused with "open access" regimes which had often in fact been brought about by state intervention.

Simultaneously, efforts were made to reduce this omnibus category of "poverty" to one or another quantifiable "indicator". In the 1940s and 1950s, the World Bank pioneered the comparison of per capita cash incomes of different countries. Many other indicators have since come into use: gross national product, distribution, "literacy", "availability of public health institutions", "degree of satisfaction of basic needs", degree of adoption of settled as opposed to "slash-and-burn" agriculture, "empowerment", "sustainability", "availability of choice" and "well-being".

What was important about these efforts was not the *type* of indicator they appealed to, but the fact that every society could now be defined as "winner" or "loser" by its position along a single (generally numerical) scale. Commensurating countries and peoples in this way brilliantly solved a number of ideological problems for Northern élites. In theory, universal adoption of a single yardstick would render any disputes about national aims quickly resoluble; all one had to do was take a few measurements. Any Southern societies agreeing to abide by such a yardstick, moreover, would *ipso facto* be admitting that Northern countries ranked higher and that their differences from the North were *lacks* or *deprivations*. This, of course, would legitimate the North's claims to be qualified to render "aid" and tutelage. Political dissatisfaction in the South could meanwhile be treated as the frustration of the have-nots in the face of the haves, and attempts by a society to move toward its own ends reinterpreted as an aspiration toward Northern-style economies. The brutal clash between radically divergent cultures which was an (often self-conscious) characteristic of colonialism could, in short, be softened.

Yet the need for order and management remained plain. Only experts could wield the yardsticks in a professional manner, and the unitary, predetermined, and quantifiable character of the "indicators" of economic success continued to hold out the promise of prediction and control. Surprise and vulnerability to circumstance were slated for elimination, together with localized adaptations and reliance on personal assessment of the particular. Setting society's ends in advance, moreover, meant that discussion could be confined to finding efficient means, making bureaucratic takeovers of indigenous political culture more easily justifiable.

The name for this new type of Northern intervention, and the solution to the newly-discovered Southern deficiencies, was, of course, "economic development". Plunder and the "civilizing" notion of progress were fused into a single program of economic and social improvement through exploitation of resources, potential markets and "comparative advantage". The more widely the North's notion of a yardstick of economic achievement was adopted, the more widely increased production and the development of industrial and scientific techniques became accepted as the way of attaining the important values of all societies.

All this was to grow out of Southern societies themselves, in an organic but preordained process called, significantly, "growth". The imagery of scientific measurement, prediction and control became wedded to that of natural unfolding and maturation. No group being reorganized as part of a money economy could possibly be oppressed since such "development", by definition, was what enabled people to reach their potential. Exploitation, resistance and liberation were defined out of the discourse.

Comparing societies by means of a yardstick carried one additional comforting implication: that they were replaceable. Provided that the source of their value lay in whatever the yardstick measured, to choose one possible society over another was not *to neglect* the separate and unique value of the rejected option, but merely to prefer a larger amount of the same value. "Everything has a cost and everybody has a price," World Bank representatives often reassured their Southern interlocutors; "you have to make trade-offs."

IS POVERTY THE PROBLEM?

Given the attractiveness of the notion of poverty-as-lack-of-development for Northern élites, it is hardly surprising that is widely used to explain tropical forest destruction. But does this explanation have any merit in itself?

Again, the answer is a firm no. First, the claim that "poverty" is responsible for the rapid deforestation of the past few decades is false if "poverty" is taken to mean, following development advocates, simply "lack of material wealth". Ways of life which are not connected to an economic system which sanctions large accumulations of wealth do not engage in forest destruction on the scale observed, and are often even oriented toward long-term forest maintenance (Westoby 1989, Banuri and Apffel-Marglin in press). Thailand's traditional *muang faai* irrigation, India's sacred groves and village forests, and the practices of Mbuti and Amazonian tribal peoples are a few examples. Nor, as is widely recognized among anthropologists, is traditional shifting cultivation the villain it is often painted as (Colchester 1990a). If such ways of life are what is meant by "poor", as is often the case, then it is simply false that poverty causes deforestation.

The particular type of "poverty" which *can* be said to have contributed to the unprecedented tropical deforestation of recent years is destitution and uprootedness. But there is no ground for saying that deforestation is caused by poverty in *this* sense which is not an even better ground for saying that it is caused by wealth and development. Wealth, after all, not only enables forests, land and water to be enclosed, cashed in, and devastated efficiently by corporations and development agencies for the sake of distant markets. It also deprives ordinary people of livelihood and independence, expropriating them and pushing them further into the forest, making them "poor". As North-Eastern Thai farmer Chalee Marasaeng puts it, "the rich make the poor poor, the poor make the rich rich." The only plausible interpretation of the claim that "poverty is responsible for the tropical forests crisis" is one which indicts development as a putative cure. While getting rid of the types of "poverty" which preserve forests (self-sufficiency, frugality, the traditions of stewardship widespread in common property regimes), development can only create more of the sort of "poverty" which destroys them.

Using a yardstick to measure societies' status, an activity which is central to the notion of poverty as underdevelopment, in itself encourages the sort of uprootedness in question. For to compare societies in this way is to give them new, external ends, whether a high rate of economic expansion or long-term "sustainability". The internal cultural and moral features of the society then become mere means to attain these ends, to be rated according to their efficiency in achieving them, and are often devalued and dismantled as a result.

The use of an economic yardstick, for example, has been associated with frugal and self-sufficient ways of life being marked for destruction unless they can be used to reproduce labour or in some other way contribute to what the yardstick measures. Screams from the "developed" — the six million in India moved since the Second World War to make room for hydro-electric dams, for instance — have had to be muffled. Shifting agriculture, whether in Finland or Laos, has been treated as a "robber economy". Risk minimization, aspirations for political liberation and other aspects of lifestyles associated with "low income" have been rendered invisible or swept away. Local technology is acknowledged only in so far as it can be commensurated with that of the West, making the Cambodian buffalo cart merely a "primitive" form of the pick-up truck and the Nepali brush dam a defective version of a concrete slab. Land is turned into real estate and local villagers are pressed into becoming migrant labour. Attempts are made to break down forests, streams, livelihoods, agriculture and communities into exchangeable bits, valued according to their contribution to national income — whose growth is viewed as synonymous with realization of inner potential and evolutionary purpose — or "global sustainability".

Throughout, United Nations agencies have taken on the job of giving advice to Southern leaders on how to take apart and rebuild their societies so that they can compete in the international race between scarcity and the growth scarcity creates. As Lloyd Timberlake noted of Africa,

> The cities where the governments live have been torn from the countryside, and development budgets have gone to filling those cities with hotels, factories, universities and cars. This has been paid for by milking the seven out of every 10 Africans who live on the land, by taking much from them in labour and produce and giving back little in money or support . . . in taking too much from

31

its farmers, Africa has taken too much from its land as well ... Soil erosion matches the erosion in farmers' political power, as they are more and more squeezed out of their nations' political and economic life. (Timberlake 1985, 9-10)

As nature itself becomes a scarce economic means for attaining open-ended growth, land, forests, water and people become treated as a commodities. Farmers who once planted diverse crops for subsistence now specialize in sugar cane, cassava, peanuts, coffee, cotton, cocoa, maize or other monocrops; sixteen African countries, for example, depend on just one crop for over 70% of their income (Timberlake 1985: 70). Close links to the global exchange economy require, moreover, that plots of land change rapidly from one simplified agroecoystem to another to exploit fleeting "comparative advantage". Crops with a narrow genetic base require inputs of chemicals, and local soil microbes adapted to diversity go extinct. Debt and loss of soil fertility force farmers to migrate and clear more forest. Roads constructed to get primary goods out and consumer goods in make it easier for profiteers in Brazil or Thailand to take over once-forested land, using the dispossessed as an advance guard. Traditions and institutions break down and opportunities for social and natural systems to coevolve in local areas are lost. Marginalized migrants unfamiliar with local techniques and landscapes tend to adopt destructive cultivation techniques. Farmers are reduced to producers and consumers whose only security depends on how quickly they can convert land and forests into cash.

Attempts to promote capital accumulation through government subsidies have often led to the same result. In Ethiopia, development policies in the 1960s and 1970s provided privileges for rapid development of large-scale commercial farms producing export crops. As cotton and sugar plantations took over the Awash valley, pastoralists were evicted from traditional lowland pastures and pushed into fragile uplands which were rapidly overgrazed and degraded. Subsidies for clearing in the Brazilian Amazon have not established permanent agriculture, but have merely made the opening up of new land more economical than more intensive management of already cleared land (Norgaard 1990:174).

As the state takes over forests in the name of development, often leasing them to corporate loggers or plantation or aquaculture interests, more local communities are uprooted and older moral rules governing forest use set aside. Timber extractors (often feeding foreign luxury markets) are allowed to devastate forests from Australia to Burma and from Cameroon to Colombia (Maher 1990: 245). The income earned can do little to prevent further destruction (Colchester 1989a; Marshall 1990). Expropriation of water for commercial agriculture or a source of energy for national industrialization, meanwhile, leads to yet more people's being driven off their land and impoverished. Ghana's Akosombo dam displaced 78,000 people from an area nearly the size of Puerto Rico, Lake Kingi in Nigeria forced 42,000 to move and China's Three Gorges project promises to uproot more than a million. Mining produces similar results. As a Bougainville landowner affected by Rio Tinto Zinc's copper mining says:

> We don't grow healthy crops any more, our traditional customs and values have been disrupted and we have become mere spectators as our earth is being dug up, taken away and sold for millions. (Moody 1991: 67)

Apologists for development have sometimes claimed that its benefits would be able to compensate people fully for being ripped away from their land and communities were it not for certain "vicious circles" inherent in the rural situation. In Thailand educated people talk about the *ngo-jone-jep* (stupidity-poverty-sickness) cycle as a block to development, while in India planners refer to a vicious circle of unemployment, low income, mental retardation and many children (Bondestam and Bergstrom 1980).

Such gambits, however, are merely sophisticated attempts to blame the victims of development policies. As even development advocates such as Robert McNamara have been forced to acknowledge since the early 1970s, poverty increases in the shadow of wealth, development widens gaps between urban and rural areas and within rural areas themselves, and national income often poorly reflects the extent to which a country's underprivileged have been marginalized. Redefining development as "sustainable growth", "health and education for all" or the fulfilment of "basic needs" does not touch underlying problems rooted in the market and the use of yardsticks to commensurate societies. Even recent moves toward "recognizing the value of indigenous practices" do little more than attempt to fit these practices into universal systems of production, thus degrading or destroying them (Marglin 1993).

Conceptions of development which emphasize the protection of nature against the effects of economic expansion — through environmental planning, environmental economics and establishment of protected areas, for example — are of little more help. They constitute merely one more way of tearing local people away from their land and knowledge, as has happened in wildlife reserves in East Africa and Thailand and forest reserves in India. People who used to be blamed for not going along with "development" are now being blamed for going along with it without the right "safeguards" — large capital investment in modern management schemes and parks. Yet such "safeguards" can only be produced by precisely the sort of economy which destroys forests and the sort of frugal, self-reliant practices which can conserve them. The mentality which regards poverty and forest destruction as lack of "development" will continue to be one associated with the greatest assaults on people and their forests.

BACKGROUND TO LAND REFORM: LATIN AMERICA, ASIA AND AFRICA

ROGER PLANT

While the world's attention has been focused on the problems of deforestation and the need for radically new approaches to forest management, there has been little concern to link these problems with the wider issues of land rights and land reform. But the link is an obvious one. Natural resources are being depleted, not only because of the well documented abuses of illegal logging, ill-advised hydro-electric and other development projects within the forests. Increasing numbers of the rural poor are having to earn their livelihood from forests, simply because they have no alternative means of subsistence. At times, it has been government policy to promote small-farmer settlement and colonization in forest regions. Equally often, the landless have undertaken spontaneous colonization because access to land outside the forests has been effectively closed off.

Some two or three decades ago a major concern of development economists and planners was the need for agrarian reform in developing countries, blending the objectives of more equitable access to the land with more efficient agricultural production. Notably in Asia and Latin America, agrarian reform laws were enacted, which challenged the existing legal basis of land ownership and provided in different ways for the transfer of ownership rights to tenants or landless rural workers, or for improved security of tenant farmers over the lands they cultivated. The heyday of the "official" land reform era was between the 1950s and approximately the early 1970s. Occasionally — as in the Peoples' Republic of

China or the several African countries that pursued the socialist path — private property was abolished altogether, and the land allocated under collectivized or co-operative forms of production. More typically, the reforms provided for limitations on private property rights, through the introduction of land ceilings, "land for the tiller" provisions, tenancy and minimum wage protection, and legal requirements that private lands should be brought under active production or be liable to expropriation.

Agrarian or land reform can involve a wide range of different policy measures. In all cases, it involves the restructuring of agrarian property and land administration, to effect changes in the use of land and labour. But differences emerge over the basic objectives of land reform law and programmes, and the weight of the relative emphasis given to economic or social considerations. Government planners and technocrats, as well as the international financial institutions that fund the reform programmes, tend to emphasize the former. They are concerned primarily, though by no means exclusively, with efficiency of production. Unless there is strong pressure "from below" for radical distribution of property, they are concerned mainly to bring all idle and under-utilized land into active production; to eliminate inefficient "semi-feudal" or exploitative labour relations in agriculture; to introduce productive technologies including high-yielding seed varieties to improve agricultural productivity; and to penalize landowners who fail to adapt to more modern systems of production. Social considerations may play a part in land reform programmes adopted "from above". Such land reforms are usually adopted in response to growing social pressure "from below", and often have the unwritten aim of defusing social tension. They tend to contain provisions for ceilings on private land ownership (with compensation), for improved security for tenant farmers, and for a measure of redistribution of expropriated land to the landless. The size of the land ceilings, the *nature* and extent of compensation, and the *form* of land redistribution, have been issues of controversy in all land reform programmes.

For peasants, rural workers and the landless, the initial concerns are inevitably different. For them, land reform is essentially an issue of livelihood, rights and justice, whether it involves land for the landless, security against eviction for tenants, communal land security for indigenous and tribal peoples, fair wages and working conditions for plantation workers, or protection against usury and moneylenders. In the longer term, of course, all peasant activists know that control over a piece of land is not enough. A small plot of land is useless without credit, infrastructure and marketing facilities, access to technological inputs and services, or without strong local-level organizations to make their demands and defend their interests. They are concerned no less than landowners with the implications of macro-economic policies, which affect prices for their agricultural inputs and outputs.

There can be no single "recipe" for land reform, and no universally applicable formula. Some broad typologies can nevertheless be developed, in assessing past approaches to land reform. One analyst, Rehman Sobhan, has distinguished between three basic types of reform. First there are radical agrarian reforms, which effect a social transition and eliminate social differentiation in the agricultural sector. Second there are inegalitarian reforms with social transition, in that they effect a transition but leave scope for differentiation in rural society. Third there are the inegalitarian reforms which take place without realizing a social transition in rural society.

To Sobhan's categories a fourth could usefully be added, namely land reforms that have effected a negative social transition, in that they have actually increased the numbers of the rural landless. As will be argued below, the problem with many land reform programmes in developing countries is that they were never premissed on the needs of the landless. Instead, they resulted in the massive expulsion of tenant farmers, as large farmers brought their lands under more mechanized and capital-intensive production, in order to escape expropriation under the provisions of land reform laws.

In any event a wide range of different development policy interventions have been included under the broad heading of "land reform". The more radical measures have included collectivization programmes, or the expropriation of lands above a certain ceiling with or without compensation. Some "land for the tiller" programmes have aimed to convert all tenants into small owner-operators. Other tenancy reforms have aimed to improve the security and conditions of tenant farmers, by fixing rental payments or providing safeguards against eviction. Others have emphasized land titling and registration, as a condition for recognized ownership. Yet others have involved land colonization and settlement, often opening up forest regions for settlement by landless and small farmers from heavily-populated agricultural areas. In some cases recent reforms have proved beneficial to indigenous and other traditional forest-dwellers, providing recognition under national law for their communal systems of land use and resource management. In other cases land reform laws and programmes have prejudiced forest-dwellers and their environment, by requiring forest clearance and crop cultivation as a condition for land titling.

Certainly, some reforms have been far more successful than others in fulfilling their stated objectives. In the development literature, the reform experience in such East Asian countries as Japan, Korea and Taiwan is usually singled out as a success, in that it eliminated large-scale and inefficient farming, and paved the way for modern and productive agriculture through fairly small-scale farm units. The experience in Latin America, where almost every country adopted land reform legislation after the 1950s, is usually singled out as a failure, in that it simply failed to address the needs of small farmers and the landless (Thiesenhusen 1989). Worldwide, some socialist land reforms have managed to combine the interests of efficiency and equity, when decision-taking has been decentralized, and when high productivity has been rewarded with incentives. Other experiments in agrarian socialization (including those in the Soviet Union after forced collectivization, and more recently in such African republics as Ethiopia and Tanzania) have had disastrous effects on productivity. The failure is generally attributed to excessive bureaucracy, centralization of decision-taking, inadequate participation of grass-roots and peasant organizations, and, of course, to coercion.

Over the past decade land reform as an equity and redistributional issue has, with the few exceptions that will be examined further below, been off the official development agenda. At the same time, agrarian reform legislation, which provides for the possibility of expropriating and redistributing private agricultural lands, remains on the statutes in the majority of Latin American countries and many countries of South and South-East Asia.

At the international level one can find a theoretical commitment to redistributive land reform in the policies and programmes of such United Nations agencies as the Food and Agriculture Organization (FAO). But this can be little more than a spoken commitment, unless the developing countries themselves adopt the agrarian reform laws and programmes for which the international donor agencies can provide technical and financial assistance.

The development literature is replete with examples of the failure of past land reform programmes to meet their twin objectives of greater equity and efficiency (Barraclough 1991; Christodoulou 1990). To a large extent, these appraisals have led to a generalized scepticism as to the efficacy of land reform as an instrument for redressing rural poverty or achieving more equitable land distribution. Some analysts stress the political obstacles, in the light of the continued influence exercised by landowners in the power structure of most developing countries. Other analysts point to the technical difficulties in devising appropriate reform models, in the light of demographic factors and the overall agrarian transformations of the past few decades.

The parameters of land reform debates will now change, in accordance with these transformations. The "land for the tiller" philosophy, which underpinned most of the moderate land reforms of the post-war decades, is only applicable to situations where tenancy is widespread, and where the agrarian structure is characterized by large and under-utilized holdings. This was the case in much of Asia and Latin America a few decades ago, but is increasingly less so today. At that time many countries had a choice of reforming their quasi-feudal agrarian systems, redistributing land to former tenants and share-croppers, and providing effective state support for small-scale production arrangements. Though legally empowered to do this, they generally failed to do so. Many large landowners resisted the reforms, evicting tenants, and bringing their lands under more active production with the benefit of subsidized machinery, other techno-logical inputs, and preferential access to credit. Modern and commercial farms were generally exempt from the reform pro-grammes, and often managed to extend their holdings at the expense of traditional cultivators even during the phase of the redistributive reforms.

Scepticism as to the efficacy of past reforms in combining efficiency and equity objectives has led to a virtual defeatism, as the political and technical obstacles to redistributive land reforms are seen as almost insurmountable. The political obstacles are fairly obvious, in that landowners retain strong political influence in developing countries, and will oppose redistributive efforts unless compensation for the state or the beneficiaries is generous. As is often argued, the state is unlikely in the current economic environment to allocate resources for redistributive reforms that target the landless. And market-based reforms are unlikely to make much headway, because the landless do not have the means to pay. Thus lack of resources is usually seen as the major impediment to moderate and consensus-based land reforms, and most policy analysis now focuses on alternative strategies for rural poverty alleviation (Binswanger and Elgin 1988; Bell 1990).

The onus is now on non-governmental organizations and activ-ists to place land reform on the policy agenda as a fundamental human rights concern. Criteria must be formulated for placing limitations on the exercise of private rights to land, and for subordinating private land rights to the interests of society at large. Equity and environmental considerations, rather than efficiency and private security alone, must be given their proper place in determining the rules of land use, access and ownership.

THE NEED FOR LAND REFORM:
RECENT TRENDS IN LAND CONCENTRATION AND LANDLESSNESS

The major problem today is that of absolute landlessness. In all developing regions, the problems of absolute or near landlessness in rural areas have become increasingly acute over the past decade. Radha Sinha calculated in 1985, using FAO estimates, that as many as 935 million people, or nearly one-fifth of the world's population, fell into the category of landless and near-landless rural workers. Nearly two thirds of landless and near-landless rural households were to be found in Asia, as against one fifth in Africa and one tenth in Latin America. In Asia, three out of every four agricultural households fell into this category, and one out of seven households was completely landless. The highest proportion of landless or near-landless rural households (at over 75%) was to be found in Bangladesh, the Philippines and Sri Lanka (Sinha 1984).

If the numbers affected are greatest in Asia, the trends are in many ways more disturbing in Latin America, where the incidence of landlessness has been estimated at 71% of all agricultural households. In most Asian countries, dense population means that the scope for redressing rural poverty through more equal land distribution is necessarily reduced. In Latin America the rapid recent rise in rural landlessness can be attributed more directly to changing production techniques and rural employment patterns, as more agricultural land has come under large-scale commercial cultivation. Over the past decade the absolute number of very small farms has in fact increased, but the total area of land they occupy and the average size of individual farms have remained the same or even diminished. At the same time there has been a marked reduction in small-farm tenancies, under tenures such as renting, share-cropping and usufruct rights provided in exchange for labour services. In Brazil, for example, the area under share-cropping decreased from 5.3 to 3.8 million hectares between 1970 and 1980. FAO cites two major reasons behind these changes. One is technical innovations such as mechanization and the use of chemical inputs, which reduce the relative cost of employing wage labour and, by increasing yields, also raise the opportunity cost to the employer of ceding land. Another is the fear of legislation which could strengthen security of tenure among share-croppers and renters, which has also led to the displacement of small tenant farmers (FAO 1988).

A further important development in Latin America, linked to the previous trends, has been the marked increase in temporary and casual labour in agriculture at the expense of permanent employment. In contrast to the situation some few decades ago, the majority of the rural labour force today may not actually reside on the plantation, but in small rural towns where they are recruited by intermediaries for a few months, weeks or even days at a time, in accordance with labour demand. It has been estimated that in São Paulo state, the growth centre for large-scale commercial agriculture in Brazil, the percentage of such workers in the total agricultural labour force more than doubled between the early 1970s and the late 1980s. The growth of such temporary labour systems has been attributed at least in part to the unintended effects of rural labour legislation of the 1960s, which aimed to improve employment conditions and security of the rural labour force.

The combination of minimum-wage legislation and other extra salary benefits including severance pay, together with the increased powers of rural unions and individual rural workers to seek redress before the labour courts, are seen as key factors behind the decision of landowners to expel permanent workers and to make increasing use of temporary labour without formal contracts of employment. Thus a Latin American irony is that attempts to improve the conditions of tenant farmers and rural workers under law has had the opposite effect of provoking their widespread expulsion, and leading to a marked expansion of technically unlawful systems of rural employment.

Problems of the above nature are most pronounced in Latin America. In most African countries, problems of rural landlessness are only now beginning to emerge, and share-cropping, instead of disappearing, is only now appearing. Recent FAO studies have pointed to the emergence of share-tenancy and landlessness in countries of sub-Saharan Africa including Burkina Faso, Ghana, Kenya, Malawi and Togo. But there are very different problems in the countries of Southern Africa (Namibia to an extent, Zimbabwe and most of all South Africa) where the land has historically been divided along racial lines, restricting the black majorities to defined communal areas too small to provide for their subsistence needs. It is in these countries, arguably more than anywhere else in the world today, that the question of redistributive land reform is now high on the agenda as a policy instrument for redressing the racial laws and policies of the past.

CAPITALIZING AGRICULTURE: REFORMS FROM ABOVE IN LATIN AMERICA

In Latin America, the agrarian and rural labour legislation adopted after the Mexican revolution of the early twentieth century has had a profound impact on the legal tradition throughout the continent. Almost all the Latin American republics have agrarian reform laws technically in force today. Some countries have imposed a ceiling on the amount of land that can be held as private property. Most national legislation provides that land that is left idle, or inefficiently cultivated, is liable to expropriation with or without compensation, depending on the circumstances.

While almost all Latin American countries now have land reform legislation, in only a small minority has significant land redistribution taken place. And in this latter group (Bolivia after the 1952 revolution, Chile during the Allende Government between 1970 and 1973, Cuba after the Castro revolution, Guatemala between 1952 and 1954, Mexico between the 1920s and 1940s, Peru between 1968 and 1975, and Nicaragua during the period of Sandinista government after 1979) the redistribution occurred usually after major social upheavals or revolution. The Bolivian social revolution was followed by an agrarian reform that nationalized all traditional *haciendas* in the highland region and distributed estate lands to former labourers and tenant farmers. The 1959 Cuban revolution brought a yet more radical land reform which confiscated large and foreign-owned plantations, abolished tenancy and share-cropping systems, and eventually provided for expropriation of private farms of over 40 hectares. In only two cases (the land reforms carried out by the Peruvian military government in the 1960s and the counter-insurgency-based land reform adopted in El Salvador in 1981, which was aborted before realizing its stated objectives) has there been significant land distribution without a radical change in government.

The historical legacy, determining contemporary patterns of land concentration, shows many similarities throughout the continent. During the colonial period, the Spanish crown attempted to safeguard traditional farming systems of the indigenous populations and to protect their communal lands against encroachment by colonists. The main concern of the crown was with the exaction of tribute, sometimes paid in cash but more generally through provision of agricultural surplus. Indigenous peoples were seen by the colonists as a source of cheap labour, and were required to perform regular forced labour on their estates. As land was in abundant supply and labour scarce, the land had no real value without a ready labour supply. This may help to explain the early concentration of land in few hands, even though most of it was left idle. Influential colonists, including the church, were keen to limit the number of landowners, in order to reduce competition for the scarce labour supply. Nevertheless, due in part to special protection by the metropolitan power, many indigenous communities did manage to maintain their communal lands intact to the end of the colonial era.

After independence in the early nineteenth century, the situation changed quite dramatically. There was a concerted effort to introduce liberal notions of property rights, recognizing only private forms of land ownership, and replacing the mixed systems of the colonial era. By the mid-nineteenth century civil codes based on the Napoleonic model had been adopted in almost every Latin American republic, providing for the abolition of communal forms of ownership, and the registration of individual property titles. After this time, the agrarian structure of different regions of Latin America evolved on somewhat different lines, depending on the extent of their integration within the world market.

In the small Central American republics, an emphasis on large-scale coffee cultivation for export led to pressure on communal lands, and to a high demand for labour on the new plantations. Laws abolishing communal systems of land tenure were rigorously enforced, and forced labour legislation was enacted requiring *comuneros* and other landless labourers to work on the plantations.

Special rural police forces and paramilitary organizations were created, paving the way for the repressive militarization that has pervaded the rural areas of countries such as El Salvador and Guatemala up to the present day, finally escalating in the civil conflicts of the 1980s. In the Andean region, where no single export crop predominated, there was relatively less pressure on the land, partly because the available land areas were so much greater, and partly because the smaller incidence of cash-crop farming for export meant that there were less demands for seasonal and plantation labour. Traditional *comunidades* survived in practice alongside the large *haciendas*, even if not recognized by law, until the exclusively liberal notions of property rights were revised in the early twentieth century. In Brazil, there was little pressure on the land in the nineteenth century. The highest population density was in the North-East of the country, on the large sugar estates that were worked by slave labour until its abolition. After that time, labour was provided by tenant farmers and "squatters" who had no legal rights to the land and were technically subject to eviction at any time. But squatting was generally tolerated and even encouraged by landowners, as long as the squatters provided personal services to the landlords and cheap labour during the harvest season.

It was in Mexico, perhaps even more than in Central America, that the alienation of Indian land was most severe in the late nineteenth and early twentieth centuries. By 1910 as much as half of the rural population were tied labourers on vast plantations, over a hundred of which were more than 100,000 hectares in size. But the Mexican revolution introduced a new legal tradition based on the principles of social equity, recognition of communal land ownership, the "social function of property", and limitations on private land ownership with absolute title to the land vested in the state. The Mexican Labour Code of 1924 was also the first to recognize the labour rights of rural workers. It provided for the abolition of unpaid personal services, debt-peonage and other semi-feudal labour systems; for minimum wage legislation; and for a series of welfare rights in which the obligation to provide social benefits for the workforce (including health care, education, housing and social security) fell not on the state but on the individual landowner in the countryside.

Labour laws based on the Mexican precedent were enacted in almost every Latin American country over the next three decades. New labour codes at first discriminated against rural workers. Many contained provisions explicitly denying the right of association, or minimum wages, to *hacienda* and plantation workers. Others contained restrictions on the right to strike during harvest periods, or restricted rural unions to larger enterprises employing more than a fixed number of workers. But militant pressure from rural worker organizations, to support demands that labour legislation be extended to rural areas, ultimately had their effect in most countries. From the perspective of the rural worker, these labour and welfare rights were seen as being of equal importance with the right to the land itself.

By the 1960s the traditional *latifundia* — with their vast under-utilized land area, their large numbers of tied labourers and poor use of capital — had been earmarked by social reformists and modernizing farmers alike as the main obstacle to progress in Latin America. It was also seen by many, including the United States Government, as a potential source of social unrest. The Cuban revolution of 1959 was an important catalyst for the agrarian reforms "from above" of the Alliance for Progress era.

But even without the Cuban revolution, the balance of economic and political power in much of Latin America would have been favourable to the limited land reforms that were carried out during this period. After the Second World War, rapid industrialization was increasing the need for more and cheaper food to cater to the needs of the rising urban population. Foreign exchange was urgently required to service the needs of import-substituting industrialization. In Brazil and the Andes in particular, political power was increasingly dominated by a new entrepreneurial class (whether urban industrial or agro-industrial) which saw the traditional *hacienda* as an anachronism. The rapid expansion of export agriculture brought new opportunities for commercial and capital-intensive farming. Economic advisers pushed for agrarian policies that would release surplus labour from the countryside, assuming that it would be absorbed in the industrial or agro-industrial sector. Population increase and changing agricultural patterns meant that there was no longer a labour shortage in rural areas. By the 1960s there were already clear signs of the rural labour surplus that was to increase dramatically over the next three decades.

The land reform measures of the 1960s have to be understood in the light of these economic and political transformations. Whatever the declared social objectives of the average land reforms, their real aim was rarely to provide land for the landless. Instead, the aim was to rationalize and modernize land use and production systems, and to replace semi-feudal and servile labour arrangements by wage labour systems. The land reform programmes tended to interpret the social function of property by the criteria of efficiency and productivity alone, declaring that uncultivated land was liable to expropriation. Except in such cases as Chile (where a moderate reform programme got under way during the late 1960s, and a progressively lower ceiling was placed on retainable private land under the Allende Government before the 1973 military coup) the land ceilings were kept high, and landowners were usually given a period of time to bring their land under active cultivation. In the Ecuadorian and Peruvian reform programmes of the 1960s and 1970s, and in the El Salvador programme of the 1980s, the enforcement of rural labour legislation has been an important criterion. When landowners could be shown to have violated the provisions of labour law (on minimum wages, for example), their lands were deemed liable to expropriation.

From the viewpoint of social justice, the deficiency of these land reforms should be easily apparent. They were premissed not so much on the *rights* of the landless or near-landless, as on the *obligations* of the landed. Landowners who could turn into efficient commercial farmers were generally deemed to fulfil the social function of property and to be eligible to retain the land. Except in Peru (where quite significant land distribution took place between 1968 and 1975, and where special agrarian tribunals were given exclusive jurisdiction over land reform cases) the courts tended to side with landowner interests. It was only when the central government was politically committed to land redistribution, and deliberately built up strong peasant organizations as political support against conservative landowner interests, that significant land distribution occurred. This was the case in Chile, Peru and, to a lesser extent, Colombia in the 1960s and 1970s; and in Nicaragua in the 1980s.

By the mid-1970s, the redistributive phase of these land reforms "from above" had generally ground to a halt throughout Latin America. In Central America, where military and paramilitary groups defended the interests of large commercial farmers producing for the export market, land reforms never got off the ground in this earlier period. In Brazil, a tentative move towards land reform ended with the 1964 military coup. In Chile, land reform ended in 1973. In the above cases, the reformist initiatives were terminated through violent military intervention. In other cases, they ended less dramatically. But the reasons this kind of reform programme began when it did, and ended when it did, are largely similar. The reforms began with much consensus among reformist politicians (mainly Christian Democrats), modernizing farmers, the US Government and sectors of the military, all of whom wished to break down the feudal remnants of rural society and make increasing use of wage labour. Peasant militancy, and growing demands for the enforcement of rural labour legislation, tenancy and minimum wage agreements, certainly played a part in the reforms. Eventually the militant demands of landless peasants and rural workers far outstripped the concessions that moderate reformists were willing to make. Moreover, the reforms often released additional labour onto the market. Landowners tended to expel *colonos*, squatters and tied labourers from the land, particularly when the agrarian reform programmes had "land for the tiller" elements that aimed to convert share-croppers and tenant farmers into small producers.

The failure of these moderate reform programmes has left a difficult social legacy. As seen above, the transformations of recent decades have seen the replacement of exploitative tenancy arrangements by a new class of landless and temporary labourers in large-scale commercial agriculture. Evicted tenants and their descendants have sought to earn a livelihood where they can, pouring into the cities, setting up new shanty towns on the fringes of the commercial plantations, or undertaking spontaneous settlement in the Amazon and other forest regions. In the 1990s, land conflicts are likely to grow and become more violent. In countries like Brazil, Ecuador and Paraguay land invasions are now almost a daily occurrence. In such Central American countries as El Salvador and Guatemala, where the incidence of land concentration and landlessness is highest of all, there can be no long-term solution to political violence until the issues of land tenure and rights are addressed directly. But the principles of land rights and agrarian justice, as they developed from the Mexican Revolution through to the land reform era, have now been overtaken by events. It is no longer a question of reforming or modernizing traditional *latifundia*. It is rather a question of meeting the demands of the tens of millions of landless rural workers.

ERADICATING AGRARIAN "FEUDALISM": THE ASIAN EXPERIENCE

In Asia, as in Latin America, agrarian systems in the immediate post-war period were characterized by "semi-feudal" structures, with the land concentrated in the hands of small and often un-productive élites. In the decades since then there have been three basic approaches to land reform: first, the socialist model of agrarian collectivization, as practised in China and to a lesser extent the other socialist countries; second, the radical "land for the tiller" approaches, as practised in Japan, Korea and Taiwan in exceptional political circumstances after the Second World War; third, the tenancy reforms, accompanied by the imposition of higher land ceilings, in the Indian subcontinent and also the Philippines.

The "land for the tiller" reforms enacted in Korea and Taiwan after the early 1950s involved the compulsory sale of tenanted and leased land, and the eradication of large scale and "feudal" hold-ings. The Taiwan reforms set a very low ceiling of only three hectares that could be retained by landlords. In terms of agri-cultural productivity, the subsequent success of these smallholder peasant economies has been widely attested. South Korea for example has virtually eliminated rural landlessness, which affected over half of all farm households in the late 1940s. According to FAO figures, rural landlessness decreased from 4% in 1980 to only 2% in 1985. It is still questionable whether these reforms are replicable elsewhere, and can provide any kind of model for other developing countries today.

In China a massive land reform programme was launched immediately after the founding of the People's Republic in 1949. Before the reforms, some 10% of the population had owned as much as 80% of the arable land. Approximately half of this land was then distributed to some 60 million peasant households. In the early 1950s the first reforms emphasized private ownership through very small plots. Subsequent policies emphasized co-operative and collective farming, which proceeded in gradual stages. The first cooperatives retained the notion of private land ownership, but by the late 1950s all private property had been abolished, and all land transformed into socialist co-operatives. After the early 1960s, China developed its village commune system. While some sources argue that the productivity record under the commune system was quite impressive, this has been contested in recent literature. Reforms enacted after the 1978 Communist Party Congress have retained collective land ownership, while devolving decisions on land use to the individual household. Further reforms since 1982 have served to strengthen individual tenure, and create a limited ability to transfer rights to land.

There have been some similar recent developments in other Asian countries that opted for the socialist path. An example is Vietnam, where after a period of collectivized farming in the North there has of late been a gradual transition towards individual land user rights. In forest areas for example, legislation since the early 1980s has permitted individual land leases. A national land law enacted in 1988 affirmed that only the state could allocate land, and that land sales were prohibited, but accorded to farmers the right to the transfer, concession and sale of the fruits of their labour and the results of their investment.

In other parts of South and South-East Asia there have been more moderate land reforms, involving tenancy protection and some limitations on private property through the imposition of land ownership ceilings. There has been some nationalization of foreign-owned estates, as in Indonesia after independence and in Sri Lanka in the mid 1970s. The ceilings have on rare occasions been kept quite low, as in the land reforms attempted in Pakistan in the 1970s. But, as in Latin America, these reforms are usually depicted in the development literature as failures, due to high ceilings, weak implementation, the tendency of courts to obstruct the reform process, failure to prevent widespread eviction of tenants, and above all failure to address the needs of the rapidly rising numbers of rural landless.

In India, land reform legislation was enacted in each state after the early 1950s, aiming first to abolish such intermediary tenures as the *zamindari* system, second to provide security of tenure to tenants, and third to impose a ceiling on land ownership. Under British rule, the *zamindari* system had vested ownership over vast tracts of land in feudal owners who generally leased it to large and small peasant farmers. In many states, *zamindari* abolition acts were quite rigorously enforced, the former owners retaining less than 20 hectares and receiving compensation in cash or state treasury bonds. Although loopholes were found, with former *zamindars* subdividing their lands and establishing fictitious land owners, this was still the most successful aspect of land reform nationwide, benefiting an estimated 20 million peasant families. Legal reforms to protect tenants and share-croppers have proved less effective. As in Latin America there were mass evictions of tenants as a preventive measure, sometimes prior to the adoption of the laws.

In India the land reform experiences in the states of Kerala and West Bengal are usually singled out as successes. In Kerala legislation in the late 1960s provided for a low land ceiling of between 2 and 8 hectares. It provided for immediate security of tenure for all kinds of tenant, with or without formal contracts, and required landowners to pay full compensation to tenants before the land could be resumed for personal cultivation. Arrears of rent were dramatically reduced, and special tribunals were established to determine the equity claims of small owners and tenants. Commercial farms were, however, excluded from the reform laws. The main components of the West Bengal land reforms have been the abolition of absentee landlordism; a low ceiling of between 2.5 and 9.8 hectares, depending on family size and irrigation; recording of share-croppers, with a view to preventing their unlawful eviction; provision of special credit facilities; and implementation of a minimum wage rate for casual agricultural labour. In a state with exceptionally high population levels, the programmes appear to have met with much success in redressing rural landlessness.

But the question of redistributive land reform has really been off the political agenda in India over the past decade. Already by the late 1960s attention was being shifted to alternative strategies for improving rural livelihood, in particular through the broader dissemination of Green Revolution technologies. A number of studies since then have argued that unequal access to these technologies has worsened the plight of those without direct access to land. A substantial middle peasantry has emerged, often absentee, usually with access to machinery and modern seeds and fertilisers, and prone to make significant use of casual wage labour. Moreover, land concentration, landlessness and rural labour abuse in India are integrally related with the caste system. Apart from tribals, the majority of the landless are the estimated hundred million members of the scheduled castes, otherwise known as the "untouchables" or *harijans*.

One Asian country where land reform has recently resurfaced as an important political issue is the Philippines. The 1987 constitution required the state to undertake an agrarian reform programme and the "just distribution of all agricultural lands", and a Comprehensive Agrarian Reform Law was enacted to this effect the following year. The drafting of the reform law, and the manner of its implementation since then, have been the subject of intense debate. In a country where for historical reasons the agrarian structure has more in common with Latin America than the rest of Asia, there have been sporadic but largely unsuccessful efforts to implement "land for the tiller" reforms on the East Asian model. A Land

Reform Act of 1955 aimed to facilitate the acquisition of large estates for subdivision and resale to tenant cultivators.

A more comprehensive Agricultural Land Reform Code, issued in 1963, established a ceiling on privately owned land, abolished share tenancy in law, and instituted a leasehold system whereby fixed rentals would be paid. Before the present Government, the land reform law of most significance was Ferdinand Marcos' Presidential Decree No.27 of 1972, issued shortly after the proclamation of martial law. Limited to rice and corn lands, this aimed to liquidate and reform feudal tenancies in the food crop sector, excluding the landless and farm workers in the commercial crop sector who were estimated to comprise almost half the rural labour force in the mid-1980s. As in Latin America during this period, there were widespread and violent evictions outside the law, with court decisions favouring landlords and severely impeding the process of land redistribution.

The 1987 Constitution now provides for land reform as a social right of the Philippine people. Section 5 of the Article on Social Justice states that:

> The State shall by law undertake an agrarian reform programme founded on the right of farmers and regular farmworkers who are landless to own directly or collectively the lands they till or, in the case of other farmworkers, to receive a just share of the fruits thereof. To this end, the State shall encourage and undertake the just distribution of all agricultural lands, subject to such priorities and reasonable retention limits as Congress may prescribe, taking into account ecological, developmental or equity considerations and subject to the payment of just compensation.

In the events leading up to the adoption of a new land reform law, controversy centred mainly on the size of the land ceiling and retention limits, and methods for the determination and payment of compensation. One Senate bill, for example, had proposed a uniform ceiling as low as three hectares, suggesting a radical "land for the tiller" programme along the earlier East Asian lines. A Congressional bill went even further, proposing a zero retention limit and the transfer of all lands to their traditional cultivators.

The Comprehensive Agrarian Reform Law was finally enacted in June 1988. The law now covered all public and private agricultural land, regardless of the tenure arrangement and the crop produced. It provided a retention limit of five hectares per landowner, on top of which adult children actually tilling the land could retain an additional three hectares each. Compensation was to be paid in accordance with general principles, to include the cost of land acquisition and its current value.

Four years later, the 1988 reform law and its implementation can be subject only to partial assessment. The short-term assessments made by either academic or advocacy organizations in the Philippines are almost uniformly critical. They single out the lack of political will, with Congress dominated by landowners, and the government giving no effective impetus to its spoken commitment to structural reforms. The basic conceptions of the land reform law and programme have also been subject to much criticism, on different grounds. First there are the views of most non-governmental and advocacy groups and a minority of Congressmen that a more radical and swiftly implemented "land for the tiller" programme is now required, and that the present law must be amended to this effect. A different set of criticisms tends to reject the Asian "land for the tiller" concept as a basis for present-day land reform in the Philippines. The argument is that, in the light of agrarian transformation over the past few decades, the earlier East Asian models are no longer applicable. Recent transformations have been more along Latin American lines, with growing commercialization and mechanization of agriculture, and the effective replacement of tenancy by wage-labour systems including seasonal wage labour. It has been argued that the present law is biased towards the protection of large-scale commercial agriculture, despite the ceiling provisions, and that there is no real scope for redressing the plight of the absolute rural landless. Thus some analysts urge the improvement of tenancy relations, rather than the legal abolition of tenancy, seeing tenancy as an important first step on the "agricultural ladder" (Hayami et al. 1990).

The recent Philippine experience reflects many of the political and technical difficulties to be confronted by the advocates of comprehensive reforms, whether in Asia or other parts of the world. The Aquino Government originally expressed a commitment to redistributive reform, which was also a major rallying point of the mass-based opposition to the former Marcos Government. But there are few signs that the current reform programme, undertaken within a democratic framework in which landowning groups retain effective political control, will go far beyond the objectives of the earlier Marcos reforms. In the less-capitalized sector of subsistence agriculture, tenants are likely to be converted into small farmers, at least where they are sufficiently mobilized to resist eviction and press their claims to the land. But the prospects for tenurial change in the more commercial sector, and for providing the landless with any kind of direct access to cultivable land, must realistically be seen as more remote.

LAND REFORM ISSUES IN AFRICA

In most of Africa — and particularly in sub-Saharan Africa — land distribution is generally more even than in the rest of the developing world. The low degree of land concentration reflects a relatively low degree of commercialization of agriculture, and widespread persistence of customary land tenure arrangements. Nevertheless, absolute landlessness, though at present a major problem in only a few countries, is becoming a cause for concern throughout the continent.

Throughout the region, there are now strong pressures on governments to reform the customary arrangements that have provided the traditional basis of land tenure. And there is an intensive policy debate, concerning the extent to which indigenous African land-rights systems constitute constraints on efficiency of agricultural production. In some African countries, land policies since independence have placed a high premium on equity, at the same time vesting powers in the state to allocate and redistribute land rights in accordance with perceived development priorities. Such approaches, as epitomized by the Tanzanian model of agrarian socialism, have been widely criticized for their bureaucratic centralism and the poor productivity resulting from the lack of incentives and security for individual producers. But the land reform debate has taken on different dimensions, in the former settler economies (Kenya in the past and more recently in Zimbabwe and South Africa) where a legacy of racially-based land law and highly-inequitable land distribution along racial lines means that the land rights of white minorities have inevitably been subject to challenge.

Thus there are two main issues of land reform and agrarian policy in Africa today. The first is how customary tenure regimes, which have traditionally provided land security for subsistence farmers, can best be integrated within national land law and policies without prejudicing efficiency of agricultural production. The second is how highly discriminatory patterns of land-use and ownership can best be reformed in the settler economies, again without severe disruption to agricultural production.

The first issue can be illustrated from Tanzania, where government policies since independence have been firmly opposed to the "commoditization" of land. Freehold title has been abolished by law and absolute title vested in the President, though considerable discretion has been given to community-based organizations to determine land-use and allocation at the local level. While the policies of the ruling TANU party have reflected a commitment to equitable land distribution they have been clouded by their coercive elements, including compulsory villagization and forced cultivation practices. After independence the TANU government headed by President Julius Nyerere adopted law and policy reforms aiming to create a unique form of village-based African socialism. In the peasant sector, the government aimed through its 1967 Arusha Declaration to promote agricultural self-reliance through the promotion of so-called *ujamaa* villages, in which the land was to be held in common. The government, concerned at the slow rate of concentration of population in *ujamaa* villages, later adopted policies of compulsory villagization. The villagization programme has been criticized from various perspectives. Some analysts argue that the coercive elements prevailed, and that villagization also failed to achieve its objectives of equity and socialized production. A Task Force on Agricultural Policy, appointed by the government in 1982, questioned the validity of collective village farms on the grounds that individually owned farms generally perform better. It advocated private rural land ownership, and the issuance of title deeds with a minimum of 33 years' duration.

At the present time, Tanzanian land law and policy seems to be beset by ambiguities. While 1982-83 marked a turning point, with a shift away from socialist agriculture towards private farming, this has not really been reflected in changes in the land law itself. Tanzania's Second Five-Year Plan (1988-93) envisaged the preparation and registration of leasehold title deeds for villages, and ultimately for subtitles for individuals. As of 1990 the pace of village demarcation, titling and registration had been slow, with much confusion even as to where village boundaries were located. Land markets are clearly developing, and concerns are being widely expressed that land allocation practices are fostering land-grabbing by those with access to government authority.

An early example of redistributive land reforms, through the transfer of ownership from white to black farmers, is provided by Kenyan policies after independence. In Kenya before 1960, ownership of the most valuable agricultural land had been limited to persons of European descent. Protection of European property rights was an important issue at the 1962 Lancaster House Conference, which prepared the independence constitution. Provisions were written into the constitution securing property rights from arbitrary government confiscation without due compensation. It was agreed that the British government would finance the transfer of a million acres of European farm land to some 25,000 landless and unemployed African families.

While much land was transferred from European to African hands under this programme, the beneficiaries in fact came from a small elite group, often comprising absentee civil servants rather than the landless. The emphasis on land settlement and the allevia-tion of landlessness, a key demand of nationalist and insurgent groups during the transition to independence, soon gave way to an emphasis on land consolidation. Kenyan policies then emphasized land titling and registration, under freehold forms of ownership. The persistence of "land-grabbing" in recent years, and problems of widespread squatter eviction in both rural and urban areas, have been amply documented by human rights organizations. In the meantime individual land registration programmes have proved highly prejudicial to pastoral communities, such as the Maasai in southern Kenya.

In Zimbabwe, the legacy of colonialism was an agrarian structure similarly divided along racial lines. A freehold sector dominated by a small number of white farmers accounted for almost 40 per cent of all farmland. African reserves or Tribal Trust Lands were occupied by some five million persons altogether. Since independence the government headed by President Mugabe has pledged to carry out land reforms to reduce these inequalities, while at the same time accepting the continued need for a significant commercial sector under predominantly white ownership and management. For the first ten years after independence, the government of Zimbabwe was legally bound by the provisions of the 1980 Lancaster House constitution, which guaranteed existing property rights during this period. Land could only change hands on a "willing seller, willing buyer" basis, except in the case of under-utilized land, which could be compulsorily acquired upon payment of the market price. Since the expiry of this independence constitution in April 1990, the land reform issue and questions of compensation have been very much at the top of the political agenda.

Law and policies since independence have had to deal with three broad categories of land use and ownership, involving the privately held lands of white settler and African farmers, and the "communal" African areas. Within the Lancaster House constraints, land reform in the commercial areas was mainly limited throughout the 1980s to the settlement of black farmers on willingly sold properties. Since the amendment of the Lancaster House constitution in December 1990, the government has pledged to pursue a more vigorous land-reform programme, involving the compulsory ac- quisition of substantial areas of commercial farm land. Inevitably, such proposals have met with resistance from large farmers' lobbies represented through the Commercial Farmers' Union (CFU). The main area of controversy concerns the government's new powers to determine compensation values without any judicial review.

In South Africa, land reform has become a keen area of controversy as the country moves towards majority rule. The land debate intensified early in 1991, when the government introduced legislation to repeal all statutory measures regulating rights to the land on a racial basis. Government proposals aiming only to repeal *apartheid* laws themselves, without addressing the practical inequalities resulting from their past application, have been widely rejected by the African National Congress (ANC) and other opposition groups. The latter have insisted that land law and policies must now address the important question of land claims and restitution, for the many blacks who have been unlawfully dispossessed by *apartheid* policies; and that future land law must be based on new principles of equity, restricting and limiting the strong ownership rights now enjoyed by white farmers.

As in Zimbabwe, the question of land rights is arguably the most difficult of the issues being negotiated in the transition to majority rule. As the ANC has dropped its earlier land-nationalization platform, there has been concern to examine the nature of competing claims to specific lands, or to the land in general, as a basis for future policy determination. Legal scholars are now examining the principles and procedures by which land conflicts and claims resulting from the *apartheid* legacy can be addressed. A common theme is that existing law lacks legitimacy, not only because of the direct legacy of *apartheid* laws, but also because the concept of ownership under South Africa's Roman Dutch law provides existing landowners with excessive powers to use and abuse their land and labour force without restriction. In this context, simply to rely upon existing title deeds as the basis of property interests would be to evade the issue of legitimacy instead of confronting it. Thus South African analysts have drawn a basic distinction between the crisis of legitimacy deriving from the *apartheid* system in itself, and the broader failure of agrarian law to recognize and build on customary and traditional land-tenure arrangements. These scholars generally advocate a more functional concept of land ownership, with restrictions on private rights and safeguards for tenancy rights similar to those involved in the concept of the social function of property that has influenced past agrarian law in Latin America.

CONCLUSIONS

In official development circles, policy work on land reform has become apathetic, defeatist and essentially retrospective. In the United Nations and other international fora, analysts pay lip service to land reform as a desirable objective in itself. They then spend most of their time analysing — with some accuracy — why past land reforms have failed, and dwelling on the political and technical obstacles to land reform as a viable policy instrument for the future. But alternative strategies have also failed, if the reduction of rural landlessness is seen as a desirable policy objective. Widespread rural poverty and exploitative labour arrangements have been translated into rural unemployment, the casualization of rural labour, and an immense growth in urban unemployment. Agricultural modernization has generally increased food production and productivity, at least where there has not been excessive emphasis on export agriculture, but usually at the expense of rural livelihoods and employment.

There is now an urgent need for more forward-looking analysis. Conceptually, the starting point must be that persons who depend on land access for their very survival, and have no alternative means of subsistence, have a clear moral right to earn their livelihood from the land. One challenge is to translate this principle into some kind of enforceable legal right or claim, as a criterion to guide future land policies.

This chapter is a condensed and revised version of a portion of Roger Plant's forthcoming book *Land Rights in Rural Development Policy*.

FOREST PEOPLES AND SUSTAINABILITY

MARCUS COLCHESTER

Development can only occur when the people it affects participate in the design of proposed policies, and the model which is implemented thereby corresponds to the local people's aspirations. Development can be guaranteed only when the foundations are laid for the sustained well-being of the region; only continued poverty can be guaranteed when the policies lead to the pillage and destruction of local resources by those coming from outside. The indigenous people of the Amazon have always lived there: the Amazon is our home. We know its secrets well, both what it can offer us and what its limits are. For us, there can be no life if our forests are destroyed. We want to continue living in our homelands.

Statement by the Co-ordinating Body for the Indigenous Organizations of the Amazon Basin, 1989

This book is focused on the crisis for tropical forests caused by the collapse of third world agricultural systems outside the forests. Yet the fatal vulnerability of the forests themselves to invasion and expropriation is also a key factor in their current destruction.

For, despite the prevalence of myths about "trackless wastes" and "virgin forests", the forests have been inhabited for thousands of years. Few tropical forests have not been subjected to modification or change by human hands. Few areas of forest are unused or unclaimed by local communities. Yet the peoples who inhabit the tropical forests are extremely marginalized and politically oppressed. Small in numbers and with little traditional interaction with state systems outside the forests, forest dwellers have thus proved uniquely vulnerable to dispossession and expropriation. Their lack of land security or political strength has meant that the forests that are their traditional preserve have been ill-defended against invasion.

DEFINITIONS OF SUSTAINABILITY

As made popular by the United Nations' World Commission on Environment and Development (WCED), the phrase "sustainable development" refers to the means by which "development" is made to meet the needs of the present without compromising the ability of future generations to meet their own needs (WCED 1987). Since the needs of future generations are undefinable and the future potential for wealth-generation of species and ecosystems are equally unknowable, the term apparently implies that total biological assets are not reduced, in the long term, through use.

In a rural context, sustainable use thus means not just conserving biological diversity, fauna and flora, but also maintaining ecological functions such as soil quality, hydrological cycles, climate and weather, river flow and water quality. It also implies maintaining supplies of natural produce — game, fish, fodder, fruits, nuts, resins, dyes, basts, constructional materials, fuelwood, and so on — essential to the livelihoods of local people.

It is important to distinguish between the WCED definition of sustainability, with its emphasis on human needs and sustaining livelihoods, and those subsequently adopted by many development institutions, whose more technical definitions of sustainability are in terms of ecosystems' continued production of goods or services or the maintenance of biodiversity (see, for examples, Pearce et al 1989: 173-185; ITTO 1990; World Bank 1991e). Many definitions strip the concept of "sustainability" of the social and political issues implicit in the notion.

As the WCED study acknowledges, achieving sustainability implies a radical transformation in present day economies. It requires a fundamental change in the way natural resources are owned, controlled and mobilized. To be sustainable, "development" must meet the needs of local people, for, if it does not, people will be obliged by necessity to take from the environment more than planned. Sustainability is fundamentally linked to concepts of social justice and equity, both within generations and between generations, as well as both within nations and between nations (WCED 1987; UNEP 1989).

Achieving sustainability thus implies major political changes. As the WCED notes:

> The pursuit of sustainable development requires a political system that secures effective participation in decision-making . . . This is best secured by decentralizing the management of resources upon which local communities depend, and giving these communities an effective say over the use of these resources. It will also require promoting citizen's initiatives, empowering peoples' organizations, and strengthening local democracy. (WCED cited in Durning 1989b:54)

Such a notion of popular "participation" in development is very close to that adopted by the United Nations Research Institute on Social Development:

> Popular participation is defined as the organized efforts to increase control over resources and regulative institutions in given social situations, on the part of groups and movements of those hitherto excluded from such control. (UNRISD/79/C.14, Geneva, May 1979 cited in Turton 1987:3)

The WCED develops this concept even further in its discussion of indigenous and tribal peoples, of whom it observes:

> In terms of sheer numbers these isolated, vulnerable groups are small, but their marginalization is a symptom of a style of development that tends to neglect both human and environmental considerations. Hence a more careful and sensitive consideration of their interests is a touchstone of sustainable development policy. Their traditional rights should be recognized and *they should be given a decisive voice* in formulating policies about resource development in their areas. (WCED 1987:116, 12, emphasis added)

The same principles are echoed by the International Union for the Conservation of Nature and Natural Resources (IUCN), which, in its *Guidelines for the Management of Tropical Forests* notes that:

> the people who live in and around tropical forests should control their manage~ment. (IUCN 1989)

In the same vein, the Tropical Forestry Action Plan states that one of its basic principles is to promote the:

> . . . active organized and self-governed involvement of local groups and communities in forestry activities, with a particular focus on the most vulnerable and on women and on commonly-shared resources. (FAO 1989)

FOREST COMMUNITIES

Perhaps the majority of the 300 million people who live in close association with the tropical forests are socially and culturally distinct from the ethnic majorities outside them. The economies of these majorities have largely developed in lowland areas of permanent, often irrigated, agriculture. Even if, historically, some of these lowland societies once had very close ties with the forests (Bandyopadhyay and Shiva 1987), today most forest communities are politically or culturally marginalized. They are thus poorly placed to exercise the "participatory" control over their resources that "sustainability" apparently demands (Colchester 1989b).

Today many of these peoples are described as "indigenous", a term used here to refer to the various ethnic groups, which are officially distinguished from the society of the national majority by a wide range of culturally loaded terms. These include the "scheduled tribes" (*adivasis*) of India, the "hill tribes" of Thailand, the "minority nationalities" of China, the "cultural minorities" of the Philippines, the "isolated and alien peoples" of Indonesia, the "aboriginal tribes" of Taiwan, the "aborigines" of peninsular Malaysia, the "natives" of Borneo, the "pygmies" of Central Africa, the "Indians" of Latin America, etc.

In recent years, such peoples have increasingly begun to identify themselves as "indigenous". In part, this is because the term carries fewer pejorative connotations than other terms commonly applied to them by outsiders. However, the main reason that they have begun to adopt the term is to demonstrate their common struggle for a recognition of their rights. By labelling themselves as "indigenous", these ethnic groups at once affirm their solidarity with others using the same term and assert their rights to land and self-determination (Nicholas 1989).

As used by outsiders, the term "indigenous" has come to have a somewhat different emphasis. The term is used in order to group together various ethnic groups with close ties to their lands which are, in some way, marginalized from the national society within whose boundaries they now find themselves (ICIHI 1987; Burger

1987). The World Bank, for example — which used to refer to "tribal peoples" (World Bank 1982c) — has recently adopted the term "indigenous" in its policy documents. As now used by the World Bank,

> the term indigenous covers indigenous, tribal, low-caste and ethnic minority groups. Despite their historical and cultural differences, they often have a limited capacity to participate in the national development process because of cultural barriers or low social and political status. (World Bank 1990a:1)

However, by no means all forest dependent peoples are members of ethnic minorities. On the contrary, many peasant peoples in Africa and South and South-East Asia — even those whose main economic activity is permanent agriculture — have a very long history of using forest produce and of regulating access to forest resources. What many of these peoples share with "indigenous" groups is a lack of land security and a politically marginal status. And while not necessarily subject to the same degree of bruising cultural prejudice, their lowly status often exposes them to similar discriminations and exactions.

Right across the tropical forest belt from South America in the west to the Pacific islands in the east, the claims that these politically marginalized peoples are making present a striking similarity. The three central claims of these communities are: the right to the ownership and control of their territories; the right to self-determination; and the right to represent themselves through their own institutions.

These claims are not without justification: to varying degrees, they all have a basis in international law. The right of tribal and indigenous peoples to the ownership of their lands is accepted in Article 11 of ILO Convention 107 and has been reaffirmed in more detail in Articles 14-19 of ILO Convention 169. The right of all peoples to self-determination is recognized in the International Covenants of Civil and Political Rights and of Economic, Social and Cultural Rights. The right of tribal and indigenous peoples to be represented through their own institutions is recognized in Article 2 of ILO Convention 169.

There is, thus, a remarkable convergence between what the

WCED has set out as the essential conditions for "sustainability" and the rights demanded by forest peoples. And this should be no surprise, for what forest peoples are demanding is no more than that they should be allowed to sustain their societies from the environments that they have always depended on.

FOREST PEOPLES AND GOVERNMENT

The gap between what the WCED has called for and the reality for forest peoples and other indigenous groups could hardly be greater. Even where government policy is notionally designed to discriminate in favour of such peoples, as in China and India, rights to traditional lands and to control development are often systematically denied. In both these countries, the state adopts the attitude that it has a duty to develop the minorities out of their "backward" state (Anon 1984, 1987; Cannon 1989, 1990).

Underlying the disenfranchising policies of governments throughout the region lie deeply held prejudices. These have been most explicitly stated in Indonesia, where so-called *suku suku terasing* ("isolated and alien peoples") are defined by government as

> people who are isolated and have a limited capacity to communicate with other more advanced groups, resulting in their having backward attitudes, and being left behind in the economic, political, socio-cultural, religious and ideological development process. (*Down to Earth* 1991)

As in the USA at the turn of the century and Australia in the 1950s, the Indonesian government pursues a policy of re-educating indigenous people to break them from their "backward" ways. They are also banned from pursuing their traditional religions (Atkinson 1988).

For example, in 1986, the Indonesian government embarked in West Papua on a new project titled "Total Development of Indonesian People" aimed at re-educating West Papuans whom it describes as "still living in a Stone-Age-like era". In order to bring these peoples "up to a par with the rest of the country", children "will be separated from their parents to keep them from settling into their parents' lifestyle". This is necessary, according to the government, "because changing their parents' lifestyle would be very difficult, and necessitate considerable expenditure and time" (Indonesia 1986).

In Central Africa, government policy towards so-called "pygmy" groups has been based on two questionable assumptions. The first is that these "backward" and "undeveloped" groups suffer from economic marginalization and exploitation by their dominant farming partners. The second is that strong national polities can only be achieved by submerging ethnic identities. Consequently, policies in such countries as Cameroon, Congo, Zaire and the Central African Republic have emphasised the rapid assimilation of all forest dwellers into the national society. At the same time, to break their dependency on the forests and on their unequal trade with farmers, they have been encouraged to settle and adopt farming (Survival International 1987a).

The aim of such policies is quite explicit. One government programme in the Cameroon is designed "to create a deep sense of belonging to the national society, to be achieved both individually and collectively ... to cleanse the human environment bathing the Baka/Bakola which hinders or blocks their aptitude and capacity to participate in the general effort of production in the country ... to adopt a sedentary agricultural life, with a view to reducing their accumulated backwardness in relation to the general rural populations of the country." This is necessary, according to the Cameroonian authorities, because the hunting and gathering way of life of the 'pygmies' "cannot offer the nation any viable mode of production, being based solely on 'luck'" (Anon 1989).

Very similar prejudices have underlain the policies towards indigenous communities in Latin America. For centuries the task of integrating the Indians into national life was entrusted by law to the religious missions who were given almost feudal powers to regulate, administer and where necessary punish the Indians. During the period of early Spanish rule Indians were resettled from their traditional dispersed forest areas into *reducciones* under strict mission supervision (Hemming 1978). Until recently paternalistic attitudes dominated church and state policy. As one Capuchin missionary put it:

> The missionary knows how to accomplish at the same time the duties imposed on him as a priest — the legacy of Christ among the unbelievers — and as a colonist — the legacy of Government among savages. These duties mutually aid and complement each other, for to Christianize without colonizing or colonize without Christianizing is to plough in the sand or build castles in the air.

Even under the secular authority of the nation states, which has taken over administration of Indian areas in most parts of Amazonia since the 1950s, discriminatory and integrationist policies have been substantially retained to this day (e.g. Arvelo-Jimenez 1980). In Brazil, until 1988, the Indians were treated by law as legal minors — denied rights to vote and sign contracts — on the grounds that they were "relatively incapable". As minors, they were treated as wards of the state. Accordingly they were unable to own land or form their own legally recognized organizations.

There have been very few local level studies of the impact of such policies (Persoon 1985; Colchester 1986a). Garna's study in West Java shows how a programme of directed development and modernization among the Baduy created a sense of dependency and fatalism, with a consequent failure of economic change. "Given the chance, the Baduy would prefer to be left alone to decide their own future," Garna concluded (1990:100).

Throughout the tropics, forced resettlement has been a central plank in government programmes to "assist" indigenous peoples. National security has often been a paramount consideration. In Malaya, for example, the Department of Aboriginal Affairs embarked on a hasty process of forced relocation in the 1950s to prevent Orang Asli villages being used as guerrilla bases. Paternalistic policies still prevail in peninsular Malaysia and have proved socially destructive, economically unsuccessful and environmentally imprudent. Today the Orang Asli are still entrusted to the Ministry of Home Affairs whose other charges include administration of the police, armed forces, prisons and civil defence (Carey 1976; Endicott 1979; Lim Teck Ghee and Gomes 1990; Nicholas 1990).

In Thailand, the "hill tribes" face equally severe obstacles. Not only are they subject to forced resettlement and imposed development programmes, but they are denied Thai nationality and residence. The Thai armed forces have even gone so far as to expel long-settled tribal communities into Burma at gunpoint (Tapp 1986; McKinnon and Bhruksasri 1986; Survival International 1987b; Sanitsuda 1990; McKinnon and Vienne 1990).

The now defunct government agency, PANAMIN (Presidential Assistance to National Minorities) must bear a large share of responsibility for the breakdown in relations between the indigenous peoples of the Philippines and the national government. The institution came into being under the patronage of President Marcos and his relative Manuel Elizalde, with the ostensible purpose of protecting the indigenous peoples' rights and interests. But far from preventing the pillage of indigenous lands by mining companies, loggers and hydropower projects, PANAMIN collaborated with the armed forces in depriving the peoples of their ancestral lands. The result was a chronic breakdown in relations between the government and the indigenous peoples, a breakdown exacerbated by the heavy-handed repression meted out by the armed forces.

Denied protection by the very institution set up to defend their interests, the indigenous people were forced into militant opposition and many even took up arms against the government by joining the Communist insurgency group, the New Peoples' Army. During all this period PANAMIN consistently failed to defend the indigenous peoples' rights to their ancestral lands. On the contrary, because Elizalde's political base and personal wealth lay in extractive concerns such as mining, logging and agribusiness, PANAMIN collaborated with the armed forces and industry in dispossessing the indigenous peoples. When PANAMIN was founded in 1968, the majority of its board members were from wealthy industrialist families, many of whom had direct financial interests in companies encroaching on indigenous lands. Elizalde maintained his own private army in Cotobato in Mindanao, near the area where the Tasaday were "discovered". In 1975 PANAMIN created its own official counter-insurgency unit and within two years "security" expenses became the single largest item in the PANAMIN budget.

In Mindanao, where the Elizalde family owned several concerns, PANAMIN actively co-operated with agri-businesses in forcing indigenous peoples to give up their lands. Tribal communities such as the Manobo were forced to relocate onto tiny reservations owned by PANAMIN. In all, according to PANAMIN's own claim, some two and a half million indigenous people were resettled in this fashion (ASS 1983; Rocamora 1979; Fay 1987).

Government policies to resettle and sedentarize "pygmy" groups in Africa have already been mentioned. In Kenya, the government has sought by force to remove Okiek ("Dorobo") communities from the flanks of Mount Elgon. Unsuccessful sedentarization programmes were an integral part of the Tanzanian authorities' attempts to bring the Hadza people into the national mainstream (Woodburn 1988; Ndagala 1988).

Mention has been made already of the historical programmes in Latin America of moving Indians to *reducciones* administered by the Catholic church. However, forced relocation still continues in some areas. One of the most extreme examples of this process is that being undertaken by the Guatemalan authorities, under which Indian communities are forcibly relocated from their traditional areas and resettled in model villages under close military supervision. Tens of thousands of Indians have been relocated under this programme, which has been widely condemned by human rights organizations and the church for undermining both the Indians' traditional social organization and their economies.

THE STRUGGLE FOR LAND

The most severe problem that forest peoples face throughout the tropical forest belt is the lack of recognition of their customary rights to their land. With the partial exception of some Latin American countries, Melanesia (James 1985) and parts of India's North-East (Furer-Haimendorf 1982), the collective ownership of traditional lands is almost nowhere legally secure.

In Indonesia, effective recognition of *adat* (customary) law extends only to areas under permanent cultivation or occupancy, and then ambiguously (Colchester 1986b; Brewer 1988). A detailed study of Indonesian law as it applies to the 1.3 million indigenous people of Indonesian-occupied West Papua concluded that:

> Current agrarian law does not adequately recognize 'adat' rights in land . . . thus frustrating environmentally sound, sustainable land management practices. This is not only unsound policy, it contravenes the goals of the Basic Law on the Environment, as well as the command of the Basic Agrarian Law that land should be utilized in a sustainable manner for the optimal welfare of the People. (Barber and Churchill 1987:10)

The study found that Indonesian agrarian law and policy persistently discriminates in favour of urban and industrial land users at the expense of traditional owners and rights holders.

In peninsular Malaysia areas set aside for aboriginal use are held by the state and may be reallocated at the stroke of a pen (Nicholas 1990). In Sarawak, "native customary rights", while tenuously recognized in law, are ignored for practical purposes and can be extinguished by simple gazettement (Colchester 1989a; 1990b). In Sri Lanka, central India and lowland Bangladesh, although laws are meant to protect "tribals" from expropriation and land sales, only individual title is recognized (Colchester 1984; Survival International 1984). In the Philippines, rights to "ancestral domain" are not respected (ASS 1983), although, after heavy lobbying, the new Constitution does grant them some recognition.

The main result of this lack of land security has been the massive take over of forest peoples' lands by the expanding lowland populations and enterprises. In Assam, for example, forest lands have diminished catastrophically over nearly a century and a half of progressive invasion by lowland settlers and tea planters. The era began in 1833 and by 1871, some 700,000 acres of forest peoples' lands were reallocated to tea plantations. By 1900, there were nearly 800 tea estates, established in areas previously given over to *jhum* (shifting cultivation), being worked by some 400,000 workers brought in from outside the area. Pressure on the forests intensified further with the demand for plywood for tea chests. Between 1930 and 1950, a further 1.5 million acres of forest lands were taken over by successive waves of Muslim Bengali settlers and Hindu migrants (Tucker 1988).

Processes set in motion in the colonial era continue unabated in India. Tribal lands continue to be classified as "wastelands" and taken over by tea plantations, thus displacing the traditional owners and obliging them to move into other already occupied areas, leading to an over-intensification of land use (Vikas and Pradan 1990).

In Africa, the legislation on land tenure is complex and varied. Although customary tenure is frequently recognized it is heavily subordinated to state interests. Communal and individual tenure may best be considered as consisting of ambiguously-defined usufructuary rights to state lands, which can be extinguished without notice or recourse to the courts (Mifsud 1967).

In Kenya, for example, British colonists, having first recognized traditional tenure through a series of treaties signed to construct a railway into the heart of the continent, proceeded to reverse their policy and completely deny traditional systems of land ownership and control in the fertile highlands which were favourable for plantations (Okoth-Ogendo 1991). To the massive clearance of the original forest to make way for the plantations was then added the problem of thousands of landless "squatters" forced onto marginal lands by the expropriation of their most fertile soils. The political resentment of these dispossessed farmers was a major force in the Mau Mau nationalist movement which forced the British to leave Kenya (Kanogo 1987; Throup 1988). Yet, since independence, the land laws have been barely changed and the skewed land distribution is as marked as ever (Okoth-Ogendo 1991: Wanjala 1990). Deforestation and soil erosion continue to be major problems (Wanjiku Mwagiru 1991).

In Francophone countries, such as the Cameroon, legislation discriminates heavily against forest dwellers and actually encourages deforestation. All land in the French colonies was declared state lands and the authorities ruthlessly alienated lands to colonial enterprises with minimal concern for local peoples' traditional economies (Martin 1991). Community land rights are not recognized while individual titles are offered to those who clear forests thereby demonstrating that they have given the land value (*mise en valeur*) (Colchester and Lohmann 1990).

Very similar land titling laws have accelerated forest colonization processes in Amazonia, particularly Ecuador, Brazil and Central America (Jones 1990). At the same time, with the exception of Peru and Colombia, mechanisms for the recognition of community land rights are seriously deficient throughout Latin America, although, due to heavy and organized pressure from the Indians, this situation is now rapidly changing (Bunyard 1989; Chirif et al 1991). Typically, forest communities can only get title by the same means as non-indigenous people — as individuals who can convert squatters' rights into tenure by the clearance of forest. Even where community tenure can be secured it is usually restricted to small areas, as in Venezuela where community-titling programmes under the Agrarian Reform Law have, for the most part, been limited to small areas suitable only for cultivation, ignoring the Indians' use and rights to their hunting and collecting territories. The Indians have, in effect, been, "peasantized" and deprived of their economies and identity (Coppens 1972: Arvelo-Jimenez 1980; Clarac 1983; Colchester and Fuentes 1983).

Legal landlessness has not necessarily been the immediate consequence of this lack of recognition of collective land title. Adjusting to the political realities, many forest peoples have used what legal avenues exist to secure individual land rights, usually to small parts of their once extensive domains. Indeed, during the colonial period in both British and American possessions, registration of individual land title under the Torrens system was strongly promoted, explicitly in order to bring land, labour and harvests into the market. The Dutch promoted a similar process in Indonesia.

The denial of communal land rights and their fragmentation into individually-owned plots undermined traditional systems of resource management. Systems of shifting cultivation, in particular, have suffered (Colchester 1990a). On the one hand, confining shifting cultivators to small parts of once extensive territories has reduced or even eliminated periods of fallow, leading to soil exhaustion, accelerated erosion and poverty. On the other hand, even where access to land has not been physically limited, lack of land security has promoted mismanagement by undermining traditional concepts of custodianship and resource allocation. A good example is Jeffrey Brewer's study of Bima in eastern Indonesia (Brewer 1988).

Chronic conflict between the state and forest peoples has actually promoted the cultivation of ecologically sub-optimal crops. Among the Hmong of northern South-East Asia, for example, the opium poppy, which is very demanding on both soils and labour, has been selected because it yields a light valuable harvest within eight months of sowing. The crop can, thus, be taken "on the run" and its considerable cash returns used to pay off corrupt army officers and government officials (Geddes 1976; Tapp 1986).

Indigenous economies have been undermined by the creation of a market in land, which many traditionally non-monetarized peoples have found hard to manage. In western Bangladesh, for example, the Santal's territories have been progressively reduced so that today they own less land per capita than the invading Bengalis (Colchester 1984). Haimendorf's studies in central India have shown how this process of land transfer accelerates rapidly with the creation of markets for new cash crops like tobacco and cotton (Furer-Haimendorf 1982). The process has also intensified sharply as a result of the so-called "Green Revolution". High-yield, high-input agriculture naturally favours farmers with greater access to land and capital, leading to a growing concentration of land and wealth (Duyker 1987; Shiva 1989).

Today the process is perhaps fiercest in Thailand where a frenzy of land speculation and commoditization is sweeping through once economically isolated provinces (Feeney 1988; Sanitsuda 1990). As an Akha from Chiang Rai province laments, "I don't think we can stay here much longer. Land is most important to our livelihood and there's almost none of it left" (Sanitsuda 1990:181).

STATE LANDS

Whereas the initial aim of the colonial powers was to gain control of trade, it was only in the 18th and 19th centuries that Western concepts of land ownership and control began to be widely applied. A major force in this process was the demand for timber to furnish colonial navies, which led to the imposition of the forestry policies over vast areas of the tropics (Fernandes and Kulkarni 1982; Shiva 1987; Richards and Tucker 1988; Westoby 1989; Peluso 1990). In the process forest peoples lost control of the major part of their ancestral lands to newly-created government agencies.

Reviewing the problems caused by this process in India, Agarwal and Narain note:

> The biggest problem lies in the alienation that the modern state has created amongst village communities towards their commons . . . The British were the first to nationalize these resources and bring them under the management of government bureaucracies . . . The laws have totally destroyed the traditional systems of village management [and] have started a free for all . . . Today nearly one third of India's lands and all its water resources are owned by the Government. No less than 22% of the national territory is under the control of the forest departments. The result is that village communities have lost all interest in their management and protection . . . This alienation has led to massive denudation of forests, over-exploitation of grazing lands and neglect of local water systems. (Agarwal and Narain 1989:13, 27; see also Morris 1982; 1983)

In South-East Asia the picture is even more startling. Indonesia's Forest Department controls some 74% of the national territory, putting it in conflict with some 30-40 million people who live in or directly from the forests (Poffenberger 1990). Special forestry laws, which override the Basic Agrarian Law, criminalize unauthorized occupation or working of official forest areas and prohibit the unauthorized cutting or harvesting of forest products (Barber and Churchill 1987:45). As the Indonesian Minister for Forestry told journalists in 1989, "in Indonesia, the forest belongs to the state and not to the people . . . they have no right to compensation" when logging destroys the forests that they depend on (*Japan Times* 1989).

The 7,000 staff of the Royal Forestry Department in Thailand administer 40% of the nation's land area, where there are 8-15 million "squatters" (Poffenberger 1990). In October 1989, Thailand's Forestry Department chief announced that all these people were to be relocated. He drew special attention to the need to expel the 700,000 hill tribespeople living in these areas (*Bangkok Post* 1989).

In the Philippines, fully 55% of the country is now classified as forest reserves after the area was greatly expanded in 1975 by Presidential Decree 704, by which all land steeper than 18 degrees in slope was so categorized. Recently it has been estimated that these forest reserves are inhabited by some 18 million people, including most of the country's six million indigenous people (Poffenberger 1990). Yet forestry policies almost systematically ignore these peoples' numbers, welfare and rights (Colchester and Lohmann 1990; Lynch 1990).

Martin (1991:187) identifies the same process at the root of deforestation in Africa:

> Actually the destruction began much earlier this century when the original forest inhabitants were stripped of their autonomy and the forest administration was centralized in the interests of commercial timber exploitation. Forest loss is the result of complex interactions between cultural and commercial factors which eventually lead to uncontrolled destruction. But the tropical timber industry plays a key role in the process.

Forestry came much later to Latin America, but the alienation of forest lands to the state was nevertheless almost total. Throughout Central and South America, the vast majority of forest lands were classified as *tierras baldias* — "wastelands" — which became the nominal property of the state. Forest dwellers continued to exercise rights in these areas not through legal or administrative sanction but through their isolation and neglect.

One of the main problems with this policy of divesting local people of control of land is that the relatively tiny bureaucracies charged with administering and policing the forests have been totally unable to prevent public access. Moreover, forest policy has leased out the same areas to private industry as logging concessions. The result of these combined pressures has been environmental devastation on an astounding scale (Repetto 1988; Porter and Ganapin 1988; Tucker 1988; Myers 1989; Colchester 1990c; SKEPHI 1991; Martin 1991).

In sum, besides replacing previously-sustainable systems of

resource use with extravagant and destructive practices, forestry has created almost insoluble political conflicts between local people and government, which have further "limited the ability of both the state and the community to effectively control forest use, and have contributed to uncontrolled exploitation and mismanagement" (Poffenberger 1990:97).

Moreover, the alienation of forest lands from local communities has long-term damaging effects on traditional regulative institutions that control access to resources (Douma et al 1989). The damage may be so severe that, even when local populations subsequently manage to reassert their rights to forest resources, deforestation only accelerates further since traditional controls no longer operate (Tucker 1988:97; Peluso 1990:43).

The policy bias against local people and in favour of timber-based economies has also severely damaged the evolution of democratic institutions in tropical countries. In Sarawak, for example, the corrupting influence of the timber trade has promoted the domination of the economy by nepotistic, patronage politics. This has undermined democratic principles and caused an increasing marginalization of rural people, who find they can no longer rely on their political representatives to defend their interests. The practice of dealing out logging licences to members of the state legislature to secure their allegiance is so commonplace in Sarawak that it has created a whole class of instant millionaires (Colchester 1989a).

The Commission of Enquiry in Papua New Guinea has revealed a similar decay in standards of public service due to the logging industry (Marshall 1990) and, in fact, the process is very widespread, having formed a crucial component in the "crony capitalism" of the Philippines under Ferdinand Marcos (Anderson 1987). In Indonesia, logging concessions continue to be one of the perks enjoyed by the ruling military clique (Hurst 1991). In West Africa, similar systems of patronage politics linked to the timber industry are also prominent and, as Witte notes below, the process is spreading south into Zaire. In Latin America, where large-scale timber extraction is a relatively new phenomenon, the traditional patron-client structures so prevalent in the political economy have readily assimilated the handing out of logging concessions.

Ironically, Western attempts to promote natural resource conservation have also foundered on this unresolved conflict between local communities and state administration. Like forestry reserves, national parks established on indigenous lands have denied local rights to resources, turning local people practically overnight from being hunters and cultivators into "poachers" and "squatters" (Colchester 1989a). The problem is very widespread. One example of many is the Dumoga Bone National Park in Sulawesi, Indonesia, where the indigenous Mongondow people, displaced onto the hillsides from their valley lands by spontaneous and government-sponsored colonization, have found themselves persecuted as "encroachers" when the hillsides were declared a national park, in turn created to protect the catchment of a dam constructed to promote irrigation agriculture in the lowlands (*Down to Earth* 1989:7-8). The last community of forest-dwellers in Sri Lanka face an identical problem from the creation of the Madura Oya National Park.

DEVELOPMENT AS EXPROPRIATION

The past forty years have seen a massive acceleration in the rate at which indigenous peoples have been deprived of their lands and livelihoods by imposed development programmes (Bodley 1982; Burger 1987). Large-scale projects such as plantations, dams, mines, military installations, nuclear waste dumps and colonization schemes have been the most obvious causes (ASS 1983; Fiagoy 1987; Tapol 1988; Colchester 1985a; 1986c,d; 1987a).

In very many cases these kinds of government-directed development initiatives are justified as being "in the national interest" and the state has thereby exercised its power of "eminent domain" to deny local peoples' rights. In Indonesia, the government feels entitled to invoke this prerogative for any project or programme in its five-year plans (Butcher 1988). In India, it is estimated that as many as two million "tribal" people face eviction from their lands to make way for proposed projects (Colchester 1987b).

Summarizing experience in India, the Delhi-based Centre for Science and Environment notes:

> In a country like India, with a high population density and high level of poverty, virtually every ecological niche is occupied by some occupational or cultural human group for its sustenance. Each time an ecological niche is degraded or its resources appropriated by the more powerful in society, the deprived weaker sections become further impoverished. For instance, the steady destruction of our natural forests, pasture lands and coastal water bodies has not only meant an increased economic poverty for millions of tribals, nomads and traditional fisherfolk, but also a slow cultural and social death: a dismal change from rugged self-sufficient human beings to abjectly dependent landless labourers and urban migrants. Current development can, in fact, be described as the process by which the rich and more powerful in society reallocate the nation's natural resources in their favour and modern technology is the tool that subserves this process. (CSE 1982)

TRADITIONS OF SUSTAINABILITY

> We hilltribes preserve the forest to protect people and animals against danger, disease, injury, soldiers and bad spirits. Having a forest belt around the village will bring happiness to the community. Big trees are like mothers, and little trees are like children, needing to be encouraged into flower and growth. If no one comes and cuts the little tree, it will grow up to be a big one in place of those there now. The forest belt and the village are things people are not to destroy.
>
> *Akha elder (cited in Witoon 1990)*

For centuries, the economic systems of tropical forest peoples have been viewed as backward and irrational. Underlying this prejudice lies a deep mistrust of peoples who are neither subject to government control and taxation systems nor contribute substantially to the market economy (Dove 1985). The Dutch summed up their prejudice against shifting cultivation in Indonesia by referring to it as the "robber economy". In India, the British classified shifting cultivation areas as "wastelands" — not because the practice laid waste the forests but because it provided no revenue to the empire (Tucker 1988). As pressure on natural resources has intensified, such systems have, in addition, been criticized as being environmentally destructive (Agarwal and Narain 1989; Colchester 1990a).

However, many detailed studies of these economies made since the 1950s suggest a quite different conclusion. Hunters and gatherers, such as the Penan of Sarawak, who explicitly see themselves as passing their lands on unharmed to the generations that follow them (Brosius 1986), consciously manage their resources to ensure sustained yield (Langub 1988a, b). The idea that present generations are merely stewards who hold the lands of the ancestors in trust for future generations is echoed in many indigenous cultures throughout the region, as in New Guinea where the people refer to future generations as "our children who are still in the soil" (Colchester 1986b).

Clear evidence has emerged, too, that these ideas are not just long-cherished ideals but actually inform and influence day-to-day behaviour. Studies of shifting cultivation reveal not only their extreme variability and complexity but the enormous reserve of vernacular knowledge on which they are based (Conklin 1954). Practices to conserve resources, restore soil fertility, mimic biodiversity and protect watersheds have been widely documented throughout the tropics.

Similarly, studies of indigenous systems of irrigation agriculture have revealed both the appropriateness of the technology and the very complex social institutions which regulate water rights (Coward 1985). In Thailand, the network of obligations and rights implicit in the traditional institution of the *muang faai* extends the management and protection of resources right up into the forested watersheds which are essential to maintain water supplies (PER 1990; Chatchawan and Lohmann 1991). In such ways, very pragmatic community-based management processes secure biodiversity far more effectively than imposed conservation plans (Lohmann 1991a).

A major obstacle to the appreciation of the value of such "common property" systems has been the myth of the "tragedy of the commons", the notion that "common properties" are free-for-all areas where each individual acts without concern for his neighbours to extract the maximum personal benefit from the land to the ultimate loss of all.

As Michael Cernea has pointed out:

> The term common property has been largely misunderstood and falsely interpreted for the past two to three decades. Common property regimes are not the free-for-all that they have been described to be, but are structured ownership arrangements within which management rules are developed, group size is known and enforced, incentives exist for co-owners to follow the accepted institutional arrangements, and sanctions work to insure compliance. Resource degradation in the developing countries, while incorrectly attributed to 'common property systems' intrinsically, actually originates in the dissolution of local-level institutional arrangements whose very purpose was to give rise to resource use patterns that were sustainable. (Cernea 1989:iii)

The point from all this is not to conclude naively that all traditional systems of resource use are indisputably "sustainable" and above criticism, but rather that they are far more diverse, complex and subtle than outsiders realize. The social, cultural and institutional strengths inherent in traditional systems of resource use need to built on to achieve sustainability and not dismissed as "backward" and "wasteful".

RESISTANCE TO DESTRUCTION

The intimate association between forest peoples and their land, and their determination to maintain their ways of life, is most obviously expressed in their opposition to imposed and destructive change. Such opposition may take very subtle forms. Von Geusau (1986), for example, sees Akha society as fundamentally shaped by centuries of passive resistance to outside interference, creating what might be called a culture of marginalization. Across the region literally hundreds of different indigenous movements have their roots in resistance to cultural, economic and political oppression (Singh 1982; Worsley 1957).

Most obvious of these, have been the mass movements of forest groups that have mobilized to confront specific threats to their future. One of the most celebrated such struggles, between indigenous peoples and loggers, is still going on in Sarawak, where Dayak peoples, denied legal or political means of defending their lands, have resorted to setting up human barricades across logging roads to defend the forests around their longhouses. The government has responded with mass arrests and by passing a new law making all interference with logging roads a criminal offence. Yet despite the intimidation and threats, the blockades have been persistently re-erected, halting timber extraction on the concessions of prominent politicians such as the Minister for Environment and Tourism. Harrison Ngau, a native activist, who was detained in solitary confinement for 60 days in 1987 without charge or trial, remains defiant. "A lot of money is being made from the trees and the Dayaks are not getting anything and they are losing their way of life. The government says this is development. If this is development, the Dayaks do not want it." (Colchester 1989a: WRM/SAM 1990)

Another celebrated example concerns an International Tropical Timber Organization project for "sustainable logging" in the Chimanes forest of Bolivia, which was promoted on Indian lands without steps being taken to secure their involvement or land rights. When it became clear that the international funds were merely accelerating the logging and invasion of Indian lands, the Indians embarked on a 750-kilometre march from their forests to the capital, La Paz, to demand a halt to the project and the recognition of their territorial rights. As a consequence the government took steps to recognize on paper the Indians' rights to land, although the legal status of the "indigenous territories" that were created by presidential decree remains ambiguous.

Alerted by the Indians, the ITTO also investigated the situation and found that the logging process was indeed out of control and far from sustainable. Funds for the project have now been frozen while new management plans are evolved that give the Indians some control over the development process.

In India, the most famous movement to halt deforestation, the tree-hugging "Chipko" movement, developed in the context of a very long history of popular mobilization against government control of forests in the Kingdom of Tehri-Garhwal dating back to the turn of the century (Bandyopadhyay and Shiva 1987). The movement to assert popular rights to forests intensified during the Gandhian nationalist struggles of the 1920s (Tucker 1988) reaching a head when on 30 May 1930 protesters at Tilari were fired on by soldiers, who killed 17 people and arrested 80 others (Hegde 1988).

After independence, Gandhian teaching was perpetuated in the region by European converts who developed a social reform programme centred on the principles of empowering women, curbing alcohol consumption, asserting rights to forest resources and promoting locally-run, forest-based industries (Bandyopadhyay and Shiva 1987). In 1970, serious floods and landslides at Alakananda, associated with the over-cutting of timber in water catchments, caused many deaths and widespread damage to property and agricultural land. The tragedy made a profound impression on local peoples, making them keenly aware of the ecological importance of forests in regulating water supplies (Das and Negi 1982).

Chipko developed on this basis and evolved as a movement of non-violent resistance to logging, in which the mobilization of women, notably tribal Bhotiyas of the village of Reni in Chamoli District, played a leading role (Das and Negi 1982). Eventually, due to the dogged determination of villagers and activists to protect the remaining forests in the face of arrests and police harassment, forest-management policies in the area were changed. While logging was reduced and finally curtailed, the Chipko grew into a tree planting movement to restore forests to denuded hill slopes. The movement has subsequently spread and diversified into many other parts of India (Hegde 1988).

In fact, Chipko is only one of myriads of popular movements within India that have challenged modern economic development. Widespread mobilizations against hydropower programmes that are displacing thousands of tribal communities and flooding their forests and farmlands have sprung up all over the country. Mass marches of protesters have led, in some places, to the cancellation of proposed dams and, in others, have resulted in police shootings and deaths.

Not all these popular movements have been environmentally benign. In Bihar, for example, where the battle between commercial plantations and communal use of forests has been symbolized as a struggle between teak and sal trees, Ho tribespeople who have lost rights to forest lands have mobilized against official forestry programmes and developed a "forest cutting movement". Despite having an ancient tradition of respect for forests, including the preservation of sacred groves for religious ceremonies, the Ho have turned to forest clearance as a means of asserting their rights to use the lands which forestry laws deny them.

Popular mobilization against forestry plantations has also developed in Karnataka state in South India. Here, attempts to take over common lands for commercial plantations of fast-growing Eucalyptus for paper, pulp and rayon led to a "pluck and plant" movement, in which Eucalyptus seedlings were uprooted and replaced by indigenous species that provide products useful to the local peasants (Kanvalli 1990). The movement eventually led to the suspension of international financial assistance from Britain's Overseas Development Administration and the World Bank to "social forestry" programmes centred on Eucalyptus planting, and to a rethink in forestry policy in the state which is still in a process of redefinition (e.g., SWDC 1990a, b, c).

Popular mobilization against state forestry policies has also been intensive in Thailand. With as many as 15 million people living in forest reserves (*paa sanguan*) (Lynch and Alcorn 1991), the government has experienced a long history of compromise and policy shifts to accommodate various vested interests. In recent years, as pressure on forest lands has intensified (Feeny 1988; Sanitsuda 1990; Hafner 1990), these popular movements have found a renewed sense of unity and courage born of desperation.

Popular pressure finally helped lead the government to declare all timber extraction illegal in 1989, after floods and landslides led to a number of deaths and a public outcry against logging. Since then, the most contentious issue has been the government's promotion of commercial tree plantations on "degraded" forest lands, on which, as in Karnataka, the livelihoods of many rural people depend. Eucalyptus plantations threaten to displace hundreds of thousands of people. The result, as Larry Lohmann notes:

> has been an explosion of rural activism unprecedented since the mid-1970s. Small farmers are standing up to assassination threats; weathering the contempt of bureaucrats; petitioning Cabinet officials; arranging strategy meetings with other villagers; calling on reserves of political experience going back decades; marching; rallying; blocking roads; ripping out seedlings; chopping down eucalyptus trees; burning nurseries; planting fruit, rubber and forest trees in order to demonstrate their own conservationist awareness . . . Their message is simple. They want individual land rights. They want community rights to local forests which they will conserve themselves. They want a reconsideration of all existing eucalyptus projects. And they want the right to veto any commercial plantation scheme in their locality. (Lohmann 1990:10)

Concerted action by rural peasants has brought a number of such plantation schemes to a standstill, and the issue continues to be of major political importance (Anon 1991).

Resistance to imposed development has been very widespread in the Philippines (ASS 1983; TABAK 1990: Regpala 1990), the most topical example being the Bagobo peoples' resistance to government plans to build geothermal power plants on the forested slopes of Mount Apo, a national park, held sacred by the Bagobo as the domain of the god Sandawa (Fay et al. 1989b). Mobilization against the project has linked the indigenous people with local environmental organizations. The protests have been met with intimidatory tactics by the military.

In some areas, relations between the national government and local peoples have become so bad that the affected populations, denied other means of protest, have expressed their opposition through organized armed resistance. A tragic example involved the World Bank-supported Chico dams project in the Philippines which threatened to displace some 80,000 Kalinga and Bontoc people from their ancestral lands (Bello et al 1982). When the locals protested against the project, the Marcos regime responded with brutal violence, leading to an escalating conflict. Many tribals took to the hills and joined the New Peoples' Army in defiance of the imposed development programme (Drucker 1985; Fay 1987). The conflict endured long after the World Bank pulled out of the project. Local villages were repeatedly bombed and subjected to counter-insurgency programmes as a result (*Survival International News* 1985 7:1).

North of the Chico, the resistance of the Tinggian people of Abra to the Cellophil Corporation's logging of the pine forests on their watersheds escalated into similar armed confrontation (Dorall 1990). In Mindanao, Higaonon resistance to the logging operations of the Nasipit Lumber Co. led to indiscriminate aerial bombardments of their communities and the displacement of hundreds of tribal refugees into the lowlands (Survival International archives).

The Philippines is far from the only country in the region where conflicts over natural resources have contributed to armed confrontations between indigenous people and the state. It is no accident that the Naxalite movement in India has thrived most in remote and forested tribal areas (Banerjee 1984; Duyker 1987), where land grievances are most acute and government institutions weakest (*Economist* 1991).

Resistance to exploitation similarly underlies the insurgency in the Chittagong Hill Tracts in Bangladesh (Survival International 1984; ASS 1984; Mey 1984), in Nagaland and other parts of North-East India (IWGIA 1986), Burma (Lintner 1990a, b; Smith 1991) and West Papua (Tapol 1988; ASS 1991). The recent liberation movement in Bougainville in Eastern Papua New Guinea, has its roots in a social conflict between indigenous peoples and a mining operation (Filer 1990).

Land conflicts have, likewise, exacerbated many of the civil wars of Africa, notably those in the South of Ethiopia, where the takeover of tribal lands by the government's resettlement programme fuelled the conflict between the country's peripheral peoples and the Mengistu regime (Colchester and Luling 1986).

In Latin America, the roots of rebellion in land disputes has a tragically long and varied history, dating from the first years of Spanish colonial occupation right up to the present day (Holland 1984; Barry 1987).

Whether violent or not, and whether successful or not, the most important and enduring outcome of these conflicts over natural resources has been the local, national and international mobilization and organization that has resulted. For example, opposition to the Chico dams and Cellophil Corporation in the Cordillera was organized around the revival of the institution of the *bodong* or "peace pact", by which warring communities would establish peaceful relations. To confront the dam, the *bodong* was extended over a very wide area, even beyond its original extent, so that it came to embrace a major part of the Cordillera (Regpala 1990). Today, although due to increased militarization people do not feel in control of their ancestral domains, there are literally hundreds of local organizations in the Cordillera concerned with educational programmes, economic development, health, women's rights, marketing and land.

CHANGE AND SUSTAINABILITY

Don't mistake us. We are not a backward-looking people. Like others we want development and we want to improve our lives and the lives of the next generations; we want better education, better health and better services. But we want to control this development in our land and over our lives. And we demand a share both in decision-making and in the benefits of development.

Tinggian Statement (cited in Dorall 1990:62)

Indigenous peoples and many proponents of "sustainability" assert that genuine "development" can only be achieved if local people control their lands and institutions and have a decisive voice in their future. Far from being reactionary forces resisting all change, practically all forest-based communities in the tropics are actively seeking development in health, education and increasing involvement in the cash economy (Gerritsen et al 1981).

This raises the crucial question: can forest peoples maintain the balance between their societies and environments when they have rising populations and increasing demands for cash and services? Many development planners are sceptical of the ability of indigenous communities to manage their resources prudently under such changed circumstances, and use this as an excuse for maintaining control of their territories and institutions or for privatizing their lands and resources.

The argument is a difficult one. If, on the one hand, there is unmistakable evidence of environmental decline in many forest peoples' areas where they are exerting increasing pressure on their resources, this has often occurred where their social institutions and environments are simultaneously under heavy pressure from outside. On the other hand, the overall record of government agencies in forest management has been far worse and undermines the claim that the forests are best entrusted to their care.

Papua New Guinea, where collective land rights are strongly protected by law, thus forms a crucial testing ground for such arguments: on the face of it the case is not encouraging. Despite apparently secure land rights, New Guinean communities have frequently negotiated away rights over their lands, by leasing them to logging and mining companies in exchange for royalties. Only later have they come to regret the massive damage that their environments have sustained from such operations. However, closer examination reveals that the issue is not so simple.

Imprecisions in the law have meant that, while the principle of collective land ownership is clearly recognized, the law does not make clear who has rights to negotiate land deals. Outside enterprises have taken full advantage of this loophole, by such means as creating fake land-owner companies, exploiting internal divisions within the societies, bribery, extortion and debt leverage (RIC 1990a; Renner 1990; Marshall 1990).

However, even once these examples are discarded, there remain cases where apparently representative land-owner associations have allowed their lands to be exploited by outsiders (Good 1986; Hughes and Thirlwall 1988). Perhaps the principal reason is that many New Guineans are very inexperienced in the cash economy and even less aware of the social and environmental implications of inviting in foreign enterprises. There is clear evidence that this situation is changing and much harder bargains are now been struck by local communities than in the past. Another factor, somewhat unique to Papua New Guinea, is that the rate of social change has been unusually rapid. As a result many New Guineans have unreal expectations about what is achievable. Crucially, many no longer believe that their own future, much less that of their children, lies on the land.

Taxation, schooling, labour saving technology, new fashions and consumerism have generated a demand for cash without the corresponding growth of a market for traditional produce. Cashing in natural resources is thus the only ready option for most communities. New technologies such as *wokabaut somils* may provide a solution to this problem (Sargent and Burgess 1988; RIC 1990b) but the social and political challenges to sustainability in New Guinea are also significant.

Melanesian political processes have traditionally concentrated power and trade in the hands of "big men". Whereas, under traditional circumstances, such leadership was both openly accountable and also, in the context of frequent inter-tribal war, dependent on the allegiance of clan members, this is no longer so true. Today, community leaders are as likely to be in an office in the local administrative centre as in the village men's house, and their wealth is more likely to be stashed in a bank in Port Moresby or Singapore than accumulated as pigs, wives and cowries. As local leadership becomes less and less accountable and responsive to community needs and rights, opportunities for making land-use decisions that increase personal gain at the expense of the social and environmental security of the community are widening.

This problem, of what I call "lairdism", is very widespread in indigenous societies and many of them are radically transforming their political institutions to take account of the problem. In Sarawak, for example, the indigenous élite, after a long history of manipulation and co-optation by the colonial and post-colonial authorities, very often sides with loggers against the local people. To overcome this problem the communities have begun to evolve new "Longhouse Associations", run under much more democratic principles than the traditional institutions, to provide themselves with truly representative leadership (Colchester 1989a).

Agarwal and Narain (1989) note a very similar situation among rural communities in India. There leaders of the *panchayats*, made up of several often large, caste- and class-divided villages, have proved wholly unrepresentative. The result has been a disastrous degradation of natural resources. Yet where communities have managed to recreate open, accountable and, crucially, equitable forums for making decisions about resource management, Indian villagers have managed to check and even reverse resource depletion (Chambers et al. 1989).

Perhaps the best known such example is the Chipko and derivative Appiko movement, which, as noted above, evolved as a community-based response to unsustainable forestry in the foothills of the Himalayas. Having successfully halted the logging of the watersheds and secured control, though not ownership, of their hillsides, women's groups have mobilized effective tree planting programmes which have begun to spread widely to other parts of India. A key feature in the success of Chipko has been the development of new political associations — what social scientists now call "user groups" (Cernea 1989) — which are democratic, open and accountable (Hegde 1988).

In the Philippines, too, the Ikalahan of the eastern Cordillera have developed a successful reforestation programme, based on a transfer of resource control from the Department of Energy and Natural Resources to community management, that has restored water quality and brought revenue to the villages involved (Rice and Bugtong 1989; Cornista and Escueta 1990). The project has encouraged the government to develop a programme of leasing out state lands under so-called Community Forest Stewardship Agreements, the legal terms of which have been improved so that indigenous signatories to the agreement are no longer deemed to have waived their ancestral land rights (Gasconia 1989).

In the Southern Philippines island of Mindanao, where indigenous communities have lost far more of their lands than in the Cordillera, land reoccupations have become a central part of their struggle. Unproductive state lands and extensive cattle ranches have been taken back by dispossessed tribal people for plough cultivation and subsistence farming (Lumad Mindanaw 1991). Reorganization into novel political institutions has been a critical step in this process and, as in the Chipko example, women have played a key role in negotiations (Edtami Mansayagan, personal communication).

The process of organizing for change has a long history in Amazonia, which started in the early 1960s with the creation of the Federation of Shuar Centres by which the Shuar people united to defend their lands on the Ecuadorean frontier. Within twenty years land title had been gained for the majority of Shuar communities; they established their own radio station broadcasting in their own language and developed bilingual and bicultural education programmes. Primary health care programmes administered by the Indians were developed with state assistance.

The Shuar experience has been repeated with numerous variations all over Amazonia. Clusters of communities along the same river valleys have come together to form local cultural associations. Regionally they have grouped their new community-based organizations into federations and national confederations. The majority of Amazonian Indian communities are now linked to these kinds of institutions and internationally they are co-ordinated through their own secretariat. Some of these institutions are so well organized and respected that western governments are directly financing their work from their overseas development budgets, recognizing that the securing of Indian political strength, land rights and economies provides the surest path to saving the forests.

Conservation groups have also begun to recognize that effective resource protection is only possible if local communities are both fully involved in protected area planning and gain direct benefits from the project. The Arfak Mountains Nature Reserve in West Papua, for example, is based, simultaneously, on a recognition of the ancestral land rights of the Hatam people and a recognition that Indonesian law does not secure them. Although the legal definition of the area as a "Strict Nature Reserve" makes indigenous resource use theoretically illegal, the project, which has local government approval, allows the Hatam to continue to use the area until the law is changed in their favour. Aware of the benefits, the local people have begun to effectively act as a "guard force" for the reserve (Craven 1990).

GOVERNMENT PROMOTION
OF THE COMMUNITY-BASED APPROACH

Many foresters and local government administrators have long realized that effective management of forests cannot be achieved without the goodwill and co-operation of local communities. Attempts to develop such relations between forestry and people have a very long history, which this chapter cannot hope to encompass. Whereas, on the one hand, foresters have sought to reconcile commercial logging with the interests local communities, mainly by providing employment in forest industries, on the other hand, so-called "social forestry" programmes — essentially plantation schemes, have also been developed with a primary focus on poverty alleviation. The latter were, in particular, promoted by the FAO's "forests for people" programme.

However, the notion that local people should not just volunteer goodwill, in exchange for benefits from forest exploitation, but should actually direct forest development and control the resource was not seriously entertained by central governments until very recently. More usually, the need for better communications with local communities has been conceived in terms of "institution building" — of building up the capacity of government to reach out to rural areas and provide for local peoples' needs more sensitively and effectively.

The political consequences of this approach have not been well appreciated but may have done serious harm to the existing institutions within forest communities. As Jack Westoby, once Director of Forestry at the FAO, noted of the craze for "institution building" in the 1960s and 1970s:

> Only very much later did it dawn on the development establishment that the very act of establishing new institutions often meant the weakening, even the destruction, of existing indigenous institutions which ought to have served as the basis for sane and durable development: the family, the clan, the tribe, the village, sundry mutual aid organizations, peasant associations, rural trade unions, marketing and distribution systems and so on. (Westoby 1987:306)

As noted, attempts in India to place local resources under the control of recreated *panchayats* has not been as successful as initially hoped because the "user groups" have been oversized and undemocratic. Resource transfers have, anyway, not gained wide political support at government levels in India. Apart from the *panchayat* experiments, the experience remains limited to those communities, like those in the Chipko areas, which have achieved *de facto* control of local forests through popular mobilization even though, legally, these remain under state ownership and administration.

Yet, as recent experiments in India since 1988 confirm, where forest users are given secure rights to the forests and have control of management and choice of tree species, forest lands can be sucessfully regenerated even though intensively used for the market (Chambers et al. 1989:197)

In Nepal, the government has been committed to a process of reallocating control (but not ownership) of forest resources to local communities since 1978. The process has been accompanied by progressive legislative changes, which have gradually ceded more and more rights and controls over forest resources to local users. Some of the crucial elements of these laws were only introduced in 1988 and further refinements are predicted.

The programme, developed with outside technical assistance over many years, has been incorporated into Nepal's Tropical Forestry Action Plan and supported by many bilateral and multilateral funding agencies, including the World Bank. The programme starts from a recognition that security of tenure (understood in this context as secure use rights) is a pre-condition to sound forest protection and management (Nepal 1988; World Bank 1989a).

The programme has not been without problems. As in India,

experience has shown that the polity appointed by law to control and administer forests, the *panchayat*, is too large a unit and too far removed from day to day decisions to effectively supervise and manage local forests (World Bank 1989a:5). Attempts are now being made, therefore, to identify and promote smaller, more wieldy "user groups" that will more fairly be able to manage forest resources (World Bank 1989a:13).

Local scientists, however, are sceptical of the results. They note that the artificial fomenting of "user groups" by outsiders rarely leads to durable or effective polities. The few successful community forestry schemes in Nepal have either been in areas where traditional management practices have endured without the hiatus of government intervention, or have been redeveloped by painstaking and highly localized NGO coaxing.

In the Philippines, the same process of resource transfer of forests to the control of local communities is now also just beginning (Philippines 1989). As in Nepal, the proposed scale of this transfer is truly impressive, but it remains to be seen what will result. Many of the political niceties, which have now begun to be teased out in Nepal, have barely yet been addressed in the Philippines case (Colchester and Lohmann 1990).

A widely celebrated example of such "resource transfer" in Latin America concerns the 18 million hectares of forest in the South-East of Colombia, where the government has recently recognized Indian land rights. The area, remote from the frontiers of colonization has been established under revived colonial legislation as indigenous *resguardos* — areas where the Indians are not only granted the right to exclusive access to their natural resources but also manage them through village councils.

CONCLUSIONS

This chapter has tried to summarize the social and political context in which forest communities operate and to outline the main obstacles that stand in the way of them achieving a "sustainable" management of their resources.

Examples have been adduced which provide evidence that community-based resource management can be environmentally benign and perhaps even "sustainable". An essential precondition for achieving success is that the state divests itself of control of land and transfers it "into the hands of those whose survival directly depends upon their careful management" (Fay 1989:8).

Summarizing their studies of community-based resource management in India, Agarwal and Narain (1989:viii) have reached the conclusion that, to achieve environmental security, "each rural settlement of India must have its own clearly and legally defined environment to protect, improve, care for and use."

In Amazonia this process is already underway. Some 50 million hectares of forest lands have already been recognized by various governments as indigenous territories. Encouragingly, there are signs too that the process is spreading into Central America, where indigenous initiatives to secure their lands are being seen for the first time as viable means of "conservation".

By itself, land security through communal tenure or collective control may not guarantee prudent resource use. Control and management of the resources must be vested in open, accountable institutions which respect the principle of equity. Moreover, long term sustainable resource use is only likely to be achieved where the community believes its future does lie on the land.

The barriers to achieving such a transformation in government policies towards indigenous peoples, development and the environment should not be underestimated (Durning 1989b:53). The promotion of sustainability is by definition political. The assertion of indigenous rights and the transfer of resources back to local communities is being, and will continue to be, resisted by those who benefit most from present development strategies.

PART TWO:

CASE STUDIES

GUATEMALA: THE CLAMOUR FOR LAND AND THE FATE OF THE FORESTS

MARCUS COLCHESTER

The clamour for land is, without any doubt, the loudest, most dramatic and most desperate cry that is heard in Guatemala. It breaks forth from the chests of millions of Guatemalans who yearn not only to possess land, but to be possessed by it . . . the serious problem of land ownership lies at the very base of our situation of injustice . . . whereby the very structure of Guatemalan society stands on the shoulders of the vast majority of Guatemalans for the benefit of a small minority.

Collective Pastoral Letter of the Bishops of Guatemala,
February 1988

INTRODUCTION

Guatemala has one of the most severely distorted political and agrarian structures of Latin America. Its economy is dominated by the production for export of a limited number of cash crops, grown on extensive lands held by a tiny minority of farmers. Meanwhile the vast majority of the rural poor, mainly Indians, who make up the bulk of the population, live on inadequate plots in the highlands, where the soils are weak and vulnerable. Many of the poor, for lack of land and livelihood, are forced to migrate seasonally in search of work on the lowland plantations or permanently into the cities. Yet half of the agricultural land, held by the landowning minority, is almost unused.

The skewed land-ownership pattern has devastating environmental consequences. Poor people, denied access to the fertile soils in the valleys and southern lowlands, are forced to clear their fields on marginal lands inappropriate for agriculture. In the uplands, deforestation is having a critical effect on the country's watersheds and river systems, while the colonization of vulnerable tropical forests in the north of the country is proceeding so fast that, at present rates, the forests could all be destroyed within 25 years. Even in these northern lowlands the pattern of land concentration repeats itself; huge areas have been taken over for wasteful and destructive cattle ranches.

Guatemala's export-orientated economy was imposed by violence at the time of conquest and has been built up and secured by powerful overseas economic interests. Attempts to change the country's development pattern in the 1950s were frustrated by US intervention on behalf of these companies and, since then, the grip of the landowners and the military on the reins of power has tightened. The position of the ruling minority, in the face of almost continuous resistance and discontent from the oppressed majority, is maintained by repression and brutal violence.

Growing calls for a more equitable distribution of land continue to be ignored by the government. Yet the economy of Guatemala is in deep recession and a change in development strategy is urgently required, not just to fulfil the needs of the poor but also to promote a more dynamic internal market in goods and services. There is a growing realization, too, that the continued expansion of agro-exports at the expense of the poor and the environment is both economically and environmentally unsustainable. The longer that Guatemala delays in bringing about change, the more painful its transition to a more balanced and stable agrarian economy will be.

ENVIRONMENTAL AND SOCIAL DIVERSITY

Guatemala is one of the most fertile, biologically diverse and geographically varied countries in Latin America. The 109,000 square kilometres of the national territory can, for simplicity, be divided into a number of zones — the southern lowlands along the Pacific coast, the piedmont of the mainly volcanic southern

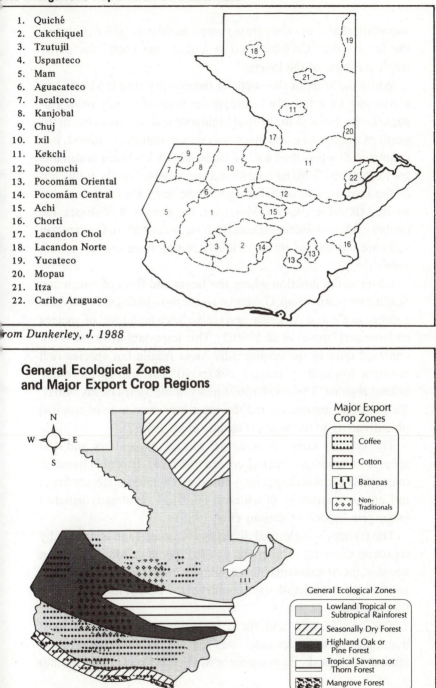

The Indigenous Population of Guatemala

1. Quiché
2. Cakchiquel
3. Tzutujil
4. Uspanteco
5. Mam
6. Aguacateco
7. Jacalteco
8. Kanjobal
9. Chuj
10. Ixil
11. Kekchi
12. Pocomchi
13. Pocomám Oriental
14. Pocomám Central
15. Achi
16. Chorti
17. Lacandon Chol
18. Lacandon Norte
19. Yucateco
20. Mopau
21. Itza
22. Caribe Araguaco

From Dunkerley, J. 1988

**General Ecological Zones
and Major Export Crop Regions**

Major Export
Crop Zones

- Coffee
- Cotton
- Bananas
- Non-Traditionals

General Ecological Zones

- Lowland Tropical or Subtropical Rainforest
- Seasonally Dry Forest
- Highland Oak or Pine Forest
- Tropical Savanna or Thorn Forest
- Mangrove Forest

From EPOCA Green Paper # 5, 1990

mountain chain, the temperate central highlands (the Altiplano), the hot tropical Caribbean coast and, to the north, the dense tropical forests of the Peten.

While the soils in the south of the country (the lowlands and piedmont) are relatively fertile, being derived mainly from volcanic rocks, those in the central highlands and, in particular, in the north of the country, are much less rich in nutrients. Indeed, it is estimated that less than half of Guatemala's land area is suitable for farming, 51% being considered apt only for forests, with 26% of the land area suitable for agriculture and 21% for permanent pasture (ICATA 1984:7). Moreover, the steepness of slopes, the quality of the soil and the climate itself mean that 65% of Guatemalan soils are considered to be seriously at risk from erosion (Anon 1990a).

Being at the junction where the fauna and flora of North and South America overlap, Guatemala is the most biologically diverse country in Central America, and it also has a high level of species endemism (Gardner et al. 1990:2). This important diversity is not confined only to the ecologically more fragile but species-rich northern lowlands (Leonard 1987:xvii), but also to the many upland regions. The coniferous forests of the Sierra de las Minas, for example, are considered the most important area of tropical pine diversity in the world (Gardner et al. 1990:2).

The country contains some 16 species of conifers and 450 species of broadleaf trees (Leonard 1987:28). It is also home to over 1,500 vertebrate species — the most diverse vertebrate fauna in Central America — of which at least 133 are already listed as endangered species (Nations et al. 1988).

The country's biological diversity is matched and enhanced by its social diversity. The country is still home to some 22 Indian peoples, the descendants of an originally much more diverse range of societies that inhabited the country at the time of its conquest by the Spanish.

The best known, and for a long time politically the most dominant, of these societies was the Maya, whose culture extended, at its peak, from southern Mexico across Guatemala into

Honduras. Mayan social organization was hierarchical and divided into warring city-states, each one divided internally so that the peasants, artisans and merchants of the society supported castes or classes of priests and warriors.

At the time of conquest it is estimated that the original population of the country may have equalled that of today (8.7 million) (Fried et al. 1983:3). And, as today, this population was not uniformly distributed, the major part of the population being concentrated in the highlands.

The traditional Indian agricultural system was based on the cultivation of a very wide variety of food crops of maize, beans, squashes and cacao, and this variety, now somewhat depleted, remains one of the country's unique resources. Early historical sources make clear too that the Indians kept aside extensive areas of forests, and later grassland, as fallow land as well as for grazing and fuelwood collection. Lands were held communally with access to land being regulated by customary laws under the authority of traditional chiefs.

THE COLONIAL PERIOD: CONQUEST AND CONTROL

The Spanish moved to assert control over Guatemala in 1524 in a bloody conflict which endured for 20 years until the Indians were finally subdued by the steel, arquebuses and horses of the *conquistadores*. Within a few years the ruling classes of Indians had been all but eliminated and the colonial society emerged divided in two parts, with a yawning economic, cultural and political chasm separating peasant Indians on the one hand from their *ladino* masters, of Spanish or mixed descent, on the other.

As in other parts of the Americas, the early years after the conquest saw a massive loss of human life to epidemics of diseases introduced from the Old World. It is estimated that for meso-America as a whole, the Indian population declined from 14 million to 2 million between 1524 and 1600 (Fried et al. 1983:12).

Because early colonial Guatemala had a large land area and a population reduced to much less than 1 million, the main concern of the colonists was not so much acquiring land as securing cheap labour. While extensive areas did come directly under colonial control, non-Indians did not own the majority of the land until later. In a context of land plenty, and with an Indian population that was almost entirely self-reliant, the recruitment of Indian labour could only be effectively achieved by force.

The violent subjugation of the Indians was thus integral to the imposition of the export-orientated economy that the metropolitan centre required. The extent to which the Indians resisted, by all possible means, this enforced assimilation into the market economy has not been sufficiently appreciated. One indication of its depth may be gauged from the fact that there has been an average of one Indian rebellion every sixteen years since the conquest of Guatemala in 1524 to the present day (Fried et al. 1983:24).

In the early years, and for lack of acceptable administrative alternatives, the Spanish set up a feudal social order in Guatemala, wherein the right to the labour and tribute of entire Indian villages or even areas was given in trusteeship (*encomienda*) to the individual Spanish *conquistadores* (Fried et al. 1983:19).

By the late sixteenth century, control became more centralized, while population decline and expanding demand for labour also created pressure for a more organized system of administration. Thus evolved the system of *repartimientos*, whereby it was the colonial administration itself which compelled each Indian village to pay tribute and supply a share of labourers each week in exchange for a nominal wage. Much of this system was administered by the Catholic missions which concentrated the Indians in 700 supervised settlements (*reducciones*), mainly in the central highlands (Gardner et al. 1990:4).

Gradually, as an export economy developed — mainly in sugar, indigo, cochineal and cacao — the settlers began to establish large plantation estates, known as *haciendas*. Labour remained the main preoccupation and to avoid competition for this scarce resource, rights to own such farms were severely limited. When land sales were held, the number of Indians that went with the land was always mentioned (Plant 1978:67).

Most of the export economy was concentrated in the fertile piedmont where the dominant crop was indigo. The crop was notable for the relatively small amount of labour it required in sowing or cultivation, but needed a very intensive effort during the short, critical period of harvest and processing (Dunkerley 1988:13). To assure a labour supply *mestizos*, people of racially mixed parentage, were by law denied access to the communal lands of the Indians and were prohibited from acquiring title to land in their own name. Many became *colonos* — workers who lived on the estates as free labour, in exchange for the use of a plot of land to supply their needs for clothing and food.

By the end of the eighteenth century, the pattern of land concentration was already well established with, according to one estimate, up to one third of the population dependant on migrant labour (Plant 1978:66). All the same, it is important to note that, even at the end of the colonial period, the principle of communal land ownership by the Indians was still acknowledged. One study suggests that up to 70% of the most fertile lands remained in Indian hands (Dunkerley 1988:14; cf. Painter 1989:10).

INDEPENDENCE WITHOUT FREEDOM

As Roger Plant has noted, for the majority of the population the declaration of independence from Spain in 1821 had nothing to do with liberation. On the contrary, the pressure on the peasantry intensified. Independence did, however, put new energy into the export economy. No longer subject to the strict trade regulations of the colonial metropolis, a rising class of would-be landowners pressed inexorably for greater access to land.

Within four years new legislation was passed allowing for the expropriation and sale of all untilled common lands (*baldios*) to private individuals. Such a law took no account of the Indians' traditional land-use practices, whereby lands were fallowed for part of the agricultural cycle to allow them to recuperate, while other lands were set aside for grazing, hunting and firewood collection. Four years later, the government introduced the first

"Vagrancy Law", to control the movement of Indians, and it reaffirmed the colonial principle of corvée labour (Dunkerley 1988:10). At the same time new taxes were imposed on the Indians in the form of a head tax and an overall tax on communal revenues.

These new policies led, six years later, to an Indian uprising in which the main demand was the restoration of the status quo of colonial days (Plant 1978:67). Polarization over land and labour intensified. By the 1850s there were clear signs that the newly emerging class of *finqueros* (landowners) was no longer prepared to tolerate the principle of communal tenure (Dunkerley 1988:14).

COFFEE IS KING

The coffee boom, starting in the 1870s, provided the economic pressure for the next major change in land use patterns in Guatemala. As the market for indigo and cochineal declined, farmers, switching over to coffee, found they required far greater extensions of land and a much larger workforce than previously (Dunkerley 1988:31). The coffee grew best at higher elevations and the overall export trade expanded exponentially. The development of the coffee trade thus directly affected the highland valleys occupied by the majority of the Indians, who were progressively dispossessed of their most fertile lands. Coffee exports rose from 95 quintales in the 1850s to 113,000 in 1870, 290,000 in 1880, 543,233 in 1890 and 846,679 by 1915 (Plant 1978:67). By the turn of the century, coffee accounted for 80% of all Guatemalan exports (Dunkerley 1988:27).

The land laws were changed to facilitate this takeover of Indian land. In 1873 a new law was passed to allow the sale of "national" lands as private property. Much of this land was actually Indian land. In 1877, a law was passed by which the Indians were obliged to register their claims to common lands — a wholly unreasonable demand on a largely illiterate population. Moreover, to further discourage them, those Indians that did register their lands became subject to a new tax on common lands (Plant 1978:66). Between 1871 and 1883 nearly a million acres of nominally unclaimed lands passed into private possession in this way (Dunkerley 1988:27). At the same time, immigrants were encouraged to buy lands, in some areas establishing virtual enclave economies such as the extensive German colony in Alta Verapaz which had its own port for export on Lake Izabal.

The process was bitterly resented by the Indians. As one attested:

> You have ordered us to leave our lands so that coffee can be grown. You have done us an injustice . . . You ask us to leave our land where our grandfathers and fathers were born . . . Is it because we do not know how to grow coffee? You know very well we know how . . . Are we not the ones who sow the coffee on the *fincas*, wash it, harvest it? But we do not want to grow coffee on our lands. We want them only for our corn, our animals, our wood. And we want these lands where our grandfathers and fathers worked. Why should we leave them? (Fried et al. 1983:25)

Despite this progressive alienation of Indian land, the demand for cheap labour was unsatisfied and further measures were introduced to service the agro-export economy. In addition to the corvée, the landowners were provided with two "main means of prising Indian labour from its communal refuge" — the vagrancy laws and enslavement through debt (Dunkerley 1988:26). Indians were forced by new laws to carry a work-book recording their debts. Indians could be prevented from leaving estates until all their debts were cleared, and political bosses were employed to control the estate workers. Indians even required passports issued by the estate police to travel off the estates where they worked (Plant 1978:68-69; Dunkerley 1988:26-28).

An official pronouncement of 1876 advised local authorities:

> You should therefore see to it . . . that the Indian villages in your jurisdiction be forced to give the number of hands to the farmers that the latter ask for, even to the number of 50 or 100 to a single farmer if his enterprise warrants this number . . . above all else see to it that any Indian who seeks to evade his duty is punished to the full extent of the law, that the farmers are fully protected and that each Indian is forced to do a full day's work. (*Official Notice*, 3 November 1876, cited in Dunkerley 1988:39)

The thirst for Indian labour was such that landowners established new estates in the highlands. Entrapped on these new "labour farms" (*fincas de mozo*), the Indians exchanged the right to continue to cultivate their lands for work in the valleys during the coffee harvest. The practice assisted in the establishment of an impressive network of large estates all over the country (Dunkerley 1988:28). Coffee is still the single most important crop for the Guatemalan economy, in 1985 constituting 42% of total exports (Painter 1989:35).

THE AGRO-EXPORT BOOM

As the process of land concentration proceeded and as rural populations rose, the problem of labour scarcity gradually receded. Land scarcity and not labour scarcity became the dominant preoccupation of the Central American agrarian economy from about the 1920s (Dunkerley 1988:186). Nevertheless harsh rules to ensure a cheap and ready labour supply remained in force in Guatemala.

Although the laws which tied indebted Indians to estates were lifted in the 1930s, a new "Vagrancy Law" was instituted which reinforced the obligation for Indians to provide labour. Under the new law, Indians with less than one and five-sixteenths of a *manzana* of land were obliged to provide 150 days work a year, while those with more land had to provide only 100 days. All peasants had to carry a notebook in which the number of days that they had worked was recorded by the farm manager. Those who failed to fulfil their quota were liable to imprisonment or forced labour building roads (Fried et al. 1983:27; Plant 1978:69).

The process of breaking up Indian communal holdings also accelerated. A decree of 1931 stipulated that common land should be split up among individual peasants, in lots of from 3 to 8 hectares (Plant 1978:69).

Coffee continued to expand, from 162,000 hectares (ha) to 270,000 ha between 1950 and 1977, while bananas leapt from 17,000 ha to 59,000 ha in the same period (Dunkerley 1988:187). Cotton production expanded from 2,000 tons on 5,000 ha in 1948 to 78,000 tons on 89,500 ha in 1967. By 1979 production of cotton was up to 146,000 tons. Sugar production also escalated from 32,000 ha in 1961 to 85,000 ha in 1977. Cattle, too, saw a substantial increase, the national herd doubling from about one to two million between 1947 and 1974 (Dunkerley 1988:189). In sharp contrast, the land devoted to producing the peasants' staple, maize, actually declined in the thirty years between 1948 and 1978 from 538,000 ha to 522,000 ha (Dunkerley 1988:197).

At the beginning of the century, the agro-export boom was financed to a large extent with foreign capital. Modern transport systems — railroads, ports and shipping — needed to export bananas called for large capital investment and created the conditions for the export of other commodities such as cotton. Sugar suddenly grew in importance after the Cuban revolution.

Leading the way in this process was the United Fruit Company (UFCO) of the United States, which commenced negotiations in Guatemala in 1899. In 1901, banana cultivators were granted tax exemption for exports and, in 1906, UFCO signed its first contract. In exchange for a grant of 69,000 hectares of prime agricultural land, it guaranteed to construct the railroad it would anyway need to export its bananas (Plant 1978:69). The deal set the pattern for the decades which followed so that, by the 1930s, UFCO was the largest employer, landowner and exporter in all Guatemala, with control of the country's only railroad and Caribbean port (Fried et al. 1983:17).

US investment in the Guatemalan economy increased further after the US-engineered coup in 1954. The domination of the Guatemalan economy by foreign companies, first as landowners and then as the principal buyers of agro-exports, has been a key factor in the development of the country this century.

Owing to the fact that the prime agricultural land was concentrated in the hands of very few families and companies, the massive increases in agricultural production achieved in the twentieth century did not translate into benefits for the rural poor. Coffee remains the prime product of the agrarian economy with 32 private exporting houses financing 65% of the national production. Cotton is even more concentrated. In 1977, 47 families controlled 70% of its production. Similarly, 84% of sugar production was processed by ten mills (Dunkerley 1988:464; Painter 1989:42). Only 482 farms occupy an astounding 22% of the cultivated land in Guatemala (Painter 1989:9).

TABLE 1
AGRO-EXPORT PRODUCTION BY FARM SIZE

	Coffee	Cotton	Sugar	Cardamom	Bananas	Beef
Value (US$m,1980)	464	166	69	56	45	29
Total farms	97,679	331	16,854	12,267	23,133	117,595
% Production on units >92 ha	83	100	95	68	83	70
No. farms	3,651	331	1,250	645	1,900	8,166
% Production on units >1840ha	19	38	41	13	3	22
No. farms	188	49	91	82	31	337

Source: *Censo Agropecuario* 1979 (Dunkerley 1988:465; Painter 1989:31)

For the rural poor, the expansion of the huge estates has meant increasing landlessness, which has in turn provided the cheap labour on which the landlords depend. This has led to growing protest on the South coast, which in recent years has focused on the figure of the Catholic priest, Padre Giron, who has challenged the stranglehold of certain landlords on the rural economy. Of one landowner he cried out:

> His plantations are today growing sugar cane. They are not producing anything for the peasants. The only thing they produce for us is hunger. The money from the sugar cultivation has always gone to the rich, is still going to the rich and will continue to go to the rich. Why, in a sugar-growing area like Nueva Concepcion, do we have no sugar? Why? Because groups like CACIF [the Chamber of Commerce] are exploiting the Guatemalan people. It is not enough for them to earn a few centavos — they want to suck us dry. (Padre Giron cited in Painter 1989:2)

As the problem of labour shortage receded, the livelihood of estate workers worsened. In a buyers' market, and without effective legal or trade union protection, their real wages have declined, making survival ever more precarious. The surplus of labour has, in particular, affected *colonos*. Between 1964 and 1979, the number of large farms on the South coast with these almost feudal workers dropped from 38% to 4% (Painter 1989:23). Even where land was rented there was a notable shift in rent from labour to money (Dunkerley 1988:186). As one planter noted: "I get all the men I want for Q1.50 a day. I have to turn them away." The legal minimum wage at the time was Q3.20 (Painter 1989:23).

ECONOMIC CONSEQUENCES

Today Guatemala's excessive dependence on agro-exports remains almost as great as ever. Agriculture, which accounts for a quarter of the Gross Domestic Product (GDP), generates two-thirds of export income (World Bank 1989b:iv). Foreign investment and development assistance alike have been shaped by a strong policy bias against the domestic agriculture sector. The almost exclusive emphasis on increased financial incentives for the development of export-oriented agriculture, has discouraged the production of basic foodstuffs intended for domestic consumption (Leonard 1987:58; Barry 1987).

Nor has the Guatemalan economy sought to redistribute the benefits accruing to the agricultural élite to the rest of the population by taxation and the provision of services. Whereas on the one hand, agro-exports have enjoyed over a century of tax exemptions and fiscal incentives, on the other hand the burden of tax at 8.8% of GDP remains one of the lowest in the world (World Bank 1989b: iii; Painter 1989:32).

Low wages and extreme poverty among the great majority of the population have meant a grave lack of disposable income. In turn, this absence of domestic consumers has put severe limits on the development of local industry for either goods or services. A model of growth based on import substitution has not been possible, although the Guatemalan economy has benefited to some degree from the creation of the Central American Common Market.

The lack of a viable domestic industrial base to invest in, has had yet further devastating consequences for the economy, as capital has fled overseas to find secure investment. It is estimated that in the first five years of the 1980s alone, US$1.1 billion left the country (Gardner et al. 1990:6).

Presently, Guatemala is in the grip of a severe financial crisis, brought on to a large extent by its excessive dependence on agro-exports whose value in real terms has fallen drastically over the past half century. By the mid 1980s GDP was 6% below its 1980 level, and external debt increased to 2.5 billion by 1987 (World Bank 1989b:ii).

To overcome this economic impasse, the medicine prescribed by the World Bank is more of the same. Guatemala, the Bank argues, has no choice but to "increase the mobilization of domestic resources" to further expand its trade in agricultural products. Further large-scale irrigation projects funded by private capital for agro-export production are recommended (World Bank 1989b:iii-iv). The Inter-American Development Bank for its part is actually lending money for these irrigation schemes. Further land alienation and the immiseration of the poor will be the inevitable consequences.

ZONES OF LAND USE

The most visible result of this model of agricultural development has been that the country has been divided up into recognizable zones of land use. To the south the coastal plains are dominated by cash crops of cotton, sugar and cattle ranches, giving way in the piedmont and the southern valleys to coffee estates.

In the highlands, where two-thirds of the country's population live (Leonard 1987:39), the economy is dominated by the small subsistence plots of the Indians, whose huts can be seen dotting the hillsides alongside tiny stands of maize and beans. Even here, in the uplands, the more fertile areas have been taken over by large farms growing highland coffee, cardamom and new crops like carnations.

The agrarian economy, crucial to the livelihood of the Guatemalan people, is thus an economy of sharp and visible contrasts. The country not only has a population density of 469 people for every square kilometre of cultivated land (Leonard 1987:41), but 53% of the total population are directly dependent on agriculture (Leonard 1987:73). In some areas the figure is much higher. In the Verapaces, for example, fully 83% of the population are in the rural sector (Davila and Castro 1990).

LAND CONCENTRATION

The visible zoning of crops is complemented by a much more fundamental differentiation of the agrarian economy, according to who owns the land, and the invisible contrasts are as stark as the crop choice that results from them. For, as the United States Agency of International Development (USAID) has noted, the inequalities of land distribution in Guatemala are the most pronounced in all Latin America (Anon 1986:i).

As Table 2 reveals, the vast majority of the agricultural area of Guatemala is held by a tiny minority, with 2% of farms enclosing 65% of the land (*see* Table 1 above). As we have noted, it is these farms which produce the bulk of Guatemala's agro-exports.

Yet not all the large farms are efficient enterprises geared to maximizing profits. On the contrary, fully half of all farms over 50 ha are, according to the USAID, seriously under-used (Anon 1986:iv). Such unused agricultural land which, in all, totals some 1.2 million ha should be classified as *tierras ociosas* and be available for redistribution. However, it is maintained by the large landowners for speculative purposes and remains unused for lack of capital investment. This pattern of land holding can be understood as a hangover from the old agrarian order of the eighteenth and nineteenth centuries.

The effect and, some would say, the purpose, of this extravagant pattern of land holding is to ensure a ready availability of labour for work on the estates. The environmental consequences, as noted below, are also severe, a result of the fact that, in Guatemala, there is actually an inverse relationship between land capability and intensity of land use: the better lands, held by the rich, are under-used while the poorer lands are over-exploited (Leonard 1987:107).

TABLE 2
DISTRIBUTION OF FARM SIZE IN GUATEMALA, 1979

	Farms		Area	
	No.	%	'000 ha	%
Less than 0.7 ha	166,732	31	55.4	1
0.7 - 1.4	121,351	23	115.1	3
1.5 - 6.9	180,385	34	508.0	12
7.0 - 44.9	49,409	9	781.0	19
45.0 - 900	13,177	2	1,817.5	43
Over 900	482	0.09	903.2	22

Source: *Censo Agropecuario* 1979 (cited in Dunkerley 1988:183).

Even where large land-holdings are being used it is often in an extravagant manner. Most notable are the extensive cattle ranches on the rich soils of the Pacific coast which could be far more productively used. In this area, while 45% of the area is given over to industrial crops and 15% to food crops, fully 37% of the area is dedicated to ranching, much of it on unimproved pasture (Anon 1986:ii).

At the opposite extreme are the 88% of the farms, squeezed onto a mere 16% of the land area, which are considered too small to provide for the needs of a family (Sandoval 1988:56). These plots are not only marginal in size but also occupy the poorer soils, mainly in the highlands.

Seriously compounding the problem of plot size is the fact that ownership or continued access to the land is not secure. Some 22% of farms in Guatemala are held by squatters with very limited rights (Dunkerley 1988:185). This has important environmental implications, for as Jeffery Leonard notes "small farmers already at or near subsistence level are reluctant to make any capital or labour investments to improve the lands that they cultivate in cases where their tenure is uncertain" (Leonard 1987:108). The lack of land security has caused a breakdown of land conservation techniques, with the traditional practice of terracing fields being abandoned over large areas, leading to escalating rates of soil erosion (Leonard 1987:130).

Provision of land security to the rural peasants would be an important step towards improving upland agriculture. The commonplace counter-claim that the traditional peasant cultivation system is inefficient and could be massively improved either to yield more food for the local markets or more cash crops to generate more export income for the country or both is largely unfounded. Yet such interpretations, which ignore the realities of the peasants' economic circumstances, underlie the recent economic programmes to promote the production of non-traditional crops in the highlands.

From the peasant's point of view, the traditional mixed crop *milpa* is optimal, being the best means of ensuring a secure and stable livelihood off a very small amount of land. Although more profitable and productive crops could be raised on such land, they also imply higher risks, which the peasant, already living on the margins of survival, cannot afford to take (Annis 1987).

Since the majority of the small farms cannot by themselves provide a living, many peasants have to find off-farm employment to support themselves. Added to this, it is estimated that there are some 309,119 landless labourers over twenty years old without permanent employment (Sandoval 1988:56).

RANCHING FOR EXPORT

As in many other parts of Latin America, Guatemala has experienced a massive expansion of cattle raising in recent years. This has been made possible by the rapid extension of the road network after the war, much of it financed by international loans or by oil exploration, as well as by the installation, at the end of the 1950s, of modern abattoirs and facilities for refrigerated transport (Dunkerley 1988).

According to one estimate, between 1960 and 1978 grazing land increased in area by 2,125% (Gardner 1990:6). The majority of the meat produced has been for export and has been priced out of reach of the ordinary Guatemalan. Indeed, despite, or rather because of, this expansion in beef exports, between 1960 and 1974 per capita consumption of beef fell in Guatemala by 50% (Dunkerley 1988:194).

Yet the overall contribution of beef to export receipts, in relation to the huge areas of land devoted to pasture, is very small (Leonard 1987:101). Stocking rates of the mainly unimproved pastures on the large ranches is extremely low, at about 1.9 head of cattle per hectare (Leonard 1987:90). Ironically, all this has been achieved while there is growing evidence that small-scale production of beef on mixed farms, where cattle can be partly fed on crop residues, is much more efficient (Leonard 1987:92).

Ranching has expanded, in particular, in the previously forested areas of the Peten and the Northern Transverse Zone — a vast swathe of territory stretching from the Mexican border across to Guatemala's narrow Caribbean outlet at the port of Puerto Barrios — where the average yield of beef is only 10kg/ha/annum. As James Nations notes, "even this meagre production plummets after 7-10 years, when soils are so degraded and weeds so prolific that production is no longer viable" (Nations et al. 1988:55).

Ranching is not only greedy for land and destructive of forests, it also creates very few jobs. Data from the neighbouring Chiapas area in Mexico suggest that ranching occupies only 1 worker per 100 ha which corresponds to 6 worker days per ha per year. In comparison beans require 37 worker days per ha per year, rice 60 and coffee 130 (Nations et al. 1988:55).

Yet, for the rancher, beef is an attractive proposition and its advantages are enhanced by the fact that the government provides credits for the conversion of forest lands to agriculture and ranching. Moreover, tax levied on unused lands is higher than for land under production (Johnson 1989:1). Between 1960 and 1980, ranching was the main force behind the burning and land clearance in the Peten, at that time running at some 40,000 hectares per annum (Godoy 1991).

COLONIZING THE FRONTIER

The 1960s saw the beginning of a major new growth area in the Guatemalan economy. Led by oil exploration, nickel mines and hydroelectric projects, the military governments pushed for the opening up of the forested Northern frontier.

The result was a growing conflict between the Indians of the region and the incoming military and landowning élite. As ranches expanded, Indians mobilized to defend their lands against the takeover. The result, predictable perhaps in the intransigent atmosphere of Guatemalan politics, was the brutal suppression of the protest. A critical moment, that can be seen as the trigger for the rebellion and government violence that followed, came when, in June 1978, K'ekchi Indians protesting the takeover of their lands were fired on by the military at Panzos in an organized massacre before their corpses were bulldozed into a mass grave.

Guatemalan President General Kjell Laugerud Garcia, who so strongly defended the military after the Panzos massacre, gave particular impetus to the development of the Northern Transverse Zone. Here, as George Black puts it, "in virgin territory the army set about creating a new geographical power base, far away from the traditional centres of agrarian power" (Black 1984:32). Indeed, the entire area is popularly referred to within Guatemala as "the Zone of the Generals".

But the excuse for opening up this territory was to provide lands for the poor and landless peasants of the highlands. The government thus embarked on a series of ambitious colonization programmes as an alternative to land reform in the more fertile lands to the south (Leonard 1987:44, 104). By 1985, the government had resettled some 60,000 people in the Northern Transverse Zone and close to 100,000 more were slated to follow in the next few years (Leonard 1987:104). According to one estimate, the colonization programme has been giving over some 30,000 ha of forest a year to peasant agriculture (Gardner et al. 1990:12).

The programme, which is overseen by the government's Agrarian Transformation Institute (INTA), has attempted to promote the establishment of viable middle-sized farms of cardamom, coffee, cacao and rubber, either as peasant co-operatives or as commercial farms under USAID guidance (Painter 1989:18). It has been strongly criticized on numerous counts.

On the one hand, Indian lawyers note that, although the INTA programme is meant to be open to all, the bureaucratic procedures present very serious obstacles to illiterate, undocumented and poor peasants who may not speak Spanish. On the other hand, the imposed communal system of co-operatives has conflicted with the private property notions of the peasants, creating quite serious obstacles to efficient production (Stewart et al. 1988:17, 53).

Yet INTA has, in any case, not even attempted to ensure that it is the poor who most benefit from the programme. In fact, very large chunks of land have been handed out to politicians, land-owners and the military (Black 1984:33). As the World Bank itself noted, far from assisting the rural poor, the INTA programme actually resulted in a "substantial distribution of large blocks of land to persons from the middle and upper income classes" (cited in Painter 1989:18). Peasants established with only provisional land titles have also proved easy prey for eviction, thus intensifying the process of land concentration in the zone (Black 1984:40).

The main beneficiaries of the colonization programme were the ranches. Between 1964 and 1973, ranches in the western two departments of the North Transverse Zone quadrupled their holdings and increased stock by 190,000 head. Further east, in the Peten, Alta Verapaz and Izabal, the stocklands expanded three-fold and the herd increased by 135,000 steers. Land prices rocketed and farmers experienced a rolling wave of dispossessions (Dunkerley 1988:466). The military made the greatest gains. Four members of government were estimated to own 285,000 hectares in the Zone, while fully 60% of the department of Alta Verapaz was reckoned to be the property of military officers by 1983 (Dunkerley 1988:467).

INTA's authority did not extend into the Peten, the vast forested area in the north of Guatemala. Here the majority of the land was held by the state (*ejidos*) and the area was entrusted to the army-run Empresa Nacional de Fomento y Desarrollo Economico del Peten (FYDEP). FYDEP, which had almost exclusive control of the natural resources of the Peten between 1959 and 1987, also began a parallel programme of land distribution that was hailed as a solution to the peasants' problems (Plant 1978:74). Some land, nearly all of very poor quality, was handed out to the small-holders, but the majority of titles were granted to the political and military élite to create further cattle ranches.

A road-building programme devoted mainly to promoting oil exploration facilitated the export of cattle and the penetration of the area by spontaneous colonists, notably K'ekchi Indians displaced from their ancestral lands in the Northern Transverse Zone further south. It is estimated that up to 20% of the entire Guatemalan cattle herd is now in the Peten and the continuing expansion of pasture in the region means that this percentage will climb in the coming years (Leonard 1987:104).

In 1960, the Peten forest still covered some 36,000 square kilometres, about one third of the national territory. As a result of FYDEP's programme, population in the area has increased from 27,000 in 1964 to 200,000 by 1984. The result of the ranching and settlement has been the elimination of at least one third of the Peten forest (Myers 1989:19). Yet the impact of the programme on the population in the highlands has been negligible (Barraclough 1988).

CONSEQUENCES FOR THE POOR

With a present population of around 8.7 million people, growing at 3.5% per year, Guatemala is likely to double in population within the next 22 years (Leonard 1987:37-38; Johnson 1989:1). The unequal development process and the lack of land and livelihood it has brought for the peasantry translates into unimaginable poverty and hardship for the majority of Guatemalans.

According to a 1982 UNICEF study, no other Central American country is poorer than Guatemala (cited in Painter 1989:4). Guatemala, the study found, had the lowest "physical quality of life index" in Central America. Government figures admit that by the end of 1985 as many as 86% of families were living below the official poverty line and 55% were classed as "extremely poor". USAID estimates that 60% of the population is living in absolute poverty (Leonard 1987). Rates of malnutrition reflect these figures. A national survey in 1980 found that only 27% of all children between six months and five years showed normal physical development, with 45% showing moderate to severe retardation in their growth (Painter 1989:3).

During a July 1896 visit, the head of UNICEF for Central America, Agop Kayayan stated: "Guatemala has the worst infant mortality rate in Central America. Every day 115 Guatemalan children under five die from such (preventable) diseases as diphtheria, whooping cough, tetanus, measles and polio." Nationally, infant mortality rates were recorded at 80 per 1000 in 1984, while locally the rates are far higher, reaching up to 160 per 1000 in the Indian areas of highlands, according to one USAID study in 1982 (Painter 1989:4).

In 1985, 46% of the population were without any access to some form of health care, with the state public health system reaching only 22% of the population. Moreover, most health centres are concentrated in the cities. Indeed, 80% of all health services are located in the capital (Painter 1989:6).

Other services and facilities are as poor. Less than half Guatemalan homes have toilets. Only 54% have piped water supplies, while 39% of rural families in towns with a population of under 2000 take their water direct from rivers, lakes or springs. The housing shortage in 1985 was estimated at 650,000 units for a population of only 8 million people. Social security benefits reach only 0.2% of the people, while fully 42% of the working population have had no formal education at all. In 1986, there were estimated to be 800,000 school children without classrooms. Another estimate was that, the same year, approximately 2.3 million children, mainly in rural areas, received no formal education whatsoever (Painter 1989:6-7).

Nor do these terrible statistics reflect a static situation. Two USAID studies in 1970 and 1980 both concluded that the situation of peasants worsened in absolute terms over the previous decade (Painter 1989:13). Observing these conditions has led many to conclude that the standards of rural subsistence are lower now than they were in the colonial period three hundred and fifty years ago (Dunkerley 1988:15, 195).

POPULATION AND DISTRIBUTION

It is commonly asserted that the basic problem in Central America is that population has expanded faster than the economy can keep up, and that, moreover, the rapid increase in the rural population is the principal cause of *minifundismo* as peasant plots have had to be further and further subdivided to provide the people with some kind of living. Although the growth of population has undeniably aggravated the situation, neither assertion stands up to close scrutiny.

In the first place, GDP has kept ahead of population. For example, between 1949 and 1982, per capita GDP for Guatemala increased from $220 to $353 (in 1950 US$ terms; Dunkerley 1988:175). In the same way, overall per capita food production in Guatemala increased well ahead of population growth, rising by 32% between 1960 and 1980. However, the bulk of these gains were made in increases in export crops. By contrast, per capita cereal production fell by 10.1% between 1975-1981 (Leonard 1987:82). As a result, while food production increased, access to food decreased. Table 3 shows in more detail this skewed growth in the agrarian economy.

TABLE 3

GROWTH IN POPULATION AND AGRICULTURAL
PRODUCTION, 1950-1980

Years	Food Crops %	Agro-exports %	Total Population %
1950-1960	2.1	9.7	4.1
1960-1970	3.8	5.1	3.6
1970-1980	3.0	7.8	2.8
1950-1980	3.0	7.5	3.5

Source: Painter 1989:17 from FAO Year Books

Similarly, land alienation rather than subdivision has been a major factor impoverishing the rural poor. In the last 25 years, despite the substantial increase in overall number of small farms of under 7 ha, the *total* area of land held in such units has declined from 37.5% to 16% of the total agricultural area (Dunkerley 1988:182).

Another cause of increasing poverty and landlessness has been the growing tendency of large landowners to expel peasants formerly allowed to live on the estates as feudal workers. These *mozos colonos* provided free labour to farm owners in exchange for the right to cultivate land. However, with mechanization and as labour has become more widely available, landholders are increasingly expelling these serfs, not least for fear they will lay claim to the lands that they cultivate (CEG 1988:27).

As James Dunkerley rightly concludes:

> In short the demographic expansion is not the principal cause of land poverty and cannot account for its exceptional acceleration over the last two decades. This is the result of a geographically uneven but general tendency for commercial farms to expand at the direct expense of the subsistence sector. (Dunkerley 1988:184)

LAND REFORM IN GUATEMALA

Ever since the Mexican revolution, two related legal concepts have been at the centre of land reform legislation in Latin America. Land, it was held, could be owned as private property, but it had to be used for the benefit of the community. Rights to lands that were "unused" (*tierras ociosas*) could be forfeit because the land was not fulfilling its "social function".

These principles found their way into Guatemalan law and even the Constitution in the reformist post-war period and laid the ground for the only real attempt at land reform in Guatemala's history. The reform was promoted under Decreto 900, the Agrarian Reform Law of 1952. Under this law, in the short period between 1952 and 1954, some 603,615 ha of private lands were expropriated and a further 280,000 ha of public lands were handed out. The total land area of 883,615 ha was redistributed to an estimated 78,000 to 100,000 peasants (Anon 1986:iv).

It is important to recognize the limited nature of the reform that was undertaken. The redistribution did not apply to *any* land that was being cultivated; no properties under 90 hectares were affected, even where the land was unused. Moreover, as is now generally agreed, the programme, far from being inspired by communist goals of abolishing private property, was conceived within the framework of a liberalization and development of capitalist agriculture. Nor were landowners expropriated without recompense. Compensation, totalling US$8.3 million, was paid for expropriated lands on the basis of declared taxable value (Plant 1978:72; Sandoval 1988:52).

All the same, considering the short time period in which the reform was undertaken, it was a substantial land transfer, especially in the Guatemalan context. Indeed, more land was redistributed in the short reform than in all the following 30 years and this includes the fact that 66% of lands handed out since 1955 have been on the agricultural frontier (Anon 1986:iv).

Potentially as significant for the future of the Indian communities, the Arevalo government in 1945 had also passed a new law designed to secure the rights of rural communities to their lands. Under this Law of Supplementary Ownership, land tenure title was recognized on the basis of proven use of land rather than the dubious titles procured by landowners over the past century (Plant 1978:71). The law, however, was never properly implemented and was annulled at the end of the reform period in 1954.

The land redistribution provoked an inevitable reaction from the landed élite whose monopoly on power was being directly challenged. Yet it was only when the land reform also challenged the power of the foreign companies that the process ran aground. Among the lands slated for expropriation were 387,000 acres of unused lands held by the United Fruit Company. This threat to US interests was unacceptable to Eisenhower, who promptly set about undermining the democratically elected Arbenz government (Black 1984:16).

Ever since 1954, there has been a tendency to characterize the reforms of the Arbenz government as part of a slide in Guatemala towards communism. Although the growth of a participatory democracy, including the legalization of left-wing and communist parties, was part of Arbenz's programme of reform, the land reforms were undertaken principally as an attempt to modernize agriculture and to replace an almost feudal agrarian economy with a capitalist system.

Indeed, in the early years of the Arevalo and Arbenz era, the World Bank itself had stressed the need to curb the monopolistic power of the fruit companies. Their control of transport facilities and prices was considered by the Bank as the greatest single barrier to Guatemalan industrial development. The political power that the companies gained from their profits, bloated by their exemptions from taxation and labour laws, also disturbed the Bank, which recommended that they should "refrain from any political activity and should accept perhaps less reservedly than they have in the past, the need to adapt their legal status and their policies to changed conditions" (World Bank study of 1951 cited in Fried et al. 1983:49).

The story of how the US government, in support of United Fruit Company, intervened in 1954 to topple Arbenz has been amply recounted elsewhere (see Fried et al. 1983:45 n1). The consequences of the CIA-engineered coup have also been well documented. It ushered in an era of severe political repression. The military, which had long been a significant player in Guatemalan politics, extended and deepened its power and economic control (Niedergang 1971 (1):306; Fried et al. 1983; Black 1984; Chomsky 1985; Painter 1989; Dunkerley 1988).

At the same time the landed élite was once again given free rein of the agrarian economy. Nearly all the land redistributed in the Arbenz land reform was once again confiscated by the state. Indeed, by January 1956 only 0.4% of the beneficiaries under the land reform retained their land (Plant 1978:73). Much of the land was returned to the original land owners; the peasants, if they were lucky, became landless workers on the estates. Reversing Arbenz's nationalist modernization programme, the new regime opened the country up to further foreign investment, while endorsing the continuing trend to diversify agro-exports.

Most important of all, the new Constitution affirmed the principle of private property and, in common with all subsequent constitutions, had the effect of closing all possibility of legal land expropriations to achieve land reform (Sandoval 1988:57). Guatemala's most recent Constitution has altogether eliminated the notion of land having a social function (Painter 1989:101).

Nevertheless, Guatemala does, technically at least, still have a land reform programme. Decree 1551, the Agrarian Transformation Law, which was passed in 1961, provides a mechanism for the expropriation of *tierras ociosas* of over 100 hectares. However, according to a USAID study of the programme, which is administered by the National Institute for Agrarian Transformation, INTA, the process is "labyrinthine". Once unused land is identified and the owner informed of this by INTA, the law allows the owner a further two years to put it under production. Only then may peasants interested in cultivating the land request use. Negotiations are then undertaken to pay compensation, not on basis of tax declarations but on evaluations carried out jointly by the owner and by INTA officials.

USAID concludes that the process is inadequate for carrying out the ostensible goals of the law, and "has the principal effect of protecting owners of unused lands from expropriation. In addition, the office of INTA in charge of carrying out the disposal of unused lands under Decree 1551 has traditionally lacked sufficient funds and staff. In reality, INTA has not expropriated any appreciable area of cultivable land since the law was approved" (cited in Sandoval 1988:58).

As noted above, INTA has instead focused its attentions on the colonization of the agricultural frontier, where new land holdings have been established on nominally unoccupied state lands (*ejidos*). It is notable that, because of the established legal mechanisms, INTA has put considerable effort into taxing these small-holders, while doing little to tax owners of unused lands, who theoretically were liable to pay INTA up to Q900,000 per year (Painter 1989:19). Between 1970 and 1981, INTA extracted Q5,300,000 from the former, while raising only Q602,000 from the latter. "In other words," the USAID study concludes, "Decree 1551 has provided a legal basis to facilitate the extraction of funds from peasants with scarce resources, while making it more difficult to recover taxes on unused lands" (cited in Sandoval 1988:58).

Given such obstacles to land reform, development agencies, especially USAID, have proposed an alternative programme to provide peasants with a cash income from their tiny fields through intensive horticulture. By growing "non-traditional crops", such as broccoli, snow peas, cauliflower, melon, strawberries and flowers the idea is to transform peasant economies from what is perceived as the inefficient production of subsistence crops into viable mini-farms producing high value crops for the export market. The proposal has the added benefit, from the economic planners' point of view, of providing valuable foreign exchange to Guatemala's flagging economy.

Environmentalists have been quick to condemn the development programme. The crops depend on intensive applications of fertilizers and pesticides, whose impact on the fragile upland soils have not been adequately assessed. Pesticide poisonings in the uplands have been on the increase in recent years. Evidence is accumulating that the initial high yields are not sustainable without increasing and costly chemical inputs. The crops, which depend on high applications of water, also risk depleting the water tables (Gardner et al. 1990:10-11).

Further doubts about the scheme have also been raised. Some fear that the transition from subsistence crops to store-bought food may have a negative impact on diet, as the wide variety of crops grown in the traditional *milpa* are replaced with a limited range of processed foods. Others doubt the wisdom of making marginal farmers dependent on the vagaries of the market, especially as the middle-men will reject any blemished crops which are not saleable to fussy consumers in supermarkets in the USA (Gardner et al. 1990:11). Making marginal farms dependent on such high over-heads puts them at risk of bankruptcy with the smallest piece of bad luck. As in many other parts of the world, the result may be to accelerate the process of land concentration as peasants are forced to sell off their lands to extract themselves from debt.

Comments one local agronomist, "Redistributing the land is the only solution. We cannot dedicate ourselves to palliatives, like improving technology so the peasant can produce a little more on terrible soil. This is no solution." (Gardner et al. 1990:14)

THE ENVIRONMENTAL IMPACT

Historically, the main environmental impact of the agro-export economy was felt in the piedmont and the plains of the south coast where forest was cleared for establishing plantations on the fertile volcanic soils. In particular, the introduction of cotton "imposed a pattern of land use which has progressively altered the ecosystem, with the indiscriminate extermination of flora and fauna" (ICATA 1984:15). In the same way, extensive areas of forest have been cleared in the Caribbean coast for establishing banana plantations, as well as rice and tobacco in the valley of the Rio Motagua.

Forest loss in these relatively fertile areas accelerated considerably in the post-war period with the massive expansion of cattle ranching. With the extension of the agricultural frontier into the much more vulnerable lowland areas of the Northern Transverse Zone and the Peten, rates of forest loss of leapt exponentially.

Today, Guatemala's forest cover is down to between 27% and 42% of the national territory, reduced from 77% in 1960 (Anon 1990a; Leonard 1987:99, 119). Forest loss, estimated by the FAO in 1981 at 720 square kilometres per annum (Lanly and Gillis. 1981), has been accelerating since, and may now be proceeding at as much as 1,080 to 1,620 square kilometres per annum (Nations et al. 1988). At this rate Guatemala's forests have only 25-40 years left before being eliminated (Johnson 1989:1).

The available data are also imprecise on the main proximate causes of forest loss, yet there is general agreement that the two main pressures come from conversion for agriculture (and ranching), especially on the northern frontier, and fuelwood collection, notably in the highlands (see Leonard 1987:123). Nations et al.

(1988:11) assess the causes of forest loss as 29% due to colonization, 6.5% fires, 1.1% industrial use, and 63% firewood (cf. ICATA 1984:11). According to the recent National Forestry Action Plan for Guatemala, of 550 square kilometres of forest being lost annually, 380 square kilometres are lost in the Peten alone, with 23% of all forest loss being in coniferous forests and 77% in broadleaf forests. The plan estimates that 90% of all deforestation is caused by colonization, 8% by fires, 2% by commercial logging. In addition some 6.8 million cubic metres of firewood is burned annually, without necessarily causing loss of forest cover (PAFG 1990b:2). Colonization has also caused the invasion of several national parks (Nations et al. 1988:14).

However, the role of logging in forest loss is higher than these figures reveal. As in tropical forests elsewhere (Leonard 1987:123; Colchester 1990c), in Guatemala logging plays a crucial catalytic role in deforestation, opening up forest lands to settlers who clear and burn forests first penetrated by logging roads. Ranching follows close behind this pioneering agricultural frontier, as squatters are displaced by those whose political connections enable them to secure title to the land.

The firewood demand, estimated by one study at 1.8 cubic metres/person/year for the entire population (Anon 1990a), is exaggerated because the wood not only supplies fuel for the majority of rural households but also for many in the cities. Some 52% of urban energy demands are met through burning firewood (PAFG 1990a:4-5). In 1982, about 40% of this fuel was coming from conifers and 60% from broadleaved woods (Anon 1990a).

Statistics on gross rates of forest loss do not by themselves give a clear picture of the seriousness of this problem in Guatemala. Much more disturbing is the fact that much of the deforestation is occurring on very fragile soils.

For example in the Verapaces region, only 7% of the land is considered suitable for permanent cultivation while some 80% should be maintained as forest. Yet, at present, over 45% of the area is already under permanent agriculture with only 40% forest cover (Davila and Castro 1989:13, 35). INTA colonization programmes have led to the clearance of 2,500 square kilometres of land inappropriate for agriculture (Davila and Castro 1989:37). Even within areas that have been set aside as forest lands, forestry is not orientated towards profitable use and conservation. Rather, a "mining type of exploitation" prevails, with felling occurring in crucial catchment areas (Davila and Castro 1989:15). Mahogany is nearing commercial extinction due to totally uncontrolled cutting (Davila and Castro 1989:49).

Guatemala's soils are extremely vulnerable to forest loss. In the southern areas this is because the highly fertile soils are largely made up of unconsolidated volcanic ash (Leonard 1987:130), while in the north the much less fertile soils under tropical forests are susceptible to rapid leaching and laterization. According to USAID, 25-35% of Guatemala's soils have already been seriously eroded or degraded. Others put the figure even higher and suggest that by the mid-1980s Guatemala had already lost 40% of the productive capacity of its soils due to inappropriate land use (ICATA 1984:12; Monteroso and Murga 1989).

Rates of soil loss increase massively once forests are cleared, rising by between 300% and 5,500% (Leonard 1987:133). The worst soil erosion problems are occurring in the severely deforested Western Highlands, where annual soil losses are estimated to range from five to thirty-five tons per hectare. Leonard (1987:130) cites one study which showed the equivalent of 267 tons of soil per hectare being lost annually in the Xaya-Pixcaya headwaters. Even higher figures, of between 700 and 1,110 metric tons per hectare, have been recorded in some deforested areas (Leonard 1987:133; WRI 1990:116).

Soil erosion from loss of forest cover has other effects apart from reducing agricultural production. Siltation is causing major problems for Guatemala's hydro-electric plants, notably to the Chixoy hydropower project, which was a centrepiece of the Northern Transverse Zone development programme. After years plagued by major constructional and resettlement problems, the plant now produces 70% of the country's electricity, mainly used for industrial purposes. The dam, which cost over US$1,000 million, was funded with 16 international loans equivalent to 39% of the national debt, including loans of US$145 million from the

World Bank and US$105 million from the Inter-American Development Bank (Black 1984:32).

The Chixoy dam is now suffering such severe silting caused by forest loss in the watershed area that the life of the dam has been reduced by 45 years (Monteroso and Murga 1989). Government officials note that the deforestation resulted primarily from clearance for agriculture, in turn caused by the unequal distribution and insecure tenure of land. Some 533,000 people live in the river catchment, of whom 82% are Indian and 43% are illiterate (Cabrera Cruz 1990).

The deforestation of Guatemala's watersheds is also having noticeable impact on the country's climate and river flow. Many parts of Guatemala now report longer dry seasons, and flash flooding and drought are also increasingly reported (ICATA 1984:16). River siltation is also reducing the rivers' carrying capacity, exaggerating the problem of flooding during the wet season. The River Motagua, Guatemala's only major inland waterway apart from Lake Izabal, has lost 192 navigable kilometres due to silting (Leonard 1987:136).

Although the attention of environmentalists has focused on the critical problem of deforestation on the agricultural frontier and in the watersheds, the continued expansion of the agro-export economy in the lowlands is also a matter for concern. Many of the infrastructural development projects to promote this expansion have been funded by multilateral development banks, whose 132 loans made to Guatemala in the past decade have, according to one study, paid "little or no attention to environmental issues" (Monteroso and Murga 1989).

Loans for tobacco production have been particularly singled out for their environmental damage, not just because they require the clearance of forest to establish the plantations but also because fuelwood is required for smoking and drying the crop. Another major concern with the expansion of the agro-export economy has been over the downstream effect of pesticides, which are considered to be one of the main causes of mangrove degradation and loss (Monteroso and Murga 1989).

In the past 30 years Guatemala has lost some 92% of its

mangroves (Leonard 1987:142), 31% being lost in just thirteen years between 1965 and 1978. Most of the destruction has been due to charcoaling and pesticides from agribusiness (Nations et al. 1988:6; Johnson 1989:1). The implications are far more serious than the small size of the areas lost might suggest. As Leonard reminds us,

> mangrove areas serve as crucial spawning and nursery areas for crabs, shrimps, molluscs, and numerous commercially valuable finfish and they produce enormous amounts of nutrients that are washed into adjacent estuarine and nearshore habitats to provide the food base for adult marine species. The links between mangrove ecosystems and off-shore marine fisheries, therefore, can hardly be exaggerated. (Leonard 1987:23-24)

Indeed, Johnson estimates that 90% of Guatemala's commercially important fish come from mangrove forests (Johnson 1989:1).

The relationship between landlessness and land degradation in Guatemala was neatly summed up at the third National Congress of the College of Agricultural Engineers in December 1982, which concluded:

> The present distribution of land, which determines in large part the use and ownership of natural resources, is affecting their rational exploitation and preventing the development of wide sectors of Guatemalan society. A great number of landowners possess very reduced areas of land, often inappropriate for agricultural production, yet, for subsistence reasons, they find themselves obliged to cultivate basic foodstuffs on this land. This has negative effects on natural resources and on the overall development of the country. The state's policy for resolving this problem of pressure on land has been to convert to agriculture lands apt only for forests. This policy has not contributed to agricultural development but, on the contrary, has generated new socio-economic and ecological problems.

RECIPES FOR CHANGE:
POPULAR DEMANDS AND THE GOVERNMENT RESPONSE

Ever since the coup of 1954, the political space within Guatemala has been severely limited. The political process has become increasingly dominated by the military, who operate in a somewhat uneasy alliance with the landowning élite. On one thing, however, they are all agreed: land reform is unmentionable and its promotion is still considered tantamount to communism. The pattern of political killings that became established in the 1960s continues to this day, a fact which seriously hampers the development of alternative policies both within government and in the public domain.

Yet the need for a change in agrarian policy in Guatemala is seen as so pressing by some sectors of the population that it continues to be advocated against all the odds. Most vociferous of the voices for change has been the *Comité Unidad Campesina*, which was formed in the 1970s as a rural workers' union and which has remained a vital force in Guatemalan politics. Central to CUC's demands has been the need for a structural change in Guatemalan society with land reform as the key to achieving this. The same position is held by the *Unidad de Acción Sindical y Popular*, which believes that land reform is a prerequisite for democracy and peace in the country.

The government's reaction to such calls for agrarian change, which have also been made by the various exiled and underground groups, has been to unleash terror on its own people, rather than countenance political reform. Just being an Indian has meant being suspected of "communism". As one Indian responds: "We are not communists. Communal, that's what we are. So, if that's what they mean by communists, well, that is their word, not ours" (cited in Holland 1984:101).

From the end of the 1970s, the killing of political opponents in Guatemala has become commonplace. Death squads and disappearances are a feature of daily life. Indiscriminate counter-insurgency during the early 1980s left a terrible toll of 100,000 killed, 40,000 disappeared, 400 Indian villages destroyed and 1,000,000 peasants displaced as internal refugees. Some 200,000 Guatemalans fled the country during these years and, according even to official figures, nearly 46,000 have still to return. In this climate of fear, popular movements' demands are now mainly limited to re-establishing basic civil rights and abolishing conscription into the militia (Nelson and Taylor 1983; Burgos Debray 1983; Americas Watch 1989).

Since the mid-1970s, the Catholic Church has been increasingly outspoken about the need for change in the country's social and political order. In 1988 the bishops issued a Pastoral Letter, titled *The Clamour for Land* , which squarely placed the blame for much of the society's ills on skewed land distribution. The Church demanded new land laws to secure title to those who work the land and allow its redistribution. It called for special measures to provide land to those who had been relocated or forced to flee by the civil war and for an integrated agricultural development package that would protect peasants from exploitative middle men and provide for their direct involvement in marketing. Changes in taxation, extension programmes, technical training and credit schemes were also demanded. Above all the Church insisted on protection for peasant organizations and respect for their human rights (Rosada-Granados 1988:39).

Individual priests have been even more outspoken, the most notable in recent years being Padre Giron, who has led a local peasant movement in Nueva Concepción in a campaign for local land redistribution. Giron has also called for nationwide agrarian reform (Painter 1989:1).

One of the few academics prepared to speak out on the issue within Guatemala is Leopoldo Sandoval, who has repeatedly and cogently argued the need for land reform. In public debate he has called for "state lands to be given out under community titles, with the aim of establishing peasant agricultural enterprises, since providing more individual parcels of land will only lead to further destruction of renewable natural resources" (*Cronica* II(93):20).

Sandoval argues that Guatemala needs much more than a mere redistribution of land, but the development of a new agrarian order in which co-operatives would play a key role. He sees as crucial for the overall democratizing of the entire political process the promotion of effective participation by the peasantry in the taking of decisions that affect their interests (Sandoval 1988:52).

Such an integrated reform would call for changes in land tenure;

systems of credit, marketing and technical assistance; the production and supply of agricultural inputs; types of agrarian enterprise; agrarian legislation; public administration; and land use planning (Sandoval 1988:54).

Sandoval puts supply of the domestic need for basic foodstuffs as a high priority. "The food security of the Guatemalan population requires a substantial change in the present use of land; the best arable land of Guatemala must pass from export crops towards products for internal consumption, especially for the production of food, of which there is presently a great deficit" (Sandoval 1988:62).

Sandoval has also addressed the difficult question of whether there is, indeed, enough cultivable land in Guatemala to meet adequately the needs of the rural poor. His calculations take as their guide the estimate that a family can adequately meet its needs, and cultivate on its own with traditional technology, an area of between 3.5 and 7 hectares. On this basis, Guatemala would need to redistribute between 2 million and 4.6 million hectares to provide land for all the landless unemployed over 20 years of age and secure adequate lands for those families presently with smaller plots (Sandoval 1988:64).

Achieving such a reform might just be feasible in Guatemala, though even meeting the lower figure would imply the redistribution of most remaining public lands, calculated at 571,342 ha, and the redistribution of about 1.5 million ha of privately owned land. It needs to be noted that not all this public land is thought suitable for agriculture by environmentalists. The inflationary effect of such a major transformation in the agrarian economy is also a serious consideration (Sandoval 1988:66).

The international development agencies have neither looked in such detail at the possibilities of reform nor been so outspoken about the need for it. (The one time that they were outspoken about the need for land reform — the CIDA report of 1964 — their report was banned by the Guatemalan authorities [Barraclough pers. comm].) Yet the recognition that reform is crucial to the political stability, economic progress and environmental sustainability of the country has been repeatedly echoed by them.

It is ironic to note that in 1961 the US signed the Punta del Este Charter establishing the "Alliance for Progress". Only seven years previously, before it had learned the lessons of the Cuban revolution, it had derailed the reforms of the Arbenz government. The Charter called, among other things, for:

> programmes of comprehensive agrarian reform, leading to effective transformation, where required, of unjust structures and systems of land tenure and use; with a view to replacing *latifundia* and dwarf holdings by an equitable system of property so that, supplemented by timely and adequate credit, technical assistance, and improved marketing arrangements, the land will become for the man who works it the basis of his economic stability, the foundation of increasing welfare, and the guarantee of his freedom and dignity. (Barry 1987:108)

Guatemala's Agrarian Transformation Law, which aimed more at the colonization of new frontier lands (see above), was the most it could do to turn this resolve into some kind of practical reality (Dunkerley 1988:440).

It should be emphasized that the US's rhetorical commitment to a programme of "defensive modernization" (Ayres 1983) was not translated into a reality by US overseas policy (Pearce 1986). Yet even the Kissinger Commission of 1983, whose main concern was to provide military assistance to wipe out insurgents and shore up existing regimes, recognized the need for major changes in the agrarian economy of Central America. The Commission emphasized the need to promote the production of basic foodstuffs for local markets and create a rural economy centred not on large agribusiness but on small and medium farms. Programmes of agrarian reform were noted as integral to such a process (Leonard 1987:66-67).

However, the resistance by the Guatemalan élite to all such suggestions has been vociferous, making up for a shortage of arguments with its vehemence. In reply to the bishops' call for land reform in 1988, the powerful right-wing lobby *Amigos de Guatemala* put out its document titled *El Clamor por una vida mejor*, which argues that land reform will only increase problems of *minifundismo*. The solution lies not in land division but in industrialization and the provision of jobs in the cities. Meanwhile, the paper argues, further land concentration, which no one disputes is occurring, will promote more productive land use (*Cronica* II(93):20).

Many Guatemalans had hoped that the election of a civilian government in 1985 would open the way for further democratic reforms and a commitment to finding a way out for Guatemala's poor. But if they had hoped that the Christian Democrat government would initiate a process of agrarian reform, they were disappointed. The government adhered firmly to the doctrine of the inviolability of private property and sided with the landowners against the rural masses (Painter 1989).

Perhaps the only hopeful sign within Guatemala is the increasing awareness of the environmental crisis confronting the country. The last few years have seen a growth of non-governmental activity which has served to highlight the problem of rapid natural resource depletion and degradation. New government agencies have been created to develop policies to deal with these problems. So far the solutions proposed remain straitjacketed by existing political priorities, but, just by seeking out the underlying causes of these problems, government planners have been forced to acknowledge the determining role of skewed land distribution in natural resource degradation.

The first draft of Guatemala's "National Forestry Action Plan", for example, notes clearly the environmental impact of skewed land tenure and the fact that while much fertile lowland and valley land remains underused, peasants are driven by poverty to clear poor land apt only for forests (PAFG 1990b). Unfortunately, even though the plan has been developed by a commission directed by the President's own son, it does not dare to challenge the status quo. The projects and policies advocated by the plan will thus do nothing to promote a more equitable use of land.

Another initiative of the Christian Democrat government was legally to secure large portions of the national territory as protected areas for conservation. The government noted the need to give local communities a stake in these areas and a place in their planning and management (PAFG 1990b:17). An interesting test case of this resolve is the Sierra de las Minas Biosphere Reserve established in 1990.

The 236,000-hectare area is a microcosm of the Guatemalan dilemma. While its mountainous spine retains an impressive diversity of forests and animals, it is under severe threat of destruction. The northern flanks of the Sierra have been settled, over the past half century, by tens of thousands of K'ekchi Indians who have been displaced from the more fertile lowlands by the expansion of logging, ranching and cardamom cultivation in the Northern Transverse Zone. The poor soils on the steep mountainsides make stable agriculture almost impossible, implying a progressive degradation of the environment as the Indians are obliged to clear new areas once their old plots become exhausted. At the same time, two-thirds of the area has been secured as private property by largely absentee landlords (FDN 1990).

The foundation which has promoted the reserve clearly recognizes that it cannot be made viable without, on the one hand, buying up the privately owned lands of the rich and, on the other hand, acquiring other areas of fertile valley land outside the reserve, or in the "Buffer Zone", to resettle the Indians (Hector Centeno pers. comm.). The case demonstrates, with startling clarity, the fact that, in Guatemala, the conservation of natural resources is inextricably linked to the need for a redistribution of land. Predictably, the landowner lobby has vehemently denounced the conservation plan as an assault on private property by taking out advertisements in the national newspapers.

Awareness of the links between the agrarian economy and the environmental crisis in Guatemala is growing, but this awareness is unlikely to be expressed through changed policies until the political space in the country is enlarged. Against all the political odds voices continue to speak out demanding a change in the social order in Guatemala, without which the forests cannot be secured. As one Indian remarks:

Ecological destruction in Guatemala is a destruction at the same time of the indigenous universe and of the Indians themselves.

Ethnocide is being carried out in Guatemala against the indigenous people, not just by killing us by the thousands, but also by the destruction of our way of life. We believe that our communities have much to contribute to those raising the problems of ecological destruction, for today in Guatemala we are facing the greatest threat to our people since the conquest. (Gardner et al. 1990:15)

BRAZIL: LAND OWNERSHIP AND THE FLIGHT TO AMAZONIA

GEORGE MONBIOT

THE SOCIAL DUSTBIN

Of all the threats to the Amazon's forests, those posed by small farmers and miners are the most intractable. While timber-cutters and ranchers are responsible for more deforestation, their activities are, in theory, possible to control through legislation. There is no hope of curtailing the cutting, burning, digging and dredging carried out by the region's impoverished immigrants while they have no viable alternatives.

While small farmers in the Brazilian Amazon are responsible for only 20% or so of the deforestation (Phillipe Lena, pers. comm.) there are no foreseeable limits to the amount of land they clear. Settlement in the Amazon is seldom final. Even before arriving there, most of the migrants settling in the west of the basin have moved through other parts of Brazil at least three times, and some, remarkably, have tried to recommence their lives on as many as twenty-five occasions (CEPAMI 1988). In the Amazon they are even less sedentary. Within a few years most move from their initial settlement sites, many travelling to fresh frontiers, where they open new plots, burning more forest. Economic, political and physical pressures make staying on the same patch virtually impossible.

Sustainable, productive agriculture and employment are desperately required in the Amazon, yet remedies within the region will have a limited impact on deforestation while, each year, tens of thousands more enter the forests from elsewhere in Brazil. To try to solve the Amazon's problems without considering

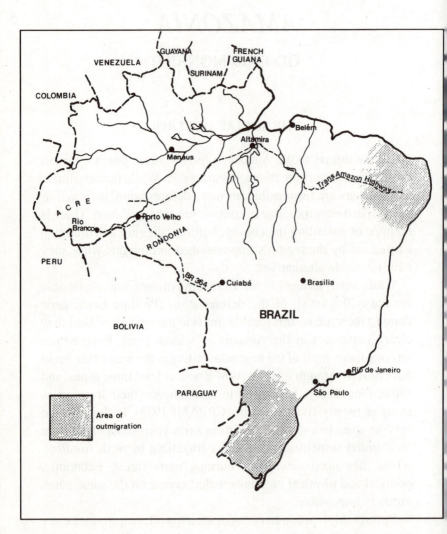

those of the Amazon's hinterland is to try to mop up an oil spill while the pipe remains uncapped.

The causes commonly blamed by governments and development consultants for the exodus to Amazonia tend to be those which bear little relation to the country's political complexion, such as population growth, inherent poverty and drought. Officials argue that the colonization of the Amazon is inevitable, as enterprising peasants move there in order to improve their prospects, or are driven there by factors beyond the government's control (e. g. Paulo Tarso Flecha da Lima, Brazilian Ambassador to the United Kingdom, personal communication). But the briefest glance at the problem suggests that such explanations are flawed.

Brazil shows all the symptoms of overpopulation. In the cities — among which are two of the largest in the world — there are desperate shortages of space, shelter, clean water, sanitation, medication and employment. In the countryside over 20 million peasants — 4.8 million families — are landless (Movimento dos Trabalhadores Sem Terra, cited in Americas Watch 1991). Throughout Brazil, 86 million people — two-thirds of the population — are considered undernourished (Americas Watch 1991).

Yet this is a country thirty-five times the size of Great Britain, with less than three times its population. At least 170 million hectares of farmland lie idle, and the country is the world's second largest exporter of agricultural commodities. Far from migrating to a land of opportunity when they move to the Amazon, the peasants are characteristically leaving fertile states which are underpopulated in terms of their farming potential, to arrive in a largely infertile region whose agricultural frontiers are already overburdened with people.

The key to this paradox is land ownership. In Brazil 0.8% of the landowners possess 43% of the land, while the 53% of landowners classed as small farmers own between them just 2.7% (*Porantim*, June 1991). While 3.3 million farmers work 19.7 million hectares of land, the 20 largest landlords own 20 million hectares, an area the size of Syria (CDPV 1991). Multinational companies own 36 million hectares of Brazilian territory.

Land and power in Brazil are indivisible. The political control of the countryside has always been the privilege of the people who own the most land. Many of the biggest landowners are the senators, ministers and army chiefs who govern the nation. Their power is often rooted in their landholdings, the local political bases from which they established their national influence. To maintain these properties they have shown themselves prepared to use all means, legal and illegal, including murder, to keep the small farmers and the landless poor from achieving a more just distribution of land.

Not content with possessing all but a fraction of the country's farmland, landowners in some parts of Brazil are actively engaged in expelling peasants from their legitimate properties and annexing them to their own. In other regions, government policies favouring certain cash crops and capital-intensive agriculture render small farming systems economically unviable, and greatly assist their displacement by existing large landlords.

The majority of the territory in the hands of the big owners, however, is unfarmed. It is used instead as a speculative asset, traded like stocks or shares, whose market value bears no relation to its productive value. While the landlords turn the countryside into a series of giant share certificates, the small farmers they displace have no choice but to leave.

Many have fled to the cities. Over the last twenty years, 30 million rural Brazilians left the countryside (*Financial Times* 15.8.91). São Paulo alone attracts 200 people every day, and already — while the farmlands surrounding it are empty — bulges with 18 million people. For the peasants squeezed into such conurbations, misery assumes proportions known to the people of industrialized nations only through post-holocaust science fiction. For most, the only employment opportunities are beggary, theft and prostitution. The only places left in which to erect their tin and tarpaulin shelters are the spaces beneath motorway flyovers or the rubble sites waiting for construction work. While property developers burn the peasants' shacks, vigilante groups torture and murder the children whose crime is to be roofless: in Rio de Janeiro two street children are murdered by death squads every day.

So, many move not to the towns but to the Amazon. They go not because it is a good prospect, but because it is a bad one: conditions there are so difficult that big businessmen have failed to clear and annex all the land. All but seven per cent of the Amazon's soils are incapable of sustaining annual crops; infrastructure, schools and health services are non-existent in most of the places still available to the peasants; malaria, tuberculosis and diseases endemic to the region flare into epidemics in the peasant settlements. Yet they go, because there is no choice. The Amazon is the dustbin of Brazil's social policies.

THE LAND OF IMPUNITY

The roots of the ownership patterns in Brazil can be found in the land tenure system prevailing in medieval Portugal. In 1375 the Portuguese crown passed the "Law of Sesmarias", which decreed that the owners of unused lands should either work them or transfer them to third parties, on pain of confiscation. While in Portugal this provided the basis of partial agrarian reforms, when later it was applied to the colony, Brazil, it led, paradoxically, to intense land concentration (Panini 1990).

In Portugal the law was designed to solve the shortage of food. In Brazil it was used to populate the territory, reducing the possibility of takeover by other colonial powers. Applicants were each allocated a *sesmaria* of four square leagues. From the very beginning of the colony's establishment, corruption and poor inspection distorted distribution policies. Unscrupulous applicants registered their wives, children and dogs for title, and accumulated vast expanses of land. (This form of cheating persists in the Amazon today: in the 1970s and 1980s it dominated land acquisition in the government's colonization sites.)

The farmers were obliged to exploit the land within six years and to pay a sixth part of the produce to the crown. These obligations led to a great demand for labour, and initially it was slave owner-ship, not land ownership, which formed the basis of power accumulation in Brazil. The sesmarial system drove the produc-tion of export crops, such as sugar and coffee. It also provided a living — albeit a sparse one — for some landless peasants, as big landlords, often unable to muster sufficient slaves, brought free-men in as sharecroppers.

By the time the sesmarial system came to an end in Brazil, in 1822, the land had already been divided into vast estates producing cash crops. Small farmers were confined to the regions of lowest fertility, furthest from the markets, and even here they had no status other than occupiers: the law made no provisions for ownership of land outside the *sesmarias*. The peasants supplied their own needs and local markets, while the landlords stoked the Portuguese — later Brazilian — treasury.

The abandonment of the sesmarial system was formalized in 1850 by the "Law of Devolved Lands". Having been arranged through grants from the crown under the old system, land-ownership was now transferred through sale and purchase, and the obligations towards the state ceased to exist. With these changes land became the principal index of wealth and status. The peasants subsisting on state-owned lands were expelled as the territories were grabbed by the private armies of the big landlords. As the supply of foreign slaves began to dry up (the trade ended with abolition in 1888), the now-landless peasants took their place, working under constraints which removed all freedom of choice.

The labour shortage faced by big landowners during the nine-teenth century was also partly offset by agreements Brazil struck with European countries, later with Japan, allowing immigrants to enter the country to farm. This, like many others, was a policy largely designed for the benefit of landlords, but also helped northern countries to ease their problems of unemployment and landlessness (there are interesting parallels here between the way Brazil was used by the colonial powers and the way the Amazon is currently used by the powers in Brazil).

When Brazil, as a republic, drew up its first Constitution, in 1891, landowners successfully lobbied for greater regional control of state-owned lands. This enabled them to accelerate their expropriation of these territories and — with it — the dispossession of small farmers.

Deprived of their means of subsistence, peasants in many parts of Brazil rebelled. Some occupied land by force of numbers; a few attempted to precipitate political change. The most famous of these movements were the 1835 Cabanagem revolt and the 1896-97 Canudos occupation. The first succeeded in deposing the state government of the eastern Amazonian state of Pará, killing the governor and briefly assuming power. The revolt was put down by federal troops, rose again, and was ruthlessly crushed.

In Canudos in the state of Bahia, a movement of 30,000 people, following a mystic revolutionary leader, took over a ranch and declared themselves to be the citizens of a free city. Though the occupation was an isolated event, landowners felt it set a dangerous example. The federal government sent four armed expeditions to destroy the free city, and the first three were soundly defeated. The fourth was successful, and all the inhabitants of Canudos — bar four — were massacred.

At the beginning of the twentieth century, landowners began to sell off some of the lands their exploitation had exhausted, moving on to newly accessible territories. This led to a slightly better distribution of land, as peasants bought small plots, but was offset by continued expulsions of the small farmers occupying state lands, as landlords expropriated them. The government turned a blind eye: coffee was Brazil's major source of income at the time, and the displacement of subsistence farmers promoted the expansion of the crop.

In the 1930s, Brazil's economic base began to move from the countryside to the towns. Political control, however, remained rooted in the countryside, many of the richest landowners simply expanding their activities into the urban business sector. With the end of the dictatorial government of Getulio Vargas, in 1954, however, the opportunities for the peasants to organize improved. As their syndicates proliferated, especially in the North-East, the landowners began to strengthen their own political organizations. The United States government, attempting to contain what it considered to be the spread of communism in Latin America, provided covert assistance to movements opposed to reform.

In 1963 President Goulart prepared a "Rural Workers' Statute", which appeared progressive, but was widely suspected by rural workers of being a means of controlling their unions. It provoked a violent reaction on the part of the landowners, backed by traditionalists in the Catholic Church. Describing it as the first step towards a socialist takeover, they intensified the expulsion of peasants from their lands.

Goulart criticized the landlords and directed several reform programmes to Congress, including a land reform measure. Within fifteen days his government had been overthrown, in a military coup backed by the United States.

The coup put an end to the progressive movements which had been developing throughout Brazil. Government critics were tortured and killed and the press was censored. Yet, at the end of 1964, a Land Statute was approved by the government, calling for sweeping land reform by means of compensated compulsory purchase of unproductive properties. It seemed an extraordinary move on the part of a government composed largely of landowners, but it soon became clear that this was no more than a classic Brazilian political trick.

The strategy followed is long tried and tested in Brazil: the government identifies a potential threat to the established order, encourages or turns a blind eye to the liquidation of its most powerful advocates, then appropriates their rhetoric. It announces, with a fanfare of publicity, a sweeping programme of reform. Then, piecemeal, it works unobtrusively to undo it, through procrastination, bureaucratic muddle, loopholes and conflicting legislation, in such a way that no one retraction is sufficient to alert the press or international attention. Such a strategy serves to douse the fire of its critics and contain the threat. Typically, Brazilian legislation is designed to do the opposite to its stated aims (Monbiot 1991).

Thus, between 1967 and 1979, not a single land expropriation was fulfilled. Landholding, by contrast, became far more concentrated. Government policies promoting the growth of big export-oriented estates favoured increasing mechanization, which began to squeeze the labour force out of settled agriculture. In the state of Parana in the south of the country, the small producers of coffee and staple crops found they could no longer get credit, as the government had channelled it towards big soya farmers. The peasants could not compete with people who could achieve vast economies of scale, and could not afford the mechanization required to convert. In the 1970s, from the state of Parana alone, 109,000 small farms went out of business, leading to the transfer of one million hectares into the hands of big landowners (Diegues et al. 1991a). Net migration from the state was 2.5 million in that decade: many moved to the western Amazon (Diegues et al. 1991b).

In 1985, following the transition to a nominally civilian government, a National Plan of Agrarian Reform was approved, with the stated aim of expropriating and redistributing unproductive farmland. In the same year the Union of Democratic Ruralists (UDR — widely known as the Ranchers' Union) was established to combat the possibility of land reform. Among its most prominent supporters were government members.

After three years, only 10% of the modest amount of land proposed for reallocation had been expropriated, and just 18,000 rural families — out of the estimated 4.8 million with no land or inadequate land — had been settled. Many others had been herded into transit camps, awaiting the outcome of the land agency's tortuous bureaucracy, living under appalling conditions (Comissão Pastoral da Terra et al. 1992). The few expropriations which did take place occurred as a result of lobbying, demonstrations and occupations of unused properties by the peasants. These actions led to violent suppression by the members of the UDR (see below).

DEMOCRACY FOR SOME

In 1988 the new Constitution re-established the principle of land reform for social ends, through "just compensation". But, as a result of intense lobbying by the UDR and a right-wing parliamentary group, the wording of the land clauses was left deliberately vague. The Constitution can be interpreted as meaning that land reform cannot take place if the land in question, even if currently unused, is potentially productive. "Just compensation" is taken to mean more than the land would be worth on the open market, rendering large-scale reform financially impossible.

The President elected in 1990, Fernando Collor, a member of Brazil's landowning class, promised to settle 500,000 landless families without resorting to colonization of the Amazon. In the first twelve months of its term his government failed to make a single expropriation of unused land. While state governments distributed land to a few families, the federal land agency failed to resettle a single small farmer (*Porantim*, January/February 1991). Five hundred expropriation requests were stuck in its bureaucracy, waiting only for the signing of the necessary decrees. While Collor's election promises suggested that an extra 5,000 staff were required in the agency, it was instead cut back (CDPV 1991).

After 18 months the land agency had succeeded in expropriating 6,000 hectares of ranches: but this was land already long-occupied by peasants who had taken the law into their own hands. Twelve thousand families were waiting in camps for the fulfilment of the government's promises (*Porantim*, September 1991). By 1992 the government had abandoned its attempts to expropriate farmlands and instead began investing in colonization projects in the Amazon states of Pará, Tocantins and Rondônia, planning settlements in areas of infertile soils, lacking adequate infrastructure (Movimento dos Trabalhadores Rurais Sem Terra 1990). These initiatives have been opposed with equal vigour by peasant organizations and environmentalists.

The efforts of the Agriculture Minister, who is one of the largest landowners in Brazil, have instead been channelled into a shameless massaging — some say pure invention — of his government's land-reform figures. His claim that 103,000 families had been settled by the government in 1990 was regarded as a sick joke by land-rights organizations. They find it hard to see how a supporter of the UDR and suspected land speculator could be trusted to oversee agrarian reform.

Another aspect of agricultural policy handled by the Collor government was credit. Until recently agricultural credit in Brazil has been, in practice, the preserve of the big farmers. Not only do they have the land title required to qualify, but they can afford the journeys and delays the application process involves, and speed up the process by means of political influence. Some have benefited enormously from subsidies: 469 farms in the Amazon, for example, cost the country an astonishing $4.8 billion (all costs accounted), while producing next to nothing (Browder 1988a). Real rates of interest on agricultural loans are negative and payback periods in some cases stretch to decades: the subsidies have functioned as free gifts to the biggest landowners. Lack of available credit for the small producers reduces their ability to remain on their land.

President Collor's government attempted to change this pattern of disbursement, and to encourage more staple-crop production. This policy reflects the abysmal prices achieved by Brazil's traditional agricultural exports — crops such as oranges, soya, coffee and cocoa — and the high import requirements for staple foods. The government increased the minimum prices paid for staple foods — of which small farmers are the main producers — and demanded that all Brazilian banks establish farmers' credit unions (*Financial Times*, 29.1.91).

However, when the Bank of Brazil announced that at least 60% of its credit disbursements should go to small farmers, Collor widened the definition of small farmers until substantial rural businesses could qualify (*A Folha de São Paulo*, 3.2.91). Despite its stated policies, in 1991 his government accepted a $140 million loan from the World Bank for agricultural export programmes (*Financial Times*, 17.8.90). It is hard to see how tariffs protecting small farmers from imports of subsidized agricultural produce from the First World — essential if domestic staple crop producers are to remain solvent — could survive Brazil's participation in George Bush's "Enterprise for the Americas" initiative.

Small farmers are unlikely to benefit from increased credit availability without significant changes in the ways in which it is disbursed. Currently farmers need to pay several visits to the towns in which the banks are located (often prohibitively expensive); wait until after their crops have been planted (i. e., until after the money is required); and wade through forms scarcely comprehensible to financial analysts, let alone to illiterate labourers.

Credit cannot be obtained without title to the land: from which most peasants are excluded by their illiteracy and inability to bribe or threaten the corrupt officials responsible for titling.

Big landowners are also greatly favoured by income tax policy. Companies pay no tax on 80% of agricultural profits, individuals on 90%. Capital investments can be completely depreciated within one year, and then depreciated up to six times more (Americas Watch 1991). As the poor farmers do not pay income tax, they receive no benefits from these provisions. Indeed they are among the principal reasons for small producers' exclusion from the land market. Low taxation makes land a highly lucrative investment for urban businessmen, and, as a result, land prices rise well beyond their productive capacity, and out of the reach of small farmers.

The droughts blamed by the government for much of the recent dispossession of peasants in the North-East have been ascribed by land-rights activists to the hand of man rather than of God. Large landowners have expropriated both the water resources and the public money destined for the development of the region (Vanette Almeida, leader of rural workers' union in Pernambuco, pers. comm.). The North-East is twice as wet as Israel and four times as wet as Texas (Pantoja 1992, cited in Comissão Pastoral da Terra et al. 1992). It should, in theory, be highly productive.

Many of the peasants' problems originate not in Brazil but in the First World nations influencing Brazilian economic policy. Brazil's production of cash crops has been promoted both by the dumping of surplus food at subsidized prices by the United States and the European Community, and through political and economic pressure exerted by the World Bank and International Monetary Fund.

The dumping of subsidized crops on world markets means that either the Brazilian government maintains high tariff and non-tariff barriers against agricultural imports — an increasingly difficult option as the United States exerts pressure on all Latin American countries to reduce protectionist measures — or Brazilian staple food producers go out of business. Brazil is going through a process which could be described as inverse import substitution:

as producers are forced to grow oranges, soya, coffee and oil crops instead of manioc, rice and beans, both exports of cash crops and imports of staple foods increase. The result is reduced food security, the loss of foreign exchange and the dispossession of peasant producers.

Both the World Bank and the International Monetary Fund have been forcing the pace of inverse import substitution, through structural adjustment programmes and selective investments. They have made it clear to Brazil that future investment and renegotiation of the external debt are dependent on the removal of protectionist barriers and the conversion of much of the domestic economy to foreign-exchange generation.

As the two agencies have been prescribing exactly the same formulae to all Third World countries, it is hardly surprising that there is a worldwide surplus of nearly all agricultural commodities. Prices, therefore, have been plummeting, to the great disadvantage of the Third World and advantage of the First. This problem is compounded by the imposition of escalating tariffs against Third World commodities, punishing processed products. Some First World countries, for instance, impose no tariff on raw coffee beans, high tariffs on roasted and ground beans, and enormous duties on instant coffee. It is economically impossible therefore for Brazil to produce instant coffee for First World markets. As all the significant profits from agricultural commodities are made by the processors rather than the producers, Brazil is condemned to sell its crops for little more (or sometimes even less) than the price of production.

As a result of such measures, Brazil is forced to produce vast quantities of agricultural commodities to generate significant amounts of foreign exchange. Having bought up or annexed much of the land in southern Brazil, for instance, soya-producers are now dispossessing both peasants and Indians in the *cerrado* (scrub savannah) belt just to the south of the Amazon. The soya produced is sold to feed European cattle destined for the EC beef mountains.

First World nations are also partly responsible for the impunity with which land owners murder peasants and annex their properties.

The 1964 coup was backed and assisted by the United States. Its subsequent suppression of land reform movements in other Latin American nations has made it clear to Brazilian peasants that their fight against the landowners' hegemony is also a fight against the world's biggest military and economic power.

All this begs the question of whether small farming is appropriate in Brazil. Landlords and government officials argue that the flight of farmers from the countryside, into the towns or the Amazon, is part of the inevitable evolution of an industrializing society.

Brazil, however, is suffering from urbanization without a corresponding degree of industrialization. For the dispossessed arriving in the towns there is no prospect of full employment. Though small farmers own only three per cent of the land, they produce nearly all the manioc, beans and maize and much of the rice Brazil consumes — all Brazil's staple crops; and Brazil is already crippled by the volume of its agricultural imports. It is not the free market but a highly protected one which is driving the peasants out of their homes. The protectionism extends to the torture and murder of people threatening the landowners' hegemony.

LAND FOR THE KILLER

Torture, murder, house-burning and crop destruction have always been features of Brazilian landlords' attempts to drive out the peasants considered to threaten their interests. In 1985, however, the amount of rural violence increased dramatically, as landlords feared the transition to civilian government would lead to a redistribution of their unproductive properties. To avert this threat they enlisted the help of police and state authorities, hired gunmen, and intensified their efforts either to terrorize the peasants into submission or to drive them out of their states.

In this they enjoyed the backing of officials at every level of government. State governors depend on the support of the local mayors, who are characteristically landlords. The police and the judiciary are controlled by the governors, so, in practice, work to uphold the interests of the landowners, against those of the peasants. Members of the federal government, who might have been expected to overrule the corrupt authority of the states, are often themselves the biggest landowners of all, and will do little to hinder the privileged minority to which they belong.

Many of the cases of torture and murder documented by Brazilian human rights groups and by Amnesty International (1988) demonstrate a disregard for the law nowhere so blatant as among the judiciary, a criminality introduced to communities only with the arrival of the police, an anarchy engineered by government. The authorities appear to have done their best to protect those least in need of protection, and persecute those who are most vulnerable. The killers rely upon an ethic of government summarized in the Brazilian proverb: "For our friends everything; for our enemies the Law".

President Collor's Agriculture Minister, Antonio Cabrera, is one of the biggest landowners of Brazil (*Jornal do Brasil*, 1.4.90). The fact that on all his 200,000 hectares he runs only 41,000 head of cattle suggests that he may also be a land speculator. He was reported by a Brazilian newspaper as having helped organize auctions to raise money for the Ranchers' Union (UDR), the body responsible for the majority of the political killings in the Brazilian countryside. His brothers were campaign managers for the bid made by the president of the Ranchers' Union to become president of the republic.

Since 1964, 1,684 rural workers and union leaders, priests and lawyers trying to defend them have been murdered by hired gunmen or police working for Brazilian landlords (Comissao Pastoral da Terra et al. 1992). In some cases the murders have been carried out to silence individual agitators, in others to frighten the remainder of the peasants into leaving their lands, both for the purposes of averting the threat of land reform and in order to expand their own landholdings.

The figures overleaf begin with the surge in killings following the establishment of civilian government, and show a gradual decline towards the present.

153

TABLE 4

CONFLICTS IN RURAL AREAS: COMPARATIVE DATA
(1985-91)

Year	1985	1986	1987	1988	1989	1990	1991
Land conflicts	636	643	582	621	500	401	383
Assassinations in rural areas	139	122	133	102	65	79	54
Attempted assassinations in rural areas	*	*	38	68	103	80	98

* Data not available

	NO. INVOLVED IN LAND CONFLICTS	NO. OF HECTARES IN CONFLICT
1985	405,456	9,557,902
1986	594,448	12,615,947
1987	667,177	17,633,879
1988	403,733	19,973,897
1989	192,533	14,480,254
1990	191,550	13,835,756
1991	242,196	7,037,722

Source: Comissão Pastoral da Terra et al. 1992

The decline in the numbers of killings is likely to reflect their increasingly selective nature. As the peasant organizations have become stronger, communities are more likely to stand firm when random members are killed. Landowners have learnt that they must select the leaders if they are to drive the remainder of the people out. Killings now seldom take place at the behest of a single landlord: gunmen are commissioned jointly by the local members of the UDR (the Ranchers' Union). As UDR members include mayors and judges, this pooled responsibility serves to institutionalize the crime.

The gunmen too have become more professional, and now have a scale of charges, depending upon the importance of the target. They are sometimes paid on receipt of the victim's ears.

Among the other probable reasons for the decline are the improved self-defence mechanisms of the rural workers and better articulation with foreign non-government organizations (Comissão Pastoral da Terra et al. 1992). Rural workers have been able to force landlords to back down, by means of demonstrations, marches, letters from abroad and security schemes for the protection of their leaders. The international outcry surrounding the death of the rubber tappers' union leader, Chico Mendes, led in that case to the only successful prosecution of the commissioner of a land rights murder. It also demonstrated that the only way of achieving substantial press coverage of these issues within Brazil is to generate widespread coverage outside: newspapers and television stations, owned by members of the landed class, refuse to cover the subject until embarrassed into action.

The states with the highest murder rates are those just within or just outside the Amazon Basin. These are the regions in which the origins of the land disputes are most recent, and in which the landlords are still jostling to secure their political control (see below).

There are no available figures for torture, but it remains widespread as a means of terrorizing peasants into submission. The methods of the police involved are crude. Peasants are held down repeatedly in water tanks, have electric shocks applied to their genitals, pieces of wood pushed up the anus, bottles, thorns or lighted cigarettes forced down the throat. "Telephone torture", beating the victim's ears with cupped hands, is common. Women and sometimes young girls are raped; in one incident a child was suspended by the hair from a beam to persuade her to reveal the whereabouts of her father.

Hundreds of rural murders were committed during the 1980s. While a very few of the gunmen commissioned by landowners have been convicted, all the rest of the instigators of these murders remain at large. Having waited two years for international attention to fade, the courts in the state of Acre reopened the Chico Mendes case and released the ranchers who killed him from their 19-year sentence. The news was greeted with celebrations and fireworks by the Ranchers' Union, and appeared to dispel the impression the conviction had created, that landlords could no longer act with complete impunity.

The police in most cases have avoided investigating the land-owners' crimes (Amnesty International 1988). They have failed to collect evidence, interview witnesses or conduct post-mortems, and records of any enquiries they do make disappear. When obliged to enquire, they have intimidated witnesses, or forced them to sign false statements. But when the police themselves are involved in a murder, or the hired assassins are issued with police uniforms or arms, investigations are unnecessary, as the survivors will not register the crime.

Sometimes, despite the efforts of priests and community leaders to restrain them, peasants use the law of the backlands to settle their disputes, and kill the landowners or gunmen who have killed their own people. It is then that the police force is transformed. Post-mortems are conducted with diligence, the most detailed evidence is collected, and witnesses are interviewed with such enthusiasm that some do not survive the experience.

When the police are forced, by legal pressure or a public outcry, to arrest or charge the gunmen, the gunmen have demonstrated a supernatural ability to escape from police cells, and they return to live among the people they have terrorized. When a series of jailbreaks begins to seem suspicious, the killers have been known to commit suicide in their cells, managing to shoot themselves several times through the head.

Similar ethics prevail among the judiciary. In the county of Rio Maria in Pará, for instance, where 17 rural workers have been murdered between 1982 and 1991, from 13 August to 16 September 1991 the courts and police released without charge the suspected murderers of seven people (CEDI 1991).

The Parliamentary Enquiry Commission established in 1991 to investigate the origins, causes and consequences of rural violence was composed of 13 members, seven of whom were ranchers or rural businessmen. A key position was held by a rancher who has been one of Brazil's most active campaigners against land reform (CEDI 1991). However, the Minister of Justice has admitted that the government is partly responsible for the rural violence and suggested that the best way to solve the problem is through land reform. He has proposed the creation of an agrarian court, in which land disputes can be heard.

RESISTANCE

The 1980s in Brazil were characterized not only by high levels of violence but also by well-organized resistance on the part of rural workers. Organizations such as the Movimento dos Trabalhadores Rurais Sem Terra (MST — the Movement of Landless Rural Workers); the Comissão Pastoral da Terra (CPT — the Pastoral Land Commission) and the Conselho Nacional dos Seringueiros (CNS — the National Rubber Tappers' Council) took advantage of Brazil's somewhat more open government to throw more weight behind the struggles of communities and their unions (these are known as Sindicatos dos Trabalhadores Rurais or STRs — Rural Workers' Unions).

The most direct means of remedying the intense concentration of landholding pursued by these organizations is to arrange occupations of unused estates. Typically, having waited in vain for the land agency to fulfil its promises to redistribute unused properties, the STRs, with the help of the MST, will bring together a convoy of vehicles and invade the land at night, hoping that by dawn there will be so many people in occupation that the police will be unable to shift them. The figures below show that, though extremely important for the families involved, these occupations have had little impact on the numbers of landless poor in Brazil.

TABLE 5
LAND OCCUPATIONS IN BRAZIL

	1987	1988	1989	1990	1991
Number of occupations	67	72	90	50	77
Number of squatter families	11,772	9,986	12,575	7,957	13,844

Source: Pastoral Land Commission (CPT), National Office

Perhaps most importantly, the MST, CPT, CNS and STRs have used their combined weights to draw attention to the plight of rural workers through demonstrations, petitions, parliamentary lobbying and attempts to interest both the Brazilian and the foreign press. Over the last two or three years, rural workers' organizations in the Amazon have begun working alongside Indians and Indian rights campaigners and environmentalists, identifying as their common enemy the concentration of land, capital and political power. In 1991 the CPT and MST were presented with the Right Livelihood Award for "their valiant action in favour of land distribution to Brazilian families without farmland and for the help they give to farmers for the adequate cultivation of those lands".

In response to the MST's increasing visibility, the federal police have established a division in Brasilia specializing in monitoring and disrupting its work. Its activities include telephone-bugging, the raiding of offices and the monitoring and harassment of the movement's leaders. This has been accompanied by a counter-propaganda campaign in the press, suggesting communist links and training of MST leaders in Cuba.

Until recently, liberation theologists in the Catholic Church were instrumental in helping the peasants to resist the violence and expropriations and call for land reform. One result of this support is that landowners — the traditional paymasters of the Catholic Church in Brazil — began turning instead towards the Protestant evangelical movements now proliferating in Latin America. These, by contrast to the liberal wing of the Catholic Church, preach not self-reliance but trust in God for the resolution of earthly difficulties. They advocate a respect for authority and adherence to the creed (Romans 13:1) that all governments are ordained by God.

Seeing both its membership and its finances falling, the Vatican launched a campaign against liberation theology in the Brazilian Church. On his 1991 tour of Brazil, the Pope condemned the "invasion of private property", referring to the occupation of unproductive ranches by peasants, rather than the occupation of productive peasant lands by ranchers. He has punished liberation theology's leading advocate in Brazil — Leonardo Boff — five times, imposing silences on him and obliging him to leave the city in which he works. Liberationists have been removed from important positions and replaced by traditionalists prepared to defend the status quo (Vanette Almeida, pers. comm.). The result has been a severe weakening of the Church's capacity to defend rural workers.

COLONIZATION

While most of the settlers entering Amazonia now pay for themselves, the infrastructure of colonization was laid down not by the peasants but by the government. Since 1970 Brazilian governments have been investing heavily in the movement of settlers to the Amazon, for several reasons. Of these it is probably fair to say that the least important was the welfare of the people being moved. Colonization has long been used as a means of avoiding land reform, and of generating substantial profits for construction companies, many of which have uncomfortably close relationships with members of the government. It increases the numbers of loyal voters in a state, and to this end certain state governments have invested in advertising campaigns in the rest of Brazil.

But above all settlement has been used to boost national prestige. In the 1970s Brazil's military leaders chose to portray their nation as a pioneer state, whose advance into the Amazon would be the first step towards becoming a superpower. Such propaganda helped to boost the popularity of the government during the time of the most ferocious state repression. Allied to this purpose was the aim of national integration, taking control of the Brazilian Amazon before it was annexed by other — unidentified — nations. To this end the people living in the Amazon were encouraged to be representative Brazilians, and much of the failure of the first farmers there can be ascribed to the fact that they were advised to farm like those in the temperate south, despite the great differences in climate, soils, infrastructure and markets.

The first big project was the construction of the notorious Trans-Amazon Highway. With the help of the World Bank and the

Inter- American Development Bank, settlers were encouraged to move from the North-East of Brazil — where most of them had been squeezed out by land expropriation, drought and financial collapse precipitated by the landowners' annexation of their states' natural and financial resources — along a road built to cut across the southern Amazon. The project took no account of the fact that only 3 per cent of the soils in the region are fertile. Despite spending $39,000 on each person settled (Browder 1988b) the administrators failed to provide them with essential supplies. Few elected to travel there, and of those who did, most soon left, but not before the road had cleft a previously inviolate part of the basin.

The other great government-funded colonization scheme was in the West, and it was this that led to one of the world's greatest environmental tragedies. The project involved the extension of a road from the South of Brazil into the state of Rondônia. By contrast to the Trans-Amazon Highway project, and through accident rather than design, the Rondônian scheme attracted vast numbers, partly as the result of inaccurate rumours that the soil there was good: regrettably only 10 per cent of the state's land is suitable for farming. Between 1975 and 1988 one and a half million people arrived in the virgin state, and by 1989, 26 per cent of its forests had been destroyed. Most of the settlers were people displaced by the mechanized farming of soya and other cash crops in the South of Brazil.

Again, a substantial part of the funding came from the World Bank, whose present attempts to make amends seem destined only to exacerbate the situation. Perhaps the most damaging result of the Rondônian settlement scheme is that the state has become the gateway to the rest of western and northern Amazonia. It is from there that colonists are now flocking towards the states of Acre, Amazonas and Roraima, the last great wildernesses of the Amazon.

Though the Collor government began to invest once more in Amazon colonization, most of those entering the region are doing so spontaneously, finding political and economic conditions in their home states impossible. The Brazilian Amazon's population now stands at approximately 16 million, of which only 225,000 are indigenous people. Though the news that settlement in the Amazon does little to solve the colonists' problems is now widespread, tens of thousands of people arrive in the region every year.

An extensive survey of peasants settled in Rondônia in the western Amazon revealed that 28 per cent considered their lives had improved since arrival in the Amazon, while 45 per cent claimed they had become poorer (CEPAMI 1988). The major problems they suffered included disease, lack of transport, inaccessible markets, poor crop prices, pests and the harsh climate, but all these were overshadowed by the nature of the soils the people were attempting to farm. Overall, only 7 per cent of the Amazon's soils are considered to be suitable for conventional peasant agriculture, and most of the places in which these soils are accessible have already been heavily colonized.

The biggest agricultural problem is a lack of available phosphate. There is a reasonable quantity in the soil, but when the neutralizing minerals released by the burning of the trees have been washed away, it becomes inaccessible to crops, and they begin to fail. On most farms in the Amazon this takes place after two to four years. The same patch of land can then be farmed again, once it has been left fallow for at least fifteen years, but most farmers who stay on their plots have neither the land nor the patience to wait that long before they return to where they first cut into the forest. When the soil is reopened too early it cannot recover for decades.

For all of these reasons, many people are moving from the land to the towns, where the majority of Amazonians now live. Some towns are now doubling in size each decade (Mitschein et al. 1989), attracting not only failed colonists, but also people from other parts of Brazil. Manaus, which now supports 1.2 million people, receives a further 80,000 each year, more than its total population in 1920. These immigrants alone require fifty new houses each day, and were the authorities in Manaus to keep pace with the needs of the population, a new school would need to be built in the city every three days. Hospitals, transport, sewerage and electricity supplies are overloaded. But in the Amazon cities, by contrast to the megalopolises of the south, nearly everyone has a house.

The city dwellers too are a serious threat to the environment. Much of the food Amazonians now consume is imported; but this situation is changing, as successive governments have attempted to make the basin productive. The inhabitants of most Amazon towns are reliant upon fish, and to this end the rivers are being exploited to the point of likely ecological collapse. In a misconceived attempt to boost meat production, the authorities have been encouraging settlers and ranchers to cut the flooded forest. The result is that the protein production falls dramatically, as the fish of the forest are replaced by unproductive cattle pastures.

VICTIMS AGAIN

Peasants' problems do not end when they reach Amazonia; by contrast land-grabbing, threats and violence on the part of big businessmen are worse there than in any other part of Brazil. In Amazonia, 1,076 people own 30% of the land, while 49% of its rural settlers possess only 1.05% of the land area. One company, the Madeireira Manasa, was registered in 1985 as the owner of 4.3 million hectares, on which it employed 68 people (*A Folha de São Paulo* 25.11.91).

On the frontiers of the Amazon there are fewer legal deterrents even than those in the badlands of the rest of Brazil. By legitimizing deforestation as a means of establishing control of the land, the government land agency has stimulated the expansion of a highly speculative land market (Diegues et al. 1991a, b). This is further fuelled by the corruption of land agency employees, who are prepared to sell businessmen titles to properties already in the possession of small farmers.

In clearing the lands they seize from their previous inhabitants, the speculators operating in the Amazon — many of them are entirely urban-based investors — have been utterly ruthless. Seventy per cent of the 488 murders documented by the Pastoral Land Commission between 1985 and 1989 occurred in Amazonia (Americas Watch 1991). Having driven the people out of their homes, landlords characteristically overfly the region, sowing grass seed, which reduces the chances of the peasants returning and growing crops successfully.

It is this continued expropriation of land which contributes to the instability of peasant settlement: an instability at the root of destructive farming practices in the Amazon. Not only are the farmers forced always to move on, abandoning their first plots and moving to new frontiers in the rainforest to clear their farms, but their insecurity means that they do not invest in the land improvements and perennial crops necessary for a sustainable livelihood. Instead they farm as if at any minute they could be forced to leave, using crops which produce rapidly, but at the cost of the exhausting the soil. This in turn increases their chances of failure and re-migration.

Among the safest places for peasants to move to are nature reserves. This is because, by contrast to the private landholdings which quickly monopolize the rest of the regions made accessible by roads, there are no gunmen in the reserves. For many Amazonian politicians the destruction of a nature reserve is a political boon, as it enables them to grant free land in exchange for votes. So when the federal government declares an area to be totally protected, there is often a rush to occupy it (Monbiot 1991).

Others stop farming and move instead to the towns or the gold mines. Mining has become one of the greatest threats to the indigenous people of the Amazon, as their reserves are invaded by armies of dispossessed peasants, trying, by the last means available, to keep themselves alive. Eighty percent of the invaders of the Yanomami territory in the northern Amazon came from the state of Maranhao where, at the time of the invasion, the levels of rural violence were higher than anywhere else in Brazil.

Without land reform, there is no chance of saving the rainforests and the indigenous people of the Amazon from destruction. The development of sustainable farming methods, birth control programmes or reserve protection measures will be little more than palliatives while the battle for land in Brazil still rages.

LAND SPECULATION AND PASTURE-LED DEFORESTATION IN BRAZIL

SUSANNAH HECHT

> These placid creatures which used to require so little food have now apparently developed a raging appetite and turned into man eaters. Fields, houses, forests, towns, everything goes down their throats.
>
> Thomas More, *Utopia*

Thomas More was writing about the expansion of sheep herding in the sixteenth century, but this description of the displacement of forests and cultivated lands by livestock could have been written last week about the Amazon basin. The majority of deforestation in Latin America is caused by pasture development, and most cleared land will ultimately end up in pasture. The environment is not the only victim. Forest peoples routinely watch their lives, livelihoods and complex agricultural systems reduced to ashes by the burning of forest for pasture. Peasants, often displaced by cattle, or as part of a short-term cropping phase before land is transformed to pasture, also have their livelihoods destroyed by this process.

WEALTH ON THE HOOF

Pasture-driven deforestation is not purely the outcome of international commodity markets — the so-called "hamburger connection" — as has been argued for Central America and has been incorrectly applied to the Amazon (Uhl and Parker 1986). Nor does the expansion of ranching only reflect the influence of misguided subsidies (Repetto and Gillis 1988). Were either of these interpretations the case, the solution — the substitution of other sources of beef and the withdrawal of subsidies — would be relatively simple. But the relentless expansion of ranching is more complex. Underlying the devastation is a combination of local processes, regional policies and national economics in which cattle and their pastures have a flexibility unmatched by other more ecologically-appropriate land uses and an ability to serve a myriad of economic purposes. It thus follows that attempts to control pasture-led deforestation and to promote more ecologically appropriate alternatives will be more difficult to achieve than simply through the manipulation of markets or policy.

PROFIT FROM LAND AND RESOURCES

There are three basic ways of capturing value through land and natural resources. First there is extraction, which takes two basic forms: renewable and irrevocable extraction. Second, there is production, which involves more direct intervention in the manipulation of biological processes through the application of energy, labour, and capital. Capital here can include the standard economic uses of the term (machinery, money, etc.), but it also implies biological/environmental capital in the form of genetic resources or soil properties and human capital embodied in knowledge and individual skill. Production implies far more complex and organized forms of intervention in the natural world than simple extraction, and incorporates the idea that energy and resources are applied to land to generate something of value not inherent in the land resource itself.

The third way to make money via land and natural resources is through their ability to capture fiscal resources, such as capital gains, through speculation; in effect, their usefulness as a means of capturing institutional rents, such as credits and subsidies, and as a means for claiming other assets. In this case, the value of the resource or land has little to do with its actual characteristics or the labour and resources applied to it. The value of the resource/land is linked to its ability to generate returns through a variety of structural features in the larger economy. Bhagwati has called these activities "directly unproductive profit-seeking activities", or DUPs (Bhagwati 1982). Value is determined less by inherent environmental characteristics (although these are not completely absent, as in the value of timber stocks), than by institutional factors such as validity of title, for example, or spatial characteristics, like proximity to roads. Land and resources thus become means of making a profit, but produce little in the way of goods and services through increased production.

LIVESTOCK AND PROFIT

In Brazil, livestock have been extremely important as a means of claiming land and tax breaks and are vehicles to a variety of other forms of financial benefits such as subsidies and immense speculative gains (Mahar 1989; Browder 1988a; Hecht 1985). I contend that the reason that livestock have played such a seminal role in the conversion of forest to pasture is that it is one of the best ways in which all three of the forms of capturing value described above (extractive, productive and DUP activities) can be achieved in the context of high environmental and economic risk. Both large and small ranchers can benefit. While the strategies for large and small cattlemen will differ, they are based on the same principles:

- The importance of land as a means of gaining access to financial benefits inherent in specific polities (credit) or those characteristic of the wider economy (speculative gains);

- The biological flexibility of the animal, which both reduces risk and permits the owner to decide the moment of sale;

- The ability to occupy large areas with little labour;

- The low risk of producing animals or pasture;

- Historic factors.

All these combine to produce the explosive expansion of a land use that produces minimal calories, proteins and direct monetary returns and maximal environmental degradation.

THE LOGIC OF LIVESTOCK: LARGE OWNERS

Most of the literature on cattle production in Amazonia focuses on the eastern Amazon and has concentrated on the dynamics of huge, subsidized, corporate ranches (Hecht 1985; Mahar 1979, 1989; Browder 1988a; Gasques and Yokomizo 1986). This is because the logistics of obtaining such information are relatively easy, and because the documentation of these enterprises can be tracked through public materials held in SUDAM, the Superintendency of Amazonia. The studies that were produced from SUDAM information thus gave the impression that only highly-subsidized livestock operations were involved in the tremendous transformation of forests to grasslands in Amazonia.

There is no question that the SUDAM ranches have been important in the deforestation dynamic since they formally control some 8,763 square kilometres of Amazonia. In areas where they dominate, such as southern Pará and northern Mato Grosso, SUDAM have been responsible for 30 per cent of the clearing, according to figures from INPE, the Brazilian Institute for Space Studies (Hardin et al. 1988). The recent data on clearing, however, suggest new trends. The explosive deforestation in Rondônia, Mato Grosso and Pará indicate that large ranches are not the only cause of the problem. Areas dominated by middle-size holdings, with few SUDAM holdings, such as those in Paragominas, Pará, are currently experiencing deforestation rates greater than 1.5 per cent per year (Woodwell, Stone and Houghton 1988).

SUDAM ranches have been highly subsidized in several ways. These have included:

- **Fiscal incentives.** SUDAM ranches received grants of up to 75 per cent of the ranch development costs in order to encourage corporate groups to invest in the region. These incentives have totalled close to $600 million.

- **Tax holidays.** Up to 100 per cent of a corporation's tax bill would be forgiven if these monies were invested in holdings in the Amazon region or the dry North-East. The net effect of these tax holidays was to permit corporations to use their monies as though they were venture capital, or simply to divert them into other more lucrative activities.

- **No import taxes.** Equipment used on these ranches was exempt from import duty.

- **Subsidized credits.** Such credits were widely available at essentially negative interest rates. Thus, while inflation leaped to well over 50 per cent, the credits were granted at 8-12 per cent. Because these credit lines were largely granted by public banks and were initially designed to favour small farmers, the loans for land development (*investimento*) — unlike those for short term costs (*custieo*) or marketing — often had 6-8 year grace periods under a 12-15 year amortization period. Many of the contracts signed in the early 1970s were not adjusted when policies shifted, resulting in a "founders rent" for early borrowers. Under the prevailing inflation rates, such funds were often diverted into the short-term financial markets ("overnights") or other kinds of investments with a rapid and high return.

- **Land Concessions.** Such concessions were provided in many areas or, alternatively, lands were provided at nominal cost. Indeed, in its economic analyses of ranching, EMBRAPA (the Brazilian Ministry of Agriculture) generally does not even incorporate a land price.

The above package of benefits — all directly tied to the clearing of forest, ostensibly for cattle ranching — made ranching enormously attractive. Dynamic entrepreneurs from southern Brazil were given extraordinary favours, in part because they helped draw up the terms of the incentives, and also because they were to take on the *mission civilisatrice* of taming the Amazon. As Mahar has suggested in his studies of Amazonian frontier policy, livestock became a vehicle for capturing both these extraordinary financial benefits and untaxed capital gains (Mahar 1989). Whether ranching was sustainable, economic or appropriate made very little difference in this context.

LAND OWNERSHIP

The SUDAM-sponsored deforestation could probably be explained on the basis of subsidies and tax holidays alone, but the focus on a few hundred mega-ranches has obscured the fact that there are more than 50,000 livestock operations in Amazonia at all scales of production. Clearing forest for pasture is clearly economically attractive even without the luxurious benefits of SUDAM affiliation. To explain this pattern of livestock expansion it is necessary to look at the role of real estate in the context of regional development strategies, subsidized credits, inflationary pressures in the Brazilian economy, the potential revenues from timber and the possibility of gold strikes — all of which contribute to the speculative value of lands.

A whole industry — the *industria de posse* — has developed around clearing land for pasture, selling that land as quickly as possible, pocketing the gains and then moving on into new forest zones. Indeed, more than 20 million hectares of the Amazon have shifted from public to private lands in the last decade — an enclosure movement unmatched anywhere else in speed and size (Santos 1984). As a result, pasture lands throughout Brazil have experienced immense rises in value, rises which also reflect large-scale infrastructure investment patterns — the development of extensive highway systems, and the clear commitment by the Brazilian government to sustain investment in Amazonia through such mega-projects as Grande Carajás and the Tucurui dam. The value of land as a commodity itself, rather than as an input into production, has helped fuel the murderous land conflicts that now characterize the Brazilian Amazon as speculators pit themselves against peasants and petty extractors.

Land ownership in Amazonia has been characterized by extensive fraud, overlapping and competing claims, and a chaotic, often corrupt process of determining definitive title (Pomper-Meyer 1979; Bunker 1985; Santos 1984; Hecht 1985; Schmink and Wood 1984). Since those who clear land have a stronger legal claim to a parcel than those who do not, there is ample incentive to clear as much land as possible. Moreover, under the laws of INCRA (the

Institute of Agrarian Reform), an area six times the size of the actual land cleared can be claimed. Thus, should there be valuable timber or potential mineral finds on adjacent sites, these can be secured through clearing. There are also obvious economies of scale associated with large clearings. Finally, under the terms of the new 1988 constitution, land in "effective use" (that is, cleared) cannot be expropriated for the purpose of agrarian reform.

PRODUCTION

In a study carried out by the Brazilian Institute of Economic Analysis (IPEA) on SUDAM ranches, it was shown that even on large operations running at capacity, the actual production and sale of livestock was a mere 15 per cent of projected productivity, while those ranches that were still developing generated a mere 8 per cent of estimated production, based on the general stocking rate of one animal unit per hectare. Take-off rates have hovered at about 10 per cent, one of the lowest rates in the world. The formation and management of pastures is quite expensive, pastures are not usually sustainable, and the value of the final animal product often does not repay the investment costs. Browder has suggested that cattle only repay about 25 per cent of their production costs, based on a 15 per cent take-off rate and fully-realized herds (Browder 1988a).

A study of the economics of livestock rearing under various price regimes — with and without subsidies and speculation, and with different types of technologies — has shown that taking the economic returns to cattle production alone (without credits, no overgrazing, and no land appreciation), ranching was only economically viable under very specific conditions (Hecht, Norgaard and Possio 1988). Overgrazing improved the economic scenario somewhat, but the major gains to the enterprise were realized through capital gains linked to the rise in land values and the subsidies. The critical issue to note is that the returns on cattle production are overshadowed by the spectacular returns available from land speculation, and the rents associated with subsidies. This is not to say that the revenue derived from the sale of cattle is unimportant, only to point out that most of the revenue associated with livestock will not be generated by production but rather through financial or DUP activities as described above.

EXTRACTION

Irreversible extraction can have a role in livestock expansion in two ways. The first, mentioned above, involves using livestock as a way to claim lands. A recognized land claim permits the holder to assert royalty rights on subsurface minerals which are technically owned by the Brazilian state. Thus, areas adjacent to gold strikes frequently experience vigorous clearing. Cattle claim what is under their feet. The other main way in which extraction is linked to pasture expansion is through the use of valuable timber to subsidize pasture-development costs. This is a more recent phenomenon due to improved infrastructure, expanding timber markets, and relatively recent policy changes, and is more widely used by smaller ranching operations.

Larger-scale livestock operations appropriate value from natural resources through their ability to capture financial resources and to claim extractive ones. They can generate revenue as producers of beef, but this rarely covers the costs of production. The fusion of all three forms of profit-making or accumulation through a given land use is not limited to cattle-ranching. Nonetheless, ranching has a special appeal due to the low cost of pasture compared to agriculture or perennial crops like cocoa, the low labour demands and most importantly, the rapidity with which cattle occupy large areas of land.

THE LOGIC OF LIVESTOCK FOR PEASANTS

Although the discussion of large-scale livestock operations has dominated the analysis of cattle and deforestation, the highest rates of deforestation in Amazonia currently occur in the state of Rondônia, where it is colonists and small producers who are mainly behind the expansion of livestock. The increase in Rondônia's herd was more than 3,000 per cent in the period between 1970 and 1988, and it has come to dominate the cleared areas.

There are several reasons why livestock figure so prominently in the strategy of small farmers. Cattle, and livestock more generally, are one means of spreading the risks in agriculture. They provide a supplement to household income in the form of milk or calves, and if there are agricultural disasters, as is often the case in the Brazilian Amazon, they provide a large "lump" of income when sold. The ability of animals to move between use- and exchange-values is also important for smallholders, as is the ready local market for animal products where beef fetches the highest price of any source of protein, and the highest per-kilo value of any basic food commodity.

Cattle provide these market benefits with less labour cost than rice, beans, maize, or manioc or tree crops, and, unlike crops, animals are capable of transporting themselves. The timing of animal harvest is determined by household need or market opportunity, and not by the biological demands of crop production which often work against small farmers since all bring their main crops to market simultaneously.

Cattle production also extends the economic life of a cleared area. Sites that have been planted with crops go out of production within three years and are usually planted with grass. This land is grazed until it becomes choked with weeds or so degraded that no forage will grow. While the productivity of these pastures is extremely low, they provide a marginal return on a piece of land that would otherwise be generating very little for the colonist household. This may be a minor gain, but for poor households its importance should not be dismissed, especially since the labour costs are relatively low.

In highly inflationary economies, such as those of most Amazon countries, investing in animals is a way for peasants to protect their assets. For people who may not be comfortable with banks, and where interest rates do not accompany inflation, such a strategy is completely reasonable.

Colonization projects have frequently enabled small-scale ranchers to gain access to credit (although the lion's share of these credits went to larger holdings). The benefit of buying a valuable asset with borrowed money whose value is evaporating, while that of the animal is maintaining if not exceeding that of inflation, is quite clear.

Throughout the Amazon, pasture is the cheapest and easiest way to claim occupation rights for both large- and small-scale producers. If, as often happens, peasant households inhabit a parcel of questionable title, and this land is adjudicated, the larger the cleared area, the greater the indemnification if they are expropriated. As areas that have been cleared for pasture have a value that is about one-third greater than that of forest, their ability to speculate with these lands is also enhanced. Among colonists, land speculation and indemnification by the state or larger landowners occurs with some frequency. Finally, a lucky minerals strike or generous profits in coca production may produce immense surpluses for a rural household. In this case, one of the few means of diversification in the regional economy involves investing in land with cattle.

Much is made of the symbolism of cattle as items of prestige in Luso-Brazilian culture, and there certainly is an element of pride in emulating the rich land owners with their huge herds. However, the diversity of economic ends that can be served by cattle make them a compelling investment for colonists with or without the symbolic overlay.

Cattle must be seen in the context of the numerous roles they fill in these very uncertain rural economies. For both large and small operators, their advantages are inescapable. Unfortunately, these private benefits have quite disastrous public costs in terms of their environmental effect and their implications for the regional economy.

UNTO DUST:
THE ECOLOGICAL EFFECTS OF PASTURES

Pastures in the Amazon do not remain productive for long, and frequently are abandoned within ten years. The rainforest survives on very poor acid soils and most of the ecosystem nutrients are held in the biomass itself, not in the soil. When forests are cleared for pasture, there is a nutrient flush as elements held in the biomass are released to soils. However, with leaching, run-off and uptake by the pasture plants, soil nutrients decline rapidly to levels below those necessary for maintaining pasture production. Cleaning the pastures by chopping down the bush, burning, and fertilizing, can give pastures a new, albeit short, lease on life, although the economics of maintaining pastures versus clearing new ones works against managing existing cleared land (Serrao and Toledo 1988). Thus new areas are constantly being cleared as old ones go out of production.

Heavily-degraded lands are exceedingly difficult to recuperate. Thus the clearing for pasture ultimately often condemns land to waste; in fact, more than half of the areas cleared have subsequently been abandoned.

In terms of regional economies, cattle generate very little employment except for that required during the clearing phase and for brush management. This is a private advantage for both peasants and large landowners, but for the regional economy it is a disaster. The standard *fazenda* uses about one cowboy for every 1,500 hectares cleared. The linkages to other parts of the regional economy are fairly weak. Implements, seed, wire, animal supplements and veterinary products all come from southern Brazil, so the major gains from these transactions accrue to merchants and transporters. Although Amazonian beef is consumed in local urban centres, and some employment is generated in the small slaughterhouses and butcher's shops, the bulk of the labour linked to pasture development is in the clearing stage, with little permanent employment. Tax revenues generated from livestock sales are low. The SUDAM ranches have produced in taxes only about two per cent of the value of incentive money they received (Gasques and Yukomizo 1986).

WHAT ARE THE REAL SOLUTIONS?

One of the solutions to pasture-led deforestation proposed in international circles is the idea that if cattle subsidies are reduced, livestock loses its attractiveness as an investment. This view constitutes the major analytic contribution of the World Resources Institute (Repetto and Gillis 1988) and the World Bank (Mahar 1989). This perspective views development processes as largely mechanistic, and ignores the fact that these processes take on a life of their own and interact with a number of dynamics within the local and larger economies. The irony is, of course, that deforestation rates have increased as subsidies to the sector have declined.

One of the central problems with those who see the solution in terms of lifting subsidies has been the excessive focus on super subsidies to a relatively small set of producers and the extrapolation of this view to all cattle operations in the Amazon. Even amongst those who received SUDAM subsidies, between 60-70 per cent of the total fiscal incentive resources were concentrated in 35 large corporate groups who often had more than one SUDAM project.

While these ranches were important in initiating a regional clearing dynamic, the withdrawal of subsidies now comes too late. The regional economy responds synergistically to a number of factors that are now beyond the control of one set of policies. What drives land speculation now are high inflation rates, the relatively low entry costs for land in Amazonia, the clear commitment to infrastructure development, colonization programmes, the threat of disappropriation of uncleared land, and the concerted promulgation of doctrines of national security, national integration and national destiny.

As the rest of the Brazilian economy goes into a tailspin, the "Amazon Card" is seen as an important means of resolving internal social tensions and assuring continued wealth accumulation for entrepreneurs who have difficulty in participating in urban investments. Given the triumph of the UDR (Rural Democratic Union, a right-wing landowners' organization that has organized against agrarian reform) in the constitutional congress, there is a large and politically powerful constituency that will support and encourage the continued occupation of the Amazon no matter what the environmental or social cost.

TECHNOLOGICAL FIXES?

A popular line of argument suggests that environmental problems in Amazonia could be substantially mitigated if better pasture and livestock practices were implemented. If each area cleared stayed in production, then the need for increased clearance would diminish. Research institutes throughout the Amazon engage in careful field testing, fertilizer trials and germplasm selection in order to find the combination that permits sustainable pasture production. While certainly a laudable goal, this assumes that destructive pasture management is largely the outcome of poor technologies.

Although better management could make a difference, I have argued throughout this chapter that production itself is of little interest in much of the regional livestock economy. It is the other things that cattle do besides grow meat that make them so profitable. Moreover, our own studies make it clear that improved technologies do not yield returns that can compete with overgrazing (Hecht, Norgaard and Possio 1988). The fact that the ancillary benefits of ranching are not linked to production and will accrue under good or bad management (indeed, in the short term, bad management brings higher returns) means that technological solutions are likely to have little impact on deforestation patterns.

In the case of Paragominas, Pará, where extensive research has been under way for more than a decade, and where the best pasture technology systems are tested and subsidized, the adoption of more appropriate technology is minimal, and deforestation rates have increased above the prevailing rates of the 1970s. If improved technologies were to make a difference, they would do so here, because of the relative proximity of ranches to the large Belém market, and because of the enormous effort in research and extension on pasture management focused there. Good management is clearly of secondary importance for landowners with pasture.

SOCIAL MOVEMENTS

Rainforests will ultimately survive because those who make their living from them have organized to protect them from destruction. Tropical forests are not empty. They are and have been home to millions of people in the Amazon, from indigenous peoples to petty extractors of all kinds. Based on systems of renewable extraction and some small-scale agriculture, informed by complex systems of local environmental knowledge, these populations have been able to generate large revenues that, in some cases, have maintained the Amazonian élites — notably the rubber barons — in fine style for centuries. Now, threatened by livestock enterprises and government infrastructure development, their resistance has become more politicized and is centring increasingly on environmental issues.

The forest peoples' movements are frail, but they have nonetheless been able to stop deforestation. The Rubber Tappers' Union of Acre, for example, claims that 1.2 million hectares of forests have been saved by their direct actions. In southern Pará, where gold-mining, logging and ranching have obliterated one of the richest forests and its fauna, the only areas that have not been routinely ravaged have been within the Kayapó and Xingu reserves.

Resistance movements, beleaguered though they may be, have managed to form alliances to bring pressure to bear at many levels. In the end, the development of non-violent *empates* (the technique of forming human chains to prevent trees from being cut down) may be even more effective at stopping forest destruction. While there is often a romantic *frisson* associated with the emergence of resistance movements, however, it is worth mentioning that the history of Amazonia has been written in crushed aspirations. The murder of rubber-tapper leader Chico Mendes is only one example of the form which the consequences of direct action can take.

CONCLUSIONS

In this chapter, I have tried to show how value can be obtained from natural resources via extractive, productive and DUP economies. This has been framed within an analysis of the logics of livestock for both large- and small-scale producers. By concentrating on strategies and rationales, I have placed less emphasis than is usual on demography and the workings of the commodity markets as causes of deforestation. In the case of Brazil, at least, the demographic model of deforestation is not valid because more than half the population is urban. The classic and well-loved "hamburger connection" and the influence of international beef markets simply do not operate in the current Amazonian context. Amazonian beef is rife with the disease aftosa and is prohibited from entry into US markets. Moreover, the Amazon is a net beef importer. The current emphasis on policy and subsidy distortions is important, but does not deal with the root causes of the problem.

Models that focus on beef as a commodity cannot capture the broader dynamics of livestock-stimulated deforestation throughout the humid Latin American tropics. Land markets, the value of ancillaries, the larger macro-economic context and individual economic strategies must also be included. The biological, market, and ancillary features of livestock make cattle quite unlike other commodities like coffee or rice.

Ultimately, control over the processes of deforestation will be resolved at the national and not the international level. This view is not popular with those who place the blame for deforestation on the vast tentacles of international capitalism, but I believe it is important to understand that the Amazon basin is not a First World colony, and that the destiny of the region will be shaped through national politics to a greater degree than international pressure.

This does not mean that one needs to throw up one's hands in frustration, but rather to realize that the logic behind livestock has a momentum that is immensely compelling, and likely to become more so, particularly since the alternatives — forestry, agriculture, and agroforestry — lack the variety of mechanisms through which value can be captured.

This chapter previously appeared as an article in *The Ecologist*.

DEFORESTATION IN ZAIRE: LOGGING AND LANDLESSNESS

JOHN WITTE

Having exhausted the timber resources of West Africa, logging companies are now turning their attention to the vast forests of Zaire. As the loggers advance, they pave the way for settlers who introduce forms of agriculture that further destroy the forest. This underclass of poor and landless farmers is the legacy of a corrupt social system, imposed by the Belgian colonialists, perfected by President Mobutu, and tacitly supported by Western commercial interests.

Increasing European concern about the fate of the rainforests has focused almost exclusively on the burning of Amazonia and the rapid logging of Malaysia's forests, while the destruction of the rainforests of Africa has been largely ignored. Perhaps it is easier to point the finger at Japanese excesses in Malaysia and cattle ranches in Latin America than to look at the involvement of European companies in the destruction of Africa's forests. Yet in the last decade it is Africa, not South-East Asia or South America, that has suffered the highest level of deforestation (Martin 1991). A study by the FAO shows that, from 1981 to 1990, Africa lost 17% of its rainforests, Asia 14% and Latin America 9%. During this period, the fastest rate of forest destruction was recorded in Nigeria — not in Brazil, Malaysia or Indonesia. Nigeria is now 90% deforested with a timber trade deficit of $147 million (Myers 1989). Over 75% of the forests of West Africa have now been destroyed.

With West Africa's forests devastated, the logging companies are now expanding their operations into the vast Central African forest, which is almost the size of Western Europe and represents 20% of the world's total rainforest cover. At present, logging is

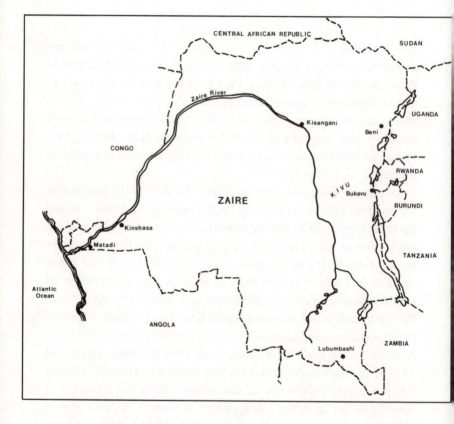

concentrated on the western fringes of the Zaire river basin in Cameroon, Central African Republic and Gabon; but increasingly, logging companies are turning to the vast interior of Zaire.

A 1991 Oxfam report concluded that "there is a major effort to open up Africa's forests to meet debt repayments and fuel future development", which will "cause an increase in poverty rather than its resolution" (Beauclerk 1991). This conclusion is supported by a report for the European Community which acknowledges that "forestry development and deforestation generally go hand in hand with the redistribution of wealth from the poorest . . . to a national élite and foreign companies [and] widen the gap between the rich and poor in tropical countries" (cited in Beauclerk 1991).

POVERTY IN A RICH LAND

Most African countries are confronted with a serious economic crisis characterized by heavy external debt, decreasing productivity, especially in agriculture, and increasing rural and urban poverty. Meanwhile, the minority ruling class "has almost confiscated the state apparatus to realize its personal interests and wealth accumulation" (Kalala 1989:8). This is nowhere more evident than in Zaire, whose foreign debt of US$8 billion, accumulated through the establishment of inappropriate prestige projects and the need to import food, is considered to be less than the personal fortune accrued by President Mobutu during his 26 years in control of the state apparatus.

Zaire (formerly the Belgian Congo) is Africa's third largest country with over 200 different ethnic groups. It is the size of Western Europe, yet has a population of only 34.5 million people, compared to Western Europe's 337 million. Zaire contains 12.5% of the world's remaining tropical rainforest; only Brazil and Indonesia have more. As well as its immense forests, it has vast deposits of cobalt, copper and diamonds, and its network of rivers are a natural transport system and a huge potential source of hydroelectric power.

Seventy per cent of Zaire's population is involved in subsistence farming on its fertile lands. The diversity of its climate and geography allows the production of a wide range of food and cash crops (Kalala 1989). Yet real wages are a tenth of what they were at independence, malnutrition is chronic, and 80% of people live in absolute poverty.

Zaire has for many years been in the grip of a social system based not on the accumulation and investment of capital, nor on a strong political structure, but on the intentional creation and perpetuation of insecurity at all levels of society. The Zairian system of government is often described as a "kleptocracy", and Mobutu at its top was referred to by Zairians as *le grand voleur* — "the big thief". The state operates through a corrupt hierarchy of institutionalized theft, involving the relentless appropriation of money, labour and fertile lands by those in a position of power. The forcible seizure of land for logging, plantations and other lucrative activities has created a class of dispossessed poor, whose only option is to move along logging roads and other roads into the forest.

The Zairian kleptocracy is not, however, Mobutu's creation; it can be traced directly back to the early days of colonialism, and to the reign of Leopold II of Belgium in particular. If we are fully to understand the causes that today push cultivators into the forests along the loggers' roads, we must look at the ways in which the traditional political structures and land tenure systems were forcibly changed by the Belgian colonialists, and the effect that this has had on present-day land use and ownership.

TRADITIONAL SYSTEMS OF LAND OWNERSHIP

Jan Vansina has described how, from about 3000 BC, Western Bantu cultivators and fishers — with an economy based on palm and root cultivation — expanded from central Cameroon into the forested areas of Gabon and the Zaire basin, previously the exclusive preserve of "pygmies" and fisherfolk (Vansina 1990).

For several thousand years, until it was destroyed by colonialism, a robust Western Bantu political tradition flourished in Equatorial Africa. Bantu cultivators and fishers traded iron and pottery artefacts and agricultural produce for the forest products of the hunting and gathering "pygmies" (about 200,000 of whom still live in the forest region). This economic and cultural exchange was often mutually beneficial, and in places such as the Ituri Forest of northern Zaire it continues to this day. The "pygmies'" traditional system of land ownership differs from that of the farming people in so far as their corporate rights to land are not related to cultivation but to gathering, fishing and hunting; and in that they see themselves as dependent on the goodwill of the forest itself rather than on the goodwill of their ancestors. However, their traditional rights to land rest on the same combination of defined territories and flexible group membership as do those of neighbouring farmers.

Even today, the Bantu farmers have very ambivalent attitudes towards the "pygmies". As French anthropologist Serge Bahuchet notes, on the one hand they see the "pygmies" as slaves and as barely human, yet, on the other, tell stories which cast the "pygmies" as civilizing beings who invented fire, farming and metallurgy (Bahuchet and Guillaume 1982:189-211). Vansina postulates that these latter views reflect the early reliance of the Bantu migrants on the long traditions of forest-living of their diminutive hosts (Vansina 1990).

Gradually, however, the importance of the "pygmies" to the Bantu's economic life decreased. New crops, such as bananas, plantains and taro introduced from South-East Asia, enabled increases in wealth and further expansion into the forest, as well as sustaining a wide network of trade routes. In Vansina's view, the logic of the environment and of cultivation of these crops combined with Bantu cultural traditions led to the evolution of a very distinct political tradition, in which the greatest degree of local autonomy was sought consistent with their need for security. It was a tradition in which each extended "household" could freely choose to which village it would belong, the frequent movement of village sites in turn being required by the process of shifting cultivation (Vansina 1990). To cope with this fluidity, land-tenure systems had to be correspondingly flexible and encompassing.

In a study of the land tenure systems of four Bantu ethnic groups in Zaire, Robert Harms concluded that land is traditionally held by small groups which are constantly dividing, merging and shifting; and the person responsible for land is relatively low in the political hierarchy. This is because of the prevalence of shifting agriculture, which means plots are cultivated only temporarily; and of the low population density, which means new plots are easily found and there is consequently little interest in maintaining permanent individual rights to land:

> Almost everywhere in Zaire large tracts of land are held by corporate groups. Individual parcels for cultivation within a tract are redistributed to the members of the group according to local laws each time the soil becomes exhausted in one place and it becomes necessary to set up new fields. Sometimes individuals move their fields, while at other times the whole village moves, causing a complete redistribution of the land. In the majority of cases the corporate group that holds the land is the lineage, though sometimes it is a political chiefdom. The land held by the group has fixed boundaries, either clearly-defined geographical features or imaginary lines. Within the tract of the corporate group there are several kinds of rights in land, such as hunting rights, gathering rights, and cultivation rights. The individual cultivator, who gains rights to a plot of land by putting it under cultivation, maintains his rights until he abandons the field for another. In land held by lineages, strangers can gain rights in land. The key test is residence [and] most systems draw a careful distinction between inherited rights, which have come down from the ancestors who first settled the land, and strangers' rights, which cannot be passed on. (Harms 1974:2; cf Fairhead 1989:2; Jewsiewicki 1981:94)

According to Bogumil Jewsiewicki (1981:112):

> From the point of view of social relationships the rationality of shifting agriculture was evident. It preserved a supple relationship between lineage or clan groups and villages . . . The traditional mechanism for the solution of conflicts had been the breakup of groups.

The establishment of Belgian rule, which forcibly kept people in the villages, halted this traditional means of resolving conflict and encouraging equitable social relations. Increasingly the rights of non-resident strangers were allowed to dominate over customary claims. Decisions about land allocation, crop choice, residence and trade have been taken out of the hands of villagers and entrusted first to colonial entrepreneurs and then to the emerging local élite. It is these interventions, far more than population growth, which have undermined rural livelihoods, causing the landless poor to clear fresh lands on the forest frontier.

THE CONGO FREE STATE

In the second half of the nineteenth century, there was a sudden rise in Western demand for African gathered and hunted materials, primarily rubber and ivory. Swahili merchants from East Africa, together with European merchants and state representatives, sought to extract and transport these products through enslaving or employing African labour. The demand for raw materials and the competition among colonial powers led to the formation of colonial states, which took over the region's economic resources. In Zaire, this began in 1885, with the imposition of the Congo Free State, the personal possession of King Leopold II of Belgium. The Free State became notorious, even in the heyday of colonialism, for cruel and violent exploitation. According to Roland Oliver, the Congo suffered more severely than any other area of Africa during the early years of colonial rule; its only tangible wealth was in wild rubber and ivory, which could most easily be obtained by forcing the agricultural peoples of the riversides, often at gunpoint, to move into the forest to gather and hunt these products. Oliver believes that the forest population may have been reduced by half during this period (Oliver 1991).

In 1885, the Congo Free State seized all so-called "vacant" land, and in 1890 declared itself to be the owner of all natural products of the forest. Although the state generally recognized cultivation rights on cleared land, it completely ignored gathering rights, which were equally well-defined and regulated by customary law (Harms 1974:11). It thus set the scene for the modern-day ownership of all forest lands by the Zairian state. Under Leopold's rule, the Anglo-Belgian India Rubber and Exploration Company (Abir) and the Anveroise Concessionary Company received vast areas of forest to exploit for a pre-determined period in order to extract rubber and ivory. Today companies such as Siforzal, a subsidiary of the German multinational Danzer, and La Forestiere, an Italian logging company, have likewise been given effective power over huge areas to extract timber. In both cases the central government was too administratively weak to exploit and manage the areas itself, and so resigned itself to indirect management through European companies.

Abir was given a concession of about 30,000 square miles in 1903 (Jewsiewicki 1983:97). The people living in the concession had to collect rubber for the company as a way of paying taxes to the state. Those men who failed to meet their quota were beaten, imprisoned or shot. As frequent tapping caused the supply of rubber to become exhausted, men had to work nearly full-time to fulfil their quotas. There was no time to clear new fields for the women to cultivate, and famine occurred.

In 1908, the Congo Free State became the Belgian Congo, when the Belgian government took over the administration of the territory from the discredited King Leopold. Two years later, it became apparent that the rubber in Zaire was being depleted. The rubber tax was abandoned, and in 1911 the British company, Lever Brothers, were given 750,000 acres of the best palm groves on "vacant" forest lands. Despite the fact that each of the groves was already owned by a local person or lineage, Lever claimed ownership of all palm groves that were not directly joined to villages. The government then instituted a tax in money to force people to work for Lever, and again people often abandoned cultivation, having to work full time for the company in order to pay their taxes (Harms 1974:13).

In the eastern Congo, farmers were forced to grow rice and other food crops, initially to feed troops and porters stationed there during World War I, and subsequently to feed the populations of the mining and urban areas. Cotton was introduced to the Congo in 1915, and each subsequent year villagers were required to extend their cotton fields in order to pay their taxes. The obligatory cultivation of cash crops greatly expanded the amount of land under cultivation and caused farmers to plant on fallow land long before it had recovered. The result was a continuous degradation of the soil, widespread undernourishment of the people and rural depopulation.

Between the 1930s and independence in 1960, the colonial authorities sought to counter this depopulation by instituting new methods of cultivation which would not exhaust the soil. The first rotation system, the *paysannat*, placed all landowners on strips side by side with one another in a block, in an attempt to "rationalize" land use and fix land tenure in individual holdings. In contrast to the indigenous sytems, whereby farmers had scattered their fields to take advantage of the best soils and other conditions, under the *paysannat* individuals were arbitrarily allocated land according to a rigid grid pattern, leaving many farmers on almost useless soils. The allocations conflicted directly with the customary systems of land tenure. "Strangers often received land belonging to the local group. . . [and so] the strangers . . . lived in fear that someday the landholding group would drive them out. Thus a system designed to provide security of tenure often increased insecurity" (Harms 1974:18).

In the Congo Free State, chiefs were the mainstay of government rule and labour policy. They often struggled to defend their people, while meeting enough of the excessive demands of the colonial authorities to retain their position. David Northrup describes how many rulers "passively resisted the ever-growing government demands for rubber, porters and food in an effort to retain the support of their subjects but soon found themselves displaced or replaced by government appointees" (Northrup 1988:44). Colonial officials often negotiated land agreements with these puppet chiefs, despite the fact that the traditional owners were generally much lower in the political hierarchy than the chiefs.

All Africans were excluded from credit, from private ownership of land and from the right to hire employees. Punitive taxes were introduced specifically to bankrupt African small businesses and so prevent the emergence of an African middle class. The learning of French was restricted to urbanized Africans, so that the different ethnic groups in the countryside would not develop a common language. The policy of "indigenization" divided people into small cultural units, tying them for life to their village and group of ethnic origin (Jewsiewicki 1983:119). Migration was controlled by passes to impede people fleeing from taxation and from obligatory cultivation or road work.

Belgian rule destroyed the dynamic nature of the traditional political and land owning system. It blocked any creative adaptation to the impact of Western institutions and demands, by maintaining a stifling system of government-appointed chiefs, taxes and laws, and by its underlying paternalism which, at best, treated the Africans as children who could never grow up.

MOBUTU'S USE OF STATE POWER

On 30 June 1960, the Congo achieved independence under the radical government of Patrice Lumumba. But a week later the army mutinied against its exclusively European officer corps, plunging the country into civil war. To contain the situation, Lumumba placed the army in the hands of some former NCOs, led by Mobutu. But Lumumba was deposed by this faction, and subsequently murdered. After five years of conflict, Mobutu, aided by Belgian and American troops, seized power.

Mobutu's promise to impose order by establishing a strong, depoliticized regime was overwhelmingly welcomed by a people sick of civil war. Parliament was dissolved, and the independent judiciary abolished. In 1967, Mobutu established a one-party state, under the *Mouvement Populaire de la Revolution* (MPR). For a while the economy appeared to recover, but Zaire rapidly built up a massive external debt to fund prestige projects such as the huge dam at Inga on the lower Zaire, or to buy industrial plant that was heavily reliant on imports. Mobutu consolidated his position by co-opting radicals and would-be opponents into his regime, a practice that proved very successful up until the early 1990s. He changed his ministers and military commanders every two or three years so that they would not create a power base to threaten him, even though it meant having no continuity in administration. The centralization of state power was accompanied by a concentration of economic revenues in the small circle around the President.

Meanwhile wages fell, agriculture was completely neglected, and the economy collapsed. This provided the justification, in 1975, for further "radicalization", in which the government took over more enterprises. This massive dislocation of the commercial economy coincided with the copper price-crash; and, a year later, many of the businesses had to be returned to the original owners in order to keep the economy going. The new Zairian partners maintained a 60% holding, however, and in this way the President himself acquired a large stake in many huge concerns. These included the major logging enterprise Siforzal; the plantation empire Celza, which is Zaire's third largest employer and produces about one-sixth of the country's agricultural exports; and Pharmakina, a subsidiary of Bayer.

Zaire's debt steadily increased, today totalling some US$8 billion, a sum estimated to be roughly equivalent to the amount the President had stolen from the country. Meanwhile, 5% of the country's profits from minerals were being paid into his overseas accounts, and in 1990, 30% of the country's operating budget was estimated to be passing through the Presidential office with no further accounting. Yet, for many years, Mobutu's position was never seriously challenged. During the Soviet-Cuban intervention in the Angolan civil war and then in Ethiopia, he was able to present himself to the West as the only alternative to chaos and communism in Zaire. With support from abroad, as well as from his own extensive security network, Mobutu's survival, until very recently, was never in doubt.

THE SPREAD OF LOGGING

At present, logging in Zaire extracts only 500,000 cubic metres of timber a year, compared to Indonesia's annual cut of about 40,000,000 cubic metres. Zaire lacks the infrastructure to handle much more than this, and consequently 86% of Zaire's rainforest is still intact. There are just over 6,000 kilometres of railways in five separate and rarely-functioning sections, and only 2,400 kilometres of roads, in a country five times the size of France. The Zaire River and its tributaries are the main transport network. It is navigable from Kisangani in the north, to the capital, Kinshasa, in the south-west; but the rapids below Kinshasa force all the timber to go overland by inefficient road or rail transport to the port of Matadi.

Zaire allocates its logging concessions on a 25-year lease. In theory, Western logging companies will return to take a second cut, but in reality this never happens, since the amount of forest destroyed in the first cut, and the influx of shifting cultivators, means that there are no valuable trees left for a second cut. Only the best trees are taken — the average is 8.7 cubic metres, less than one tree, per hectare — and this low yield effectively quickens the pace at which further rainforest is opened up. Logging is thus both highly selective and completely unsustainable. Since the massive trunks can only be taken out of the forest on feeder tracks and logging routes before travelling down river, these selectively logged areas are criss-crossed with roads.

The heaviest logging has occurred in the region of Bas-Zaire, close to Kinshasa and its ports; and settlers have followed in the wake of the loggers to clear extensive areas for farming. Logging companies pay Zairian workers the least they can possibly get away with, and feel no responsibility to their workers once they have finished logging an area and moved on. Those who have moved into the forest to work for the company often have to switch from logging to clearing the forest for agriculture, in order to feed their families. Today, there is virtually no primary rainforest left in Bas-Zaire.

Huge increases in logging are planned. The Tropical Forestry Action Plan for Zaire, which held its final meeting in 1990, plans to increase logging to 5,000,000 cubic metres by the year 2020. The TFAP also suggests the "promotion of Zairian timber in the ... EC, US and Japan", where "Zaire can recuperate the markets" of the major African producers of the 1970s, whose exports "crumble year by year" (TFAP 1990:123-124).

The vast forested central basin is sparsely populated and has a non-existent or abysmal road system. The TFAP plans a "road network in the interior of the country" as far east as Haute-Zaire. The Kisangani-Bukavu road, already being constructed by the Chinese and the Germans, will permit an increase in the export of timber to East Africa from its present low level. Thirty-seven per cent of the total exploitable area of Zaire's rainforest has already been allocated as timber concessions (in the neighbouring Central African Republic the figure is 90%) (Kenrick 1990). Eleven German, French, Belgian, Italian and other foreign-based companies or joint-ventures account for 90% of logging in Zaire. Of these companies the largest is Siforzal, which accounts for 40% of Zaire's logging, and has ten concessions, mostly in Equateur and Haut-Zaire provinces, three of which are over one million hectares in size.

Timber from Africa's rainforests is exported in its cheapest, raw material form. Of EC timber imports from Central Africa, 1,726,000 cubic metres arrives in the form of raw logs and 213,000 cubic metres as sawn wood. In contrast, the EC imports 6,800 cubic metres of raw logs and 1,356,000 cubic metres of sawn wood from its second largest supplier, Malaysia. In Zaire, for exports worth $16 million a year, Siforzal pays less than $10,000 to Zaire's government (Grantham 1990). Of the taxes the government receives, far more goes into the President's personal account than is spent on education, health and transport combined. Few of the profits from logging reach the local population.

LAND CONCENTRATION IN KIVU

The pressure of increasing landlessness upon the forest is nowhere more evident than in the province of Kivu, which borders Uganda, Rwanda, Burundi and Tanzania.

Kivu is highly fertile, a fact which did not escape the notice of the Belgian colonialists. In 1927, the administration of the Belgian

Congo gave tax and plantation rights in Kivu to a private company, Comité National de Kivu (CNKi). However, they were only allowed to occupy "vacant" lands, far from the relatively heavily populated areas, which were most favourable for *arabica* coffee production (Fairhead 1989:3). CNKi therefore had cultivated land declared "vacant" by corrupt chiefs, and then set up their own plantations on it. The chiefs benefited through "selling" land that was not really theirs, especially land belonging to their political rivals (Fairhead 1989:7).

Plantations of coffee, tea and cinchona (quinine) were very labour-intensive. Recruitment to plantations was achieved initially through forced labour; and later through the raising of taxes, combined with the destruction of any alternatives to paid labour on the plantations or in the mines. From 1937 until 1956, the labour shortage was partly solved by the relocation of populations from the densely-populated regions of Rwanda and Highland Bwisha. Land was forcibly reallocated to the immigrants, to the benefit of the chiefs and the detriment of local people.

The means used in the colonial period to force people into paid employment are still in use today. State and local authorities collaborate in forcing people off their land. Those with power, wealth and influence, are now more than ever able to manipulate the land-grant system to appropriate occupied land. The local élite claim the land is theirs by tradition, while the state élite uses state laws and central government influence to support their claims; the original farmers often end up as dependent labourers. Since land is increasingly valuable, "repression, including arrests, extortion and crop destruction have been employed against peasants who have refused to abandon their homes and fields. Many have been forced off the land; others now work in exchange for squatter's rights" (Fairhead 1989:7). By creating a dispossessed landless class, the landowners can pay low or no wages by offering people land to cultivate, in return for personal security and labour obligations.

In Kivu, concessions for ranching (and consequently the appropriation of land) are in increasing demand by those with influence in the state system:

> In the highlands of Kivu, home of a principal immigrant group, the Nande, an expanding entrepreneurial class is buying up land from village chiefs to convert it into cattle-ranches and plantations. A study by a Nande anthropologist found that as early as 1980, 25 percent of Nande farmland in the zones of Beni and Lubero (in Kivu) was owned by wealthy businesspeople and private cash croppers. Land put into cattle ranches is often very inefficiently used or left unexploited, thus locking up land that could be used more efficiently and sustainably for food production. The resulting land scarcity leaves few choices for Nande rural producers; it is leading to their dispossession and immigration onto the lowland forest frontier. (Peterson 1990:58)

Agricultural land has also been lost to various aid projects. Loans for small- scale projects such as roads and buildings have benefited the local kleptocratic élite and enabled them to take over large amounts of land. Larger schemes are imposed at the international level. Most prominent of these is the Ruzizi dam in Kivu on the Zaire/Rwanda border, funded by the World Bank. In 1989, six years after the project was approved, no resettlement and rehabilitation plan existed. The number of people to be displaced had originally been estimated at 200. In fact, "a total of 12,600 people suffered expropriation of their property and productive farmland. They were left with inadequate or non-existent compensation in one of the most densely populated and cultivated areas of Zaire" (Beauclerk 1991).

The situation is aggravated by the continual conflict between different ethnic groups. Often one group will claim traditional land rights over an area, by insisting that other groups are untitled immigrants. In many cases, the only recourse of the poor is the Catholic church, but in its battle against ancestor-worship the church usually opposes traditional land claims and supports those who have purchased land contrary to customary land rights. Although in some cases this may protect poorer immigrants from dispossession, it may equally support the moneyed élite against poorer farmers' traditional land claims. James Fairhead points out that different church sects have often come to represent different ethnic groups, supporting different land claims (Fairhead 1989:19).

He also documents the continuing existence of compulsory labour and the violence meted out to villagers by the army, secret police, gendarmes and state officials.

PRESSURE ON THE ITURI FOREST

Sixty years of exploitation and corruption in Kivu have left vast numbers of people landless and powerless. The result is poverty in the midst of plenty:

> Outside observers are sometimes astonished when malnutrition or famine is talked of in Kivu. It is a region where strawberries are harvested all year round, where quail's eggs and luxurious fruits and vegetables of every description are packaged and shipped to Kinshasa, and where rich soils and abundant rainfall leave the landscape green and lush. It is a region which commonly feeds Kinshasa and Rwanda with its 'surplus', earning it the title of 'Grenier du Zaire' (Zaire's Granary). Kivu is simultaneously "food deficit" in aggregate statistics, and yet a food exporter, which indicates that food security there is not just about aggregate food supply, but about access to that supply. (Fairhead 1989:3)

The lack of access to food, the insecurity of land tenure and the climate of political corruption are all placing increasing pressure on the forest in Kivu and the Ituri forest in Haute-Zaire. In 1971, the town of Oysha in North Kivu was completely surrounded by forest; today the women have to walk more than 15 kilometres to reach the forest and collect firewood. From Oysha south to Beni the Zairian firm ENRA has replaced almost the whole forest with tea and coffee.

ENRA is also logging in this area, exporting the timber to East Africa. The building of logging and other roads, enables people to move from Kivu into the Ituri and other forested regions, threatening the forest and the livelihood of its traditional inhabitants. The logging roads connect previously remote areas to the regional and urban markets, opening them up to the establishment of cash-crop estates, farms and plantations. The forest is also cut to supply the more-populated areas with charcoal and firewood. These activities put pressure on the "pygmies" and other hunters to provide more meat for the incomers, and to export to the towns.

Gold is another attraction in the Ituri Forest. The Nande people are as much drawn by the possibilities of looking for gold or clearing the forest for large plantations as they are by the pressure on land in the areas of Kivu from which they originate. Indeed, Janet MacGaffey has described how successful they have been as an ethnic group trading between Kivu to the east of the Ituri and Kisangani to the west (MacGaffey 1986).

However, the basic pressure on the Ituri Forest is from the unequal distribution of land in Kivu. The continuing concentration of land ownership, the growing of cash crops, the expansion of ranching and the general insecurity fostered by those in power combine to force farmers in Kivu into either becoming dependent labourers or else migrating into the forest.

Richard Peterson has studied the effects of immigrant agriculture in high population density areas in the Ituri Forest. He explains how incoming farmers

> ... practise both more extensive and intensive agriculture than the Ituri's indigenous farmers, for whom agriculture is just one among several forest-based means of subsistence, along with trapping, fishing and gathering. These activities, coupled with exchanges with Mbuti, allow the indigenous farmers to survive on relatively small fields. In contrast, for many immigrants coming to the Ituri, agriculture is their primary economic activity ... [Their fields] are an average of 10 to 25 percent larger than those of local farmers ... Larger garden plots, coupled with rising populations in villages experiencing immigration, increase the extent of primary forest clearing dramatically ... The use of longer farming periods per field, with shorter or no use of fallow ... can also cause the soil to deteriorate to the point of permanently preventing the forest from regenerating naturally.

> Immigrants also bring with them the cultivation of cash crops, most notably coffee, and to a lesser extent, oil palm and beer bananas ... In Eringeti, the study site experiencing the most advanced immigration, garden clearing has been extended from five to fifteen kilometres on each side of the road in less than two years. (Peterson 1989:1-2, 58-60)

Traditionally, there has been a continual exchange of garden and forest produce between the farmers and the Mbuti "pygmies", which has also involved the Mbuti working for specific farmers at certain times. But now, since the new immigrants have less need of forest products, the Mbuti have less bargaining power. "It is primarily the Mbuti who are providing a cheap labor pool for immigrants' needs . . . The rigidity and heavy labor demands of the wage-for-labor system do not allow Mbuti the freedom to 'borrow' food from the villagers' gardens, nor the flexibility to follow their own agenda of hunting and gathering" (Peterson 1989:60). The Mbuti are left alienated and far less independent, with the forest on which they depend shrinking fast.

AFTER MOBUTU

There is a growing international consensus that unsustainable logging must be stopped and that solutions must be found to halt the influx of the landless into the forest. Some suggest that this could be achieved by reimbursing governments through "debt-for-nature" swaps, whereby Third World debt would be cancelled in exchange for the creation of protected forest areas. Another solution put forward is to provide financial incentives for companies to pursue sustainable timber production in areas that have already been devastated.

It is vital, however, to recognize that sustainable logging can only be achieved if it takes into account not just the need to stabilize logging, so that it can maintain a sustainable yield of timber into the future, but also the needs of the local people to establish a secure livelihood, and to maintain the vital functions of their local ecosystem. In these terms sustainability is only possible when it is the local people themselves who benefit from both logging and other forest product revenues and from the mainte- nance of their long term financial, social and ecological security. This, in turn, is only possible if measures are taken to institute land reform, redistribute wealth and secure people's livelihoods in the areas from which the landless settlers are fleeing. In this sense the protection of the environment goes hand in hand with democrati- zation and the structural alleviation of poverty.

At the start of 1992, inflation was out of control, food scarce, the mines closed, and the shops in Kinshasa and the other main cities looted systematically by the army and the poor. Mobutu was working to divide the opposition, but it seemed unlikely that his promise of multi-party elections would stave off his downfall. If it is true that revolutions are born out of the fusion of hope and despair, then Zaire is set to explode. But given the continuing Western demand for timber, copper and cash-crops at the lowest possible prices, and the well-established hierarchy of corruption, it is very possible that a new regime may simply replace Mobutu with another "big thief".

The gradual ending of white rule in South Africa, the people-power movements of Eastern Europe and the end of the Cold War have led directly to a situation in which Mobutu's regime might topple. The "Sacred Union", a movement for the introduction of multi-party democracy, is gathering support. But in order to ensure the political security that may be possible with the introduction of democracy, and subsequent environmental and economic security, the international context may prove to be critical. Altering the exploitative relationship between North and South, putting environmental sustainability high on the agenda, and replacing Cold War paranoia with positive support for democratic institutions, may be the long overdue apology the West owes to the people of Zaire, from whom it has attempted to steal both their past and their future.

LAND, POWER AND FOREST COLONIZATION IN THAILAND

LARRY LOHMANN

The whole problem lies in the inability of the élite to bring about proper political and economic development in which political power as well as natural resources and wealth are equally distributed among citizens of different ethnic and cultural backgrounds . . . This can ultimately be achieved only through democratic struggle by the people. Only when the people have secured access to natural resources and benefited from them will they participate fully in conservation . . . The time has already arrived for the élite, should they want to stay on, to return the forests to the people.

Shalardchai (1989)

It's like a fish being hit on the head, then shivering with pain until death takes over. That's what it's like to be evicted.

Khampai Boonkorb, assistant village head,
Baan Tad Rin Tong, Chaiyaphum, January 1992

Thailand, bordered by Burma in the west, Malaysia in the south, and Laos and Cambodia in the north and west, covers over half a million square kilometres in South-East Asia. The country is commonly divided into four geographical zones. The North is mountainous, with wet-rice cultivation possible only along relatively narrow valleys and flatlands, and forms the catchment area for the marshy plains which occupy much of the Central region. The latter, which enjoys deep alluvial soils, lies mainly below 50 metres in altitude and is mostly given over to rice cultivation; for centuries it has dominated the other regions politically and economically. The long, narrow South, bounded by Burma, Malaysia, the Andaman Sea and the Gulf of Thailand, is largely an extension of the country's western mountain spine.

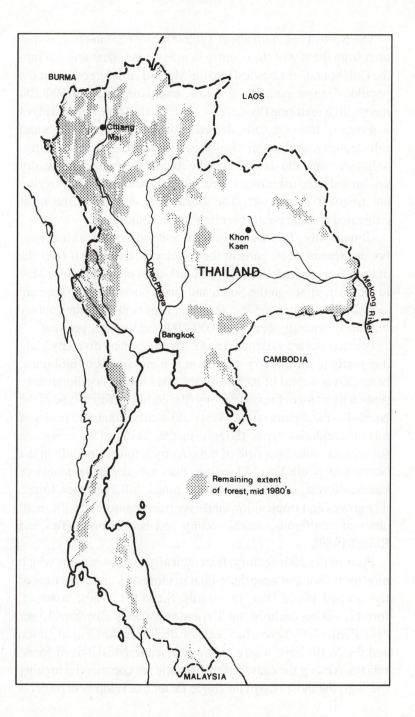

The North-East, with about 170,000 square kilometres, is distinct from the rest of the country in many ways. Draining not into the Gulf but rather eastward into the Mekong, this largest and most populous region consists of a low, undulating plateau 100-200 metres high featuring floodplains, terraces and some steeper ridges and ranges. Here the soils, derived from marine sands, clays and salt deposits, are poorer than those in the rest of the country, although some alluvial soils can be found along rivers. In the dry season soils tend to become baked, while flooding and waterlogging are frequent in the wet. The North-East is at once the most cultivated and the poorest section of the country.

Climatically, Thailand is tropical and monsoonal with a long, hot dry season. Most parts of the country receive over four-fifths of their annual rainfall during the south-west monsoon, from May to October, although the South and small pockets of the East are substantially wetter and less seasonal. Across most of the country rainfall is generally between 1000-2000 centimetres per year.

Forest types are variegated and native biological diversity high, due partly to the country's location at a crossroads of biological zones. Over a third of its forests are savannah or dry dipterocarp types with non-continuous canopy (the dominant forest type of the North-East and parts of the West) and nearly a quarter consist of mixed deciduous types (largely in the North). Dry evergreen formations make up a fifth of the country's forests, mainly in the North and North-East. There are also substantial remnants of bamboo forest, semi-evergreen rainforest, hill evergreen forest, mangroves and tropical lowland evergreen rainforest, with small areas of coniferous, scrub, swamp and beach forest (Jira and Round 1989).

Prior to the 20th century, the ethnically diverse regions which now form Thailand were three-quarters forested, and at the time of the Second World War, two-thirds. Since the 1950s, however, forest cover has declined rapidly, and now stands at perhaps 15 per cent. Particularly severe has been the decline in the Central region and the North-East, where only a few scattered islands of forest remain. Among the causes of this decline are commercial logging (perhaps the most important single factor), development projects and conversion to agriculture. Since the Second World War, farm holdings have increased approximately fourfold to cover nearly half the country's land area (Kamon and Thomas 1990; Scholz 1988; Napat 1988; Uhlig 1988; Saphaa Phuu Thaen Rassadorn 1990). Between 1961 and 1985, 125,000 square kilometres, or a quarter of the nation's land area, is estimated to have suffered encroachment. The country's National Reserve Forests (many if not most of which are now forests in name alone) are estimated to contain between eight and 15 million people in 15,000 villages or more (out of 60 million people and 60,000 villages in the entire country) farming a quarter to a third of the country's agricultural fields (Hirsch 1990a).

This boom in forest colonization cannot be explained simply by population increase. Statistical correlations between human numbers and forest loss or growth in cultivated area are poor. Between 1960 and 1985, for example, while population roughly doubled, the amount of land cleared went up between two and a half and three times or more (WRI 1990; Shalardchai 1989; RFD 1985; Myers 1989; Uhlig 1988). In the mid- to late 1970s, official figures show rates of forest loss abruptly doubling or tripling, driven partly by a surge in colonization, before subsiding to roughly previous levels. A more complete explanation of colonization requires examination of three additional, often concurrently-effective factors: traditional incentives, economic and development mechanisms associated with increased state control of the countryside, and the use of forest areas as political safety-valves.

THE PRECOLONIAL-ERA LEGACY

In sparsely-settled precolonial-era Siam, élite revenues and power depended more on control over people than on control over land. Corvée labour, taxes, and conscripts had to be mobilized, and at one time perhaps a third of the population consisted of debt slaves. Authorities had incentives not to exploit subjects so severely that there would be mass migrations to frontier areas outside their reach and to attempt to increase the population through resettlement and pronatalist policies. Property rights over land had yet to emerge in their modern form. On the one hand, the king exercised nominal control over all national territory, forbidding commoners to buy or sell land, and the status of nobles was measured according to the maximum amount of rice-land they were entitled to claim. On the other, commoners were encouraged to farm virtually any land they had cleared (customary *jàpjong* rights to forest claims have continued to be recognized by villagers through the latter 20th century (Hafner and Yaowalak 1990)), and nobles were seldom in a position to make use of all the land they had been granted rights to. "Ownership" by commoners was registered for tax purposes, but the state did not enforce individual land rights, and land effectively had no price. Allocation of usufruct rights was often made by village heads, many of whom allocated (and periodically reallocated) rice lands among local residents, according to their ability to work it, soil fertility, family size and so on. Local forest was treated as commons and used for swidden agriculture, timber, game (subject to certain local regulations), and a source of tax payments and trade goods. Labour and land was provided to village heads, who as a matter of course had to be responsive to village mood in order to maintain their positions. Such precolonial-era concepts and practices of land rights remain more prevalent today in Thailand, which was never formally colonized and which until recently had a large forest frontier, than in many ex-colonial countries.

As well as being a form of "avoidance protest", migration to the forest frontier has also been a traditional response to growth in numbers. Although in most areas land is traditionally subdivided among children when they marry, it can be fragmented only so far in a situation in which land is abundant, fertility moderate and productivity static, and the need not to try to acquire the land of neighbours who are also labour partners is strongly felt. In the dry North-East, the largest, poorest and most populous region of the country, sons-in-law have customarily been encouraged by their wives' parents, with whom they traditionally live for some time, to seek new land if enough is not available at the family homestead.

Increasing clearance of land around villages has often been followed by segmentation into separate villages under the leadership of local strongmen, and villagers have traditionally tended to migrate in groups in order to be able to pool their agricultural labour. This pattern continues, but today's migrants, whether seasonal or permanent, tend to cover ever-larger distances and to colonize locations together with groups from other regions. Annual Buddhist merit-making ceremonies function to provide farmers with opportunities to return periodically to villages of origin, spread the word about land available elsewhere, and collect new converts. Moving villages in response to epidemics or natural disasters has also been common.

MARKET ECONOMICS
AND NATIONAL DEVELOPMENT

During the 19th and 20th centuries, the expansion of agriculture and state control under international influences has transformed and added immeasurably to pressures on Thai villagers to colonize forests, as land has increasingly been put to purposes other than local subsistence or traditional revenue gathering. To a degree unseen prior to the last few decades, villagers have been both pushed off land in long-settled areas and pulled into new and destructive roles in frontier society.

Both pushes and pulls have to a large degree been a result of mutually-beneficial deals Thai élites have made with foreign commercial and military powers. Exporting of teak from the North began in earnest in the 18th century, and in the early and mid-19th century, forests further south were cleared to plant sugar cane to feed export markets. Following trade concessions given to the British in 1855 in return for an agreement not to annex Siam, much of the alluvial plains of the central region was transformed into a ricebowl feeding Western colonies elsewhere in South-East Asia. Previously unused land was brought under cultivation by both nobles and peasants, and land began to acquire a price, leading to land scarcity in the region by 1900-1925. By co-operating with colonial powers, Bangkok élites were moreover able to extend their power over more territory. In the early 20th century, railway construction was chosen over central-region irrigation, delaying the intensification of agriculture and facilitating long-term commoditization, expropriation, and colonization of land and forests in outlying regions (Hirsch 1990b). In 1896, Bangkok established firmer control over the North by giving to the newly-formed Royal Forestry Department (under a British director with experience in India) the power to allocate and regulate British teak concessions which had previously rested with autonomous local nobles. In 1899 the king formally claimed all forest lands.

With the demise of the absolute monarchy in 1932, these lands passed to the state, but leases continued to be restricted in practice to corporations in accordance with the philosophy of the Royal Forestry Department (RFD) that the forest was essentially a cash crop under its jurisdiction. The 1938 Protection and Reservation of Forests Act, still primarily focused on foreign companies, authorized local logging firms to extract for free as long as the cut was not exported, and the National Forest Reserves Act of 1964, which led to expansion of state holdings of forest land in accordance with international recommendations, only opened up the forests to further commercial exploitation. Enclosure of forests for timber cutting was encouraged not only by export policies (Thailand ceased to be a net timber exporter only in the 1980s), but also by domestic development strategies favouring the emergence of a large timber-consuming urban middle class.

Mutually-beneficial state-foreign alliances continued after the Second World War, when the government lavished foreign loans and "aid" on dams and roads (including "strategic highways" built during and after the Vietnam War) — at the same time neglecting distributional issues and instituting an export tax on rice to provide revenue to the swelling bureaucracy and keep labour costs low for foreign industrial investors in Bangkok.

In addition to depriving villagers of some of the control over local resources they had previously exercised, such factors also created a strong "pull" on ordinary peasants to clear forests. The expansion of infrastructure under state and military aegis, as well as construction of logging roads and partial clearance by timber companies, has provided pathways to hitherto remote areas for farmers marginalized by the development process. Between 1969 and 1979, 516 timber concessions were granted, covering nearly half the country's land area. Concerned at the widespread destruction that followed, the government cut the concession area in half in 1979, but capitulated to pressure from influential loggers in 1984 by allowing timber harvesting to be stepped up again. Some 300 concessions were still valid when logging was banned in 1989, a measure which, in addition to slowing timber extraction, cut forest encroachment by more than 83 per cent within a year (PER 1991).

Enclosure of forests both in remote areas and on land which had previously been subject to rules of community use laid the basis for "open access" in government forests. As forests were transformed from a commons into a scarce national resource to be competed over, the rational attitude for villagers became: "Why not cut down the trees ourselves, when those *naai toon* (capitalists) from town will definitely come to cut them down anyway?" (Shalardchai 1989; cf. Bromley 1991).

A further "pull" was created following the Second World War by the growing, World Bank-promoted integration of Siam's agriculture into the international economic system to fuel indus- trialization and "development". This brought demand for new crops, first kenaf, then sugar cane, maize, cassava, pineapple, coffee, prawns, and others, which have been mainly exported to Japan, Taiwan, the EEC and other regions to finance "development" and repay debts. Partly because these crops were suitable for non- rice areas, the country expanded and diversified its agricultural production not by intensifying rice production and planting a variety of crops in lowland areas but by clearing upland forests for export crops. Fifty thousand square kilometres of forests were declared opened for agricultural use under the First Five-Year Plan of 1962-1966, leading to a massive influx of forest settlers even in areas which were simultaneously to be "reserved". At the same time, farmers were encouraged by the government to plant the new land to export crops. While rice-land increased 68% between 1950 and 1978, the area under upland crops went up 618%, replacing tens of thousands of square kilometres of forest (Uhlig 1988). Between 1978 and 1988, the trend continued. Official figures for the decade show forest cover declining by over 32,000 square kilometres, while the area under non-rice crops increased more than 19,000 square kilometres and that under rice only about 1,350 square kilometres (PER 1991).

To the east and west of Bangkok in the central region, much land was planted to sugar cane following logging operations, while cassava currently plays a huge role in the East and North-East. In the lower North and along the border of the North-East, maize and more recently cassava have been planted along broad fronts following road construction. The mountainous far North has retained more forest cover, clearance having been along valleys and up the sides of hills, but increases in accessibility and attempts to reduce opium cultivation have led to large-scale highland clearances for maize, tobacco, and high-value temperate-climate cash crops. Other crops with high export value, such as ginger and sesame, have also played an important role. Between 1979 and 1988, while paddy cultivation in the North increased by only 1,644 square kilometres, non-paddy cash-crop cultivation went up 8,273 square kilometres. In the peninsular South, meanwhile, many forests have been taken over by rubber plantations and mining operations. In 1986 rubber plantations covered over 14,000 square kilometres of the country — including many slopes highly vulnerable to erosion — four times the area they had covered in 1950. Aggressive promotion of tiger prawn farming for export led to the destruction of nearly 30 per cent of Thailand's mangrove forests, or nearly 850 square kilometres, between 1980 and 1986 alone. Side-effects have included the displacement and impoverishment of thousands of small fisherfolk, who are then forced to try to eke out a living in other ways (Hirsch 1987; Feeny 1988; Uhlig 1988; PER 1991; Thai Development Research Institute 1987).

Patron-client networks, together with farmers' desires for advancement, agricultural extension, malaria eradication programmes and other factors, have articulated with the new export economy to pull more farmers into forests. Since the 1960s, merchants, millers, traders in forest products, timber companies, speculators and strongmen have encouraged and financed a large proportion of the settlers who have cleared forests in the Eastern, Central, lower North, and North-East regions which are then planted to maize, sugar cane, cassava, rubber and eucalyptus. These new rural patrons have provided marketing, seeds and credit at astronomical interest rates of 5 per cent monthly and up (mainstream sources of credit are often not available) to buy food or hire labour or tractors. In some areas peasants have been bought out or otherwise pushed on to occupy new land after a few years and to dislodge any isolated subsistence cultivators they may encounter there. After an interval, the peasants have been again displaced by their corporate patrons, and the cycle has been repeated (Uhlig 1988).

As the frontier vanishes and the government cracks down on peasant colonizers, the latter have been forced into an increasingly marginal existence as casual agricultural labour. Where villagers have a stronger hold on land, contract farming is an important trend. Here again, businesses — including highly vertically-integrated multinational agribusiness corporations such as Charoen Phokaphan — find it to their advantage not to assert immediate legal control over land, but rather to improve their hold on resources involved in its exploitation and on markets for its products. Production and legal and market hazards are in large part passed on to individual growers, who have to turn over their output to agribusiness in exchange for costly inputs. As in other patronage-mediated systems, further clearance of land often follows, whether to clear debts or to provide more income in a cash economy.

Over the last century, and particularly in the last three decades, this "pull" has been combined with the "push" of land deprivation to draw ever more settlers into the forest. This deprivation can be ascribed to roughly four causes related to the patterns of economic development promoted by the Thai state and its international benefactors. The first is economic differentiation, the accumulation of land and other resources in the hands of a minority, and the migration of the deprived seeking new access to them. This pressure is subject to positive feedback from environmental degradation resulting from the cultivation of migrant-cleared upland forests, and from cultural change undermining previous protective attitudes toward local land and forest. Third, outright seizure or enclosure of land by élites for "economically productive" purposes such as logging or plantations forces still more peasants into forest colonization. Finally, rising land prices and speculation make it difficult even for those smallholders who have kept control of their fields to resist pressures to sell and move on elsewhere.

The age of "development" pioneered by the military dictator Sarit Thanarat and his US and World Bank patrons in the late 1950s and early 1960s has led to increasing land alienation in a number of complex ways. For an ordinary farmer, holding land formerly meant, very roughly, having cleared and occupied it as a member of a community which helped work it. It also meant having access to traditional non-land means of subsistence such as buffaloes, family and communal labour, a water supply whose reliability was ensured by environmental integrity and community obligations of maintenance, traditional knowledge of the forest, seeds and agricultural techniques, access to leaders whose position was based on largely non-economic factors, and other common goods. As land has acquired economic value, however, holding it (as well as holding one's position within the community) has come to entail being able to obtain and maintain instead a whole range of "modern" non-land means of production. These include cash, credit and the legal title needed to obtain it cheaply, tractors, mechanized tillers, transportation, modern irrigation, chemicals, wage labour, fuel, connections with influential people outside the village, access to market-empowered leaders within the village, legal and economic knowledge, and so on. (Unsurprisingly, legal landownership often does not coincide with control over the land itself. In the central region, for example, land registered in the name of smallholders may in fact be controlled and "mined" for short term profits by creditors who rent it at nominal rates from their debtors or who monopolize other non-land means of production. This type of control may lead in the long term to smallholders' impoverishment and migration, yet it is the wealthy who show up in statistics as "tenants" of such plots and the larger number of smallholders as "landlords") (Hirsch 1990b).

Without some command of this multiplicity of new tools provided by the market and the state, and the power which lies in accumulation achieved through their rental, through trade, and through interest, many farmers have found it difficult to defend land against those who would buy, rent, seize or degrade it. While these tools have enabled a sizeable minority to enrich themselves, many others have suffered. Meanwhile, the older tools are no longer either available or efficacious. Their usefulness has been undermined by the collapse of practices of sharing farm labour; the growing inability of the family production unit to reproduce itself; the loss of labour implied by the dispersal of extended families into geographically far-flung profit-making activities; the decline of participatory or democratic local institutions with the increase in state control; the increased voice of merchants and money-lenders in crop choice; development projects; legal measures; the growing need for consumer goods, modern education, and non-agricultural professions as indicators of social position; and government imposition of modern inputs and cash cropping.

The consequences of this economic differentiation and loss of relevance of traditional cultural tools have all favoured migration. Landownership has declined while maldistribution increases, as peasants are forced into foreclosure or into renting their land at low prices to profiteers. Pressures mount to open new areas, either as permanent homes or as seasonally-occupied land, to provide cash to families with new market-derived needs. Competition between poor and wealthy colonizers for the use of newly-valuable unoccupied areas exacerbates pressures for the former to move on.

Environmental factors have added a number of positive feedback effects to colonization pressures. Deforestation has led to flood-drought cycles that have cut into fertility and crop growth in both new and old areas of cultivation. Rainfall has dropped or become more irregular. The recent migration of perhaps three million lowlanders into the hills of the North is forcing the half-million minority people there to exert ever-greater stress on watersheds through reduction of fallow cycles, with disastrous effects on soils and run-off, accelerating the marginalization of those downstream. One quarter of the national area is affected by severe or very severe soil erosion, and many watercourses have silted up or become intermittent.

The colonization prompted by such effects becomes all the more extensive the further frontiers are pushed outwards, since the land there tends to be of lower quality and available inputs are spread more thinly, necessitating more clearance of land for the same unit output. Each time forest pioneers eliminate obdurate and malarial forest environments which had previously constrained settlement, meanwhile, the floodgates are opened all the wider. Land degradation and invasion by *Imperata* grass has meanwhile resulted from the cultivation of the export crops favoured by the international market, local money-lenders, and government extension services. High-altitude market gardens in the North have led to disruption of livelihoods downstream due to erosion or pesticide contamination, further increasing pressures to colonize remaining forest areas. Peasants impoverished by development, meanwhile, are often forced to over-harvest forest products for subsistence or income, particularly during hard times. Many villagers participate, together with commercial and official interests, in small timber scams involving sale of homemade furniture or easily-dismantled "houses" to earn extra income. All this reduces the availability of the natural forest "insurance clause" to local residents and fosters colonization of more distant areas. In Southern Thailand, finally, declining fish yields due to overfishing by commercial trawlers have forced many small fisherfolk into trying their luck with forest farming.

Appropriation or enclosure is the most direct and the longest-established form of dispossession. Railway authorities have displaced farmers for a century. Road mileage increased nearly fourfold between 1960 and 1988, displacing still more. Since 1964, peasants have been displaced from fertile lowlands to make way for the construction of hydroelectric dams intended to feed the urban industrial sector; the dams' reservoir area alone amounts to nearly 3,000 square kilometres. Compensation, where given, has generally been inadequate and resettlement areas of inferior fertility and often already occupied; this has tended to set off a chain-reaction of further forest colonization. The military has also continued a tradition of dislodging peasants from commercially-valuable properties in the Central and North-Eastern regions and has taken a leading role in evicting tribal peoples from protected and watershed areas.

The most widespread processes of enclosure have taken place on state-administered forest reserves, first, as mentioned above, by foreign and then domestic logging firms, who have often dispossessed villagers indirectly, by damaging their sources of agricultural water and forest products. Following the 1989 logging ban, forest reserves have been rented out increasingly to plantation interests, resort-builders, golf-course builders, ranchers, dairy farmers and the like.

Eucalyptus plantations alone threaten to dispossess millions of peasants, as the RFD, the military, and other bureaucratic and business interests have promoted plans to lease as much as 40,000 square kilometres of so-called "degraded" forest (consisting mainly of farmland, pasture, and community woodlands) to commercial planters to feed foreign and domestic wood-chip and paper-pulp demand while supposedly "reforesting the country". Eucalyptus operations have received boosts from the Asian Development Bank, United Nations Development Programme, the Japanese, Australian, Canadian and Finnish aid agencies, Britain's Commonwealth Development Corporation, as well as the army-initiated Green North-East programme (Lohmann 1991b). Through 1990 they were pushed by Ministers of Agriculture whose political parties were funded by plantation interests or who were themselves potential beneficiaries. Following the 23 February 1991 *coup d'état*, the Internal Security Operations Command began evicting villagers from National Reserve Forests (NRFs) through its US$2.76 billion *khor jor kor*, or Land Allotment Programme for the Poor Living in Degraded Forest Reserves — a stupendous projected military operation described by Professor Saneh Chamarik of Thammasat University as an "inhumane measure" which would "hurt the people on the most massive scale we've ever seen in our history". *Khor jor kor* called for the resettlement of over five million people on small plots of degraded land in preplanned villages, partly in order to free up approximately 14,700 square kilometres for conversion to private sector tree plantations. (The programme boasted the motto, "Forests for the state, Land for the People"). No title was to have been provided, and many resettlement areas were already occupied. According to some estimates, forty thousand families had already been forcibly displaced by early 1992 in the North-East, with repression especially severe in areas targeted by the military as hotbeds of resistance (Anon 1991b; Sanitsuda 1992).

Khor jor kor and other programmes to move villagers off state land classified as forest tend, paradoxically, to undermine forest conservation. First, they displace peasants to forests elsewhere (very little unused cleared land of good fertility remains by now anywhere in the country, and urban opportunities are generally unattractive or lacking for migrants). Second, they disrupt local forest conservation practices rooted in long-standing traditions or in recently-developed resistance to modern resource expropriation. Among lowlanders in the North, such practices often revolve around protection of sources of water used in traditional irrigation; among Lao villagers in the North-East, around establishment of new orchards or protection or regeneration of local woodlands used for fodder, mushrooms, vegetables, medicines and game; among Southern fisherfolk, around protecting local mangrove forests which serve as breeding areas for fish and sources of firewood; and among Karen in wildlife sanctuaries, around complex and long-tested systems of rotating agriculture. Eviction programmes thus damage many of the social roots of indigenous conservation at the same time they create and unleash floods of deracinated "disposable people" on Thai society.

Many of the contradictions involved in evicting farmers from NRFs in order to "save" the forests were recently illustrated by the case of Nong Yai village in Nakorn Ratchasima province. As part of a forest conservation network set up by a local Buddhist monk to fight illegal logging and eucalyptus plantations, the village had resisted military attempts to evict it from the reserve forest area fringing Thap Lan National Park. After the monk was assaulted and arrested during a confrontation with armed troops in 1991, villagers were beaten and their houses torn down and cassava crops destroyed. Several hundred families were forced to construct makeshift shelters at a state resettlement site five kilometres away while they waited for land assignments. These turned out to be both insufficient for the number of resettlers and already occupied. Other Nong Yai families, meanwhile, took up residence at a local monastery from whose pavilion they draped a protest banner reading "Thai people's refugee camp". Faced with an influx of still more thousands of *khor jor kor* refugees from other provinces, authorities could only find new land for the old occupants of the resettlement area by compelling them to burn and clear-cut 15 square kilometres of lush forest in Thap Lan National Park. The timber disappeared and the RFD obligingly redrew the park boundaries to exclude the clear-cut zone and include Nong Yai village. When, after 10 months of misery, some Nong Yai farmers returned to reclaim the flattened site of their old village in June 1992, they were attacked, beaten, driven away and 17 of their number detained. Working to the advantage of the villagers, however, was the democratic movement which had gained strength following the massacre of hundreds of unarmed civilians by Prime Minister Suchinda Kraprayoon's troops in Bangkok in May and Suchinda's subsequent resignation. Massive protests by Nong Yai villagers and their North-Eastern allies and shrewdly managed meetings with government ministers finally forced officials to allow the villagers and others to return to farm their old land for the 1992 growing season. Those who have not yet been resettled have been given permission to stay temporarily in their old homes, and national-level reconsideration of *khor jor kor* was under way by July. Local officials and their business allies, however, are working overtime to undo the villagers' gains (Apisak 1992; TDSC 1992).

A final mechanism of land deprivation is speculation, which has occurred wherever former frontier areas have been drawn into the market economy, driving up land prices hundreds of times within a few years. The "winners" of the development process of the last three decades, which has resulted in increasing gaps between rich and poor, are, in company with foreigners, using their increasing amounts of disposable income to invest in land held by people with low and diminishing bargaining power. Investment-promotion privileges, development projects and a boom in industrial estates, golf courses and garden resorts, in addition, have helped transform rural lands into a valuable commodity for speculators (international tourism, the country's largest foreign-exchange earner since 1985, is viewed as the major bulwark against trade deficits and debt repayment difficulties).

Speculators include both local- and national-level government officials, politicians and business figures who are in a position to anticipate the entry into a particular area of resort and second-home builders, plantation companies such as Soon Hua Seng or Shell, or other firms. Their tools are formidable and include fraud and legal chicanery, political and bureaucratic connections, inside information, access to credit, threats, murder, arson, beatings, co-option of village elders, lack of demarcation of commons land, villagers' indebtedness, lack of title and status consciousness. Many of those bought out, in addition, are illegally occupying government land, making them vulnerable to charges of "forest encroachment" brought by officials working hand-in-hand with speculators. Although not as brutal, dramatic, and direct a mechanism of land deprivation as government eviction programmes, land speculation is comparable in its sweep and scale. Between 1986 and 1990 there was a sevenfold increase in the value of land transactions, while the number of transactions has risen by 250%. Boom areas include the Eastern Seaboard, the far North, and the South (Anderson 1977; Pornjai 1991).

FORESTS AS A POLITICAL SAFETY-VALVE

As in Indonesia and Brazil, forests in Thailand have often been used as a political safety-valve relieving land pressures caused by increasingly skewed distribution of resources in the centre. But the meaning of flight to the forest has shifted. Instead of fleeing exploitation by a feudal state, most of today's migrants are fleeing an economy in which they have no secure place. In previous times, forest colonizers relied heavily on traditional forms of horizontal solidarity and non-confrontational, personalized, superior-inferior relationships. As the government increased its grip on remote areas and closed out alternative patrons and means of avoidance, however, many farmers found more confrontational and class-based forms of resistance of greater use. The nature of social organization in the forest haven itself also changed, partly due to the presence of merchant-patrons closely linked to officialdom and partly due to political polarization. By the 1960s, the option of peaceful flight or marginal resistance had in some areas been transformed into the threat of armed insurgency under the aegis of the Communist Party of Thailand (CPT). Other partly class-based threats to the current distribution of power and resources followed in the period after the decline of the CPT in the early 1980s.

Such threats helped maintain migrants' bargaining power while completely transforming its basis. Unable simply to wipe out the guerrillas, the army followed until the 1980s a policy of trimming away frontier refuges by (among other things) encouraging "friendly" migrants to clear forest in sensitive areas, motivating them with the offer of land there. By the same token, the government had found it more expedient in the 1970s not to take action against most illegal colonizers of government forest land than to run the risk of forcing them into the arms of the CPT, then at the height of its influence, or of threatening the upland export-crop economy and its merchant-patrons.

Following a student-led rebellion against the military dictatorship in 1973, farmers' organizations and students were freed to pressure the state for genuine land reform. Unable to meet this pressure head-on, the government deflected it by promoting yet further colonization of the frontier. In 1974 an amnesty for farmers illegally residing in state forest reserves was enacted, making an informal policy official. This is often linked with the huge upswing in forest clearance during the mid- and late-1970s (Anat 1989).

Even by the mid-1980s, fewer than 10 per cent of illegal occupants on government forest land had been evicted in four sample provinces, a figure hardly higher than for those living outside such land (Feder et al. 1988). This lenience, however, never extended to tribal groups, who, due to their lack of political power, have been constantly subject to brutal "resettlement" programmes carried out by RFD and the army which force them onto unfarmable land or over the national border. Despite the fact that these groups constitute less than one per cent of the population, are "responsible" for at most five per cent of annual deforestation, and live almost exclusively in the North, they are often treated as the primary cause of the country's entire deforestation problem by high officials and PhD technocrats.

Through the mid-1970s, a series of assassinations of farmer leaders and, finally, the massacre and right-wing coup of October 1976, blunted the agrarian movement, encouraging a return to "avoidance protest", including migration. In more recent years, however, dwindling forest land has become too valuable a commodity (as, e.g., substrate for industrial plantations or golf courses) to be treated as a safety-valve to absorb the potentially disaffected. At the same time, untouched forests have come to be viewed by the élite as *loci* of ecological values rather than simply as dangerous obstacles to development or (as is the connotation of the words for forest *pàa* and *thùen*) areas of wild, illegal, subversive or uncivilized activities. Since the 1970s the protected areas system has expanded greatly to cover more than 11 per cent of the national land area. Equally importantly, there is less of a perceived need to placate forest colonizers. The bargaining position of individual groups of forest "squatters" in the country's political economy has weakened due to the demise of the CPT by the early 1980s, the decline in the importance of agriculture in the country's export profile, the rise of the non-labour-intensive commercial plantation option, the continuing improvement in the government's administrative position in remote areas, and the ability of officials to provoke different groups of impoverished villagers into conflict over the same resources (e.g., resettlement areas). Yet at the same time, élites have little desire to draw migrants back from the frontier. The modern agribusiness, manufacturing and service sectors are already equipped with a plentiful reserve army of unemployed. The consequence is that recent forest colonizers are becoming, in élite eyes, increasingly expendable in economic terms. This was evident well before *khor jor kor* in, for example, the growing number of police and military attacks on villagers attempting to defend local resources from metropolitan interests in 1990 and in the use of Eucalyptus-growing companies as proxy eviction agents. Recognizing this, peasants in forest reserves and elsewhere, among whom the sense of a "moral economy" encompassing *de facto* land rights is often still extremely strong, began some years ago to seek new political sources of bargaining power (Lohmann 1991b).

The age of direct or indirect élite promotion of forest colonization as a painless "development option" is clearly at an end. As has been clear since the 1970s, it is impossible to treat the frontier as a safety-valve absorbing social tensions created by maldistribution elsewhere and extend agriculture indefinitely, yet simultaneously to enclose forest reserve land for corporate use and development projects, establish conservation areas, maintain traditional patron-client relations, deny tenure to restive forest colonizers, and follow industrial-oriented patterns of development in a context of continuing growth in numbers.

LAND LAWS AND COLONIZATION

The emergence in Siam over the last century of land "ownership" in the modern sense has on the whole only favoured the mechanisms which spur dispossession and forest colonization. This has been true since the beginning of the shift from a regime favouring property rights over humans to one favouring property rights over land — a period marked by the decline of the corvée, increasing population, the phasing out of legal slavery between 1874 and 1915, the invasion of foreign timber interests, the availability of Chinese immigrants for wage labour, and the 1901 law which provided the first state protection for agricultural land rights.

Laws governing rights to agricultural land outside state reserve forests have done little to provide security for the most disadvan-taged. There are, of course, a number of documents for this type of land, most deriving from the notoriously ambiguous and conflict-ridden Land Act of 1954. These include full land title (NS-4), a transferrable certificate of use (NS-3), a pre-emptive certificate authorizing temporary occupation (NS-2), and a claim certificate legally unusable as collateral (SK-1). But only 15% of private lands have full title (NS-4) and only 53% the relatively secure certificates of use (NS-3 or NS-3k). This leaves a full 32%, or over 62,000 square kilometres, without proper documentation. In *thûng kùlaa rông hâi* (Weeping Prairie), the poorest section of the coun-try, only 0.02% of agricultural land has full title, and less than 2.5%, NS-3k and NS-2 documents (Amara 1985).

Lower-grade land rights, moreover, though often intended to stabilize land use, generally do the opposite by legitimizing and encouraging forest colonization in a context of economic expan-sion, widespread patron-clientage and growth in numbers. False claims of prior occupancy using SK-1 certificates, for example, have been used by officials, profiteers and others to stake out unoccupied forest for sale or transfer, and legitimately-acquired documents often end up in the hands of the rich (Hafner 1990). Even legally secure tenure, which provides access to credit at normal commercial rates, does not in itself assure control over production. Where others hold power over capital, crop choice, timing of ploughing and planting, legal resources and means of violence, titling programmes can easily even reduce land security by favouring investors and speculators over ordinary villagers. Apologists for land concentration pronounce themselves hopeful that a "humane way" can then be found "to reduce resident independent small farmers to farm hands", but evidence to date suggests that this is unlikely. Meanwhile, the widespread lack of secure land rights facilitates government expropriation of land to build dams, roads, and other forest-destroying infrastructure projects.

Laws governing state forest land are at least equally crucial to agrarian issues in Thailand. Evolving partly out of a desire to see official forest conservation measures go beyond the simple regulation of teak-cutting — the concern of original royal timber concession system — the current forest reserve system has made settlement of over two-fifths of the country, now occupied by 8-15 million people, illegal (see Table 6). No transferrable documents can legally be granted in National Reserve Forests (NRFs), even in the 56,000 square kilometres which is estimated to be currently under cultivation, though many NRFs were gazetted in areas already occupied by villagers who were candidates for title deeds. The growth of the protected area system as a result of increased urban conservation concern, tourism and availability of foreign assistance, has also shut out farmers from legal occupation of an ever-larger proportion of the country's land area. As with NRFs, National Parks and Wildlife Sanctuaries began to be gazetted during the 1960s, often on top of territories already occupied by tribal groups or others. Much government and foreign expenditure is now being used, ironically, in attempts to "keep those who could have been the best protectors out of the parks or sanctuaries" (Ghimire 1991: 10). Peasants' lack of title has of course always encouraged their intimidation and dispossession by powerful or wealthy individuals wanting to lease state land for plantations, resorts and the like.

Reservation of forests and gazetting of national parks in areas previously used as commons are often regarded as absurd by the ordinary villagers no longer allowed legal access to them. For many of them, there remain two categories of land: that used for family farms, and forest commons. The introduction of a third category of "public" but unusable land is unacceptable. Partly this is connected with the traditional absence of concepts or practices demarcating public space (as opposed to royal, individual or common space). But villagers' puzzlement and outrage is compounded when the demarcation of National Reserve Forest is followed by encroachment of private companies onto the land which has just been declared "public". It is hardly surprising that the end result has often been the establishment of a free-for-all zone looted by both marginalized peasants and business. The

TABLE 6
PER CENT OF NATIONAL LAND AREA UNDER
JURISDICTION OF THE ROYAL FOREST DEPARTMENT

Harvest concessions, plantations, and/or NRFs		National Parks and Wildlife Sanctuaries (may overlap NRFs)
1953	13 (almost all in North)	-
1967	21	1
1968	50	-
1980	36	6
1985	39-42+	9
1992		11

Sources: Kamon and Thomas 1990: 167-186; Hirsch 1990a; Ghimire 1991

livelihood security of minority nationalities occupying hill areas is also at odds with forest land laws. Occupation of watershed areas has been made illegal, and the position of minority groups is further weakened by lack of citizenship rights. In addition, land laws, by mandating more or less constant use of agricultural land, have made no allowances for Karen and Lua patterns of agriculture according to which land was traditionally left fallow for long periods.

Creating additional problems are conflicts between modern land law and customary law, which provides for squatters' rights enforceable by the ability of the claimant to mobilize a following. Even the various arms of the "modern" bureaucracy are at odds with each other. The Agricultural Land Department, for example, follows precolonial-era precedent by collecting land taxes from illegal "encroachers", and the receipts are widely used in lieu of title deeds. Up until 1986, meanwhile, the Interior Ministry routinely kept extending its administration to "illegal" villages in government forest reserves and protected areas; the provision of infrastructure, administration and services to villages within NRFs by various government agencies added to villagers' sense of official acquiescence in their settlements in National Reserve Forests. Even when villagers are officially resettled, it is typically onto lands already unofficially occupied.

Patron-client systems and traditions of royal or dynastic powers have meanwhile not been replaced by, but have rather partially absorbed, modern law and bureaucracy in a way which often further disadvantages ordinary farmers. The bureaucracy, as the heir since 1932 of some of the powers originally vested in the absolute monarchy (the main positions in the bureaucracy were originally occupied by nobles), capitalizes on the tradition of royal powers over land in a number of ways. Any development project which has a vestige of royal imprimatur — dam, highland agriculture scheme, or palace — has little difficulty in meeting its land needs, a fact which the government electricity authority has repeatedly taken cynical advantage of by naming many of its hydroelectric dams after members of the royal family. The Thai language itself makes resistance to displacement by development schemes difficult by preserving the customary dual class distinction between government officials, who are referred to as "royal servants" (*khâarâatchagaan*), and ordinary villagers (*chaaw bâan*). Property deals benefiting Siam Cement Company or other firms in which the Crown Property Bureau participates, meanwhile, have privileged status. The feudalistic rights of lesser figures persist as well. In the late 1980s, for example, a member of the dynastic Sarasin family illegally began to develop prime protected forest land in Kanchanaburi into a resort under the protection of two relatives, the national police chief and a deputy prime minister. Traditionalists and cynics alike often conceptualize ministries and departments concerned with land and forests as (very roughly) lucrative concessions given to loyal clients of high status rather than as guardians of lands in the "public" interest.

Partly out of concern over increasing forest colonization, the Royal Forest Department embarked on several programmes over the last decade or so to try to stabilize land use in NRFs without undermining its own hold on them (and its power to rent them out to private firms). The STK programme launched in 1982, for example, granted temporary, renewable cultivation rights, transferrable only by inheritance, inside NRFs. The Agricultural Land Reform Office (ALRO) issued similar usufruct licenses called SPK on the condition that NRF-occupying families to whom they are issued reforested degraded land around them. Although STK ostensibly provided 11,500 square kilometres of land, or over 10 per cent of denuded lands, to more than 700,000 households, these programmes failed. Squatters' land security was not improved, partly since the documents could not be used as collateral to obtain ordinary commercial loans, a consideration especially important to farmers in the lower North and North-East. This made titleholders vulnerable to partial or full dispossession by informal money-lenders charging astronomical interest rates. In addition, it lowered the price of these (supposedly untransferable) documents. The ALRO, in addition, was legally unable to force landholders to sell unused or excess land at stipulated prices. Moreover, managing agencies' regulations did not always allow occupants to maintain an adequate standard of living on their land. The result, in an atmosphere of economic boom, differentiation and corruption, was that documentation tended to collect in the hands of local notables, merchants and money-lenders through purchases and foreclosures, with few benefits accruing to the sellers.

Dispossession thus continued unchecked, with merchants and money-lenders rapidly following migrants to the frontier. At the same time, more migrants arrived, probably spurred by hopes of getting land documents. Influxes of settlers drawn by rumours of legal land distribution also plagued an integrated-development programme of forest villages set up under RFD and international agencies, whose other woes included unequal or inadequate land allotments, inability to meet land demand through degazetting, conflicts between villagers and foresters due to top-down management, failure to take account of village needs, conflicts with previous settlers claiming squatters' rights resulting in further encroachment, planting of inappropriate species in reforestation areas, and unreplicability due to high cost (Hirsch 1990a).

WAYS FORWARD:
VIEWS OF PEASANTS, NGOS AND ACADEMICS

Pressures for new approaches to land and forest rights are growing rapidly. The most important of these new approaches have been forged not in universities, government ministries, think-tanks or aid agencies but cumulatively through a series of concrete, practical battles for land and livelihood fought by grassroots groups in local areas over the past several years.

Some of the most visible peasant struggles in the North of the country have been to secure local control over community forests. In 1975, 500 villagers in Nan province blockaded a local watershed forest, halting logging there. In 1987, villagers in Chiang Mai embarked on a two-year, ultimately successful struggle to stop logging in part of Samoeng District. In 1988, 5,000 villagers in Phayao province invaded a district office for five days until the government suspended another local logging concession. In 1989, farmers in Baan Toong Yao in Lamphun province opposed the gazetting of a local community forest as a national park and commercial resort area, reasoning that the forest and the subsistence guarantees it provided would be destroyed; the government was forced to shelve the plan. In the same year, villagers of Baan Huay Kaew in Chiang Mai, after a year's concerted resistance to a commercial concession granted to the wife of a Member of Parliament, in which they were joined by academics, students, the mass media and non-government organizations (NGOs), compelled the government in an unprecedented decision to declare the local forest to be officially under the stewardship of the community itself. Earlier in the year, in what could be viewed as a culmination of previous protests in the North and other regions of the country, the government had acceded to a nationwide logging ban.

Later in 1989, villagers from provinces across the North-East, speaking at a seminar held at Government House in Bangkok, capped two years of protest by calling on the government to suspend planting of commercial tree farms until land rights problems in NRFs were solved and to recognize that forest conservation and land rights for the people go hand in hand. They also asked that the government acknowledge the existing role of ordinary people in forest conservation by enacting a community forest law rather than simply to brand them as "encroachers", and issue documents certifying villagers' claims to farmland and communities' claims to local woodlands in NRFs. In 1990, 19 NGOs working with farmers' groups issued a 10-point proposal reiterating some of these points and demanding that the government shift its emphasis in NRFs from law enforcement to promotion of local participation in forest management. The proposal called for surveys of 276 forests formerly leased to logging companies, gazetting of all remaining untouched forest as protected area, and legal status for community forests now under the care of various villages. In addition to land rights for individual farmers in NRFs, it called for measures to prevent the loss or illegal transfer of such rights. The proposal also demanded a review of the long-standing Food and Agriculture Organization-inspired policy calling for 40% forest cover. Some months later NGOs issued a "no-confidence" statement in the National Forestry Policy which sets the 40% figure and gives privileged treatment to corporations who wish to lease forest areas. More than 200 Thai NGOs mainly working in rural development then joined together in calling for a moratorium on Finnish funding for a Forestry Master Plan on the grounds that it would encourage just such treatment. In February 1991, NGOs forced Jaakko Pöyry Oy, the Finnish contractor, to agree to suspend work on it until grassroots communities had more of a say in national forestry policy, although Jaakko Pöyry has since broken this promise.

The proposal on land rights put forward by an umbrella group of about 200 rural-based NGOs shortly before the February 1991 military coup stresses economic justice. It calls for the following measures to be implemented in NRFs, beginning in areas where village organizations are most prepared:

- demarcation of forest land, including community forest, and its separation from agricultural and residential areas;
- fair distribution of land taking into account characteristics of land and family size;

- issuance of land documents in accordance with these principles to promote land security;
- provision of an agricultural fund by the government;
- support for ecological farming by the government;
- a solution of farmers' debt problems;
- implementation of the above to be carried out by a board consisting of government bureaucracies; villagers including representatives of village-level farmers organizations; independent qualified people such as NGOs, Buddhist monks, teachers, and professors;
- a halt to arrests for encroachment in NRFs.

Echoing the demands of peasant groups across the country, the Project for Ecological Recovery, one prominent environmental NGO, has called in addition for the shelving of forest-affecting commercially-oriented projects such as dams and resorts and suggests that unoccupied or unused forests, whether degraded or not, be protected from commercial plantations. Land speculation, while also a crucial issue, offers few entry points for popular movements that do not challenge the entire pattern of "development" in Thailand over the past decades.

The 1991 coup and subsequent institutionalization of *khor jor kor* was a setback for popular movements in National Reserve Forests, but with the decline in military influence after May 1992 and the appointment of a new civilian government, resistance and discussion have emerged once again into the open. Following major demonstrations by North-Eastern villagers including the blockade of the region's principal highway, the temporarily-appointed Agriculture Minister has conceded that the private sector should not be involved in "reforestation", and proposes to replace *khor jor kor* with a new land and forest management programme stressing community forest rights, freedom from forced eviction from NRFs, and the leasing to villagers of plots purchased from the private sector. A community forest Bill long proposed by NGOs is also under discussion.

Some academics, meanwhile, have favoured sweeping grants of full land title to occupants of NRFs regardless of their settlement date, accompanied by other measures which would improve these farmers' access to cheap credit, increase government control, and so on. The reasoning is that titling would allow villagers to hold their own better in the market economy, increase their economic productivity, or lead to consolidation of land holdings in a way which would enable them to be put to maximum use.

This view, however, ignores distributive issues both within NRFs (where much land is already in the hands of large holders) and outside them. Without redistribution, titling programmes are bound to stimulate further colonization. In addition, although titling would help farmers gain access to cheaper credit, improved local control over water, mechanization, trade, and other factors is needed as well. The imputed links between economic productivity and increased security are also questionable given the Thai experience with cash crops and debt. Finally, the assumption that the consolidation which would follow titling would enable land to be put to maximum use is highly dubious. First, consolidation of holdings in recent years has tended if anything to be associated with directly unproductive uses of land, for example in speculation. Second, what is "maximum use" for landholders or for the economy as a whole may not be a "maximum use" which enhances local peoples' security, as for example when land is planted to nontraditional export crops. The moral of these objections seems to be, however, not that titling would be a mistake, but that much more is needed before colonization can be checked.

Most independent observers agree that current systems of land management need to be made more "collaborative", bottom-up, sensitive to the multiplicity of local knowledge and needs, and more reliant on village- and local-level institutions as opposed to the central government administration. Villagers and NGOs, however, tend to insist on more: the primacy of land rights and planning which starts from small farmers' own organizations, rather than using them as an instrument in implementation. They agree, moreover, that full citizenship rights must be granted to minority groups in protected watershed areas, that military suppression must be halted there, and that some form of land rights must be granted to the inhabitants.

Disagreements and uncertainties have persisted, for example about whether unconditional ownership of forest land should be granted, whether there should be a distinction between NRFs and protected areas, whether it is premature to push for genuine redistribution of land (rather than simple titling programmes), whether more progressive taxes should be imposed, whether land reform outside NRFs should be demanded at present, and so on. Farmers from different regions of the country, moreover, tend to have varying demands. Villagers in the lower North, for example, value full land title because of the improved access to credit it makes possible, while many in the South are holding out initially only for assurances they will not be evicted from land to which they have no title. But there is no disagreement that an effective response to the Thai forest crisis hinges on local people's taking greater control of the land, forests and water around them.

INDONESIA: LAND RIGHTS AND DEVELOPMENT

SKEPHI AND RACHEL KIDDELL-MONROE

Indonesia, an archipelago of 13,500 islands covering nearly two million square kilometres, can be divided roughly into two parts. "Inner" Indonesia consists of most of Java, Madura, south Bali, Flores and west Lombok. The much larger "outer" Indonesia encompasses Sumatra, Kalimantan, Sulawesi, the Moluccas, Nusa Tenggara, and Western New Guinea. (The latter territory was given the name Irian Jaya by the Indonesian government in the 1970s. It was formerly known as West Irian, and to many of its indigenous residents goes under the name of West Papua.)

The contrast between the two Indonesias is sharp. Java, with its fertile volcanic soils, swift rivers, irrigation-friendly topography and moderately humid climate, is the heartland of productive wet-rice cultivation, and most of the island is under crops. "Outer" Indonesia, with its poorer soils, mountainous or swampy topography, and over-wet or variable climates, is more conducive to swidden than to wet-rice cultivation, and remains largely uncultivated. Generally unsuitable for large-scale agriculture, the rainforest soils become leached and eroded when exposed to monsoon rains after the trees are removed. Most of the country's forest area, the second largest in the world, covering somewhere between 45 and 60% of the land mass, is to be found in "outer" Indonesia.

Another area of contrast between "inner" and "outer" Indonesia is human numbers. Due to its fertility, to factors associated with rule by the Dutch (who superimposed a colonial economy on the islands from the seventeenth century to the Second World War), and to cultural patterns, Java's population began to expand rapidly after 1830. Today, with a mere 7% of the land area, it is home to nearly 60% of the nation's 190 million people. The less hospitable

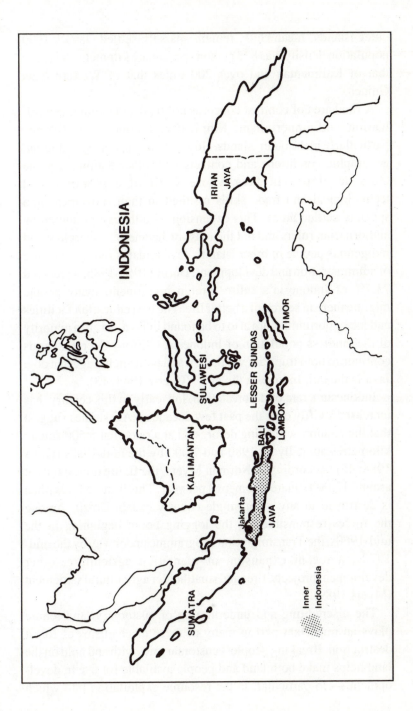

outer islands, meanwhile, remain sparsely settled. Java's 1990 population density was 838 persons per square kilometre, 52 times that of Kalimantan and over 200 times that of Western New Guinea.

A final area of contrast concerns political and cultural centralization and imperialism. Ethnically, Indonesia is diverse, particularly in the outer islands. However, due to demographic and geographic conditions and contacts with other nations, a noble class developed in Java whose spirit of exploration and technological and trade skills resulted in their movement into sparsely-settled areas. This expansion — although promoted by authoritarian rulers and not the mass of Javanese — marginalized indigenous people of other islands. Java remains today the centre of administration and development. During 1965-1985, it received 73.7% of Indonesia's entire foreign investment; many people migrate there in search of a better life. The best education facilities and job opportunities are also to be found in Java. So are a majority of the landless population of Indonesia. Clifford Geertz's words continue to hold true: "if ever there was a tail which wagged a dog, Java is the tail, Indonesia the dog" (Geertz 1963: 13).

Indonesia's rate of deforestation, low early in this century, has increased swiftly over the past few decades. FAO studies suggest that the country was being deforested at a rate of at 5,500 square kilometres annually by 1980 and 7,000 by the mid-1980s (Gillis 1988: 45). According to Norman Myers, the figure now stands at around 12,000 square kilometres per year. This is more forest than is destroyed in any other single country except Brazil. Among the forces responsible are the logging boom beginning in the mid-1960s, the Transmigration Programme under way by the mid-1970s, a recent expansion of plantation agriculture, other development projects, fires and smallholder agricultural settlement (Myers 1989).

The discrediting and undermining of customary land tenure plays an important part in many of these mechanisms of forest destruction. Breaking people's customary ties with and hold on the land helps make both land and people available for use in development — in particular, in the resource exploitation into which

Indonesia has been prodded by international agencies, by Northern corporations and consumption, and by its own élites. Logging operations, industrial projects, plantations, tourist developments, parks, dams and other private or state activities are enabled to take over land to foster economic growth in the "national interest". In the process of internal colonization known as "transmigration", meanwhile, people from "inner" Indonesia are transported to the outer islands, where, it is intended, they will appropriate land for development, inculcate the Javanese ethic in diverse ethnic groups, and relieve pressures for land reform in "inner" Indonesia. (It must be stressed, again, that this is an attempt by a particular traditional élite, in collaboration with international interests, to use Javanese culture for its own purposes and is not an intrinsically "Javanese" initiative.) Those displaced, if they are not put to work on forest-destructive development projects, are often driven to clear large areas of forest for cultivation or in turn to displace others. Many transmigrants, in addition, serve as the advance guard of Javanese expansionism, disrupting traditional systems of land and forest use and conservation. This chapter introduces three aspects of the land rights issue as it relates to deforestation: conflicts between customary and Western systems of tenure, transmigration, and new forms of plantation agriculture.

TRADITIONAL SYSTEMS OF TENURE

Land is our cultural heritage and our blood; even if it is only as wide as our forehead and as long as our finger, we will defend it with our blood.

Javanese saying

The huge cultural diversity of Indonesia has resulted in a complex system of indigenous, and largely unwritten, laws relating to land. Religions have had an important influence, with Islamic law playing a strong role in some areas.

Under the traditional *adat* land rights system, land is regarded as the common property of the community. This communal right to land, known as *hak ulayat*, cannot be bought, sold or leased: it is inalienable. Traditionally people do not own the land on which they live and work; they merely control it. Humans are merely a transient part of this world, and land belongs to God as the creator.

The traditional community has always had strong ties with the land on which it lives. The land gives the people life, it gives life to the trees which in turn give life to various micro-organisms (known as "little lives"), and it provides a resting place for the dead. The community's rights centre on the three life-giving elements of land, air and water, and refer to rivers, beaches, trees, wild plants and wildlife, among other things. While customary or *adat* law varies widely over the archipelago (sixteen broad forms of *adat* law have been identified), two general patterns of traditional land rights are present. One consists of rights which are used by the community as a whole. The other consists of rights which belong to the community but are granted to its individual members. The former pattern is more important in smaller and very traditional communities, the latter in more extended communities. However, the community never abrogates its responsibility even where individual rights are granted. In this way, respect for the land and its resources is maintained for the benefit of the community as a whole.

Rights to collect forest products and to hunt have created close ties between the community and the land covered by the forest, often expressed as religious restrictions on overexploitation of trees and animals. These "animist" controls are very tight, with systems of taboos which require communities to fulfil a host of activities before, during and after collection from the forest. Where the individual or community violates these, the community must make amends. In areas closer to the community settlement, members of the community have rights to work the land for agriculture. If a community member is given the right to cultivate a fish pond, a relationship will be formed by the community member with the land and the fish pond. If the relationship is severed the rights are withdrawn and the land and fish pond revert to the community, becoming common property once more. In other words, individual rights over land may exist within the *adat* community, where a person opens up and works on community land for a consistent period of time. The right of that person will be accepted by the community if it is in the community interest. If the right is abandoned or neglected, it will be recontrolled by the *hak ulayat* system.

Adat law has been subject to a variety of contradictory influences. During the feudal era in Java and South Sumatra the concept of ownership was introduced. It was claimed to be in accordance with the traditional belief that the land could only be owned by God; it was argued that, since the king was descended from the Gods, he was the ultimate owner of the land. Under this system it became increasingly difficult to assert the communal right to land, and the kingdom distributed land only to villagers who fulfilled certain qualifications, such as being members of the local ruler's family. Officials appointed by the king controlled the land in his name, and people were obliged to pay tribute to the king by paying a share of goods collected or produced from it (CCCIL 1988).

The arrival of the Dutch in 1602 had little effect on the majority of what they termed the "Dutch East Indies". Initially concerned mainly with monopolizing the spice trade, then with the extraction of cash crops, the Dutch East Indies Company and later the Dutch colonial state confined the implementation of European land law to Java, Madura, and, to a lesser extent southern Sumatra. Thus a system of "dualism" was instituted. European law ousted traditional law where the needs of colonialists dictated, but otherwise traditional law was treated with indifference. The removal of this colonial legacy of dualism became the major basis of land reform attempts after independence.

During a brief British interregnum between 1808 and 1816, despite an ostensible "humanitarian" recognition of traditional systems, a system of land rental reform was introduced which firmly entrenched European principles of private land ownership. The British claimed that all land in Indonesia was their property and that they therefore had the "right" to regulate land rents, which were payable to the state. Facilitated to an extent by the presence of the feudal system, the introduction of land rent enabled the territory subject to direct European administration to be greatly extended, and financial value given to land, rather than its produce, for the first time.

233

When the Dutch returned in 1816, they assumed the "right" to carry on the policy of land rent. In 1830, the Cultivation System (*cultuurstelsel*) was introduced. This system obliged peasants, instead of paying rent or taxes, to plant cash crops for the state on one-fifth of their land (or, alternatively, to work 66 days a year on government-owned estates or other projects). The key to Dutch success in "prying agricultural products out of the archipelago" (Geertz 1963: 47) in this way, without stimulating markets for industrial goods (which would have brought in the British) or pressing the subsistence economy too far, was to leave alone the existing communal form of village government. All threats to the communal land rights structure were thus rejected (CCCIL 1988).

After 1848, responsibility for Java's profitability began to be turned over to private enterprise. A highly-capitalized sugar-milling industry helped transform the Cultivation System into a corporate plantation system. In 1870, the Dutch government adopted the Agrarian Act, which both entitled the state to let uncultivated "waste" land in bundles of up to 500 hectares for up to 75 years and enabled Indonesians to lease land to non-Indonesians for up to 20 years. While the Act ostensibly offered protection for indigenous land rights, a proviso that alienation was allowed if it was in "the public interest" effectively negated any safeguards.

Using this law, corporations backed by a network of banks took over cultivation of cash-crops. Privately-planted sugar cane made up about 9% of the total cane crop in 1870, but 97% in 1890. By 1938 there were 2,400 cash-crop estates in Indonesia, equally divided between Java and the outer islands, occupying about 25,000 square kilometres and controlled for the most part by a few large, interlocked companies.

In Java, this brought into being a social entity which was half plantation, half peasant community. In the areas where they rented land through persuasion or coercion, corporations would often wind up filling a third or two-thirds of a village's rice land at any one time with sugar cane, which would rotate with rice and other crops. Local mills staffed by Europeans would process the output of around 10 square kilometres of plantings. Peasants served the needs of this system as casual seasonal industrial wage-labour and at the same time pursued community-oriented household farming:

> The need on the mill's side for a simple, flexible and comprehensive land-owning unit within which cane cultivation could move freely from one block of terraces to the next, unobstructed by a cloud of separate, individualized land rights, and the need on the villagers' side for a reasonable equitable sharing throughout the community of the burdens imposed by the system as it so moved from field to field, made the collective apportionment procedures of traditional communal tenure functional to both parties. (Geertz 1963:91)

In Java, the colonial system thus did not result in the creation of huge landed estates worked by an oppressed landless class demanding land redistribution. Rather, peasants responded to the encapsulation of their society within a colonial structure, and to increased numbers, by adjusting and limbering their own techniques and customs to ensure subsistence and homogeneity. They did this through, among other things, intensifying agriculture by increased application of labour, dividing the economic pie into a steadily increasing number of minute pieces, expanding and elaborating labour exchanges, shareholding and other tenancy systems. While the plantation sector became irremediably capital-intensive to boost productivity, the peasant sector reinforced its labour-intensivity and dependence on traditional tenure systems (Geertz 1963: 98-100). It was only later that land reform emerged as a central rural issue.

In parts of Sumatra and elsewhere in the outer islands, however, a different pattern was followed. Export agriculture was established in enclaves worked by Chinese and Javanese shipped in from outside. Land use was extensive rather than intensive, and traditional swiddening agricultural patterns were progressively excluded from rather than incorporated into the new economy. Smallholder agriculture meanwhile became more oriented towards the production of export crops such as rubber, coconut, coffee, tea and pepper than was the case in Java, pushing back the forest frontier. The percentage of Indonesian exports from the outer islands increased rapidly from 1870 to 1930. As the world economy penetrated deeply into the outer islands' agrarian economy, land tenure became more flexible and less subject to customary community control. The depression of the 1930s, the Second World

War, and nationalist revolution disrupted the estate economy, but a pattern was established of localized plantation and mining enclaves using capital-intensive techniques and uprooted labour in a matrix of low-density swidden agriculture.

POST-INDEPENDENCE LAND LAW

After independence President Sukarno declared land reform to be "an indispensable part of the Indonesian Revolution" (CCCIL 1988). The first effort to design a national land law was made in the form of *Undang-Undang Pokok Agraria* (UUPA), the Agrarian Law of 1960. A land reform programme based on the UUPA was to provide the foundations on which the "green revolution" planned for 1965 was to have developed. In his Political Manifesto, Sukarno referred to this as the "nucleus of the Indonesian Revolution in the phase of socialistic reconstruction of the nation" (CCCIL 1988).

The UUPA followed the principle of eminent domain set out in the Indonesian constitution of 1945:

> land and water, and the natural resources contained therein, shall be controlled by the state and used for the maximum benefit of the people. (Article 33 (1))

This, combined with the prevailing desire to abolish any remnants of the colonial domination, made one of the major purposes of the UUPA the abolition of Western-*adat* dualism by basing agrarian law on *adat* land law. And in fact the law incorporates traditional concepts in passages such as the following:

> The agrarian law over the earth, water and space is a *hukum adat* (traditional law) so long as it still exists and in does not hamper the national and state needs . . . (Article 5).

> The right to own traditionally can be represented by the regional authorities and *hukum adat* community so long as it is in line with national needs and government regulations. (Article 2(4).

Yet the law also recognizes Western-type property rights in the form of absolute private ownership. Even non-tillers are permitted to own up to 5 hectares of *sawah* (irrigated rice land) in areas with population densities of over 400 per square kilometre and up to 15 hectares in areas with population densities of 1-50 inhabitants. The figures rise to 6 and 20 respectively in *ladang* (dry-land) areas. These ceilings are quite high given that by 1963 real property per capita in Java had dropped to only 0.151 hectares and that the island was home to three million landless peasants, many of them sharecroppers tilling other people's plots of land and often badly exploited by their landlords (CCCIL 1988). The law also provides for sweeping state powers:

> The earth, water and air space, including natural resources contained there, in the highest instance are controlled by the state, being an authoritarian organization of the entire population. (Article 2(1))

Article 3 clearly reveals the inherent *adat*-state conflict:

> The implementation of communal property of the *hak ulayat* (the communal rights of an *adat* community), and rights similar to that of *adat* community, in so far as they exist, shall be adjusted as such to fit in the national and state's interest, based on the unity of the nation and shall not be in conflict with the acts and other regulation of higher level.

The *adat*-Western conflict is evident in the widespread practice of dismissing traditional rights as "undocumented" or "unevidenced". This requirement for documentary proof of title is irrelevant in traditional law. Evidence of the existence of the *hak ulayat* is shown in the recognition of the power of community leaders to allocate plots of land for cemeteries and wet rice fields, and in the requirement for members of other communities to seek permission and pay for the right to work on a plot of land or harvest forest products in what they see as another community's territory. Of course, if documentary evidence is required, these traditional rights could be expressed in writing.

Adat law is also at odds with the UUPA's insistence that

> every person and every corporate body having a certain right on agricultural land is in principle obliged to cultivate or to exploit it actively by himself while avoiding extortionate methods. (Article 10)

This clause opens swidden agriculturalists such as the Kayan in Kalimantan to charges of violating the law if they follow their customary practice of leaving their land fallow. Yet attempting to cultivate Kayan land continuously in order not to violate the first clause would cause environmental damage, thus violating the clause about "extortionist" methods (Ngo 1991).

THE FAILURE OF LAND REDISTRIBUTION

The redistributive aims of the UUPA fell far short of expectations (CCCIL 1988). Ceilings were high, legislation and implementation rested on compromise, and landowners' interests received priority. Loopholes allowed prohibitions on absenteeism and on keeping a land surplus outside the range of the land reforms to be eluded. Opposition on the part of landowners and the frequent fraudulent manipulations committed by the land-reform committees made redistribution difficult. In addition, no system existed for registering land. By 1964, reforms were far behind schedule. Yet by lowering ceilings and by treating the 55,910 absentees in 1960 less leniently, double the 337,445 hectares actually obtained for the more than 3 million landless peasants could have been found (CCCIL 1988).

Despite the landowners' attitude, the peasants, backed by left-wing organizations, continued their land struggle. In the first half of 1964, mass organizations of landless peasants used the Agrarian Law as a basis to demand land reform in Klaten (Central Java), Banyuwangi (East Java) and Bali. At the same time, land-grabbing became a weapon of landlords, who sought the support of unorganized, self-styled "anti-nonbelievers" groups resembling youth organizations in their attempts to oust sharecroppers from their estates in defiance of the sharecropping agreements. Small-scale warfare broke out between landless peasants and landlords. Under pressure from the army and the police, many peasants were forced to leave their newly won pieces of land.

After the alleged Communist coup of 1965 and the subsequent massacre of over half a million people, land reform was stopped, having from the start been stigmatized by its opponents as Communist. Many peasants dared not return to their plots of land due to the routing of Communists and their sympathizers, and much redistributed land gravitated back into the hands of the former owners. Little new land was redistributed between 1966 and 1971.

Since then there has been no further implementation of the 1962 land reform scheme. The law has been manipulated in such a way that Western concepts of land ownership and possession prevail and has often been deliberately violated for gain by government officials themselves.

LAND AND FOREST LAW AFTER 1965

The "New Order" government has attempted to reinforce the powers of the state. Nowhere are these powers more sweeping than in Indonesia's forests. More than 70% of the country's land has been designated as forest lands, i.e., an area of 143 million hectares out of the estimated total land area of 193.6 million hectares. A single government department, the Department of Forestry, is responsible for forest management — concession policy, log harvests, reforestation and conservation-area development programmes — over this entire area.

The Forestry Department tends to view forests merely as producers of wood. From 1967 to 1983 the explicit goal of forestry policies was to maximize wood production (Gillis 1987), with no specific forest-management pattern. It was only in the mid-1980s that a management pattern was drawn up, although this was not based on accurate field data. The Department of Forestry began to classify forests following consensus-seeking meetings between the government of each province, the Transmigration Office and the Department (local people were not consulted). The result was that over 16% of Indonesia's land area has been set aside as "regular production forest", over 14% as "limited production forest", another 14% as forest to be converted to agriculture, 9% as conservation area and 14% as forests intended primarily for watershed protection. These areas often overlap. By 1989, 600,000 square kilometres had been leased out to 561 state and private concessionaires, 50 of which can be considered major. By comparison, rotating cultivators, who are blamed by the World Bank for the bulk of deforestation in Indonesia, occupy approximately 75,000 square kilometres, half of which is outside forest lands. According to some estimates, logging causes 8,000 square kilometres of deforestation annually.

In exercising jurisdiction and control over the fates of the millions of people who depend on the forests, the Department of Forestry has ignored traditional rights in forest areas. The 1967 Basic Act on Forestry, unlike the 1960 Agrarian Law, contains no mention of traditional rights. It states that land in Indonesia is considered state property, and the government reserves all rights to decide what is to be done with a certain plot of land in a given area. In production forests, the sole right to harvest timber lies with concession holders; local communities are often barred from entering the concession area. Regulation No. 21 of 1970 on Logging and Forest Product Concessionaires states that the rights of traditional communities to harvest forest products are "frozen" in concession areas and can be exercised only with the permission of the concessionaire. Although a Forestry Agreement passed in 1975 mandates that logging companies "observe the rights of local people, for example to trees and products", it is not adhered to by logging companies and, in fact, is rarely referred to by the Forestry Department which enacted it. Similarly, although both the Basic Forestry Law of 1967 and the 1970 Regulation on forest exploitation are legally subject to the 1960 UUPA, few courts are likely to give precedence to the earlier law where the interests of business and finance are at stake. When conflicts arise, local villagers are blamed as backward, primitive people who do not understand the need for foreign exchange. They are accused of hampering development and are agents of forest destruction in the eyes of the government, foreign and domestic consultants and the business community. Many local people are not even aware of the UUPA, putting them at an additional disadvantage when confronted with contract papers owned by logging or mining companies.

The concept of protection forests, particularly National Parks and Nature Reserves, also alienates people from the forests. Conversion forests, meanwhile, are often meant only for development projects such as transmigration and estate plantations. In effect, forests are considered "empty", with no human inhabitants or dependants. This policy is bound to create landlessness and to result in stress on areas outside those being "developed" — in effect forcing the "encroachment" of people upon forests.

Government bodies other than the Department of Forestry also directly affect the utilization of the forest. The Agriculture Department controls policies affecting conversion of forest lands to estate crops; the Transmigration Department identifies land sites cleared for resettlement of families from the heavily populated islands of Java and Bali to the outer islands; the Department of Public Works handles the actual land clearing for the transmigration programme as well as construction such as dams and irrigation systems; and the Energy and Mines Department issues oil and mineral concessions on both forested and unforested lands as well as being in charge of hydroelectricity projects in forested and unforested areas. Conservation as a whole is meanwhile the responsibility of the state Minister for Population and Environment (whose acronym is KLH — *Kependudukan dan Lingkungan Hidup*), although the Department of Forestry has its own Directorate General of Forest Protection and Nature Conservation (PHPA). KLH attempts to introduce environmental considerations into the policies of various departments such as the industry, agriculture, mining and transmigration departments. Where conflicts between economic return and conservation occur, however, economics inevitably wins out, and the KLH has proved to be powerless against the interests of forestry and transmigration. The KLH Minister himself has admitted that KLH is "merely an implementer, not a policy maker" (Emil Salim, pers. comm., 1991); in fact, the KLH acts largely as an environmental screen for the destructive practices of other departments.

Conflicting goals and interests among the many government departments involved in this cross-sectoral approach contribute to deforestation and land conflicts. Lack of co-ordination often leads to severe land disputes which none of the departments are willing to settle. Corruption also plays a significant role. Consequently, forests are exploited and converted to other uses without regard for conservation and long-term sustainability. Where state claims to ownership conflict with traditional law, it is hard to determine which institution should handle the matter — the Department of Internal Affairs, which handles land ownership matters, or the

Department of Forestry, which handles forest management.

Agrarian matters, meanwhile, have since 1988 been under the jurisdiction of the Internal Affairs Department and the recently-formed National Land Agency (*Badan Pertanahan Nascional* or BPN), a body directly responsible to the President. In dealing with land cases the BPN formulates policy and planning for land use, control and ownership, and enforces principles of the social function of land as stipulated in the Agrarian Law. Empowered to grant land title, it is also supposed to settle the hundreds of land disputes across the country (at least 300 are pending in Java alone) which have resulted from the unequal distribution of land caused by the corruption of the principles on which the Agrarian Law was founded and by the absence of legal safeguards for the people dispossessed (SKEPHI, pers. comm., 1992). The BPN, however, has shown no more ability to regulate land control and no more sympathy to people's problems and indigenous land-rights systems than the body it replaced, *Direktorat Jendral Agraria* (the Agrarian Directorate General) under the Department of Home Affairs.

DEVELOPMENT AND LAND RIGHTS

Official hostility to customary land rights and land reform is closely connected to the pressure on Indonesia to develop, to integrate itself more closely into the global economy, to provide goods for Northern consumption and to reduce its dependence on oil and natural gas. In responding to these pressures, the country is sacrificing the needs of its people for land and resources, as well as long-term national goals, to the need for foreign exchange and the repayment of debt.

Indonesia's economic position exaggerates the drive to develop cash crop and natural resource exports, tourism and industry, all of which push people off land. The first wave of economic development following Suharto's takeover in 1965 concentrated on exploitation of crude oil, minerals, timber, fishery products and other natural resources, mostly with foreign investment. During the second wave, in the late 1970s, with oil prices rocketing on the international market, the emphasis was on development and protection of import-substitution industries. The third wave occurred when the oil price decline led to the deregulation and debureaucratization of various other sectors of the economy and of production. This phase emphasized export-led growth and the further encouragement of foreign investment.

With declining oil prices, annual growth in Gross Domestic Product slowed to 3.4% in the period 1980-1986 from its 1965-1980 average of 7.9%. A Structural Adjustment Programme suggested by the World Bank was introduced in 1983, and the government began to embark on reorientation of the country's economic policies. The first step was an economic liberalization campaign which devalued the rupiah by 28%, launched an austerity budget, liberalized trade and substantially deregulated the financial sector. The ultimate goal was to restore economic stability and decrease the country's dependence on oil. In 1986, the international oil price plummeted and the country's terms of trade declined 34% due to fluctuation in US currency valuations, inducing the government to intensify economic liberalization and devalue the rupiah by an additional 31%. With the approval of the World Bank, the deregulation campaign has reached into every sector of the economy.

The consequent emphasis on non-oil sources of foreign exchange has been reinforced by the country's debt plight.

Indonesia has generally relied on two main sources of development funds. One was the Inter-governmental Group on Indonesia (IGGI), a donor consortium formed in 1967 to assist the country in its development and consisting of about 14 donor countries plus multilateral development agencies such as the World Bank and the Asian Development Bank (ADB). (This has now been replaced by the Consultative Group on Indonesia (CGI).) The second source consisted of oil revenues, which were largely spent on development projects such as expansion of agriculture, industry and infrastructure. The boom in oil revenues during the 1970s, however, although it led to improved aggregate income, literacy, health and food security statistics, also encouraged massive corruption, growing disparities in wealth and the marginalization of many. Consequently, Indonesia's development programme is still very much dependent on foreign aid. By 1991/1992, IGGI loans amounted to US$4.75 billion. Although the government keeps assuring the public that foreign loans are used only to supplement existing development funds, foreign monies funded 37.5% of the country's development projects in 1990/1991. The proportion of government revenue that has to go to servicing the foreign debt has risen from 25% in 1983/1984 to 53.1% in 1988/1989. The government's savings have meanwhile declined drastically from 7.3 trillion rupiah in 1985/1986 to 1.7 trillion in 1988/1989. In 1988, Indonesia received US$6.377 billion in foreign "aid" while its debt service amounted to US$7.296 billion. Trapped by these burgeoning debts and debt service ratios, the Indonesian government is pushing hard to attract foreign investors and increase its export earnings. In this way it hopes to be able to pay off its massive $60 billion debt.

The result has been pressures to steer the economy away from oil dependence and toward other sectors. These include timber production, the main non-fossil-fuel earner, which brought in more than US$2 billion during the first three quarters of 1989, and agricultural production, which employs over half of the nation's workforce and earned the country over US$1.5 billion in the first three quarters of 1989. Non-fossil-fuel mineral exports totalled more than US$1 billion during the same period.

This pattern of resource exploitation requires large amounts of land — for timber extraction, palm-oil and other tree plantations, dams, mines, tourist facilities and industrial estates. Communities displaced by this process, if not given an alternative form of livelihood, must either relocate or operate within a smaller landholding. The results are well-known: new land is cleared, fallow periods become shorter, the environment suffers. The cleared land becomes useless and new land must be opened again. This vicious circle, combined with rising numbers on ever smaller areas of land, results in the use of more destructive agricultural methods and consequently an increase in deforestation.

To date exploitation and development have been concentrated in the western parts of Indonesia, mainly Java, Bali, Kalimantan and Sumatra. While natural resources including forests are dwindling fast on these islands, roads, communication facilities, transport systems, education, industries and infrastructure have progressed (except perhaps in Kalimantan) — as have land disputes. In an effort to balance the situation, the government is attempting what is called the "East Indonesia Development" (EID) programme in the West Nusa Tenggara islands, Sulawesi, the Maluku islands and Western New Guinea. This means an expansion of natural-resource extraction in these regions, including exploitation of forests. As logging shifts from its 1970s boom centres in Kalimantan and Sumatra to Western New Guinea and other parts of East Indonesia, deforestation and land problems will follow.

TRANSMIGRATION:
DEMOGRAPHIC DESTRUCTION

Transmigration involves moving huge numbers of people from densely-settled areas of Java, Madura, Bali, Lombok and Flores to the "sparsely" populated outer islands, mainly Sumatra, Kalimantan, Sulawesi, Maluku and Western New Guinea. By 1984, between 2.5 and 3.6 million people had been moved under official programmes scheduled to shift a total of 65 million (Uhlig 1988; Colchester 1986c). The World Bank estimates that unofficial migrants outnumber official ones by two to one.

To take one of the more striking examples of migration, local authorities in Lampung in southern Sumatra estimate 100,000 spontaneous migrants enter their province each year; Javanese in this province alone already numbered 3 million by the 1980s (Uhlig 1988). Partly as a result of this influx, the area under coffee in the mountain zone of Lampung jumped from 530 to 1,290 square kilometres between 1973 and 1980 (Scholz 1988).

Although transmigration has had an immense impact on the outer islands, it has had little noticeable demographic effect in Java. Between 1905 and 1950, Java's population was 30 million; by 1979 it had risen to more than 91 million. In 1989, it soared to 99 million.

The first government-sponsored programme of relocating

population in Indonesia can be traced back to the early years of the century when the *kolonisatie* (colonization) programme was introduced by the Dutch colonial government, with the aim of "improving the welfare of the people". This justification for the programme was the belief that Java was overpopulated and that this "surplus population" created landlessness, unemployment, deforestation and was hampering the progress of development. By redistributing population to the "sparsely"-populated islands, these factors would theoretically be eliminated. In 1905, the first batch of 155 families were sent to Gedong Tataan in Lampung, South Sumatra. Eighty-five years later, Lampung is facing the same acute population problem as Java.

In reality, *kolonisatie* was simply an attempt to get cheap labour from Java to work on Dutch-owned plantations (state and private) in Sumatra. During this time the Dutch government opened up forests for rubber and oil palm plantations in Sumatra to supply raw materials to industries in The Netherlands. When commodity prices fell a few years later, many transmigrants who worked in plantations as "contract labourers" were sent back to Java. This caused social unrest due to increased unemployment and poverty. By 1940, 35 years later, the Dutch government had only been able to transfer 150,000 people permanently out of Java.

Today, the same arguments, and more, are being used by the Indonesian government to justify transmigration. Just as the Dutch colonialists failed, so the Indonesian government is failing. Social and environmental costs are high, and transmigration does not come close to achieving its official aims of population redistribution and assisting economic growth and development for the outer islands. Over and over again the programme has failed to attain its targets and has done nothing to alleviate the pressure on Java, Madura and Bali. On the contrary, transmigration has caused despair and poverty both for the transmigrants and those living in the recipient areas.

Transmigration is a process of internal colonization through land and resource appropriation. Using Javanese culture as a tool for political and cultural engineering, the New Order government seeks to assimilate and unify the varying cultures of Indonesia into a single dominant way of life, that of the Javanese, who have been regarded and treated as the "true" Indonesians both by European colonialists and by the present administration. The political system is based on the Javanese principles of harmony and consensus, confrontation being an anathema.

A programme called *bedol deso*, for example, aims to deposit a "typical Javanese village package" from Java to the outer islands, so creating Javanese-style villages all over Indonesia. These Javanese village enclaves are similar to colonies and are expected to be able to dictate the culture and community of the outer islands. Such initiatives make social and cultural conflict intrinsic to transmigration.

As part of this general approach, Javanese are publicly declared as superior and essential to Indonesia's overall "development". For example, the head of the Land Planning Agency, Bappeda, in West Sumatra, in defending the transmigration of 20,000 families from Java to the Mentawai islands, branded the 18,000 traditional Mentawai people of Siberut Island as backward. "With the current inhabitants, Mentawai has no chance of developing. The work ethic of the Javanese is excellent. Their agricultural methods are far advanced and they can be imitated by the Mentawai people" (SKEPHI 1991b). Newcomers from Java, Madura, Bali, and Nusa Tenggara are thus being encouraged to work on traditional Siberut lands, threatening the local lifestyles which had preserved the forest for some 3,000 years. Primary forest will be clear-cut to make way for palm-oil plantations and 10,000 families will be transmigrated in a deliberate attempt to displace or forcibly assimilate local people, whose customary community land rights will be ignored (SKEPHI 1991b).

The Transmigration Programme, as well as assisting in the appropriation of land in the outer islands, also serves as a tool to remove people from "inner" Indonesia to make way for development projects, industrial sites, and tourism facilities. Since the 1980s, the government has conducted large-scale land appropriations in the name of development. People and communities have been forced off their land and to solve the resulting landlessness problems, the government has stepped up the already existing transmigration scheme, which is the only form of compensation for those displaced. Demographic pressure, as well as unrest in Java arising from lack of employment opportunities, inability to solve regional planning problems and the people's subsequent dissatisfaction due to poverty and land appropriations, has always resulted in the eviction of people from "problem" areas through transmigration (although, at the same time, people are often settled in such areas).

Increasingly, as during the Dutch colonial era, transmigration has also become a method of supplying cheap labour to pioneer industrial projects, such as timber estates, mining and plantations.

Transmigration to Western New Guinea, where the aim has been to resettle the majority of transmigrants along the border with Papua New Guinea, has had military and political objectives since it was used in an attempt to eliminate the intensive rebellion of *Organisasi Papua Merdeka* (OPM, or Free Papua Movement) and so ensure the integration of Western New Guinea with Indonesia. Indonesian development activity is widely considered in Western New Guinea to be an act of imperialism, colonialism or expansionism; by some, transmigration is even seen as an "act of genocide towards the indigenous Melanesian people, or even a military strategy to one day annex Papua New Guinea." (Aditjondro 1986). The same process has occurred in the annexed East Timor.

Rather than fulfil its official objectives, transmigration firstly eats up development funds and increases debt. Secondly, while depriving people of land and livelihoods, it overstresses the land. In Western New Guinea, most arable land is already used for the rotating or shifting agriculture of the one million indigenous inhabitants.

Unsurprisingly, traditional or customary lands are often forcibly appropriated to resettle transmigrants, who cut forests rapidly to fulfill short-term demands. Transmigrants are even shipped to areas where the population density exceeds the government's own targets. The government in now launching transmigration in Kamu Valley, Baliem Valley, and Batom/Kwirok in spite of the fact that the population density there is already 200 persons per square kilometre, well over the 50 persons per square kilometre permitted for the site. Traditional landowners who are advertised as having voluntarily contributed their customary lands to the government for transmigration have usually in fact either been intimidated to release their land or enticed with promises of compensation and socio-economic improvements by the government. Compensation for prior residents— often, where it is given at all, in the form of building materials — is inadequate.

Cultural conflict between Javanese and the people of the outer islands is an inevitable and destructive part of transmigration. For many indigenous communities outside Java and Bali, wet-rice cultivation is alien. The positive Javanese cultural attitude toward forest clearing (the spirit of a traditional epic in which a prosperous kingdom was created through clear-cutting is often evoked) is also at odds with the perceptions of, say, indigenous people in Western New Guinea, who tap forests for fruits, game, vegetables and sago but conserve them as homes of ancestor spirits and sacred animals. At Prafi, a transmigration site near Manokwari, a violent confrontation occurred in March 1987 between transmigrants from Sikka, East Nusa Tenggara and the Meyakh tribe. The indigenous people of Salor village have also protested against contractors clearfelling their traditional forests for transmigration sites.

The negative impacts of transmigration are also suffered by transmigrants themselves; Javanese are tricked by the programme no less than the indigenous inhabitants of the outer islands. Workers on pioneer industrial projects do not have security or guarantee over land ownership, not even over the land on which their houses stand, and are very dependent upon their employers. There are no work contracts or free trade unions within these industries, which are often located in remote, isolated areas. Drought and the cost of fertilizing acidic soil has forced many transmigrants to resort to prostitution or to work illegally outside the site. At the Kurik I transmigration site in Merauke, transmigrants are plagued by floods, infertility, pests and lack of potable well-water. Transmigrants settled on inadequate sites are often forced to abandon them and colonize forests in order to survive. Many transmigrants have died of starvation or disease. Thus, although transmigration can be described as an attempt at Javanization, its connotations are quite different from those of, say, Zionism. Unlike migrants who settle the Occupied Territories, Javanese migrants are typically unaware that their role is to acculturate, colonize and attack the prior occupants of the land.

Massive deforestation is an inevitable consequence of transmigration. During 1984-89 alone at least 3,000,000 hectares of primary forests in Western New Guinea were opened up for transmigration. Even before then, 80% of transmigration sites were created by cutting down forest. Erosion, flooding and malaria epidemics have resulted. Rotting wood left after land clearance, moreover, attracts large numbers of rats, creating a market for the ICI rodenticide Klerat. Deaths due to Klerat poisoning have resulted in Lampung (Southern Sumatra), South Kalimantan and the southern part of Western New Guinea. The introduction of new species has meanwhile led to the loss of indigenous species. Forest clearing also results in loss of protein sources due to depletion of deer, pigs and monkeys.

New pest infestations are brought in by transmigrants, and consumption of DDT in Western New Guinea has tripled since the late 1970s and early 1980s. One of the major US DDT manufacturers, Montrose, which has supplied DDT to Indonesia through USAID, has even built a subsidiary in Ciracas, West Java, in anticipation of a large market among transmigrants. Use of chemical fertilizers has meanwhile damaged many soils (SKEPHI 1991a;*The Ecologist* 1986).

Transmigration cannot even achieve its own targets. In the early 1980s, there were plans to resettle one million people to Western New Guinea alone. By 1983 this figure dropped to 700,000. The actual number transmigrated was only about 125,000. The number of migrants abandoning resettlement sites, meanwhile, has increased over the years. Out of 21,000 families relocated in Western New Guinea between 1979 and 1989, 1,500 families have abandoned their sites for unknown locations. Failing to solve demographic problems, transmigration is in fact causing a whole new range of problems based on landlessness and the ensuing poverty of both transmigrants and displaced local people.

Meanwhile, landlessness in Java continues to rise, due not only to the increase in human numbers but also to development pressures and the eclipse of customary land rights by those vested in the state and in individuals. In 1973, 3.2% of farmers on Java were landless, but by 1980 the figure had increased five-fold to 14.9%. In the same period the proportion of farmers owning less then 0.5 hectare rose from 45.7% to 63.1% (Colchester 1986c: 63). On Java, in 1963, 73% of rural households had a farm of more than 0.1 hectare; in 1983, only about 57%. Between 10 and 20% of rural Javanese households control all plots of land more than 1 hectare in extent.

PLANTATIONS AND DEFORESTATION

In 1976, the Indonesian government began to implement the *Perkebunan Inti Rakyat*, or People's Nucleus Plantations scheme (PIR), supposedly as another response to poverty and landlessness. Under this scheme, state-owned nucleus estates become nuclei for surrounding smallholder tree-cropping, "supported by a business system of food- and tree-crop commodities whose activities of production, processing and marketing are promoted and performed in an appointed place" (Special PIR Team 1976). Each nucleus estate is expected to assist surrounding smallholdings with culti-vation, processing and marketing.

The PIR scheme has roots in the colonial "Cultivation" and corporate plantation systems, which obliged farmers in surround-ing areas to supply land and labour. Like the earlier colonial schemes, PIR deprives small farmers of control over production and marketing processes, transforming them into landless labourers no longer able to use traditional methods of agriculture. Meanwhile, the fixed-capital component of production costs increases throughout the agricultural sector, and production units grow in scale. This draws new technology and state-backed credit and subsidies, allowing further capital to enter rural areas.

The majority of PIR schemes today are Special PIR (PIR for transmigration), backed by the World Bank. Special PIR schemes do not serve to rationalize abandoned land but instead clear areas of virgin tropical rainforest and displace thousands of indigenous

TABLE 7
TYPES OF PIR

Type	Location	Participants	Settlement	Land
Local	around existing nucleus estate	local	partly subsidized	2 ha
Assisted	new area	local people are priority within Java	full cost met	2 ha (Java: 1.5)
Special	new area	20% local 80% trans-migrants	full cost met	2 ha

people, giving opportunities on the estates to transmigrants. Through Special PIR, the new plantations have a ready supply of cheap labour both to produce the crops and to work in the processing plant as well as a sure supply of the produce needed to make the profits.

The original aim of PIR was to redistribute the land in former plantations, which had been abandoned after the exit of the colonial powers, to the peasants. The smallholders would benefit by having security of tenure through a clear titled landholding with a guarantee of a permanent market for the their crops and a secure income. However, the need to find an alternative source of foreign exchange to reduce the heavy dependency on oil and liquified gas led to a drive to export increased quantities of palm oil and other plantation products such as rubber, coffee, coconuts, cloves and tea. The Indonesian government hopes that by 1993 around 80% of Indonesia's exports will be non-timber forest products. The PIR scheme is now used to open up areas outside Java for natural resource exploitation to feed this export drive. In particular, oil-palm exports are scheduled to double, comprising 42.1% of total plantation exports, by 1994. By June 1986, oil-palm PIRs covered a total of 140,261 hectares (35,189 hectares of nucleus estate and 105,072 hectares of plasma estate, where smallholders plant trees) out of a total of about 400,000 hectares of plantation estates; the target is for 1,381,000 hectares to be planted before 1994. Projections are for some one million families to be transmigrated in association with the PIR programme, largely to Sumatra, Kalimantan, and Western New Guinea. Two hundred thousand families are currently allocated for plantation transmigration. The Transmigration Department also plans to send 40,000 transmigrant families to work on timber estate projects, 90,000 to fisheries and 40,000 to tertiary industry developments in the outer islands.

Another major reason for PIR is that it facilitates transmigration. Transmigration came under heavy international criticism in the mid-1980s because of its disastrous social, environmental and economic effects, culminating in the suspension of any new funding by the World Bank (*The Ecologist* 1986). PIR provides a screen behind which large-scale transmigration can proceed with funding from the international community. By 1987, some US$132.5 million had been invested in PIR by the World Bank and others.

Special PIR has many advantages for the Indonesian government. Because of the involvement of the private sector, initial operations on the sites are very economical from the government's point of view: land clearance is the task of the private or state-owned companies developing the project and the government has only to arrange and pay for the transport of the transmigrants and to provide a supply of rice for one year. As for investors, they are able to penetrate new potential areas of Indonesia's forests with the support and backing of the Indonesian government, and the Transmigration Programme provides them with a cheap source of labour. As in colonial times, the "labourers" are under their control as is the land they are given to occupy. Transmigration can be provided with additional sources of financial support through loans for the private sector and state-owned companies on an unspecified basis or under the name of programmes other than transmigration. The Transmigration Sector Review financed by the World Bank has recommended a shift to more tree-crop transmigration models in upland schemes.

The schemes themselves, however, have been failing due to mismanagement, corruption and mistreatment of smallholders. The areas cleared are being abandoned by companies and small-holders alike, leaving the destroyed forest areas redundant and worthless. In addition, the plantations introduce pesticides, and pollution has reached alarming proportions. Smallholders and transmigrants working on the estates have found that rather than gaining a secure future, they are far poorer than before.

Traditional land rights have been disregarded in appropriating land for the plantations. Projects have begun on land with private title and, in local schemes, people have had to give up their land for 1.5 or 2 hectares on the plantation without any compensation for areas lost. Farmers are "persuaded" to hand over their rights to the project without receiving any compensation or promise thereof. The social and economic benefits the farmers are supposed to receive by being involved in the PIR scheme are seen as being more than adequate compensation. In Special PIR projects, tradi-tional landowners have been forced off their land to make plots available for transmigrants. In areas such as Western New Guinea, traditional communities have been forced to move deeper in the forest to exploit new areas for food and homes.

Entitlements to land, in addition, have not been forthcoming. Smallholders in West Java are supposed to receive 1.5 hectares of land and 55,000 rupiah to buy seeds, fertilizers and pesticides necessary to begin tree crop development as well as materials to improve their homes. Provisions for allowances, as well as houses, seeds and land, have been handed out erratically or not at all. Smallholders actually have to pay for the privilege of being involved in the PIR scheme, whether they are local farmers or transmigrants, in that they are required to repay some development costs to the estate owner. These costs include credit items of tree crop plants, subsistence payments, settler housing, roads and telecommunications development overheads. This further enforces the lack of regard for traditional land rights.

In areas of local PIR, farmers have often been working on the project land for over 50 years. Yet they now find themselves paying for land which they already own. In the case of oil palm and cocoa, smallholder loans are made for a period of 17 years with a two-year grace period and repayment beginning in the sixth year. For rubber, there is a grace period of three years and repayment begins in the seventh year. Interest is set at 10.5% per year which, while possibly being below the rate of inflation, is cumulative.

The promise that farmers will gain security of tenure has proved empty. Smallholders are expected to work for three years before title to the land (*hak milik*) is in principle due to them. At the end of that period there are various additional requirements smallholders must fulfil. The most insidious is that they must prove to be "satisfactory labourers" and to be willing to work and live on tree-crop holdings. Just how this level of satisfactoriness is judged is unknown and undocumented.

Until loans are repaid, moreover, the Bank of Indonesia is to hold land certificates as security. These certificates, however, often turn out not to exist and so, even if repayment is made, maladministration and corruption deprives smallholders of documentary land security. And repayment often turns out to be impossible even if the smallholder does qualify for *hak milik*. This is partly due to the nature of PIR projects themselves. In many cases, the central processing factory is never built and the "secure" market for the produce never materializes. When unable to sell their crops, the people face major problems, especially where, for example, oil palm has been given precedence over food crops. In other cases, the interest accumulation proves prohibitive and the smallholders barely make enough to live, let alone to repay the bank.

Cases of corruption and malpractice are widespread. The monopoly created by the nucleus over the produce and therefore over prices has meant below-market crop prices. Unable to sell crops on the open market, farmers face poverty; the possibility of ever being free of the estate loan slips still further from their grasp.

Land granted for commercial utilization is often not utilized to the maximum and sometimes even left idle, merely being used as security for concessionaires to obtain loans.

On top of all this, the "oil palm fever" rampant in Indonesia means large companies are ousting smaller enterprises, whose smallholders can no longer afford to plant oil palm seedlings. This obviously has serious repercussions for transmigrants waiting for the promised work. Another concern is the price of oil palm, which is heavily affected by fluctuations in the world commodities market. With a glut on the market, prices are liable to fall heavily, causing the bankruptcy of large numbers of companies.

INDUSTRIAL FORESTRY

Because colonial loggers concentrated mainly on Java, it was not until the enactment of the Basic Forestry Act in 1967 and the Regulations on Foreign and Domestic Investment in 1972 that intensive commercialization of the forest in the outer islands began. Through the 1972 regulations, the Indonesian government invited foreign capital and technology to exploit the forest under a "profit sharing" system. The first foreign investors were FDC (Japan's Forestry Development Committee) in East Kalimantan, while Kodeco (Korea Development Corporation) and Mitsui (Japan) were based in central Kalimantan. By 1986 there were at least 537 logging companies covering an area of 55 million hectares located in 19 provinces, and the current figure is likely to be far higher (SKEPHI 1990).

Since 1967, the rate of logging in Indonesia has risen at an alarmingly rapid rate. By 1970, some 7 to 10% of the total forest area was being logged. By 1979, the log harvest reached 25 million cubic meters, ten times the harvest recorded in the 1960s. The timber boom made Indonesia the largest log exporter in the world (the total exports being in excess of those from all African and Latin American countries combined), contributing 41% to the world's timber market. Some 93.5% came from the islands outside Java, 60.9% from Kalimantan alone.

After 1979, the log harvest fell sharply following an increase in the log export tax and the enactment of policies encouraging exports of more lucrative processed wood. In 1985, a total log export ban was imposed. Timber export earnings fell sharply between 1981 and 1984, but by 1987, Indonesia's production of sawlogs and veneer logs was 10% of world production and 38% of ASEAN production. Today Indonesia controls 70% of ASEAN production in the plywood market. It is projected by FAO that this share will further increase to 81% by 1995 (SKEPHI 1990). This is despite stiff international opposition which has resulted in protectionism from other manufacturers such as Japan, forcing Indonesia to sell its timber products at lower prices. By 1990, the Indonesian forestry industry sector was earning over US$3 billion annually, that is, 16% of the total exports, ranking second only to petroleum and natural gas (GoI/FAO 1990: 37). In July 1992 the log export ban was lifted, which, together with the increased demand from the new lumber industries, will accelerate logging once more.

Logging operations often violate the land rights and undermine the security of local communities. Bintuni Bay, a highly biodiverse mangrove area of Western New Guinea, of which 450,000 was gazetted as a strict nature reserve in 1982, is one example. Following the degazetting of part of the reserved area in 1986 through a single signature from Jakarta, 11 logging and fishing companies invaded the bay, including an Indonesian partner of the Japanese conglomerate Marubeni and another firm, PT Agoda Wai Hitam, which illegally exports raw logs to Taiwan to be used to produce paper money. Many of the local Iraratu people, who previously enjoyed clan use rights to the area, have become landless, and fishing communities' catch has been reduced. Compensation paid has been inadequate or non-existent (*Setiakawan* 1991, No. 6).

The World Bank has supported a study to introduce new contracting procedures to ensure recovery of commercially valuable timber through "tree crop transmigration models" in East Kalimantan. Such timber estate schemes fulfil the Indonesian government's objective to create plantations for industrial timber production, and logging companies and others are currently given incentives to "reforest degraded lands" through timber estate projects. Although until 1987 timber estates were being openly established in natural forests, government officials and foresters claim that such estates, by producing wood efficiently on small areas of land, will take pressure off already over-exploited natural forests (GoI/FAO 1990: 37). They add that timber estates in Java have proved successful for over 30 years. Current plans call for an expansion of the estates from 2.2 to 6.2 million hectares by the year 2000.

The schemes plant monocultures of exotics such as eucalyptus, acacia, albizzia and mahogany on what is officially described as logged-over land or other degraded areas, where apparently worthless scrub has taken over. In fact, however, the estates often invade old-growth rainforest. The projects granted to Astra Scott Cellulosa in Western New Guinea, for example, were in primary natural rainforest stands. Astra planned to clear-cut some areas first and then replant with eucalyptus. Like PIR, timber estates also fall victim to pest infestations and sometimes invade surrounding farmlands. On some estates, land has been underplanted due to mismanagement and corruption, and plant care has often been totally absent.

It is often argued that the real aim of timber estates is not reforestation, but ensuring a supply of raw materials for the pulp and paper industries. As the FAO notes, paper production is rising fast, and Indonesia has recently become a net exporter of paper products (GoI/FAO 1990:19), yet newsprint is subsidized by the government.

The environmental and social threats of pulp and paper companies have been all too visible. PT Inti Indorayon Utama, a pulp and rayon mill in North Sumatra, was sued by an Indonesian non-government organization on the grounds that it was causing visible ecological damage to its locality. Although the company won the case, it was then embroiled in controversy once again when ten North Sumatran women claiming that the company had appropriated their ancestral land for eucalyptus were sued in 1990 for damaging eucalyptus saplings. Environmental and social concerns expressed by the international community meanwhile forced Scott Paper Company to withdraw from its partnership with PT Astra International to establish a wood chip and a pulp mill in Western New Guinea. In August 1992, PT Astra withdrew for similar reasons, although Indonesian firms still hope to carry out the plans with funding from Japan. Concern has also been directed towards the pollution damage to local water sources caused by pulp mills.

OTHER DEVELOPMENT PROJECTS

Other industrial or foreign-exchange-oriented development projects are also important causes of landlessness. Gold mining concessions, often involving multinational companies from Australia, are frequently granted over land which originally belonged to the local community under the *hak ulayat* system. At least 100 gold mining permits have been granted, mainly on forested land.

Tourism, too, takes up a vast amount of land either bought at an unreasonably cheap price or appropriated from the people. Sumber Kelampok, a village of nearly 10 square kilometres with 2,000 inhabitants in Bali, for example, is to be demolished to make way for tourism developments, including the development of a national park. The government has arrogated all land rights to itself, nullifying titles granted to resident families in the early 1940s by the Dutch and promises of further titling from local plantation managers after independence. When a National Park was gazetted in the area in 1984, local people were branded as "poachers", prohibited from bee hunting and gathering, and prevented from using electricity and water. In 1990 it was announced that the inhabitants were to be transmigrated. According to a government official, they are not considered "educated enough" to be a suitable workforce at the luxury hotels slated for the area. After fruitlessly petitioning the government for land rights, they have since November 1991 refused all officials entry to the village.

The current trend in tourism of "experiencing the rainforest" has led to the opening up of forests or agricultural land in remote areas for the construction of resorts. For the construction of a golf course in the buffer zone of the Gunung Gede Pangrango National Park in West Java, for example, lands which local people have cultivated for more than 50 years were appropriated by the developer for a price of 30 rupiah (0.15 US cents) per square metre, without the knowledge of the people themselves. Future potential threats to community lands and forests include resort developments in remote areas of the eastern part of Indonesia.

Hydroelectricity dams, meanwhile, require vast amounts of land, not merely for the reservoir, but also for resettling displaced people. A phenomenon of "double landlessness" is thereby created: the dam deprives local people of land, and the displaced people then invade the land of others, depriving them in turn. For example, in Central Java, the controversial Kedung Ombo dam funded by the World Bank, the Export-Import Bank of Japan and the National budget displaced 30,000 people and flooded 6,000 ha of fertile farm land. Some families transmigrated to Bengkulu, Sumatra where forests had to be opened up for them, some of which belonged to the area's indigenous people. Many families refused to move because compensation was too low, only 730 rupiah (37.5 US cents) per square metre. They demanded to be resettled near the dam. Part of the state production forests surrounding the reservoir were finally handed over to some families who had refused to move. All in all, the project "ate" up more forests than originally intended (SKEPHI 1991c).

The proposed Japanese-funded Koto Panjang dam in a forest area of Riau and West Sumatra is almost five times larger than Kedung Ombo and will create even more serious landlessness and deforestation. Local people are to be given farmland in compensation that belongs to the neighbouring villages. Conflicts are inevitable, and the project is facing resistance from local people as well as from environmental groups in Japan and Indonesia. Many other dam projects are now being started in Sumatra, Kalimantan and Sulawesi. One is even being planned in the Sentani lake, Western New Guinea, which will displace the traditional fisherfolk and appropriate their fishing waters.

WAYS FORWARD

Blaming deforestation on population pressure and shifting agriculturalists has enabled the Indonesian government to pursue a whole series of "regreening" policies which do not attempt to deal with landlessness as a central cause of deforestation. Ignoring the need for land reform, as well as the poverty which development schemes create, the government has embarked on reforestation, forest protection and social forestry schemes. These schemes, however, are only for show, and in fact exacerbate the deprivations of the people they are supposed to benefit. Communities deprived of land rights and values become dependent, landless peasants or labourers working at the behest of the state.

Hope for Indonesian forests lies not in such programmes but in local people standing up for themselves. Growing numbers of local people travelling huge distances to Parliament House over land disputes. Protesting inadequate compensation and environmental and social destruction, local people have demanded recognition of their rights to ancestral land.

While the Indonesian press covers the majority of such representations and the parliament promises to help the people, the political structure in Jakarta effectively prevents fruitful practical action. Often, instead, local military presence is increased, local organizers put under surveillance and local civil servants replaced. In the case of the Koto Panjang dam, villagers were driven to travel all the way to Tokyo to appeal to the Diet to reconsider Japanese funding for the project. As a result, Japan expressed concern to Indonesia and the project is in limbo (SKEPHI, pers. comm., 1991).

Since action through official channels is proving insufficient (although vital in putting pressure on the government, international development agencies and multinational investors), local people have turned to direct actions on their land. More and more local people are risking all because they see that if they do not, there will be no life for future generations, let alone their current dependents. In Siberut, indigenous people have been blocking logging trucks and planting fast-growing crops on land the state would otherwise claim to be empty and thus under its ownership. In Bintuni Bay, Western New Guinea, a community went to the company office to claim compensation. In Ophir, West Sumatra, smallholders attacked the offices of the state company which had defrauded them of their land and entitlements. Effective protest is difficult, however, due to political, economic, and social repression. Every protest non-Javanese people undertake offends the Javanese principle of non-confrontation and confirms the élite view that people become increasingly backward the further away from Jakarta they live. Yet protests by dispossessed Javanese people, although they sometimes make more of an impact on Jakarta leaders who seek ways of channelling them, are not necessarily given proper consideration, either.

Non-governmental organizations (NGOs) in Indonesia are working to try to formulate popular demands with which to lobby both the Indonesian government and international opinion. Many NGOs are pressing the case for community forestry under the control of existing traditional institutions as the key to forest conservation. They are trying to block the increasing abuse of the term to cover timber estates and PIR, so that the concept can work instead for the people and the environment. Local NGOs have also suggested that communities should be assisted by formal representatives in the House of Representatives. NGO work too, however, is proving very difficult. The government has turned its attention to suppressing the organizations through laws banning free association of over five people and through the cutting off of financial assistance to them from overseas NGOs.

On the official level, land reform is a mere slogan in Indonesia. The New Order government would consider genuine land reform to be a Communist threat (although in reality the pre-1965 Communist élite's interest in the issue was no more sincere than that of the New Order). Hence to demand land reform is to call up memories of the slaughter of hundreds of thousands of suspected Communists in 1965-66. Yet in the face of the political dangers, a land reform which would benefit landless farmers on Java, together with a proposal for their representation by a strong mass organization in Parliament, is being publicly pushed as a way of removing the need for transmigration. Government solutions to deforestation have proven so ineffective that the land movement is seen by many concerned about the issue as the only hope for the future.

Action at an international level must support the local and national initiatives by which Indonesian people are risking their lives to save their land, their homes, and their future; the North must learn to stop blaming environmental destruction on local people. Northern funding of destructive development projects in Indonesia simply continue the cycle of forest destruction and landlessness, and the economic demands and consumption rates of the North encourage and indeed force the Indonesian government to put its people and forests second to rapid economic expansion. Thus many Indonesian NGOs are demanding a moratorium on the timber trade at the international level until post-logging rehabilitation measures have proved their efficacy. Such a moratorium must be coupled with the development of sustainable, people-oriented non-timber forest production. In addition, all forestry sector lending to Indonesia should be halted, and disbursements and implementation of already-approved loans delayed, until communities are able to participate in, and help revise, all stages of the National Forestry Action Plan, which co-ordinates forestry aid. International support for the outcry in Indonesia following the 1992 lifting of the log export ban is also necessary if this protest is not to fall on deaf ears.

None of this will be possible without a moratorium on Indonesia's debt and more humane international relations. This means a fair international trading system has to be created and excessive rates of Northern consumption decreased.

The contributions of Suyanto Wongsomenggolo, Maurice Rademaker and Claire Peusens to the writing of this chapter are gratefully acknowledged.

THE PHILIPPINES: DWINDLING FRONTIERS AND AGRARIAN REFORM

MARVIC M. V. F. LEONEN

. . . .What is the most precious thing to man? Life. If life is threatened, what ought a man do? Resist. This he must do, otherwise he is dishonoured and that is worse than death. You ask if we own the land and mock us saying "where is your title?" Such arrogance of speaking of owning the land when we are instead owned by it. How can you own that which will outlive you? Apu Kabuni-an, Lord of us all, gave us life and placed us in the world to live human lives. And where shall we obtain life? From the land. To work the land is an obligation not merely a right. In tilling the land, you possess it. And so, land is a grace that must be nurtured. Land is sacred and beloved.

Macliing Dulag, during the Chico River Dam Controversy, 1980

The Philippine archipelago is a cluster of some 7,100 islands extending about 1,800 kilometres from north to south along the south-eastern rim of Asia. With a population of well over 60 million, it is bordered on the east by the Pacific Ocean, on the west by the South China Sea, and is separated by straits from Taiwan to the north and from Malaysia and Indonesia to the south.

The Philippines may be divided into six distinct island groups: Luzon, the Visayas, Mindanao, Mindoro, Palawan and the Sulu archipelago. The two largest islands, Luzon in the north and Mindanao in the south, account for 65% of the total land area of about 30 million hectares. The Philippines are endowed with varied, rugged terrain and a coastline indented with gulfs and coral bays. Mountains divide the islands into coastal strips and shallow interior plains and valleys.

The warm, humid climate of the Philippines, together with its high rainfall and rich soil have produced a diverse and abundant

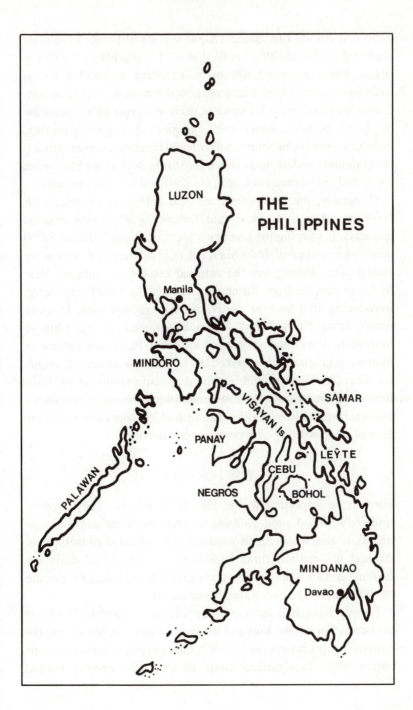

plant and animal life. Some 12,000 species of plants have been recorded in the country, more than 8,500 species of flowering plants. There are over 3,500 species of native trees and 300 or so introduced tree species. Many are now threatened with extinction. Larger mammals include monkeys, deer, wild pigs, and the tamaraw or dwarf buffalo. Kingfishers, junglefowl, pigeons, parrots, hornbills, bulbuls, babblers, sunbirds and flowerpeckers are among the common resident birds. Some rare birds, such as the Philippine eagle and red-vented cockatoo, are confined to mountain areas.

Culturally, the Philippines are also extremely diverse, with Negritos, Malays, Chinese and Europeans all having had an influence in shaping the country's identity. Some 7,000 to 8,000 years ago, waves of Indo-Malayan migrants arrived, venturing inland after driving out the original coastal inhabitants. New Malayan peoples from Borneo appeared about 2,000 years later, introducing iron and the cultivation of irrigated land. In more recent times, Spanish and American colonialism and Chinese immigration have had a profound impact on Philippine culture. A number of languages are spoken but none forms an overall majority. There are over a hundred ethnolinguistic groups in the Philippines. Eight million people belong to what are called indigenous cultural communities, divided into around 35 major ethnolinguistic groups, each with its own component sub-tribes.

THE FORESTS

Forests are important to the Philippine people. They provide timber, fuelwood, food, clothing material, medicine and other raw materials and wood-based products for domestic consumption. Around 6.7 million rural households use fuelwood daily for cooking and about half of this comes from forest lands. Forests are also critical to soil and water conservation.

Forests have had an important role in the country's export economy. For a time, logs and lumber products ranked among the country's top ten exports. In 1982, lumber ranked sixth as export earner while logs ranked ninth. In 1987, the country earned

US$306 million from the export of wood-based products. During that year forest products were the second-largest foreign exchange earner among traditional Philippine exports. Forest-based industries, though they employ only about 16,000 people, contribute US$500 million per annum to the country's foreign exchange.

Deforestation, however, has greatly eroded the important economic contributions of the forestry sector and reduced the availability of forest products to villagers. Deforestation rates over the past 60 years have been among the highest in the world. In 1934, more than 17 million hectares, or 57% of the entire land area, was forested, with virgin forests covering about 11 million hectares. Today, although statistics vary due to the lack of a national inventory and the high rate of extra-legal deforestation, it is estimated that only 6.5 million hectares of forest remain, covering a mere 21.5% of the country. According to some reports, less than 800,000 hectares of this is old-growth. Between 1948 and 1972, cultivated land increased from 38,000 square kilometres to 65,000 square kilometres and to 91,920 by 1980 (Uhlig 1988: 28; Putzel 1992b). Alienable and disposable lands are now said to cover 13.8 million hectares, or 48% of the country. Between 1969 and 1988, the country's forests were depleted at a very fast rate of 210,000 hectares per year. The rate was as high as 300,000 hectares a year in the late 1960s, declining to 150,000 hectares per year in the early 1980s. At present, it is estimated at less than 100,000 hectares per year.

Deforestation, in addition to threatening the livelihoods of local villagers, particularly indigenous peoples, has increased soil erosion. In 1987, Celso Roque, Undersecretary to the Department of Energy and Natural Resources, said that 75% of arable lands in the Philippines were menaced by severe soil erosion due to deforestation. Recent floods and droughts have been blamed in part on forest loss (Putzel 1992a).

Forests dominated by trees of the family *Dipterocarpaceae* are the most important sources of commercial timber, minor products and biological diversity. Of the total of 4.4 million hectares remaining in 1988, only a fraction were old-growth stands. Although

267

not as commercially viable, other forest types, including mossy and sub-marginal forests, perform vital roles in the protection of watershed areas and in maintaining ecological balance. Pine forests are of local commercial use for timber and resin production.

North-Eastern Luzon has always been considered as the most important timber region of the Philippines. Its 1.5 million hectares of forest occupy 43% of its land area, the highest proportion among all the regions, and the region contains more than 40% of all dipterocarp old-growth forests. Other large forested areas are in the Southern Tagalog area with 1.18 million hectares forest cover, Northern Mindanao with 1.09 million hectares, and North-Eastern Mindanao with 0.87 million hectares. Palawan also has large areas of hardwood forest. Pine forests are concentrated at altitudes of 800 meters and above in the Central Cordillera mountain range in Northern Luzon, and large mangrove areas in Mindanao.

CAUSES OF DEFORESTATION

Philippine deforestation must be seen as a process which involves both logging and the spread of small-scale subsistence agriculture in the uplands, of which shifting cultivation is only a small part. Logging converts primary into secondary forests; an influx of people along logging roads, many of them marginal farmers from the lowlands, then degrades forests further. Commercial logging and small-scale subsistence agriculture are said to be responsible for the destruction of 1.24 million hectares of commercial dipterocarp forest in a mere 10 years.

Logging and colonization are driven not mainly by high population densities but rather by a "comprador economy" and by the overall failure of development in the Philippines over the past 40 years. On the one hand, an unstable, export-oriented economy and political order encourage those with available capital to concentrate on rapid mining of natural resources for quick profits. On the other, development has failed to raise living standards or provide food and income for the majority of Filipinos, spurring migration to the uplands and the spread of frontier agriculture along logging roads and through other means. Between 1950 and 1973 alone the agricultural area of the country is estimated to have increased by 30,000 to 40,000 square kilometres, mainly through the work of spontaneous settlers (Uhlig 1988: 24). This dual mechanism of deforestation is closely connected historically with patterns of land ownership in both lowlands and uplands.

HISTORICAL BACKGROUND TO LAND OWNERSHIP

Although social stratification was developing before the beginnings of Spanish rule in 1571, it was the Spanish who introduced private property to the islands. Colonizers acquired communal land from village heads and all uninhabited lands were declared reserved for the Spanish king (Putzel 1992b; IBON 1988). Tribute districts were established and part of the produce of the tillers on these *encomiendas* was extracted as tribute. Much of the best land granted by the crown to conquerors and early settlers soon passed to Catholic friars, who formed *haciendas* which were farmed increasingly by tenants who paid a fixed rent in grain. At the end of the Spanish period, the monastic orders possessed more than 1,850 square kilometres of land, or more than 6% of the land then under cultivation. The Church's demands for tribute and forced labour outside its estates, its disruption of communities, and finally its encroachment on villagers' rice land and enclosure of commons began provoking strong resistance by the 18th century (Putzel 1992b; Hayami 1990).

Export cropping began to be promoted by Spain in the late 18th and early 19th centuries. This triggered a rush for land among friars, native officials and Chinese traders who had established sugar mills and intermarried with the Spanish élite. Chinese-Spanish *mestizos* and other entrepreneurs moved into outlying areas and rented blocks of unsettled land to subtenant sharecroppers with whom they contracted to grow indigo, sugar and rice (Hayami 1990: 46). Foreclosure and landgrabbing increased. The Spanish created a *Guardia Civil* to guard large landholdings, setting the pattern for both the Philippine constabulary and the paramilitary squads of the present day. In 1857 the British set up their first sugar mills in Negros; by 1900, 274 were in operation. Later in the 19th century newly-emerging élite families such as the Cojuangcos (Corazon Aquino's family) began to acquire huge tracts of land which were then put under cultivation by tenants to take advantage of the export economy. Gains from exports and sale of imports tended to be invested not in industry but in land and consumption.

Lowland peasants provided important support for the emerging Filipino élite in their 1896 Revolution against the friars and the Spanish. Underlying conflicts of interest between the peasantry and the élite could not be contained for long, however. While the Filipino landed oligarchy soon came to an understanding with the Americans, who annexed the islands in 1898 as a way of gaining access to the markets and resources of Asia, peasant resistance continued. More than a quarter of a million Filipinos were killed in the course of a war which at one point involved 100,000 American troops.

The Americans took pains to protect the property relations which had been established by the Spanish. In 1902 the Philippine Commission passed the Land Registration Act calling for the issuance of Torrens titles for private and public lands. This mainly benefited large landholders and landgrabbers. Americans were given rights to acquire agricultural lands for large-scale farming. To cool peasant unrest, prime land belonging to Catholic friars was bought up, but in the end this was sold rather than redistributed free to the 60,000 share tenants working it. As a result the land ended up in the hands of the landed oligarchy, absentee leaseholders, better-off tenants, American-backed colonial administrations and US corporations. As land values rose, big landowners concentrated in Manila and increased their political power and share of national production.

Laws were passed in the 1930s to regulate landlord-tenant relations, but little was done to implement them. Corporations got around legislated land ceilings by leasing land at low rates from the government-owned National Development Corporation, which

EXPLOITATION FOR EXPORT

In the late 18th and early 19th century, the Spanish divided their lands in the Philippines into regions, each specializing in a different crop. Northern provinces were compelled to produce cheap tobacco the colonial government could sell on the international market; other areas were planted to abaca, sugar and indigo. As the original mixed cropland was converted into *haciendas*, and farmers into plantation workers, subsistence needs of local farmers were sometimes disregarded, triggering starvation (Miranda 1988: 18). American and Spanish firms shared the trade in agricultural goods, much of which went to the US.

The American takeover around the turn of the 20th century geared the Philippine economy even more closely to producing for US markets. The US accounted for 18% of Philippine exports in 1899, but a full 83% in 1933. With a sure market for sugar, *hacederos* expanded the area under cane from 720 square kilometres in 1902 to 2,300 in 1928.

Over the same three decades, the US share of Philippine imports, mainly manufactures, went up from 9% to 64%. After the Second World War, foreign aid, together with World Bank and International Monetary Fund influence over the financial sector, ensured that the US continued to have special access to the Philippines to sell its growing industrial output. American transnational companies (TNCs) gained monopolies over key industries. The accession to power of Ferdinand Marcos in the 1960s further facilitated an export-orientated economic policy, and national debt accumulated. Resources badly needed by the rural sector, which employs a majority of the population, have gone instead into luxury goods and industries which benefit only a few.

Agribusiness TNCs own little land formally. But they form joint ventures with local business, link up with contract growers and lease land from the government. This has resulted in both clearance of forest and displacement of indigenous people and peasants whose presence interrupts the contiguity of plantation areas. In co-operation with their affiliates, pineapple and banana TNCs such as Dole and Del Monte controlled more than 527 square kilometres of Mindanao alone by 1980 (IBON 1988). Under the direction of Marcos cronies, the coconut and sugar industries also consolidated and accumulated more land. By 1980 the area under these two crops amounted to 31,557 square kilometres. At the same time, the area producing rice and corn staples has declined — a trend which has been reinforced by agrarian reform legislation exempting land under export crops from redistribution. In a country in which a majority of children suffer from malnutrition, 40-45% of all cultivated land is given over to export crops (Ateneo de Manila University 1991; Putzel 1992b).

had been set up to increase state landholdings for use by foreign investors and was exempt from the ceilings.

A HALF-CENTURY OF "AGRARIAN REFORM"

All presidents of the Philippines have had their own versions of agrarian reform. The first few pieces of legislation regulated relationships of actual tillers. It was only later that a full programme of land transfer was envisioned.

Manuel L. Quezon, who was commonwealth president under US authority from 1935-42, was instrumental in the passage of the Rice Share Tenancy Act. The Act provided for a 50-50 sharing arrangement between landowners and tenants and established a 10% interest ceiling for loans extended to tenants. For it to be implemented, however, an official petition by the municipal councils was required. This proved to be its greatest obstacle, since most of the councils were dominated by landowners. Hence the law was hardly implemented at all. Implementation of the law was then made mandatory in all Central Luzon provinces. Contracts for a 50-50 sharing arrangement, however, were good only for one year. By refusing to renew contracts, landowners were able to eject tenants and circumvent the law.

Manuel Roxas and the charismatic Ramon Magsaysay, who headed the second administration after independence from the US was achieved, were faced with the more serious task of defeating an insurgency movement, led by the revolutionary Hukbalahap movement, which grew out of the People's Anti-Japanese Army of the Second World War and focused on land reform. Several types of legislation were enacted during Magsaysay's tenure. Resettlement areas were established under the National Resettlement and Rehabilitation Administration to attract farmers-turned-rebels in Central Luzon to a peaceful life by giving them homelots and farms in pioneer areas of Mindanao and elsewhere. Widespread forest clearance was encouraged, yet the number of beneficiaries did not even reach one-tenth of one per cent of landless peasants. With the Hukbalahap threat receding, US interest in land reform faded. A USAID official said in 1972, "If the Huks had been perceived as more of a threat, we would have [imposed land reform as] we did in Japan, Korea and Taiwan" (IBON 1988).

The Agricultural Tenancy Act followed closely on the heels of the resettlement project. The law allowed share tenants to shift to leasehold. Rent was limited to 30% and interest rates to 8-10% per annum, but these were not enforced. The law also allowed the purchase or expropriation of private lands for redistribution to tenants at cost. Its major flaw was that it exempted lands less than 144 hectares in size.

The 1955 Land Reform Act, also passed during Magsaysay's administration, provided for the expropriation of lands of over 300 hectares of contiguous area if owned by individuals and 600 hectares if owned by corporations. The inclusion of the contiguity requirement exempted many landowners of huge but parcelled-out landholdings. Also, lobbying by landlords ensured that expropriation could be started only if a majority of the tenants petitioned for it. As tenants who did so were threatened with eviction, this Act accomplished little. After seven years only 41 out of 300 estates had been purchased by the government.

The outright abolition of the share tenancy system was envisaged by the administration of President Diosadado Macapagal (1962-65). An Agricultural Land Reform Code, passed in 1963, called for, among other things, the establishment of owner-cultivatorship and economic family-size farms as the basis of Philippine agriculture. The Code made share tenancy on most lands illegal, instituted the leasehold system with a fixed 25% rent (as a step to full ownership) and lowered the retention limit from 300 to 75 hectares. A land-to-the-tiller programme was set up to cover rice and corn lands.

Landowners found several ways to avoid this law. They continued to evict tenants through the personal cultivation clause and uncontrolled conversion of farms to uses exempt from coverage. Moreover, no timetable was set for the law's implementation, although priorities were indicated. And while the code was a monumental piece of legislation, Congress, largely controlled by landholding interests, did not provide for its funding.

It was during the second term of Ferdinand Marcos as president (1969-72) that the Code of Agrarian Reforms was enacted. This code created the Department of Agrarian Reform (DAR) and declared all share tenancy to be contrary to public policy. Unfortunately, the code never had a chance to be fully implemented. Less than a year after it was enacted, martial law was declared. Simultaneously, the whole country was decreed a land reform area. A month later, the president issued Presidential Decree No. 27 which immediately mandated the outright expropriation of private rice and corn lands. Operation Land Transfer, which was supposed to execute the decree, targeted 822,069 hectares for acquisition and distribution. Acquiring title, however, was a long and complicated process, and loopholes allowed landlords to evict tenants or shift to crops, such as sugar, which would exempt them from having to comply with the legislation. After more than thirteen years, the Marcos administration had distributed full titles to only 1.3% of the targeted land, leaving 810,870 hectares for the Aquino administration to distribute. Even if it had been fully implemented, however, Presidential Decree No. 27 would only have benefited a small fraction of landless and near-landless farmers. Nor could landless workers, tenants on non-rice and non-corn lands, or farmers on public lands have benefited.

THE AGRARIAN SITUATION TODAY

Through the 20th century, land distribution and poverty have steadily worsened. The percentage of farmers without their own lands who have to rent from landlords has gone up from 18% in 1903 to 22% in 1918, 35% in 1933, 37.4% in 1948, 48% in 1956, and 50% in 1961 (ASS 1983: 140). By the late 1980s, about 72% of the rural households which make up three-fifths of the Philippine population were landless or near-landless, including tenants paying rents of between 25 and 90% of production (Putzel 1992b; ASS 1983: 140). Usury at rates of 100% in three months or 50% in one month is common. Half of all people earning a living from agriculture are farmworkers, living in conditions even worse than those of tenants. Much work is only seasonal. Pay is often of the order of US$1 a day.

According to government figures, not more than 5% of all families own 80% of the land, and 67% of rural families live beneath an income level necessary for minimum nutritional requirements (Putzel 1992b: 17, 27). Two per cent of coconut farms occupy 1.25 million hectares, or 40% of the entire coconut area, while 91% of farms occupy only 33% of the area. In the early 1980s, 24% of sugar landowners owned 79% of sugar lands. Plantations covered one-fourth of the country's land area in 1984 (IBON 1988). Since 1975, the Philippines has had the highest degree of social inequality in Asia. The Gini coefficient measuring inequality in landownership reached the stratospheric level of 0.647 in 1988 (Miranda 1988, Putzel 1992b).

TABLE 8
LAND CONCENTRATION AND INEQUALITY

Farm size (hectares)	% of owners	% of area
<3.0	65.7	16.4
3.1-7.0	20.6	19.2
7.1-12.0	7.9	14.7
12.1-15.0	1.8	4.7
15.1-24.0	2.4	9.3
24.1-50.0	1.1	7.1
50.1-100.0	0.3	4.4
>100.0	0.2	24.2

Source: Putzel 1992b: 30.

RECENT DEVELOPMENTS

By the time Corazon Aquino came to power in 1986 as the seventh president of the Philippines, the peasant movement had matured. Steeled by the failures of the past administration to provide for a genuine solution to pressing agrarian problems, it had organized on a national scale over a large portion of the archipelago. Political mobilization consisted of a mixture of protest and proposal (see People's Demands and Actions, pp.279-280).

Partly as a consequence, the agrarian problem found its way into the new constitution drafted during the Aquino administration, as it had into previous ones. According to Section 4 of the constitution,

The State shall, by law, undertake an agrarian reform programme founded on the right of farmers and regular farmworkers, who are landless, to own directly or collectively the lands they till or, in the case of other farmworkers, to receive a just share of the fruits thereof. To this end, the State shall encourage and undertake the just distribution of all agricultural lands, *subject to such priorities and reasonable retention limits as Congress may prescribe, taking into account ecological, developmental, or equity considerations, and subject to the payment of just compensation.*

The clause to which emphasis has been added contains several hedges of which landowners were soon to take full advantage.

On 18 June 1988, almost one and a half years after the constitution was promulgated, the Aquino administration inaugurated the Comprehensive Agrarian Reform Programme (CARP). Unlike its predecessors it was proclaimed to be comprehensive, covering, "regardless of tenurial arrangement and commodity produced, all public and private agricultural lands as provided in the Constitution". A special fund known as the Agrarian Reform Fund (ARF) was established to finance the critical components of the programme, with an initial amount for 1987-1992 set at 50 billion pesos. CARP included not only the distribution of land but also the integrated delivery of a package of support services. Beneficiaries were to be assisted with credit, roads, irrigation, post-harvest facilities, technology transfer and organization to ensure their success as farm entrepreneurs. The programme was to be implemented not only by a strengthened DAR but by virtually the entire government machinery for rural development. The task of co-ordinating the implementation of CARP was given to the Presidential Agrarian Reform Council, or PARC, to be chaired by the president herself and to have as members the heads of more than

10 major governmental agencies. The programme was to involve greater consultations with the affected sectors, particularly the beneficiaries, and was to tap the skills of people's and non-government organizations (NGOs). A total of 10.3 million hectares was targeted for distribution over a ten-year period. Some 6.5 million of these were public, alienable and disposable lands and Integrated Forestry Areas to be distributed by the Department of Environment and Natural Resources. Only 3.8 million hectares of private agricultural lands and resettlement areas were to be distributed.

After almost four years of implementing the agrarian reform programme, the DAR claimed that it had distributed 1.9 million hectares as follows:

Public lands, Free Patent	497,300
Public lands, Integrated Social Forestry	416,200
Private lands	1,000,000
Total	1,900,000

Two points should be made here. First, the Integrated Social Forestry Programme and the Free Patent System, which the DAR claims as part of its agrarian reform programme, are in fact administered by the Department of Environment and Natural Resources for quite different purposes: in the ISF's case, supporting the private sector in the establishment of industrial tree plantations. Second, farmer beneficiaries cannot possibly have received 1,000,000 hectares of private lands. Jurisprudence requires that no title will actually pass to the state and eventually to the farmer beneficiary without full payment having first been made to the landowner. Yet the DAR has admitted that of all areas covered by Notices of Acquisition only 140,000 hectares were actually valued and paid. In addition, landowners have been able to escape redistributing land through a number of legal alternatives, including exemptions, exclusions, suspensions, deferments, stock distribution plans, and leaseback arrangements with farmer beneficiaries. Between 1987 and 1990, only 9,949 hectares of privately held land, or 4.6% of the target for the period, were distributed; this figure includes land covered by stock-distribution schemes (Putzel 1992a). Landowners have also been able to take advantage of the fact that valuation of holdings under the present law is a time-consuming process. The administration demonstrated insufficient political will to pursue its ambitious agrarian reform programme fully even on the president's own estate, Hacienda Luisita.

TENURE AND LAND CONFLICTS IN THE UPLANDS

Issues of land rights and deforestation intersect especially clearly in the uplands, which form more than three-fifths of the Philippines' territory. Forestry monitoring officials and academics estimate that altogether there are about 18 million upland dwellers, of which 6 to 8 million live within forest zones (EMB 1990: 69-85). The World Bank calculates that eight to ten million people farm upland areas (World Bank 1989c). The DENR puts the population on forest lands at about 5.95 million indigenous people and 2.55 million migrants. Non-governmental organizations meanwhile point to a study estimating that in 1980 the uplands were occupied by at least 14.4 million people, or 30% of the total population of the country (Cruz 1986).

Among indigenous peoples in the Cordillera, where much of the Philippines' remaining forest is located, the concept of *ancestral domain*, or territory under recognized occupation by an indigenous group "since time immemorial", is widely recognized.

Within ancestral domain there are typically three classes of land rights: communal, indigenous corporate, and individual. Communal land rights are exercised by all members of the community, and usually cover forest lands on which no improvements have been made. Indigenous corporate rights are exercised by families, clans, or "wards" (*ators*). These are lands on which some improvements have been made by an ancestor or predecessor, and which have been continuously used since. Family rights typically cover land on which considerable improvements have been made, such as rice terraces. In taking a legal approach to indigenous tenure, it would

278

PEOPLE'S DEMANDS AND ACTIONS

Peasant organizers and environmental activists alike argue that redistributive agrarian reform is essential both to stop the flow of landless lowlanders to the already crowded uplands and to provide security for peasants already there. Little unoccupied or unclaimed arable land is available by which redistributive reform could be avoided (Putzel 1992a: 80). Such redistributive reform, however, would have to be coupled with a recognition of indigenous cultural communities' claims to their ancestral homelands.

In the Philippines, there is no lack of participants in the debate on agrarian reform; landowners, the government, the insurgent New People's Army, peasant groups, minority organizations and academics have all formulated proposals. Land occupations, alliances of indigenous peoples against expropriation and destructive development projects, and underground armed movements have kept the issue constantly in the political spotlight.

One of the more active farmers' groups on the national scene is the Kilusang Magbubukid ng Pilipinas or KMP — the Peasant Movement of the Philippines — which was formed in the 1980s and claims a membership of over 750,000. The KMP's programme calls for free distribution of tenanted land to tillers, beginning with that controlled by Marcos cronies, and a moratorium on or reduction of land rent in areas where free land distribution cannot be immediately enforced. It also mandates the nationalization of agribusiness plantations controlled by TNCs, targeting especially large sugar and coconut holdings, whose redistribution could benefit 250,000 families. These, it suggests, can be transformed into co-operatives. Idle and public lands, including logging concessions suitable for agriculture, are to be distributed to individuals. KMP "believes that the government is incapable of implementing genuine land reform and it is up to the peasants to draft and implement it . . . the degree of implementation of land reform depends on how well peasants are organized" (IBON 1988; KMP 1986: 237). Seizure and occupation of abandoned lands, and negotiation with landlords for rent reduction have been accomplished successfully in some areas.

PAKISAMA, another farmers' organization, also calls for land to the tiller and says that land reform must cover all agricultural lands, regardless of crops planted. Rights are to be based on stewardship. Non-cultivators will not have the right to retain land.

The umbrella Congress for a People's Agrarian Reform emphasizes in addition the primacy of the right of all members of the agricultural labour force (there are more than 3 million seasonal workers on export plantations alone) to own and control the land, have full access to other natural resources, and gain full disposition over their produce. All arable public lands and idle lands are to be made available.

The last 20 years have also seen an increasingly organized mobilization of the indigenous peoples of the Philippines. Spurred into determined opposition by the invasion of their ancestral domains by loggers and hydropower projects during the Marcos era, indigenous communities have now built up formidable community associations, development organizations, "peace pacts" and regional groupings. Nationally the indigenous peoples' organizations have united as KAMP — the National Federation of Indigenous Filipinos.

KAMP's demands include a nationwide recognition of ancestral domains and the right to self-determination. KAMP argues that the formal and effective recognition of the right of indigenous peoples to manage their own affairs on their own lands is crucial to their demand for ancestral domain. It is *control* of their territories, not just ownership title, which they seek, as title by itself is meaningless so long as the expropriation of tribal lands in "the public interest" can always be invoked against the interests of minority groups.

KAMP and KMP have begun to work together to campaign for effective agrarian reform, recognizing that securing indigenous rights to ancestral domains requires a simultaneous resolution of the problems of peasant colonists forced into the uplands by landlessness and marginalization in the lowlands.

---

thus be inappropriate either simply to grant land titles to individuals (since according to indigenous systems much land is not owned by individuals) or simply to impose communal tenure (since very valuable land does tend to be individually owned).

Community boundaries have often been defined and settled in the course of competition with neighbouring communities over resource usage. These boundaries define the limits of a community's power to decide how land, water, minerals and the like would be allocated, used, or managed, and may have developed partly as a result of the evolution of permanent wet-rice terracing among Cordillera groups. All communities have systems constraining alienation of any type of land to outsiders (which makes citizenship rules in the community quite important). In general, more densely-populated areas have built up more developed notions of territorial boundaries than less-populated areas. For many groups leadership tended to reside in councils of elders. Some groups have established mechanisms for intervillage diplomacy. Among such groups, the concepts of land rights and ancestral domain are inseparable from the question of their societies' survival.

They are also inseparable from forest conservation. Traditional cultures have always been concerned with sustainability, and are not less able than others to adapt and evolve. Thus government and FAO officials' attacks on upland farmers as practising a uniformly destructive shifting agriculture are misplaced. Many minority groups practise long-established fixed-field agriculture even in steep valleys, with rice yields per hectare above the national average (ASS 1983: 96). In addition, as Harold Conklin observes, swidden farming in the Philippines comes in several varieties. Some swidden farming is undertaken merely to supplement crops grown in permanent fields. Some is undertaken by colonizers with little prior knowledge of swidden techniques who import perma-nent-field concepts of agricultural land-use to zones where they are inappropriate; this is the most destructive form of swidden. More traditional systems, usually practised by indigenous com-munities, include pioneer shifting cultivation (where significant portions of climax vegetation are customarily cleared each year), and established swidden farming (where tree crops are plentiful and relatively little or no climax vegetation is cleared annually). The latter type of farming uses a great deal of intercropping and multiple cropping (Conklin 1957: 3) and is increasingly recognized as being non-destructive to the environment. Not surprisingly, two of the more successful social forestry sites in the Philippines are inhabited by indigenous cultural communities. As elsewhere in the world, tribal peoples inhabit some of the best-preserved forests.

Shifting cultivators have long suffered from encroachment and been displaced by logging firms, plantations, and lowland farmers. State systems of land tenure have conflicted with indigenous systems in a way which has contributed to widespread deforesta-tion. This problem is rooted partly in the fact that the legal framework for the allocation and management of the public domain in the Philippines was patterned after US public land and resource laws, despite large differences in land endowments and habitation (Hayami et al. 1990: 42). The Public Land Act of 1905 declared as public all land unregistered under the 1902 Registration Act, making indigenous cultural communities squatters on their own land. The Mining Law of 1905 declared this land open for occupation and purchase by American miners. Then, in 1929 and after, huge areas of forested land inhabited by half a million Igorots was declared "inalienable" or parkland and was subsequently invaded by loggers and miners. Today, under the law, the Philippine government, through the Bureau of Forestry, claims ownership of all the uplands in the country, or more than 62% of the nation's total land area. Four-fifths of this land, located mainly in the mountainous interiors of the major islands, is officially classified as forestal and inalienable; yet most of this land is also claimed by communities of indigenous peoples. Only 15% of these public lands have been classed as agricultural, that is, as alienable and disposable; 5% remain unclassified.

This monopoly ownership by the government allowed much of the uplands, following the Second World War, to be leased to domestic logging companies — some owned by US corporations — under 25-year Timber License Agreements (TLAs) typically covering 40,000 to 60,000 hectares each. One concession alone — awarded in the 1970s to Cellophil Resources Corporation and its sister company, under the control of a Marcos crony — covered 1,973 square kilometres on the territory of five minority groups (ASS 1983: 75). These groups' status as illegal "squatters" was thereby confirmed and local pacts and demands to respect community forests, watersheds and pasturelands were ignored.

Forest conservation was regarded as the responsibility not of the companies but of the forest dwellers and farmers, who were blamed for the deforestation mainly caused by loggers (ASS 1983: 66). Presidential Decree 705 in 1975 made it possible to accuse occupants of public forest land who used forest products without license of "theft" and to strip them of traditional rights. Through this process, trees planted by the Ifugaos for conservation and

MIGRATION

Sometimes officially sponsored, sometimes not, migration of farmers into Philippine forests has accelerated rapidly during the 20th century. In 1903 the Public Lands act allowed distribution of up to 16 hectares of uncultivated public land to Filipinos, but provided no financial assistance. State-backed agricultural colonies began to be established in frontier areas of Mindanao and the Luzon Cordillera foothills as early as 1913. In 1933 colonies were set up in Cotabato province of Mindanao to defuse peasant unrest in Central Luzon (IBON 1988; Hayami 1990: 44). Land laws were promulgated to encourage the peasantry of the Visayas and Luzon dispossessed by land concentration and export plantations to acquire "public" land in Mindanao. Peasants were deliberately brought into conflict with the indigenous groups already living there. President Manuel Quezon (1935-42) attempted to quell agrarian unrest in densely-settled areas of the country by setting up a National Land Settlement Administration. Migration increased after large expenditures on roads and land surveys.

Subsequent attempts at planned colonization of forests include the establishment of the Land Settlement and Development Corporation in 1950 and the National Resettlement and Rehabilitation Administration in 1952. The Economic Development Corporation organized by the armed forces tried to settle former Hukbalahap rebels from Central Luzon to Mindanao in the 1950s. By 1977 the Department of Agrarian Reform was administering settlement schemes with an aggregate area of 7,358 square kilometres (Uhlig 1988: 27).

Between 1948 and 1970 roughly 1,562,000 people, mostly spontaneous migrants, arrived in Mindanao, and more in the 1970s. Sulu, Palawan, Mindoro, and Sabah in Malaysia are other important destinations. Tending to group themselves according to region of origin, migrants often set aside unofficial reserves of forested land for latecoming friends and relatives (Uhlig 1988). Those already living in colonized areas, if they do not resist or accommodate the newcomers with a division of land, are forced to flee to areas occupied by others or to take up plantation work.

"Providing land for the landless" has often provided a good ideological cover for efforts by élites to expand their landholdings and dilute and divide indigenous resistance. Without sufficient support from the government, peasant colonizers have often been unable to make ends meet and have been forced to move again, the land they had cleared then falling into the hands of landlords, bureaucrats, and American plantation companies and ranchers. Land speculators, meanwhile, have often used government policies or programmes encouraging colonization in order to gain land title from settlers who cannot prove ownership in court. This they then resell to plantation interests, who in turn use force to drive out the original occupants under the sanction of the law. Between 1974 and 1976, the Bukidnon Sugar Company used such methods in order to shift 230 square kilometres of Bukidnon land, most of which had previously supported local minority groups and settlers, to sugar production (ASS 1983: 51- 53). In their attempt to cool off peasant unrest in more densely-settled parts of the Philippines, resettlement schemes have also helped to ignite the Muslim separatist movement in colonized areas of Mindanao.

Military conflicts have in turn caused further dislocation and disruption of agricultural production, marginalizing still more peasants (Putzel 1992a). The burning and plundering of villages in the southern Philippines, including resettlement projects, has set, according to government estimates, as many as a million refugees on the move, with perhaps 60,000 casualties by the mid-1980s. Strategic hamleting has added to the problems, and forested areas are still sometimes cleared to deny sanctuary to those resisting the government (ASS 1983: 162; Putzel 1992a). Increased funding from international bodies has meanwhile given the government greater power to intervene in Luzon's Cordillera on behalf of miners, dammers, and other outside interests, making the area more militarized than ever.

---

against future use have become the property of the state and then of logging companies (ASS 1983: 73).

In 1988, 137 timber license agreements (TLAs) still covered 4.4 million hectares of forest land. Joint state-private ventures have since taken over a portion of these, reducing the number of privately-worked TLAs to 63 on 2.3 million hectares by 1990, but increased state involvement in the remainder is unlikely to have benefited local communities.

Reforms since the overthrow of Marcos have done little to resolve conflicts over land and forest rights in the uplands. Although a mandate for the protection of the rights of the eight million members of indigenous cultural communities to their ancestral lands was introduced at the national policy level — not for the first time — in Article 12, Section 5 of the 1987 Philippine constitution, implementation of this policy under the Aquino administration, in terms of law and jurisprudence, has failed. There is no clear governmental definition of ancestral domain. The Public Land Act, as amended by Republic Act No. 6940 (1990), does not recognize the private nature of lands held since time immemorial. The definition of ancestral domains found in the Organic Act of Mindanao is limited only to those places where the Act was ratified, while the Cordillera Autonomy law was rejected by the Cordilleras. No law provides for recognition, delineation and registration of ancestral domain rights or title to ancestral lands. For this reason, several development projects located in the heart of tribal lands, like the Mt. Apo geothermal plant project on Mindanao, are not legally contestable as violations of tribal rights to ancestral domains. This makes it more difficult for local communities to protect their natural heritage. Indigenous cultural communities remain objects to be displaced or relocated when development projects are set up within their domains. They are generally seen as human resources to carry out private or governmental commercial activities in these areas. Community consultations, if they occur at all, are half-hearted and carried out only for the purpose of getting pre-planned projects implemented, never for the purpose of modifying targets as a result of community feedback or for the purpose of opening projects to possible veto.

Resource management patterns of indigenous communities have also been given short shrift. In August 1989, the Philippine Strategy for Sustainable Development (PSSD), which had been initiated by the Department of Environment and Natural Resources (DENR) and refined by a process of national consultation, was adopted in a joint meeting of the Cabinet Assistance System and the Chapter on Rural Development. The PSSD is intended to integrate economic and tenurial concerns with adequate protection for biological resources, diversity, and vital ecosystem functions. People's participation and community-based forest management were seen as essential to PSSD initiatives. These include the Forestlot Management Agreement, the Community Forestry Programme, and a proposed shift from reforestation by administrative initiative to reforestation by private corporations, non-governmental organizations, local government units, communities, and individual families. In addition, bills were to be promoted banning logging in all provinces, establishing an Integrated

Protected Areas System, and recognizing and delineating ancestral lands of indigenous cultural communities (DENR 1989).

The majority of existing private natural resource users, however, are not parties to the DENR's schemes of natural resource utilization in the uplands. In contrast to the vast areas still covered by logging concessions, only some 260,843 hectares were targeted in 1992 for Social Forestry, to be distributed among 118,565 beneficiaries. That amounts to a concession of only 2.2 hectares per person, a figure which is inconsistent with the DENR's own Administrative Rules and Regulations which say that at least 7 hectares must be allocated per individual social forestry contractor. The Contract Reforestation scheme, according to a survey of the Upland NGOs Assistance Committee, involves few people in reforested areas and is riddled with technical and administrative difficulties. Since the contractors are mostly outsiders, there is little or even no local participation in the preparation of development plans, selection of species, seedling production and related activities in plantation establishment. Permits for gathering non-timber forest products have meanwhile largely been given to non-resident or migrant speculators in disregard of indigenous cultural communities who have long been on the land. Indigenous peoples' participation in government and foreign-assisted forestry programmes is marginal and solicited only for the purpose of lending projects cultural credibility.

Forest land use for 1987-1992 reflects a continuing bias in favour of production forestry. Approximately 60% of forest lands are allocated for activities such as timber production-sharing agreements, industrial tree plantations, tree farms, mangrove production-sharing and reforestation projects. Protection forests cover only 18.81% of forest lands, which include areas for reforestation projects, national parks, game refuge and bird sanctuaries, wilderness areas and watershed reserves. The remaining areas are set aside for various non-forest activities such as grazing, agroforestry, social forestry, military and naval use, civil use and fish ponds. Hunting and gathering, swidden farming and terrace agriculture have been made either illegal in themselves or illegal when conducted on public lands. No recognition has been given of prior rights or priority needs of local people.

The government, together with the United Nations Development Programme and other international organizations, is also actively encouraging mining in the uplands. Mining patents, mineral production-sharing agreements, and energy-related explorations are being pursued at the expense of the local peoples and the environment and in violation of the nation's sustainable development strategy. Large- and small-scale mining outside the indigenous framework is promoted by the government to compete with existing indigenous mining methods.

Since 1979, meanwhile, many watersheds have come under the control of the government power corporation. Dams threatening indigenous territory, streams and forests have provoked determined community resistance (ASS 1983: 113; Drucker 1986). Geothermal and coal-fired power plant developments undertaken to accommodate present and future energy requirements of the country have also encountered resistance, due to lack of consultation and information dissemination by government field personnel and staff.

Seeking to accelerate the "land for the landless" programme of the government, the DENR has adopted a land management policy involving lot and cadastral surveys. DAR issuances of emancipation patents and certificates of land ownership awards are made possible by DENR delineation surveys, many conducted outside the upland areas to which its jurisdiction is formally limited. Whereas DAR was reported to have issued 26,215 homestead patents covering 80,343 hectares from 1981-1987, DENR issued a total of 242,621 land patents nationwide, from 1987-1990. Yet in doing so it has failed to address the issue of ancestral domain delineation, survey and titling. Several tribal communities have indicated willingness to avail themselves of cadastral or any other kind of surveys in the Cordilleras, Agusan del Sur, Surigao, Bukidnon, Mindoro and Palawan, under any scheme protective of their domains. They remain unassisted by the government.

A total commercial logging ban, meanwhile, is still under consideration. In 1991, a promising intermediate and administratively viable step was taken when logging was banned in virgin forests, in residual forests with a slope of 50% or greater, in areas above 1,000 meters elevation, in areas within 20 meters of either side of stream or bank, in wilderness areas, proclaimed watershed reservations, in areas identified with historical value and in other areas proclaimed for ecological and environmental protection, effective 1 January 1992. A TLA-holder who does not undertake a timber inventory of logged-over areas automatically forfeits the right to continue logging operations within six months or one year. Then-DENR Secretary Fulgencio Factoran Jr. stated, however, that until Congress passed a total log ban law, he could not impose this partial ban. DENR announced in 1992 that it would issue temporary logging permits to TLA holders to enable them to work specific sites within their concession areas even without the mandatory inventory of residual and second-growth forest areas within which they are supposed to operate.

In addition, while a general logging ban is supposedly in force in part or all of seven regions of the country, and a moratorium in parts of three regions, no administrative regulation contains any specific information on the scope and implementation of this policy, and its implementation has been largely *ad hoc* and discretionary on the part of the Secretary of the Department of Environment and Natural Resources and the Forest Management Bureau. Illegal logging meanwhile continues "unabated and uncontrolled", according to a report on the state of the Philippine environment in the 1980s by the Environmental Management Bureau of the DENR. The DENR has insufficient facilities and field personnel to monitor either illegal logging or compliance with mandatory conditions like reforestation, thus gravely impairing its power to cancel existing licenses of TLA holders found violating them. Low forest-product prices only exacerbate the logging problem (EMB 1990: 87).

REFLECTIONS AND CONCLUSIONS

Control by the government of forestry resources contributes significantly to the process of deforestation. Yet neither a logging ban nor a recognition of the rights of indigenous people to control their own land will be sufficient to reverse this trend unless the issue of the Philippine economy is addressed as well. Development models which fail to be participatory make tropical deforestation possible — in some cases, even inevitable. Without the basic ingredient of a genuinely liberative development plan, the economic conditions that encourage logging as well as unsustainable types of swidden farming will remain. The many development plans relating to the forest — USAID's US$125 million for Natural Resource Management Planning; the Asian Development Bank's US$400 million in sustainable development loans; World Bank-backed programmes for National Parks and biodiversity conservation (which in reality will be used to repay old debts); the Philippine Forestry Master Plan — will be rendered pointless.

A holistic, viable and responsive upland resources utilization policy is critical at this point in Philippine history. This should take into account the concrete needs of the majority of the Filipino people. Statistical projections about development, particularly about industrialization, the stabilization of dollar reserves, and energy consumption and needs, must yield to local priorities and indicators. Respect, recognition and sensitivity to the prevailing culture of the communities found on the sites of energy projects will have to be a priority of government, if only to preserve the remaining indigenous knowledge of indigenous people, which is key to authentic and genuine sustainable development.

The failure of government-controlled programmes of agrarian reform in lowland areas plays a large part in skewing the current socio-economic structure and further endangers the forest stands that remain. Proper agrarian reform, taken as a political and not an economic issue, and based on the premise that there is enough land for everyone, is a key to any development model capable of challenging the dominant model.

Many types of such agrarian reform exist. There is no formula. It can be said, however, that:

- Agrarian reform is generally not something that comes from outside, but is a matter of recognizing existing initiatives, which may be very diverse.

- Agrarian reform need not be imposed by the state, which sometimes need only recognize rights endogenously generated: for example, indigenous ancestral domain.

- Agrarian reform means rural transformation. Titling is necessary and redistributed lands must be reasonably valued. Land must go to the tiller, but support services are also needed.

PART THREE:

CONCLUSION

THE INTERNATIONAL RESPONSE: POLICIES OF THE INTERNATIONAL AGENCIES

MARCUS COLCHESTER

Dominant development strategies have, of course, emphasized rapid economic growth and modernization. In societies where the control of wealth and income is highly unequal, this almost inevitably results in greater polarization and growing rural landlessness and poverty.

Solon Barraclough 1991:102

Poverty reduction initiatives must often operate in socio-political environments that are structured to perpetuate the established order, and by implication to preserve patterns of distribution of wealth and power . . . Unless project design incorporates specific measures for ensuring representation of all socio-economic groups at the local community level, they may serve to reinforce or worsen existing inequalities in rural communities.

World Bank 1991c:10

International development agencies continue to provide a significant proportion of the finances used by Third World countries for rural development. This source of revenue is likely to increase in the present climate of concern about the environment. Yet, historically, the development agencies have long fought shy of the kind of "bottom-up" approach which the previous chapters have argued is both intrinsic to "sustainability" and crucial for successful land reform.

Concepts of development have seen a progressive shift over the past forty years. In 1950s and 1960s, the heyday of centrally-planned development, the new multilateral development banks led the way in imposing top-down prescriptions on Third World economies. Roads, dams, mines and agribusinesses were assumed to provide a sure route to peace and prosperity.

The Cuban revolution forced a rethink of this simple strategy, as it was recognized that wealth generation without redistribution actually increased poverty and social unrest. In Latin America the new resolve to make development more sensitive to the needs of the poor gave birth to the rhetoric of the "Alliance for Progress" (Pearce 1986), while internationally it was expressed right through the 1970s — the MacNamara years at the World Bank — in an emphasis on "poverty-focused lending" and "redistribution with growth". As part of a strategy that has been described as one of "defensive modernization" (Ayres 1983: 227), the Bank adopted a policy of promoting land reform in Third World countries (World Bank 1975). Even forestry lending was revised to have a social welfare focus (World Bank 1978).

For all this, the top-down approach remained essentially unchanged and the result was an overall failure of development assistance to alleviate poverty. As a World Bank review recently admitted: "The principles guiding beneficiary participation in Bank-financed projects have been quite abstract and of limited operational impact. Beneficiaries were not assigned a role in the decision-making process, nor was their technological knowledge sought prior to designing project components." (World Bank 1988 cited in Hancock 1989:126)

In the 1980s, the emphasis shifted yet again. Programmes aimed at poverty alleviation, it was widely noted, were not working. For development really to benefit the poor and marginalized, it had to be made culturally sensitive (World Bank 1982a, b; Chambers 1983; Mair 1984; Cernea 1985; Hughes and Thirlwall 1988).

Development policy also came under two conflicting new pressures during the 1980s. On the one hand, the rise of governments with monetarist policies, simultaneous with a massive rise in interest rates, put poverty-focused lending onto the back burner (El-Ghonemy 1990), while, at the same time, the development community came under heavy attack for the environmental ruin caused by its projects and policies.

The evidence for the environmental destructiveness of conventional development programmes has been overwhelming and the development agencies have been obliged to grope for new ways of making development environmentally sensitive and "sustainable". One attempt to achieve this end has been to "internalize" environmental costs and benefits into project accounting (Warford 1987; Pearce et al 1989). However, as Bank officials admit, some "externalities", notably social, cultural and political considerations, are "intangible" and cannot be accommodated by number-crunching development planners.

This book has argued for a quite different approach. If agrarian reform is to benefit the poor, meet their needs, nurture their cultures and accommodate itself to their external political, economic and environmental circumstances, it must be under their control. Only if the natural resources that these communities depend on are controlled by them can they be expected to commit their initiative, labour and financial resources to their prudent management. Only if local communities have a decisive voice in their use is sustainability achievable.

These are not new principles. On the contrary, rural communities have been managing their resources for millennia. The challenge today is to reassert these values and to show that, far from being backward and irrational, the principles for which rural peoples are struggling are the very ones to which advocates of "sustainable development" should be paying attention.

Alan Durning has argued that, if, in the future, development is to be made sustainable, "international development agencies might look on their role broadly as building the groundwork for grass-roots-government partnerships" (Durning 1989b:53). Many others have argued that the North should impose more rigorous conditions on its financial flows to the South as a means of creating such political space for local peoples (George 1989; Tomasevski 1989).

However, as this book has clearly revealed, the political obstacles to achieving such a transformation of development relationships are formidable. As Susan George notes (1989), and as this study has persistently highlighted, some of the main barriers to a socially just and sustainable development process inhere in the social orders of Third World countries themselves. Institutionalized injustice, land and wealth concentration, patronage and "cronyism", censorship and repression, are the main enemies of sustainability and these are now as deeply embedded in the social orders of the Third World countries as they are entrenched in their relations between them and the industrial North (Colchester 1989c).

To date international development assistance has done more to shore up these forces than challenge their hegemony; and this should be no surprise, for Western economies remain heavily dependent on the cheap resources that the Third World provides. The North is unlikely to give up easily the advantage in trade relations that it currently enjoys thanks to the collaboration of Third World élites, much less use the conditionality of its aid to undermine their control of natural resources. Nothing makes this clearer than the way the development agencies have dealt with the issue of agrarian reform.

AGRARIAN REFORM AT THE UNITED NATIONS

Among the family of United Nations agencies charged with promoting development, that entrusted by mutual agreement with the lead role in promoting agrarian reform has been the Food and Agriculture Organization (Christodoulou 1990:180). Yet the FAO, despite long ago promising to devote its energies to agrarian reform, has since done nothing effective to achieve it. On the contrary, the main activities of the FAO have directly promoted the development of cash cropping and chemical farming systems which have undermined rural livelihoods and increased the disparities of wealth between rich and poor (Griffin 1979).

In 1979, the FAO convened a massive World Conference — with delegates from 145 countries, including four heads of government — on the subject of Agrarian Reform and Rural Development (WCARRD). Recognizing that two decades of development had failed to benefit the rural poor and that "trickle down" had not worked, the conference expressed an international commitment to "growth with equity" and formally endorsed what it called the "Peasants' Charter".

According to this document, agrarian reform was an essential component of development for many developing countries. "The rural poor must be given access to land and water resources," Edouard Saouma observed in an introduction to the report of the conference (FAO 1981:iii). "Agrarian Reform", according to the Charter, "is a critical component of rural development and the sustained improvement of rural areas" (FAO 1981:1).

The Charter strongly emphasized the need for popular participation in development. According to the Charter, "participation by the people in the institutions and systems which govern their lives is a basic human right, and also essential for realignment of political power in favour of disadvantaged groups and for social and economic development" (FAO 1981:13). According to the Charter, rural development strategies could not achieve their full potential without such participation "through the motivation, active involvement and organization, at the grassroots level, of rural people" (FAO 1981:13). This would require respecting the right of free association and recognition of the rural peoples' own organizations (FAO 1981:13).

Participation, the FAO agrarian reform programme later added, included among other things increasing the access of rural poor to productive assets and taking part in decision-making through organizations of their own choice (FAO 1981:2).

The Charter noted that programmes to alleviate landlessness and rural poverty should include a "substantial reorganization of land tenure and land redistribution to landless peasants and smallholders" (FAO 1981:10). It called for increased security of tenure for the rural poor, "broad-based community control and management of land and water rights" and programmes to "ensure the conservation and management of fishery and forestry resources through arrangements involving local communities" (FAO 1981:11-12).

The Charter was explicit that frontier settlement schemes should only be undertaken where environmentally appropriate and "should be supplemental to, not substitutes for, agrarian reforms necessary in already settled areas" (FAO 1981:12).

Agrarian reform should be undertaken by setting ceilings for landholdings to ensure an "equitable distribution and efficient use of land, water and other productive assets, with due regard for ecological balance and environmental protection", while measures should be set in place to prevent the reconcentration of land and the evasion of ceilings through land transfer (FAO 1981:3,10).

The bold programme was welcomed by many non-governmental organizations while others were sceptical of the intent behind the rhetoric (Whittemore 1981). It is still held up by the FAO as the "main mandate for FAO for its development activities" (FAO 1988:ii).

Ten years on the FAO carried out a commendably candid evaluation of the progress made towards achieving the goals set out in the Charter and agreed to by the 145 governments that attended the conference. The conclusions of the study make dismal reading. According to the FAO, the programme has, overall, failed to reach its goals. Targets for land reform may have been set in some countries but they have not been achieved. Target groups may have been identified but action has not reached them. Investment in agriculture continues to be a tiny part of national budgets.

There has been no evidence of effective agrarian reform. "In practice very few governments adopted any significant programmes for agrarian reform during this period," the study noted (FAO 1988:3). The result was a general decline in land availability per capita. Large inequalities in land holding remained, while small and marginal holdings had increased. Landlessness had increased massively (and *see* FAO 1984).

In general there had been a fall in the availability of credit to the rural sector. Irrigation and fertilizers, where provided, had tended to be given more to the richer farmers. Meanwhile real farm prices were falling, as export crop prices fell and terms of trade declined. There was little sign of any increase in foreign assistance to the sector, while private capital investment had declined rapidly. As a result of all these factors, malnutrition levels remained as high as ever, with the exception of Africa, where the situation was much worse.

Only three aspects showed any sign of improvement. Literacy had progressed world-wide, there had been slow progress in health and popular participation and an awareness of women's needs had made some ground, notably in the promotion of community forestry where programmes had sought direct participation in forest management and use.

The report concluded that "mounting pressure on scarce resources, combined with inappropriate policies and institutions, has already brought about an increase in 'natural disasters', in which the poor have been the main victims" (FAO 1988:4).

The FAO's reaction to this generally frank appraisal is what is perhaps most shocking. Instead of calling for a serious re-evaluation of the way it and the other development agencies have gone about promoting rural development, it has restricted itself to pious and vacuous exhortations. "Agrarian reform and rural development", the FAO noted, "cannot be achieved without making concerted efforts needing continuous action at various levels. They require professional competence, political commitment and the willing cooperation of all concerned: beneficiaries, governments and international agencies." (FAO 1988:ii)

What was obvious to observers, however, and was made so startlingly clear by the FAO's report, was that the development process was failing to promote the needed changes in land ownership patterns because the rural development process was not open and accountable. Participation, so strongly urged by the FAO, was not structured into the WCARRD programme itself. On the contrary, despite all the rhetoric, development assistance programmes remained the preserve of donor and borrower governments, freed from real scrutiny by so-called beneficiaries in whose name it was all being carried out. Even the FAO's WCARRD programme suffered from being marginalized within the FAO, unable to influence the wider activities of the organization, let alone the wider development community. Moreover, despite the dismal conclusions that the FAO had to draw about the effectiveness of the whole WCARRD programme, the rest of the development community maintained a grave silence. The result, inevitably, was business as usual at the FAO, with only the muted protests of academics and development research agencies suggesting that anything untoward was actually going on.

Riad El-Ghonemy (1990:3), ex-Deputy Director of the FAO's Human Resources Division, concludes:

> Land reform as a policy issue has virtually disappeared as a fundamental development issue in international debate in the United Nations forums, only to be replaced by ambiguous integrated rural development programmes and environmental concerns which avoid landed property distribution issues.

In sum, land reform, once seen as the central issue for the UN development agencies, has been dodged. Development in the name of the people but in the interests of the rich has successfully taken over the UN development agencies' agenda.

THE WORLD BANK

As the world's single largest development financing agency, currently lending some US$28 billion per annum, the World Bank has played a major role in the transformation of Third World agriculture since the 1950s. Initially oriented towards the "modernization" of Third World farming to increase "efficiency", overall production, exports and foreign exchange generation, the World Bank moved slowly to incorporate concerns for poverty alleviation, customary tenure, cultural considerations and the environment into its agricultural lending portfolio.

The Bank has thus lent heavily to promote cash crop agriculture for export, and continues to do so. By providing funding for agricultural credit schemes, the Bank has skewed the advantages of its lending programmes towards the already rich (World Bank 1991c:19), inadvertently but inevitably promoting rising land prices, land speculation and land concentration, while at the same time displacing farm workers and peasants from the countryside.

World Bank finance for large dams and irrigation programmes has favoured capital- and technology-intensive farming systems which, far from proving "scale neutral", have benefited rich farmers and urban investors at the expense of the poor (e.g. World Bank 1987).

However, during the MacNamara years and under the influence of the Alliance for Progress, Bank documents began giving increasing attention to the plight of small farmers and the landless poor. In 1975, the World Bank came out with a little-noticed policy statement which accepted that land reform was consistent with the Bank's objectives of "increasing output, improving income distribution and expanding employment" and concluded that "the Bank group should support reforms that are consistent with these goals" (cited in El-Ghonemy 1991: 138, n.14). The Bank even went so far as to state that "in countries where increased productivity can effectively be achieved only subsequent to land reform, the Bank will not support projects which do not include land reform." (cited in El-Ghonemy 1991:60)

However, the self-imposed limits on this commitment to land reform have been very great. In the first place the Bank, and its sister organization the IMF, will not support countries which expropriate private property for redistribution to the poor, arguing that this is against the Bank's founding charter. The threat of losing favour with the Bank and the Fund has acted as a powerful disincentive to African governments, in particular, that have contemplated the expropriation of European farms at independence.

What the Bank's articles of agreement actually state is that the Bank's resources are to support the creation or improvement of productive assets and not the transfer of existing assets. "Thus Bank financing of land improvement (including cadastral surveys and registration of title) that enhance land security — but not the acquisition of land — is permissible." (World Bank 1991d:11)

So, even where land redistribution is to be achieved through the buying out of large landowners, the Bank will not provide direct financial assistance. Bank staff give various additional reasons for this. The first is that the efficiency gains that result from investment in land redistribution are not considered adequate to allow effective cost recovery. The Bank argues that if small farmers are expected to repay the costs of compensating large farmers for their loss they will be plunged into unrepayable debts. The newly established smallholdings cannot generate an adequate income to fund start-up costs and overheads, and pay back interest and principal, at the same time as providing a livelihood to the small-holder family (Binswanger and Elgin 1991). In other words, land redistribution achieved through compensation requires grants, not loans. These grants are best raised, the Bank argues, from the government's own revenues since there is no need for foreign exchange and since this ensures that the government has a real policy commitment to redistribution, not an artificial one stimulated by external financing.

It is important to understand that the principal commitment of the Bank is to improved "efficiency" and production, with poverty-alleviation or livelihood issues getting secondary consideration. Thus, for example, where the economies of scale of export crops favour large land holdings, Bank staff tend to reject redistribution options, apparently ignoring the possibility that smallholders might make quite different crop choices that favour food security rather than the generation of foreign exchange (Binswanger and Elgin 1991:745).

In fact, as Christodoulou has noted, the Bank has supported very few initiatives that assist genuine agrarian reform. Some that it did, such as the Malawi Lilongue Project, were actually programmes that took over and commoditized customary rights areas for the benefit of civil servants and urban dwellers (Christodoulou 1990:190). Such projects have been part of a long-term strategy within the Bank to stimulate the creation of markets in land and overcome what are seen by the Bank as cultural obstacles to the effective mobilization of land for development. Thus, for example, in Papua New Guinea, the Bank has lent money both to accelerate the registration of alienated lands and to loosen up tribal land holdings. To get around the cultural impossibility of tribes relinquishing their communally-owned lands, the Bank has stimulated "lease-lease-back" arrangements by which tribal owners lease customary lands to the government which then leases them back to land developers. The developers, often members of the tribal élite, can then use this "leased-back" land as credit for land development schemes (World Bank 1988). Growing income disparities and migration to the cities are part of this process, although actual landlessness is not a widespread problem in Papua New Guinea (Good 1986).

Similar programmes to break up and commoditize tribal land holdings for ranching schemes have been carried out in Africa under a large number of the Bank's livestock projects. The results have been an increasing concentration of land and wealth among tribal élites and politicians, the overstocking of land leading to environmental decline, the fencing off of areas with a devastating impact on wild game, and the displacement or marginalization of hunting and gathering groups (Davis 1992; Mikesell and Williams 1992: 181-184; World Bank 1992:20).

At the same time, also ostensibly to promote agricultural development among poor farmers, the Bank has supported numerous forest colonization schemes. The most notorious of these have been the Polonoroeste scheme in Brazil and the transmigration programme in Indonesia (Rich 1985; Colchester 1986c). Both have substituted *in situ* agrarian reforms with programmes to move "surplus people" onto tribal lands on the tropical forest frontiers. The Bank now admits that these programmes have had serious ecological and social impacts and claims to have learned lessons from them (Conable 1987; World Bank 1992:14). In fact, however, the Bank continues to promote frontier colonization in Brazil (Feeney 1992).

Most observers agree that the Bank's belated commitment to support land reform waned to insignificance by the early 1980s, despite the fact that the conditions of the rural poor and particularly the landless had worsened over the intervening years (Christodoulou 1990; El-Ghonemy 1991:61). On the contrary, the emphasis of the Bank shifted increasingly towards reliance on market forces and monetarist principles and away from all kinds of state-directed interventions — this, despite the fact that the Bank's own policy on land reform had admitted that rural development without land reform could not reach its full potential and might even adversely affect the poor. Indeed, as El-Ghonemy has noted, where the distribution of land ownership and opportunities is highly skewed, the market works for the benefit of traders, large and medium farmers and multinational corporations, whilst harming the poor peasants and the landless workers (El-Ghonemy 1991:61). This shift in emphasis corresponded to the Bank's increasing involvement in policy-based adjustment lending, which overshadowed the Bank's focus on poverty (World Bank 1991d:1).

Just how far the Bank could go in ignoring the issue of agrarian reform was signalled by its World Development Report of 1990, titled "POVERTY", in which there was a complete absence of any discussion of land tenure issues (World Bank 1990). Disturbingly, this approach threatens to be "operationalized", to use the Bank's jargon. The policies outlined in the report have now been transformed into a new Operational Directive, OD 4.15, which makes no commitment to support structural reforms in land ownership and virtually ignores land tenure questions (World Bank 1991d). The policy of "redistribution with growth" — the Bank's slogan of the 1970s — seems to have been forgotten. The Bank appears to have reverted to a trickle-down model emphasising that "poverty reduction, in the first instance, depends on sustained economic growth" (World Bank 1991d:3).

SIGNS OF CHANGE ?

The apparent shift in Bank policy away from a concern with distributional issues is especially ironic considering the increasing attention paid by the Bank to the connections between poverty and environmental degradation. When, in 1987, the Bank finally admitted that previous Bank projects had been costly environmental mistakes and promised a major reform in its lending policies in the future, it also clearly identified that individual and collective land ownership "improves conservation practice by stabilizing the use of resources and thus promoting sustainable methods of land use" (Warford 1987).

It has thus been disappointing to note that the new Environment Department of the Bank has moved very slowly to articulate a policy regarding land tenure issues (World Bank 1990b; 1991a). Steps in the right direction have, however, gradually become apparent. Notable has been the Bank's re-evaluation of the notion of the commons and a growing appreciation that communal tenure, far from being either an obstacle to productivity or a formula for open access and land degradation, may make a good deal of economic and environmental sense (Bromley and Cernea 1989; Cernea 1989).

In particular, studies by Bank staff of customary tenure in sub-Saharan Africa have revealed that these systems are dynamic and flexible, astutely balancing demands for increases in productivity with long-term concerns and the welfare of less well-off members of the community, thus effectively cushioning farmers against poverty (Migot-Adholla et al 1991; Blarel et al 1992; Place and Hazell 1992).

Summarizing these studies in its 1992 *World Development Report* , the Bank noted:

> Landownership in Sub-Saharan Africa traditionally resides with the community, but farmers are assigned rights to use specific parcels. These rights give sufficient security for growing crops and, where bequeathed to children, foster a long-term interest in land management. Farmers may have limited rights to transfer land they use to others without permission from family or village elders, and other people may have supplementary use rights over the same land — to graze the land during the dry season or to collect fruit or wood. Such restrictions, however, do not appear as yet to have had a significant effect on investments in land improvements or on land productivity. Moreover, as population growth and commercialization make land scarce and increasingly valuable, land is increasingly privatized. The indigenous systems of communal tenure appear flexible enough to evolve with the increasing scarcity of land and the commensurate need for greater security of land rights. At the same time, the retention of some community control over landownership helps to prevent the emergence of landlessness. (World Bank 1992b:144)

Some powerful policy recommendations are emerging from the Bank's rethinking of land tenure issues. The Bank now advocates "that Governments guarantee security of land tenure" (World

Bank 1992b:143) by "giving poor farmers rights on the land they farm" (World Bank 1992b:1) and "formalizing community rights" (World Bank 1992b:12). It argues that, while recognizing that communal systems may break down under pressure from the market and population increase, the "strengthening of existing institutions should be the first line of action" (World Bank 1992b:20). "A compelling reason", the Bank notes, "for supporting community resource management is its importance for the poor" (World Bank 1992b:142). "Governments need to recognize that smaller organizational units, such as villages or pastoral associations, are better equipped to manage their own resources than are large authorities and may be a more effective basis for rural development and rational resource management than institutions imposed from the outside." (World Bank 1992b:143)

The Bank may even be moving back towards a realization that redistributional reforms are necessary if the exigencies of environment are to be taken into account and "development" made "sustainable". The Bank now notes that "stopping environmental damage often involves taking rights away from people who may be politically powerful" (World Bank 1992b:14), and since "industrialists, farmers, loggers and fishermen fiercely defend their rights to pollute and exploit resources" (World Bank 1992b:14), "governments need to build constituencies for change to curb the power of vested interests (and) to hold institutions accountable . . ." (World Bank 1992b:3). "Sound environmental policies", the Bank notes, "are likely to be powerfully redistributive" (World Bank 1992b:2).

The omens are mixed on whether this rhetoric is directed only at others or whether it will apply to the Bank's own development programmes for the future. The Bank's Annual Sector Review for Agriculture and Rural Development for 1991 makes only one mention of land tenure issues. The report scrutinizes the year's project reports for evidence of a concern for poverty alleviation, noting that the "requirement is simple: a project or program claiming to help the poor should say who the poor are — and how they are to be helped". Only a few projects measured up to even this simple task, leaving the reviewers to conclude that "all that can be said about the year's agriculture sector projects is that . . . their potential impact on the poor remains unclear" (World Bank 1991c:13).

Other evidence is a little more encouraging. If the Bank is not actively adopting projects aimed at restructuring agricultural property relations, it is at least involved, principally through its sector loans, in attempts to secure gains made under previous partial agrarian reforms. In Honduras, Costa Rica and Nicaragua, for example, Bank loans include in their objectives efforts to secure the tenure of, and provide services to, those who have recently acquired lands through reforms — principally by streamlining land titling and registration. However, the assistance has a cost — which many may feel is unacceptably high: while the gains of past reforms are consolidated, further reforms are being suspended.

At the same time, the Bank is also moving to correct the policy environment which favours large farms. In Brazil, in particular, spurred by the international outcry about forest destruction in Amazonia, the Bank was active in identifying the fiscal, legislative and economic policy incentives that have promoted the expansion of large ranches in Amazonia (World Bank 1987; Mahar 1989; Binswanger 1991). It has actively pressurized Brazil to cancel these incentives, so far with only limited success (and see Monbiot, this volume).

A number of more progressive policy changes are beginning to find their way into internal Bank documents and thus have at least a chance of being translated into practice. A draft policy paper circulating within the Bank as we go to press, which outlines the Bank's future agricultural strategy (World Bank 1992b), advocates, inter alia, securing communal tenure, land titling and the removal of the tax and policy incentives which favour large farms. The Bank's emphasis is placed on support for small and medium-scale farms. However, land concentration and landlessness are not highlighted as problems to be addressed and the Bank steers clear of suggesting that it should support, either directly or through sectoral lending, national programmes of agrarian reform (World Bank 1992a).

CONCLUSIONS

Agrarian reform has been in and out of fashion with the development agencies for forty years. The rhetoric of the World Bank today is disturbingly reminiscent of the rhetoric of the FAO in the 1970s. The reality, however, is that the development agencies, working with the political grain, have been unable or unwilling to challenge the power of those who control Third World agriculture. They have thus been unable to transform the rural economies of the Third World into more equitable and stable patterns of resource use and management. They have failed, even though they know that such transformations are structurally necessary for effective poverty relief and for environmentally sound development.

There are many who would anyway be sceptical of the value of international agencies directly promoting or funding agrarian reforms in the Third World. Given these organizations' track record, the fact they work in a very top-down manner through government agencies and are rarely able to work effectively with grassroots movements, the possibilities of their really effecting change in agrarian structures seems remote. Better, some may feel, that they stay out of it.

Yet if, as it seems, it is unreasonable or even unwise to expect the international agencies to involve themselves directly in promoting effective agrarian change, still there is much they could do to create a policy climate that favours such change. At the least, we could ask that detailed evaluations, preferably by independent agencies, are made of their past projects and technical assistance programmes to discover to what extent and by what means their interventions have in fact accelerated land concentration and destabilized rural livelihoods.

Future lending should be radically revised to take account of these findings and more earnest efforts made to transform the policy climates in Third World countries so that they are more "scale-neutral".

THE WORLD BANK AND THE SÃO FRANCISCO VALLEY

Brazil's North-East has been an area of intensive agricultural development since the seventeenth century. Initially supplied with Indian slave labour from the Amazon and then black slaves from Africa, the region has long experienced cycles of boom and bust, owing to the vagaries in the international trade in tropical crops. The São Francisco Valley lies in the centre of this region.

By the time of the World Bank's early interventions in the 1950s, the valley had over the centuries developed the patterns of land and wealth concentration typical for much of Brazil. Large estates and plantations dominated the political economy, leaving the vast majority of the population — employed as sharecroppers, tenants, squatters and labourers — in extreme poverty.

Initial attempts to "develop" the waters of the São Francisco river focused on hydroelectricity generation. Several dams were constructed to provide power to local industrial centres. In 1974, the World Bank provided further financing for the Paulo Alfonso IV dam, which caused the displacement of some 70,000 people by the Sobradinho reservoir.

These people have fared badly. A colonization scheme meant to absorb half those resettled 1,000 kilometres into the interior failed and was subsequently abandoned by most of the settlers. The others, resettled on the lakeside, have not prospered. Many settlers have left the area, some selling their land to larger commercial farms, thus contributing to the concentration of rural holdings.

The Paulo Alfonso IV dam provided for a dramatic expansion of capital-intensive irrigated agriculture geared towards higher-value commercial and export crops, with associated agro-industrial processing enterprises and sophisticated transport and communications networks. This has resulted in a transformation in land tenure and land use. Small-scale subsistence agriculture has been largely replaced by more capitalized and commercially-oriented larger farmers. Out-migration from the rural areas has been matched by rising urban squalor and spreading shanty towns.

The dam also caused changes in the river flow, which necessitated further emergency interventions by the World Bank to regulate downstream flooding. Dykes and polders were created allowing the redistribution of land to some 4,600 small farmers. But the disruptions to agriculture in the lower river in the late 1970s, due to extensive flooding on the one hand and the rapid expansion of sugar cane plantations on the other, caused the dislocation of some 50,000 rural dwellers and the net displacement of as many as 30,000 people. No attempts were made to resettle those affected, leading to massive out-migration.

Environmental problems have also surfaced. Inadequate drainage and increased salinity have resulted in low cropping intensities and highly variable farmer income. Farmer indebtedness has led to the abandonment of land. At the same time, the trapping of sediments by the dams has resulted in reduced soil fertility in the lower valley, necessitating increased application of chemical fertilizers. Rice monocropping is increasing the risk of pest infestations and allegedy encouraging the excessive use of agrotoxic chemicals.

In 1985, the Bank made a substantial loan to the Brazilian Power Sector, thereby indirectly supporting the development of the Itaparica dam on the same river. To ameliorate the impact of the dam, the Bank made two additional loans, one of US$132 million to assist in the resettlement of some 40,000 people and another of US$100 million for irrigation works and agricultural development.

Further problems have ensued for those resettled. Despite an estimated cost of US$63,000 per family, there have been extensive delays in implementing the resettlement plan. Incidents of intra-communal violence, alcohol abuse, family disintegration and low morale have occurred as a consequence of a growing climate of uncertainty and frustration.

Source: *World Bank Approaches to the Environment in Brazil: a Review of Selected Projects* (Five Volumes), 1992. Volume 1: *Overview.* Operations Evaluation Department, Report Number 10039, World Bank, Washington DC: 16-22.

FUTURE OPTIONS: PUSHING ON A PIECE OF STRING?

MARCUS COLCHESTER

> Those from the outside who would advocate the peasant would do
> better to help him acquire economic and political strength than to
> encourage a land reform of a benefactor's making.
> *John P. Powelson and Richard Stock (1990)*

The need for structural changes in Third World agriculture is
acute. Denied alternative lands and livelihoods, impoverished
people are moving into the tropical forests in increasing numbers.
Massive and accelerating deforestation is the inevitable result.
This process can only be reversed by broad-based agrarian reforms
which make it easier for the poor to secure lands and defend their
livelihoods in the areas they are presently fleeing.

Advocates of agrarian reforms have long argued their case in
terms of poverty relief, social justice, human rights, national
security, economic productivity and the strengthening of democracy. This book has added another dimension to the argument, by
showing that agrarian reforms and the safeguarding of rural
livelihoods are essential to the survival of forests.

Present agricultural development initiatives directed by the UN
agencies and multilateral development banks are not providing
peasants with viable alternatives. On the contrary, the agencies
have not only avoided promoting structural reforms, they have
promoted the very processes that have worsened the lot of the very
poor, increasing landlessness and insecurity by promoting the
rapid modernization and industrialization of agriculture and other
sectors. They have often, at considerable expense, provided funds
for the colonization of marginal ecosystems, to the long-term loss
of all.

For their part, the voluntary development agencies have been calling for structural reforms in Third World agriculture for more than twenty years, having learned through painful experience that assistance programmes directed merely at increasing food production have not relieved poverty. This is because they do not address themselves to the root causes of impoverishment and, in so doing, have not only failed to solve the problems of the poor but, in the end, have only served to shore up the very mechanisms which perpetuate poverty (Whittemore 1981).

The need for structural change in Third World agrarian systems has been readily admitted by bodies as diverse as the Vatican, the World Bank, the FAO and blue-chip think-tanks in Washington, DC. Such bodies even admit, albeit in muted tones, that agrarian reform is crucial to saving the tropical forests. Thirteen years ago, no less than 145 government members of the United Nations committed themselves to agrarian reform as an integral part of rural development.

Above all, the call for such reforms comes from the rural poor themselves. Right across the tropics, and despite vastly different cultural backgrounds and political circumstances, popular movements have been pushing for change — for rights to land and the means to take control of their lives.

PATTERNS AND PROCESSES

In discussing the possibilities for change, it is important at the outset to recognize the very wide range of situations confronted by the rural poor. This book has purposefully focused on a very wide variety of national situations to show up this diversity.

The case of Guatemala presents, in a somewhat extreme form, problems prevalent throughout Latin America. An almost feudal landowning élite has retained its grip on power in collusion with the military and with the assistance of foreign companies and US interventions. An export-orientated agricultural development model which favours large mechanized farms has further limited peasant opportunities for development. Attempts by the desperately impoverished peasantry to seek change have been met with cruel violence. Massive deforestation has been the inexorable result. Reviewing the failure, so far, of popular movements to secure agrarian reforms, Rupert Scofield concludes that Guatemala "is virtually guaranteed another major social upheaval in the decades to come" (Scofield 1990:173).

In many ways, the Guatemalan situation is not very different from those in El Salvador, Honduras and Panama. Although all these countries have undertaken limited land reforms, the basic disparities in wealth and power remain little changed. In El Salvador, the skewed land distribution and rising populations have meant the virtual elimination of natural forests and it is now doubtful if adequate lands exist to meet the needs of the landless (Pearce 1986; Leonard 1987).

In Honduras, strong pressure from peasant movements has obliged the government to undertake limited reforms and legalize peasant land occupations (Alvarado 1987). If this pressure is sustained, it seems inevitable that the government will have to take action to redistribute the lands presently occupied by large cattle ranches (Scofield 1990).

In Panama, the same problem of giant cattle ranches remains unaddressed (Leonard 1987). The presently forested lands of the Embera and Kuna Indians in the Darien isthmus are under increasing pressure from landless settlers and ranchers, migrating south from the northern provinces of Panama.

Even in Costa Rica, once unique in Central America for its relatively equitable distribution of lands, problems of landlessness and land concentration are growing worse, exacerbated by mechanization. Land occupations and rural violence have increased markedly, while at the same time there has been an encouraging mobilization of small farmers and landless labourers who are pushing, through parliamentary and non-governmental channels, for broad agrarian transformations.

The pattern of land concentration, resistance and repression in the Philippines is startlingly similar to that in Latin America, almost surely a reflection of the agrarian and political structures that took root under Spanish and US colonial rule. Imposed legal notions from Europe have been substituted for traditional systems of land ownership, control and management, thereby undermining not only practical traditions of land use but also the delicate balance of power between community leaders and those who work the land. The new legal structures were set in place because they favoured the interests of a landowning élite that took over large areas of land for export. This export-orientated agricultural model has deepened over the centuries, with the result that landlessness and migration to the forested frontiers have become critical problems. Land reform has been a central political issue from well before independence, but despite agreements about the need for reform and strong pressure from peasant movements, attempts to redistribute land more fairly and to secure the lands of upland indigenous groups have been strongly resisted by the land-owning élite who remain a major group in Philippine politics.

At this level of generality, the Brazilian example also shows a surprisingly similar pattern. While land reform laws have been promulgated, the political will to institute them has been absent, as the higher echelons of government are dominated by landowners. Far from effecting reform, the policies pursued by the landowning élite and the state have favoured cash-cropping on large mechanized farms, increasing land concentration throughout the country. Subsidized rural credit and tax relief has favoured, in particular, ranching in Amazonia and soybean and wheat farms producing for export in the south. The national programme of producing sugar cane as a petrol substitute has similarly favoured large farms. As Anthony Hall has noted:

> From 1960 to 1980 the area planted to soybean jumped from 0.2 million to 9 million hectares. The area planted to sugarcane more than doubled . . . from 1.5 million hectares to 3.8 million hectares in 1985. Over the same period, output of beans and cassava, the two most important staples in Brazil, fell by 8 per cent and 14 per cent, respectively. By 1983, per capita food production in the country had fallen to three-quarters of the 1977 level. (Hall 1990:215)

According to one study, in the ten years after 1970, the poorest 50% of the rural population saw its share of total income in the

WHY MODERNIZED FARMING DOESN'T BENEFIT THE POOR

The introduction of modernized farming technologies and marketing systems has often been held to be "scale neutral", offering advantages to small and large farmer alike. History does not bear this out. The reasons that modernization favours large farms are complex. Large farmers tend to wield more political power than peasants and so skew fiscal, tenurial, legal, subsidy and extra-legal processes in their favour. However, many technical factors also favour the large farm.

Small farms have problems raising and repaying the necessary capital for "lumpy" investments like farm machinery, modern management systems and technical advice. Bulk buying and transport of seeds, fertilizers, herbicides and pesticides also provide economies of scale to the large farmer. Many cash crops and modern markets demand complex processing of food. Threshers, driers, grainstores and transport infrastructures make for dauntingly large overheads for the small farmer, which can only be partly overcome through co-operatives and time-sharing arrangements.

Waiting in a queue to process crops can make or break a small farmer. Sugar cane, for example, only maintains its quality for 12 hours between cutting and processing to achieve a good yield. A farmer selling bananas on the international market has only 24 hours after harvest to get his crop into storage on a cold boat.

Small farmers have far less bargaining power with middlemen, trucking companies, processing mills and farm hire agencies than large farmers, who can often dispense with these outside services. The small farmer is obliged to accept poor prices for his produce and second rate services. Living far nearer to the margins of survival the peasant farmer has to adopt farming strategies that minimize risk rather than optimize yields.

The bureaucratic processes related to modernized farming are often time- consuming and favour the large farmer, thus providing preferential access to equity, tax breaks, credit and legal security.

Modernization means turning farming from being a way of life into a business geared towards maximizing production for the market. It means laying off permanent farm-workers and replacing them wage labourers and machinery. Social values are replaced by the single criterion of efficiency. Costs are incurred in the form of landlessness, poverty, migration, urban squalor, frontier expansion and environmental decline.

countryside fall from 22% to 15%, while the wealthiest 5% enjoyed an increase from 24% to 45% (Hall 1990:215).

In Brazil the size of land holdings among the rich is truly staggering and the availability of potentially redistributable land outside the forests is obvious. According to official figures, nationally 2% of rural properties with more than 1,000 hectares occupy 57% of agricultural land. Most of these *latifundia* are not put to productive use but are held as a real estate investment and as a speculative hedge against inflation (Hall 1990:206). Moreover, as the chapters by Monbiot and Hecht show so clearly, the politics of land in Brazil means that these patterns of inequity have replicated themselves in the forests.

In Amazonia, we find that land holdings are larger and land is even more concentrated than in the rest of Brazil. While two-thirds of farmers have properties of less than 100 hectares and occupy only 13% of the land, the 6% of landowners with more than 1,000 hectares hold 80% of the farmland. Even in areas like Rondônia and Acre, intentionally opened up to colonists fleeing landlessness in the south of Brazil, land concentration is vicious. By 1985, 60% of farmland in Rondônia and 90% in Acre were concentrated in estates of more than 1,000 hectares (Hall 1990:210).

With the exception of the Philippines and some parts of India, these kinds of gross inequities in land holding are not so common in Asia. While very large areas of land and forest are held by the state or tied up under the control of parastatals and plantations, large *latifundias* of unproductive lands are rare.

Yet land concentration and its stultifying effects on agrarian systems are a common problem in South Asia. In Bangladesh, for example, at a conservative estimate 12% of rural households own 56% of all land. The top 25% own 79%. The difference is that in this case the "top" quarter of households are classified as those with over two acres of land. Despite the small size of most holdings, the need for reform is as clear in Bangladesh as anywhere. The present extremely hierarchical system secures rights in land in very few hands, hands which do not till the soil but which live from the exorbitant rents paid by the mass of rural tenants and sharecroppers, who pay for all inputs to the land but must share 50% of the output with the owners. The inevitable result is that neither owner not occupier have clear incentives to improve land or manage it efficiently (Tomasson, Jannuzzi and Peach 1990). Chronic landlessness and insecurity contribute to the massive out-migrations into the surrounding forested areas of central and northern Bangladesh, the Chittagong Hill Tracts and neighbouring north-east India.

In Thailand, the picture is different. The problems of the peasantry inhere not so much in their lack of access to land or in land concentration as in their lack of land security and control. Millions of farmers are vulnerable to dispossession by the forestry bureaucracy and the military. Clientelistic political structures dominate the agrarian economy, yoking peasants into exploitative patron-client relations that deny them initiative or real decision-making power. These hierarchical patterns of control, which evolved in a context of labour scarcity, subsequently intensified as Siam integrated itself into the world market and became a major primary product exporter. While the state arrogated all forest lands to itself for logging, cash cropping increased massively. Export crops like kenaf, sugar cane, maize, pineapple, coffee and prawns expanded exponentially, spreading the agricultural frontier far beyond the traditional wet rice area. Lacking land security and political autonomy, peasants have been unable to resist heavy pressures to "modernize" and expand their farms. Even those who have been drawn onto marginal and forested land are pursued by land speculators, developers and creditors.

In generalizing about Indonesia, the common approach is to distinguish between the "overpopulated" inner islands of Java, Madura, Bali and Lombok and the "underpopulated" outer islands, such as Sumatra, Kalimantan, Sulawesi, Western New Guinea and Nusa Tenggara, which make up the rest of the archipelago. Attempts to balance these perceived inequalities, or rather to export "surplus people" from one part to another, have been a major feature of development policy since the turn of the century. Yet the impositions of agricultural policy and law on the peasantries of both regions have had similar destabilizing effects leading to chronic insecurity, population growth and mobility.

Since independence in both the era of "guided democracy" and since the imposition of the "New Order", Indonesia has experienced an increasing interference by government agencies, parastatals and monopolized marketing systems in agrarian affairs. The result has been the undermining of peasant traditions of self-management and communal farming. Since the massacres of 1965, when over half a million people were killed for allegedly holding radical views - including support for agrarian reforms - political repression in the countryside has been intense. As a result, overt popular opposition in the countryside has been limited to apparently spontaneous outbursts against instances of acute land alienation or bureaucratic inefficiency. Agrarian reforms may be desperately needed in Indonesia but the political obstacles are too great for the notion to have wide currency. The present pattern of accelerating loss of both the upland forests of the inner islands and the large areas of forest on the outer islands thus looks set to continue.

In Africa, agrarian systems are in a state of turmoil and even collapse after the sudden and late intrusion of the colonial powers and the very wide-ranging changes that they set in train. In the Sahelian zone, the problems have arisen principally from the imposition of policies that favour the cultivation of export crops such as groundnuts and cotton. The process continued after independence with the central governments offering peasants subsidized inputs of seed, fertilizer and pesticides, technical assistance and guaranteed purchase prices. As a result farmers have been cultivating more land more intensively than was customary and, where they have had to make a choice, cotton has been chosen before millet as the farmers know the state will collect it at harvest time (Timberlake 1987:62; Barraclough 1991).

The result has been over-intensive land use, shortening fallows and gradual ecological decline. Studies by the United Nations Research Institute for Social Development have found that cash-cropping, not rising populations, is the principal cause of ecological degradation in West African drylands (Barraclough 1991:30).

Programmes to develop cash cropping have squeezed farmers off the more fertile lands into marginal, low rainfall zones not suited for dryland agriculture. This has accelerated land degradation and "desertification", with yields per hectare and per farmer falling drastically. It is these processes, coupled with drought, which have triggered widespread famines (Timberlake 1987).

Migrants have not only been moving north. Many have flooded south into the high rainfall, forest belt along the coast. Moving into the forests along logging roads, the migrants have delivered the *coup de grâce* to West Africa's forests, which have experienced some of the fastest rates of deforestation in the globe (Myers 1989).

Witte's account of the situation in Zaire suggests that similar processes are now underway in Central Africa. While international companies are creaming the forests of their best timber, growing disparities of wealth and in access to land threaten to unleash a wave of forest colonization. Witte's chapter highlights the problem of an emerging, black African, urban, land-owning élite who are taking over large areas of land for cash cropping, creating local landlessness and poverty. It prompts the question: how best can customary land rights be secured so that the process of land concentration is curbed, without undermining the flexibility and relative autonomy of customary tenure systems which have cushioned Africans from experiencing the degree of landlessness common in Asia and Latin America?

Landlessness is a more serious problem in those parts of Africa which have experienced white colonization. In the colonial era, the expropriations of Africans' lands by white planters and ranchers provoked frequent rebellions (Pakenham 1991) and, since independence, have led to Africa's few faltering experiments with land reform. For example, land reforms were initiated in Kenya after independence but were very limited in their extent, despite the fact that the Mau Mau movement was based on the grievances of landless squatters dispossessed by the establishment of a plantation culture in the so-called "White Highlands". Money was not the limiting factor, as considerable international financial assistance was made available to the government to compensate expropriated white farmers and provide services and credit to newly established small-holders. Rather, the reforms halted because the interests of an emerging black African entrepreneurial and land-owning élite coincided with externally imposed agricultural development priorities, which favoured the promotion of export-orientated modernized agriculture.

Zimbabwe now faces exactly the same political impasse. At independence the Mugabe government inherited a country divided by race and with a highly skewed land ownership pattern. Some 6,000 white farms accounting for only 0.1% of total holdings covered 15.3 million hectares of the best agricultural land concentrated in the fertile northeastern highlands — 39% of the total land area. At the other extreme, 750,000 black households were squeezed onto "communal areas" in the marginal and arid lands to the south and west — only 42% of the land (Bratton 1990:268).

Agrarian reform was a high priority of the independence government and a significant land redistribution did occur, although the beneficiaries were not granted secure rights to the lands on which they were resettled. However, the impetus has flagged. Just as in Kenya, an emerging bureaucratic élite of black Africans have secured substantial land holdings, biasing land policies in favour of the "haves", which include the remaining 4,400 white farms and their powerful Commercial Farmers Union (Bratton 1990; Ivor 1992).

The Zimbabwe case also warns us not to over-react against those who argue that rising populations contribute to the crisis in Third World agriculture. As Michael Bratton points out, despite the government's success in providing land to 52,000 households between 1980 and 1990, due to population growth the total number of landless increased from 330,000 and 370,000 households in the same period (Bratton 1990:289).

Despite the extreme diversity of situations, two common themes emerge. First, peasants' welfare is being steadily undermined by their rapid integration into the market and their domination by urban and export demands. Secondly, peasants lack land, or clear rights to land. Agrarian reform has the potential to help resolve these problems, not only by providing land security but also by shifting the balance of power in the peasants' favour. However, for exactly this reason, agrarian reform has been strongly resisted.

OBSTACLES TO CHANGE

Agrarian reform, although recognized as essential, has been dodged. The main reasons are political. Agrarian reform challenges the power of the élites who benefit from the present economic structures and who control the political process. International agencies which work through governments and within narrowly conceived mandates are poorly placed to support, let alone work alongside, the popular movements in the Third World that are pushing for reform.

Dennis Rondinelli has described this "power paradox" in the following terms:

> A paradox inherent in agrarian reforms is that strong political commitment is unquestionably necessary to initiate them, [while] they cannot be effectively implemented or sustained without diffused political support and widespread participation by intended beneficiaries. But such a diffusion of participation and power is often considered a serious threat by those whose political commitment is necessary to initiate the reform. (Montgomery 1984: 18)

Rondinelli argues that to escape this paradox of power it is necessary to break the hold of clientelistic politics and to "create" an organizational base of political support and local participation. The reality in very many countries, however, is that the élites who control land continue to react with startling brutality to suppress the emergence of such movements for change.

Indeed, it is often objected that the only successful examples of agrarian reform that have been carried out this century have been in the context of massive social upheaval, when the political obstacles to reform have been weakened or removed by war or revolution. The cases of Taiwan, Korea and Japan are paraded as unique examples of land reform being successfully carried out, from the top down, in circumstances that could neither be wished for nor planned. Other countries, by implication, should accept the *status quo*.

However, the argument does not stand up to close scrutiny. A number of Third World countries have embarked on major land reform programmes under democratically elected governments — such as Guatemala, Brazil, Nicaragua and Kerala state in India. The problem, as in the Brazilian and Guatemalan cases, is that outside interests have intervened to destabilize these reformist governments and crush the reforms.

Yet another of the paradoxes of land reform experience in the Third World is that where land reforms *have* been imposed from above they have rarely worked. Especially where land reforms are directed by development agencies, there is the serious risk that international involvement may undermine peasant processes of self- determination.

Securing property rights through the registration of land holdings itself has two inherent risks. On the one hand, the legalization of tenure can lead to an increasing commoditization of land, which undermines environmentally appropriate, customary management systems by promoting short-term, individualist profit-seeking. On the other hand, the formalization of title even as communal land may create undue rigidity and inflexibility in customary systems, rendering them unresponsive to changes in peasant use and ownership.

Cultural factors are frequently overlooked by eager reformers. For example, except in the case of "land to the tiller" programmes, land redistribution implies massive resettlement programmes which, while they may be voluntary, have to overcome serious social and cultural obstacles. Land claims often endure long after areas are taken over by large landowners and are not therefore as "free" for redistribution as land reform laws may imply. In ethnically diverse countries, especially in Africa, resettlement may exacerbate ethnic frictions by bringing together groups which do not have a tradition of living together.

Land reformers also face the dilemma of how much assistance to provide without creating dependency and undermining peasant initiative. Newly resettled farmers may require the provision of considerable agricultural extension facilities and infrastructural investments (roads, housing, schools, dispensaries), before they can become familiar with their new surroundings and able to work their new lands well.

During the 1960s and 1970s, the development agencies were enthusiastic in applying "integrated rural development programmes" to the Third World. It became World Bank dogma that to ensure the rapid conversion of backward peasants into efficient modern smallholders, it was essential for the government to provide the farmer with a complete package of seeds, chemicals, credit and marketing — frequently part of a Green Revolution programme — ostensibly to cut out the middlemen and promote self-reliance. Where, as in the Philippines case, this process was tied to land reforms, the peasants were also expected to put up their lands as collateral (Bello et al. 1982).

As Grace Goodell has argued, the result in the Philippines was to increase the power of state agencies and erode the economic autonomy of the peasants, many of whom are now worse off under the exactions and impositions of state bureaucracies and monopolies than they were under the landlords. In her view, the peasants would have been far better served by the existing middlemen and entrepreneurs, whom they have learned to deal with and who have learned to be responsive to peasant needs and demands. Yet the reform programme systematically undermined the private sector: rural banks, private retailing chains, Chinese middlemen and moneylenders all went out of business, depriving the peasants of alternatives to the state-imposed structures (Goodell 1990).

John Powelson and Richard Stock (1990) have developed this line of argument in their broad-reaching survey of agrarian reforms, *The Peasant Betrayed*. They are scathingly critical of top-down reforms, which they argue have, willy-nilly, benefited the state rather than the peasant.

> In fact, many (probably all) peasant societies have their own well-developed systems of credit, supply, saving, investment, and communications technology. The supposition that peasants do not have these capabilities is one of the gross ethnocentricities of the development profession. (Powelson and Stock 1990:6)

Yet the lesson that should be drawn from these studies is not that it is enough to hand peasants their lands in the form of tenure that they choose and then leave them to get on with their life. On the contrary, in a context in which a broad range of top-down economic and political initiatives are impinging on peasants' lives, such a policy, if pursued by itself, would only condemn them to further marginalization and poverty.

Mexico is a case in point. There, energetically prosecuted land reforms unique in Latin America have redistributed approximately half of the country's farm area, creating over 70% of its farmed units. Yet, as Merilee Grindle has shown, despite the extent of the reform, underproductivity, landlessness and marginality characterize most of the country's rural people. Grindle traces these conditions to government policies that have encouraged the emergence of large-scale commercial agricultural units and given little or no support to those who gained land from the reforms (Grindle 1990:179). In 1940, after the fall of the Cardenas government, which at the same time that it vigorously initiated the land reform had pursued a policy of support for small-scale farmers producing staple food crops, Mexican development strategy changed tack towards the promotion of large-scale farms for export and to supply growing higher-income demands for livestock products and high value foods. In the process, notes Solon Barraclough, "its agrarian bureaucracy, originally established to aid land reform beneficiaries to become independent producers, was gradually converted into an instrument for extracting basic foods at low prices from the peasantry" (Barraclough 1991: 105).

Experience shows that both agrarian reforms that include integrated state-directed packages and land reforms that leave small farmers to the mercy of the forces of modern agricultural "development" have failed. Where comprehensive reforms tied to "Green Revolution" packages rely on what Powelson and Stock naïvely refer to as the peasants' "own" middlemen (who are in fact usually local usurers and profiteers viewed with the greatest animosity by ordinary peasants) to provide them with the requisites for modern farming, the common result is an erosion of peasant autonomy. Frequently, the consequence is the reconcentration of land or control of land in fewer hands —

landlessness, land insecurity and impoverishment then intensify (Duyker 1987; Harriss 1988; Shiva 1991). In nearly all cases, top-down reforms have had disappointing results.

The answer to this dilemma is that agrarian reform must be perceived as a political process which builds on community initiatives, secures community control of land, and involves local peasant organizations in policy-making, to ensure that they have a decisive voice in the execution of the reform programme and influence over the wider trade, fiscal and credit policies which shape agrarian change.

For example, Ronald Herring has argued that the relative success of the land reforms in Kerala in southern India has been due to the mobilized coalition of the rural poor behind a reformist political party. The reforms brought sweeping benefits to tenant farmers who gained land, and the political nature of the process ensured that even though landless labourers did not make commensurate gains in land, their situation has nevertheless improved in terms of wages, services and employment opportunities (Herring 1990; Powelson and Stock 1990:185-206).

PUSHING ON A PIECE OF STRING

All this has important implications both for international agencies and those that support calls for agrarian reform. The historical record shows that top-down interventions, even those ostensibly in favour of peasant welfare and land redistribution, can undermine peasant solvency, autonomy and initiative. The peasants may appear to gain some material benefits through reforms "from above" but, if the cost is a simultaneous weakening of their political strength and economic independence, such gains will at best be ephemeral. Unless an enduring shift of power in favour of the peasants is achieved, the same forces which ensured land concentration before reform will work to undo reforms immediately after they are achieved.

The structural and political nature of effective agrarian reform thus creates a dilemma for the international community. During the colonial era, the industrial countries of the North tied the South into the global market and used their superior political strength and weaponry to haul cheap agricultural surpluses out of the peasantries of the Third World. The effect was to distort the political structures of southern countries — often taking advantage of existing indigenous inequities — into new forms that favoured this one-way flow of unprocessed goods towards the industrial countries of the North.

The post-war era of "development" has entrenched this same political economy, with an increasing domination of the agrarian systems of the Third World by local urban élites working in collaboration with international agencies and businesses. It is not just the countries of the North which are yanking cheap goods out of the southern peasantries, but the urban élites of the South as well. The political structures that favour this one-way flow reach down deep into the communities themselves, in the guise of patron-client structures, racial and ethnic discrimination, and caste and class differences.

In this context, top-down reforms are as effective as pushing on a piece of string. Entrenched political structures, locally and nationally, will frustrate imposed reforms and ensure that enduring changes do not come about. The same is true of top-down macro-economic reshuffling. The benefits of debt relief and improved terms of trade for cash crops will not "trickle down" to the peasants, any more than they ever have. On the contrary, real change will only come about when the peasants themselves are able to reassert their political will. Only action from the grassroots can undo the political structures that at present, ratchet-like, ensure that all shifts in prices, policies and power move wealth in favour of the already wealthy.

FUTURE OPTIONS

There are no quick fixes to "save the rainforests". Immediate action is certainly necessary to halt the depredations of logging, mining, hydropower development, road-building, forestry master-planning and top-down land-use zoning, but the long-term solutions depend on the emergence of genuine grassroots movements of those forest- dwellers and peasants whose lives are rooted in the land. The processes by which these peoples secure rights to their lands in the forests and gain rights to land outside the forests are bound to require slow and painful political change.

This does not mean that there is no place at all for outside action or support. What it does mean is that outsiders must learn to be accountable to those whom they would help. In the first place it must be clear that, even if "pushing on a piece of string" can undermine peasant self-determination and be frustrated by local vested interests, an essential change is for the North to stop pulling on the string. Capital flows and development agency interventions must be checked, excessive demands for the products of agribusinesses operating on land in the South curbed, and Third World economies redirected towards policies that promote national food security and the supplying of internal markets. This alone will entail major reforms in the agricultural development strategies of the international development agencies, as well as life-style changes in the North.

The international community can also take action to encourage the enlargement of political space in Third World countries to promote an environment in which power can shift back in the peasants' favour. Whatever international development assistance remains should be used to promote the creation of national policy environments that do not favour large-scale, mechanized farming and ranching. Price changes, subsidies, credit systems and tax breaks should be revised so that they are either at least more "scale neutral" or else skewed in favour of the small farmer.

In the past, development assistance — and the international arms trade — have been used to support regimes that have employed extreme violence to suppress peasant movements. This must be stopped. Human rights and "good governance" criteria should play a far more central role in decisions about the allocation of "aid", in place of the considerations that prevail in decision-making today.

This "democratization" of development assistance implies immediate, fundamental changes in the agencies' own regulations about freedom of information. "Participation" of affected groups in project planning and implementation should become routine, but this is relatively meaningless if the participants are deprived of information about what is planned and why. Development agencies thus need to elaborate very clear mechanisms by which the general public can be informed about and effectively involved in decision-making at all levels — both in the evolution of national and sectoral policies and in the elaboration of specific projects. The token reforms so far undertaken in this direction by the World Bank and other agencies fall far short of what is needed.

If these kinds of reforms in development assistance become routine, international assistance to national processes of legislative reform could be helpful. In the first place, legislation could be assisted which secures customary tenure systems in accordance with the demands of local movements and representative organizations. There is no common prescription for what this legislation should be like, since local situations are so variable. The important point is that they be determined by those affected.

Certain types of agrarian reforms, in this wider sense, are already underway. Moves to secure Indian territories in Latin America are one example, while various experiments with "resource transfers" in the Philippines and South Asia are beginning to be replicated through local and national policy changes. Legislative changes which recognize the "legal personality" of customary rights-holders can be a crucial part of this process.

Anthony Hall of the London School of Economics, who has made a detailed study of the politics of land in Brazil, believes foreign assistance could play an important role in two ways. Governmental and multilateral assistance should be directed to building up the capacity of governmental institutions charged with the implementation of agrarian reform programmes. At the same time, Hall argues, non-governmental assistance should be to provide "financial and technical support to incipient forms of community organization", the aim being to "encourage community mobilization both within and across communities, so that such groups acquire a collective voice and a degree of bargaining power to be able to negotiate with land reform institutions". Such "bottom-up" participation and a certain autonomy of decision-making are thus essential if land reform settlements are to avoid being either totally neglected or manipulated by technocrats for their own ends. "To the extent that participation in project implementation can build upon pre-existing forms of community activity rather than attempting to create such involvement from scratch, so much the better." (Hall 1990:230)

Too often, books about agrarian reform pile up one cautionary tale after another to the point where the obstacles to effective reform seem overwhelming. The desperate need for the reforms is then lost sight of and attention shifts to more politically easy options. The new means then justify a new end, and the problem remains.

The ills of landlessness and rural poverty have indeed been with us for a long time. The massive loss of tropical forests is, however, a much more acute problem. Unless decisive action is taken soon the vast majority of these forests will be destroyed forever. Agrarian reforms based on indigenous and peasant initiatives provide the only credible means of averting this biological and social catastrophe. The political difficulties have to be confronted.

Indigenous peoples, peasant movements, environmental organizations and human rights groups in the Third World have been challenging these political forces for a very long time. Their continuing struggles against the odds for land, social justice and against the relentless commercialization of natural resources offer the main grounds for hope. Change must come from below if it is to be effective.

The most immediate contribution that the North can make to help these struggles is to curb its pressure on the South. Reducing the demand in the global marketplace for Southern-produced agribusiness products and alleviating the pressure from externally financed development projects and assistance is the first essential step.

APPENDIX

APPENDIX

NEW YORK DECLARATION
STATEMENT TO THE FOURTH
PREPCOM OF THE UNCED, NEW YORK,
2 MARCH 1992

We, representatives and activists from indigenous peoples, nomadic pastoralists, peasant and environmental organizations from various parts of the world, recognize the strong links between landlessness and tropical deforestation, both of which are symptoms of an unjust and unsustainable development process. Increasing landlessness and rural poverty are devastating rural environments and are causing the widescale destruction of tropical forests.

We are extremely concerned that the nearly two billion peasants of the developing world are not even considered by UNCED as one of the "Major Groups" that will implement Agenda 21.

The reports presented at the first workshop, convened by the World Rainforest Movement in New York from 28 February to 1 March 1992, on "Agrarian Reform and Tropical Deforestation", have revealed very clearly that the development programmes implemented by different Governments of the poor countries of the Pacific, Asia, Africa and Latin America have failed to guarantee even the survival of a great part of humanity. The programmes have increased the misery and insecurity of the majority of the population throughout these continents and have destroyed natural resources. Aside from this, no solution to the foreign debt problem has been found. Increasing land concentration is a problem affecting rural people in both the developing and industrial worlds and is driven by the same forces.

These development programmes were designed and implemented by international organizations, transnational corporations, technocrats and Governments, especially of the North, and imposed on indigenous peoples, peasants and the population as a whole, who had no meaningful voice in their design and did not participate in their execution.

We see that the failure of these development programmes is caused by the imposition of a model of economic development which is depriving people of their means of survival by expropriating and degrading their basic resource — land. Therefore we feel strongly that, both to ensure the survival of these people and of the resources they depend on and to restore their creative potential, alternative development models are urgently needed. The rural peoples themselves have the right and ability to define their own lives and manage the resources basic to their livelihoods. They must be assured the means to express their initiatives, at local, regional, national and international levels, based on their long experience.

Fundamentally, such development must assure them secure access to, and control of, land and all resources necessary for their present needs and future development. The optimal use of their resources can only be achieved if there is full scope for the expression of their traditional systems of decision-making, cultures, knowledge and technologies.

The UNCED notion of sustainable development must recognize as its central goal the sustaining of the livelihoods of the people based on their own control of their lands and resources.

We, therefore, insist that the UNCED recognizes peasants as one of the "Major Groups" that will implement Agenda 21 and demand that the UNCED acknowledge that:

- the rights of rural communities to the land and commons that they depend on should be respected and secured. This must be achieved by recognizing and securing customary systems of land ownership and use, and through meaningful agrarian reform, including the redistribution of land, in accordance with their priorities and demands;

- their rights to control the land, water and the other natural resources that they depend on must be respected and secured. They should be given a decisive voice in the formulation of policy on the use and conservation of resources in their areas;

- the development of their lands and resources should be subject to their informed consent as expressed through their own representative institutions;

- their indigenous knowledge systems and technologies must be respected and secured against the depredations of transnational companies claiming intellectual property rights over them.

We are convinced that a just social order which will permit real sustainable development — that meets the needs of present generations without sacrificing the needs of the future — cannot be achieved until these principles are respected.

We strongly feel that urgent attention should be paid to the extremely violent and suppressive character of the political processes that accompany the present model of development at all levels, which demands serious thinking of a totally different approach to survival, growth and development.

It is imperative that these principles are discussed at the Prepcom IV and the Earth Summit with a view to establishing both real political commitment and concrete mechanisms for their realization. As a start toward opening the way for local people to regain control of their lands and their economies, all members of the United Nations attending the Earth Summit must ensure that these principles are clearly articulated in the Earth Charter; in the international agreements and declarations of principles being prepared on Climate, Biodiversity and Forests; and in the content and functioning of Agenda 21.

Arvind Kumar, Lok Jagriti Kendra, India
Gail Omvedt, India
Vandana Shiva, Foundation for Science and Ecology, India
Sarath Fernando, Devasarana Development Centre, Sri Lanka
Hamid Ansari, Nepal
Ivo Polleto, Comissão Pastoral da Terra, Brazil
Francisco Menezes, IBASE, Brazil
Roberto Bissio, Instituto Tercer Mundo, Uruguay
Carlos Campos, Consejo Nacional de Productores — Justicia y Desarrollo, Costa Rica
Kenny Matampash, Development Education Programme, Catholic Diocese of Ngong-Maasailand, Kenya
Egnankou Wadja Mathieu, Université Paul Sabatier, Côte d'Ivoire

Barbara Carl, Melanesian Solidarity Group, Papua New Guinea
Marvic Leonen, Legal Rights and Natural Resources Centre, Philippines
Srisuwan Kuankachorn, Project for Ecological Recovery, Thailand
Nanang Subana Dirja, SKEPHI, Indonesia
Martin Khor, Third World Network, Malaysia
Rachel Monroe, SOS Siberut, UK
Larry Lohmann, The Ecologist, UK
Roger Plant, UK
Chad Dobson, Bank Information Center, USA
Korinna Horta, Environment Defense Fund, USA
Marcus Colchester, World Rainforest Movement, UK

REFERENCES

REFERENCES

Aditjondro, George J.
   1986   Transmigration in Irian Jaya: issues, targets and alternative
           approaches. *Prisma*, Jakarta.

Agarwal, Anil and Sunita Narain
   1989   *Towards Green Villages.* Centre for Science and the Environ-
           ment, Delhi.

Alvarado, Elvia
   1987   *Don't be Afraid, Gringo.* Institute for Food and Development
           Policy, San Francisco.

Amara Pongsapich
   1985   *Panhaa daan sathaaban lae kaan jatkaan rueng thii din.* Mimeo,
           Chulalongkorn University, Bangkok.

Americas Watch
   1989   *Persecuting Human Rights Monitors: the CERJ in Guatemala.*
           Americas Watch Report.

   1991   *Violencia rural no Brasil.* Nucleo de Estudos da Violência,
           University of São Paulo, São Paulo.

Amnesty International
   1988   *Brazil: authorized violence in rural areas.* Amnesty Interna-
           tional publications, London.

Anat Arbhabhirama
   1989   Introduction. In: Siam Society (ed.) *Culture and Environment in
           Thailand.* Siam Society, Bangkok.

Anderson, Ben
   1977   Withdrawal Symptoms: social and cultural aspects of the Octo-
           ber 6 coup. *Bulletin of Concerned Asian Scholars* 8 (2): 13-30.

Anderson, James N.
   1987   Lands at Risk, People at Risk: perspectives on tropical forest
           transformations in the Philippines. In: Peter Little (ed.) *Lands at
           Risk in the Third World: local level perspectives.* Westview Press,
           Boulder: 249-267.

ANGOC
1989   *People's Participation and Environmentally Sustainable Development*. Asian NGO Coalition For Agrarian Reform and Rural Development, Manila.

Annis, Sheldon
1987   *God and Production in a Guatemalan Town*. University of Texas Press, Austin.

Anon
1984   *China's Minority Nationalities*. Great Wall Books, Beijing.

1986   Resurge problema de la tierra en Guatemala. *Inforpress CentroAmericana*, 19 June 1986, Informe Especial, No. 694.

1987   *Minority Peoples in China*. China Pictorial Publications, Beijing.

1988   El retorno de los refugiados guatemaltecos en el extranjero. *Revista de la Universidad de San Carlos de Guatemala* 4: 44-49.

1989   *Projet: integration socio-économique des populations Baka et Bakola du Cameroun*. Ms.

1990a   Principales problemas del medio ambiente. Seminario Taller *Migración Interno y Recursos Naturales del Guatemala*.

1990b   Politicas ambientales. Taller Coban. Ms.

1991a   *The Effect of Martial Law on the Grassroots in Thailand*. By a friend of the Coordinating Committee for Democracy in Thailand, Bangkok, 7 May 1991, mimeo.

1991b   Konkai rat ruk khaat phra prajak. *Phuu Jatkaan Raai Sapdaa*: 16-23 September.

Apisak Dhanasettakorn
1992   New Land and Forest Programme Proposed. *The Nation*, 20 July.

Arcilla, Grace Punongbayan (ed.)
1990   *Lupa at Bayan: agrarian reform in the Philippines*. Philippine Development Forum, Amsterdam.

Arvelo-Jimenez, Nelly
1980   Programmes Among Indigenous Peoples in Venezuela and Their Impact: a critique. In: F. Barbira-Scazzocchio (ed.) *Land, People and Planning in Contemporary Amazonia*. Centre for Latin American Studies, Cambridge: 210-221.

ASS
1983   *The Philippines: authoritarian government, multinationals and ancestral lands*. Anti-Slavery Society, London.

1984   *The Chittagong Hill Tracts: militarization, oppression and the hill tribes.* Anti-Slavery Society, London.

1991   *West Papua: plunder in paradise.* Anti-Slavery Society, London.

Atkinson, Jane M.
1988   Religion and the Wana of Sulawesi. In: Michael R. Dove (ed.) *The Real and Imagined Role of Culture in Development: case studies from Indonesia.* University of Hawaii Press, Honolulu: 41-61.

Ayres, Robert L.
1983   *Banking on the Poor: the World Bank and world poverty.* MIT Press, Cambridge, Massachusetts.

Bagwati, D.
1982   Directly Unproductive Profit-seeking Activities. *Journal of Economics.*

Bahuchet, S. and H. Guillaume
1982   Aka-Farmer Relations in the Northwest Congo Basin. In: E. Leacock and R. Lee (eds.) *Politics and History in Band Societies.* Cambridge University Press.

Bandyopadhyay, Jayanta and Vandana Shiva
1987   Chipko: rekindling India's forest culture. *The Ecologist* 17 (1): 26-34.

Banerjee, Sumanta
1984   *India's Simmering Revolution.* Zed Books, London.

Banuri, Tariq and Frederique Apffel-Marglin (eds.)
1992   *Who Will Save the Forests?* Zed Books, London.

Barber, Charles and Gregory Churchill
1987   *Land Policy in Irian Jaya: issues and strategies.* United Nations Development Programme INS/83/013.

Barbira-Scazzocchio, F. (ed.)
1980   *Land, People and Planning in Contemporary Amazonia.* Centre for Latin American Studies, Cambridge University.

Barraclough, Solon
1988   *The Rich Have Already Eaten.* Transnational Institute, Amsterdam.

1991   *An End to Hunger? The Social Origins of Food Strategies*. Zed
         Books, London.

Barry, Tom
1987   *Roots of Rebellion: land and hunger in Central America*. South
         End Press, Boston.

Beauclerk, John
1991   *Hunters and Gatherers in Central Africa: on the margins of
         development*. Draft report produced for Oxfam.

Beauclerk, John, Jeremy Narby and Janet Townsend
1988   *Indigenous Peoples: a field guide for development*. Oxfam,
         Oxford.

Bell, Clive
1990   Reforming Property Rights in Land and Tenancy. *World Bank
         Research Observer* 5(2).

Bello, Walden, David Kinley and Elaine Elinson
1982   *Development Debacle: the World Bank and the Philippines*.
         Institute for Food and Development Studies and the Philippine
         Solidarity Network, San Francisco.

Berryman, Philip
1984   *The Religious Roots of Rebellion: Christians in Central Ameri-
         can revolutions*. Orbis Books, New York.

Binswanger, Hans
1988   What are the Prospects for Land Reform? World Bank Discus-
         sion Paper. World Bank, Washington.

1991   Brazilian Policies that Encourage Deforestation in the Amazon.
         World Development 19 (7): 821-829.

Binswanger, Hans and Miranda Elgin
1991   What are the Prospects for Land Reform? In: Allen Mander and
         Alberto Valdez (eds.) *Agriculture and Government in an Inter-
         dependent World*. Proceedings of the 2nd World Congress of
         International Agricultural Economic Associations. Dartmouth
         Publishing Co.: 739-754.

Black, George
1984   *Garrison Guatemala*. Zed Books, London.

Blaikie, Piers and Harold Brookfield
1987   *Land Degradation and Society*. Methuen, New York.

Blarel, Benoit, Peter Hazell, Frank Place and John Quiggan
1992   The Economics of Farm Fragmentation: evidence from Ghana and Rwanda. *World Bank Economic Review* 6 (2): 233-254.

Bodley, John H.
1982   *Victims of Progress.* 2nd edition. Benjamin/Cummings, Menlo Park.

Bodley, John H. (ed.)
1988   *Tribal Peoples and Development Issues: a global overview.* Mayfield, MountainView.

Bondestam, Lars and T. Bergstrom (eds.)
1980   *Poverty and Population Control.* Academic Press, London.

Bourne, Richard
1978   *Assault on the Amazon.* Gollancz, London.

Branford, Sue and Oriel Glock
1985   *The Last Frontier: fighting over land in the Amazon.* Zed Books, London.

Bratton, Michael
1990   Ten Years After: land redistribution in Zimbabwe, 1980-1990. In: Roy L. Prosterman, Mary N. Temple and Timothy M. Hanstad (eds.) *Agrarian Reform and Grassroots Development: ten case studies.* Lynne Riener Publishers, Boulder and London: 265-293.

Brewer, Jeffrey D.
1988   Traditional Land Use and Government Policy in Bima, East Sumbawa. In: Michael R. Dove (ed.) *The Real and Imagined Role of Culture in Development: case studies from Indonesia.* University of Hawaii Press, Honolulu: 119-135.

Bromley, Daniel R.
1991   *Environment and Economy: property rights and public policy.* Blackwell, Oxford.

Bromley, Daniel W. and Michael M. Cernea
1989   The Management of Common Property Natural Resources: some conceptual and operational fallacies. World Bank Discussion Paper No. 57, Washington, DC.

Brosius, J. Peter
1986   River, Forest and Mountain: the Penan Gang landscape. *Sarawak Museum Journal* XXXVI(57): 173-184.

Browder, J.O.

1988a The Social Cost of Rainforest Destruction: a critique and economic analysis of the "hamburger debate". *Interciencia* 13 (3): 115-120.

1988b Public Policy and Deforestation in the Brazilian Amazon. In: R. Repetto and M.Gillis (eds.) *Public Policies and the Misuse of Forest Resources*. Cambridge University Press.

Bunker, S.

1985 *Underdeveloping the Amazon*. University of Illinois Press, Champaign-Urbana.

Bunyard, Peter

1989 *The Colombian Amazon: policies for the protection of its indigenous peoples and their environment*. Ecological Press, Wadebridge.

Burgos Debray, Elisabeth

1983 *I, Rigoberta Menchu: an Indian woman in Guatemala*. Verso, London.

Burger, Julian

1987 *Report from the Frontier: the state of the world's indigenous peoples*. Zed Books, London.

Butcher, David

1988 *A Review of Land Acquisition and Resettlement under Four World Bank-financed Projects in Indonesia*. World Bank, Washington, DC.

Cabrera Cruz, Ruby

1990 *Degradación en la Cuenca Alto del Rio Chixoy, Guatemala*. Ms.

Cabungcal, Minerva C. et al.

1991 *The Philippines Today: a situational analysis*. Centre for Community Services, Ateneo de Manila University, Quezon City.

Cannon, Terry

1989 National Minorities and the Internal Frontier. In: David S.G. Goodman (ed.) *China's Regional Development*. Routledge, London: 164-179.

1990 Colonialism from Within. *China Now* 135: 6-14.

Carey, Iskander
1976   *Orang Asli: the Aboriginal tribes of peninsular Malaysia*. Oxford University Press, Kuala Lumpur.

CCCIL
1988   *Collected Commentary and Cases on Indonesian Law*. University of Sydney, Sydney.

CDPV
1991   *Quinzena* 121, 1 August 1991. Centro de Documentação e Pesquisa Vergueiro, São Paulo.

CEDI
1991   *Aconteceu:*, 4 October 1991. Centro Ecumenico de Documentação e Informação, São Paulo.

CEG (Conferencia Episcopal de Guatemala)
1988   El clamor por la tierra. *Revista de la Universidad de San Carlos* 4: 23-34.

1990   Comunicado de la Conferencia Episcopal de Guatemala. *Prensa Libre*, 29 January 1990.

CEPAMI
1988   Realidade das familias de migrantes no estado de Rondonia — 1987. *Cadernos do CEAS* 119.

Cernea, Michael M. (ed.)
1985   *Putting People First: sociological variables in rural development*. Oxford University Press.

1989   *User Groups as Producers in Participatory Afforestation Strategies*. Harvard Institute for International Development, Development Discussion Paper No. 319, Harvard University.

Chaiyon Praditsin
1990   *Settasaat kaan muang waa duay kaan waang phaen khrawp khrua khong thai: suksaa jaak kaan nayobaay* (The Political Economy of Family Planning in Thailand: a study of policy process), master's thesis, Thammasat University.

Chambers, Robert
1983   *Rural Development: putting the last first*. Longman, London.

Chambers, Robert, N.C. Saxena and Tushaar Shah
1989   *To the Hands of the Poor*. Intermediate Technology, London.

Chatchawan Tongdeelert and Larry Lohmann
  1991   The Muang Faai Irrigation System of Northern Thailand. *The Ecologist* 21(2): 93-98.

Chirif, Alberto, Pedro Garcia and Richard Chase Smith
  1991   *El indigena y su territorio*. Oxfam America/ Coordinadora de la Organizaciones Indigenas de la Cuenca Amazonica, Lima.

Chomsky, Noam
  1985   *Turning the Tide: US intervention in Central America and the struggle for peace*. South End Press, Boston.

Christodoulou, D.
  1990   *The Unpromised Land: agrarian reform and conflict world-wide*. Zed Books, London.

CIMI
  1992   Brazilian Rural Workers Leave Paraguay. Electronic mail bulletin, 3 July 1992.

Clarac, Gerald
  1983   *Las comunidades indigenas del país*. IAN, Caracas.

Colchester, Marcus
  1984   The Crisis of Ownership: the plight of the tribal populations of Northern Bangladesh. *Survival International Review* 43: 29-35.

  1985a   An End to Laughter? The Bhopalpatnam and Godavari Projects. In: Edward Goldsmith and Nicholas Hildyard (eds.) *The Social and Environmental Impact of Large Dams*, Vol. 2. Wadebridge Ecological Centre: 245-254.

  1985b   Piaronoia: Venezuelan indigenism in crisis. *Survival International Review* 44: 94-104.

  1986a   Unity and Diversity: Indonesian policy towards tribal peoples. *The Ecologist* 16(2/3): 61-70.

  1986b   The Struggle for Land: tribal peoples in the face of the Transmigration Programme. *The Ecologist* 16 (2/3): 89-98.

  1986c   Banking on Disaster: international support for the Transmigration Programme. *The Ecologist* 16 (2/3): 61-70.

  1986d   Wereldbankprojekt in India: ramp voor tribalen. *Derde Wereld* 5 (2): 31-39.

  1987a   The Tribal Peoples of the Narmada Valley: damned by the World Bank. In: Sahabat Alam Malaysia (eds.) *Forest Resources Crisis in the Third World*. Sahabat Alam Malaysia, Penang: 284-297.

1987b   The Social Dimensions of Government-sponsored Migration and Involuntary Resettlement: policies and practice. Paper prepared for the Independent Commission on International Humanitarian Issues, Geneva, January 1987.

1988   Respecting Forest Peoples' Rights: a strategy for survival. Paper presented to the Oxford Forestry Institute's conference "The Future of the Tropical Rain Forest: a forum for discussion", Oxford University 27-28 June 1988.

1989a   *Pirates, Squatters and Poachers: the political ecology of dispossession of the native peoples of Sarawak.* Survival International and INSAN, Kuala Lumpur.

1989b   Unaccountable Aid: secrecy in the World Bank. *Index of Censorship* 18(6/7): 8-16.

1990a   Shifting Cultivation: rational resource use or robber economy? Paper Presented to the Third World Network and Asia-Pacific Peoples Environment Network Conference on "The Destruction of Asian Agriculture", Penang, Malaysia,10-13 January 1990.

1990b   A Future on the Land? Logging and the Status of Native Customary Land in Sarawak. *Ilmu Masyarakat* 19: 36-45.

1990c   *The International Tropical Timber Organization: kill or cure for the rainforests?* World Rainforest Movement, Penang.

1991a   Peoples of the Tropical Forests of Asia and Pacific. In: Mark Collins, Jeff Sayer and Tim Whitmore (eds.) *The Conservation Atlas of Tropical Forests: Asia and the Pacific.* Macmillan, London: 25-29.

1991b   Sacking Guyana. *Multinational Monitor*, September 1991: 8-14.

Colchester, Marcus and Emilio Fuentes (eds.)
1983   *Los Yanomami Venezolanos: propuesta por la creación de la reserva indigena Yanomami.* Edicampa, Caracas.

Colchester, Marcus and Larry Lohmann
1990   *The Tropical Forestry Action Plan: what progress?* World Rainforest Movement, Penang, 2nd edition.

Colchester, Marcus and Virginia Luling (eds.)
1986   *Ethiopia's Bitter Medicine: settling for disaster. An Evaluation of the Ethiopian Government's Resettlement Programme.* Survival International, London.

Collins, Mark, Jeff Sayer and Tim Whitmore (eds.)
1991   *The Conservation Atlas of Tropical Forests: Asia and the Pacific.* Macmillan, London.

Comissão Pastoral da Terra et al.
1992   BRASIL: uma analise do campo. Topic 195, conference ax.brasil, Alternex electronic mail network, 26 May 1992.

Conable, Barber
1987   Speech to the Board of Governors. September. World Bank, Washington, DC.

Conklin, Harold
1954   *Hanunoo Agriculture*. University Microfilms, Ann Arbor.

Coppens, Walter
1972   La tenencia de tierra indigena en Venezuela: aspectos legales y antropológicos. *Antropológica* 29: 1-37.

Cornista, Luzviminda B. and Eva F. Escueta.
1990   Communal Forest Leases as Tenurial Option in the Philippine Uplands. In: Mark Poffenberger (ed.) *Keepers of the Forest: land management alternatives in Southeast Asia*. Kumarian Press, West Hartwood: 134-144.

Corry, Stephen
1984   Cycles of Dispossession: Amazon Indians and government in Peru. *Survival International Review* 43: 45-70.

Coward, E. Walter, Jr.
1985   Technical and Social Change in Currently Irrigated Regions: rules, roles and rehabilitation. In: Michael Cernea (ed.) *Putting People First: sociological variables in rural development*. Oxford University Press: 27-51.

Craven, Ian
1990   Community Involvement in Management of the Arfak Mountains Nature Reserve. World Wide Fund for Nature (Indonesia), Jakarta. Ms.

Cruz, C.J.
1986   Population Pressure and Migration in Philippine Upland Communities. In: S. Fujisaka, P. E. Sajise and R. A. del Castillo (eds.), *Man, Agriculture and the Tropical Forest: change and development in the Philippine uplands*, Winrock International Institute for Agricultural Development, Bangkok.

CSE
1982   *The State of India's Environment*. Centre for Science and the Environment, New Delhi.

Das, J.C. and R.S. Negi
1982   The Chipko Movement. In: K.S. Singh (ed.) *Tribal Movements in India* (Vol. 2). Manohar, Delhi: 381-392.

David, Rosalind and Mary Myers
1991   Nature's Nurturers Hit by Male Exodus. *Panoscope* 26: 17.

Davila, Amilcar and Rene Castro
1990   Monografia Ambiental de la Región de las Verapaces. Paper presented to a regional seminar on environmental policies in the Verapaces region, 20-22 June 1990, ASIES/CONAMA. Asociación de Investigación y Estudios Social, Guatemala City. Ms.

Davis, Shelton
1976   *Victims of the Miracle*. Cambridge University Press.

1992   *Indigenous Views of Land and the Environment*. World Development Report, Background Paper No. 10, World Bank, Washington, DC.

Dick, John
1991   Forest Land Use, Forest Use Zonation and Deforestation in Indonesia: a summary and interpretation of existing information. A background paper to the UNCED prepared for the State Ministry for Population and Environment and the Environmental Impact Management Agency.

Diegues A.C. et al.
1991a   *The Social Dynamics of Deforestation in the Brazilian Amazon. An Overview*. United Nations Institute for Social Development, São Paulo, June 1991.

1991b   *Social Dynamics of Deforestation in Brazilian Amazonia: two case studies*. United Nations Institute for Social Development, São Paulo, June 1991.

DIGEBOS
1990   II reunión de trabajo sobre el recurso mangle (varios documentos). Ms.

Dorall, Richard
1990   The Dialectic of Development: tribal responses to development capital in the Cordillera Central, Northern Luzon, Philippines. In: Lim Teck Ghee and Alberto G.Gomes (eds.) *Tribal Peoples and Development in Southeast Asia*, University of Malaya, Selangor: 37-67.

Douma, Willy, Wim Kloezen and Paul Wolvekamp
1989   The Political and Administrative Context of Environmental Degradation in South India: how changes in political and public administration determine natural resource management by inhabitants of two villages in a drought-prone area. Centre for Environmental Studies, Leiden.

Dove, Michael R.
1985   The Agroecological Mythology of the Javanese and the Political Economy of Indonesia. *Indonesia* 39: 1-30.

Dove, Michael R. (ed.)
1988   The Real and Imagined Role of Culture in Development: case studies from Indonesia. University of Hawaii Press, Honolulu.

Drucker, Charles
1985   Dam the Chico: hydro development and tribal resistance. In: Edward Goldsmith and Nicholas Hildyard (eds.) *The Social and Environmental Effects of Large Dams* (Vol. 2). Wadebridge Ecological Centre: 304-313.

DTE
1991   *Pulping the Rainforests: the rise of Indonesia's paper and pulp industry.* Down to Earth, London.

Duden, Barbara
1992   Population. In: Wolfgang Sachs (ed.) *The Development Dictionary.* Zed Books, London: 146-57.

Dunkerley, James
1988   *Power in the Isthmus: a political history of modern Central America.* Verso, London.

Durning, Alan B.
1989a   Mobilizing at the Grassroots. In: Lester Brown (ed.) *State of the World: 1989.* Worldwatch Institute Report. W.W. Norton, New York: 154-173.

1989b   *Action at the Grassroots: fighting poverty and environmental decline.* Worldwatch Paper No. 88, Washington, DC.

Duyker, Edward
1987   *Tribal Guerrillas: the Santals of West Bengal and the Naxalite movement.* Oxford University Press, Delhi.

REFERENCES

Ecologist, The

1986   *Banking on Disaster*. Special issue on transmigration, Vol. 16(2/3).

1992   *Whose Common Future?* Special issue on UNCED, Vol. 22(4).

El-Ghonemy, Riad M.

1990   *The Political Economy of Rural Poverty: the case for land reform*. Routledge, London.

Endicott, Kirk

1979   The Impact of Economic Modernization on the "Orang Asli" (Aborigines) of Northern Peninsular Malaysia. In: James C. Jackson and Martin Rudner (eds.) *Issues in Malaysian Development*. Heinemann Educational Books, Singapore: 167-204.

Environmental Management Board (EMB)

1990   *The Philippine Environment in the Eighties*. EMB, Quezon City.

Fairhead, J.

1989   *Food Security in North and South Kivu (Zaire)*. ZAK 630, Oxfam.

FAO

1980   *Tropical Forest Resources*. FAO, Rome.

1981a   *The Peasants' Charter: the declaration of principles and plan of action of the World Conference on Agrarian Reform and Rural Development*. FAO, Rome.

1981b   Report on Indonesia. FAO, Rome

1984a   *Landlessness: a growing problem*. FAO, Rome.

1984b   *Studies on Agrarian Reform and Rural Poverty*. FAO, Rome.

1985   *The Tropical Forestry Action Plan*. FAO, Rome.

1988a   *World Agriculture: Towards 2000, an FAO Study*. Belhaven Press, London.

1988b   Potentials for Agriculture and Rural Development in Latin America and the Caribbean. Annex II on Rural Poverty. FAO, Rome.

1988c   *Overview of Indonesia's Forests*. FAO, Rome.

1989   *Note on the Basic Principles of TFAP*. Rome, May 1989. Ms.

1990   *The Tropical Forestry Action Plan: report of the independent review*. FAO, Rome.

1991   *A Review of Indonesia's Forests* (4 volumes). FAO, Rome.

Fay, Chip
   1987   *Counter-Insurgency and Tribal Peoples in the Philippines.*
          Survival International USA, Washington, DC.

Fay, Chip (ed.)
   1989   *Our Threatened Heritage.* Seminar Series Vol.124, Solidarity
          Foundation, Manila.

Fay, Chip, Nonette Gatmayan and Gus Gatmayan
   1989   The Destruction of Mt Apo: defense of Bagobo ancestral
          domain. In: Chip Fay (ed.) *Our Threatened Heritage.* Solidarity
          Foundation, Manila: 136-145.

FDN
   1989   Resumen de Seminario de Taller *Elaboración de la estrategía
          nacional para la conservación de la biodiversidad de Guate-
          mala,* 8-9 May 1989. Fundación Defensores de la Naturaleza.
          Ms.

   1990   *Estudio tecnico para dar a Sierra de las Minas la categoría de
          Reserva de la Biosfera,* Fundación Defensores de la Naturaleza.
          Ms.

Feder, Gershon, Onchan Tongroj et al.
   1988   *Land Policies and Farm Productivity in Thailand.* Johns Hopkins
          University Press, Baltimore.

Feeney, Patricia
   1992   Wrong Signal from the Bank. *Crosscurrents* 18 June 1992.

Feeny, David
   1988   Agricultural Expansion and Forest Depletion in Thailand, 1900-
          1975. In: John F. Richards and Richard P. Tucker (eds.) *World
          Deforestation in the Twentieth Century.* Duke University Press,
          Chapel Hill: 112-143.

Fernandes, Walter and Sharad Kulkarni (eds.)
   1982   *Towards a New Forest Policy.* Indian Social Institute, New Delhi.

Fiagoy, Geraldine
   1987   *Death Stalks the Isneg: report of three fact-finding missions to
          Lower Kalinga-Apayao, Northern Philippines.* Cordillera Re-
          sources Center, Baguio.

Filer, Colin
    1990   The Bougainville Rebellion, the Mining Industry and the Process of Social Disintegration in Papua New Guinea. *Canberra Anthropology* 13(1): 1-39.

Fried, Jonathan L., Marvine E. Gettleheim, Deborah T. Levenson and Nancy Peckenham
    1983   *Guatemala in Rebellion: unfinished history.* Grove Press, New York.

Furer-Haimendorf, Christoph von
    1982   *The Tribes of India: the struggle for survival.* University of California Press, Berkeley.

Gadgil, Madhav
    1989   *Deforestation: problems and prospects.* Society for the Promotion of Wasteland Development, Delhi.

Galeano, Eduardo
    1973   *The Open Veins of Latin America: five centuries of the pillage of a continent.* Monthly Review Press, New York.

Gardner, Florence with Yaakob Garb and Marta Williams
    1990   *Guatemala: a political ecology.* Green Paper Number 5, The Environmental Project on Central America, San Francisco.

Garna, Judistira
    1990   The Baduy of Java: a case study of tribal peoples' adaptation to development. In: Lim Teck Ghee and Alberto G. Gomes (eds.) *Tribal Peoples and Development in Southeast Asia.* University of Malaya, Selangor: 89-111.

Gasconia, Donna Z.
    1989   Breaking the Minority Myth: a step towards resource transfer. In: Chip Fay (ed.) *Our Threatened Heritage.* Solidarity Foundation, Manila: 114-118.

Gasques, J. and Yokomizo C.
    1986   Resultado de 20 años de incentivos fiscais de Amazonia. *ANPEC*, Brasilia.

Geddes, William Robert
    1976   *Migrants of the Mountains: the cultural ecology of the Blue Miao (Hmong Njua) of Thailand.* Clarendon Press, Oxford.

Geertz, Clifford
1963   *Agricultural Involution: the processes of ecological change in Indonesia.* University of California Press, Berkeley.

George, Susan
1989   *A Fate Worse than Debt.* Penguin, Harmondsworth.

Gerritsen, R., R.J. May and M. Walter
1981   *Road Belong Development: cargo cults, community groups and self-help movements in Papua New Guinea.* Working Paper No. 3, Department of Political and Social Change, Australian National University, Canberra.

Ghimire, Krishna B.
1991   *Parks and People: livelihood issues in national parks management in Thailand and Madagascar.* United Nations Research Institute for Social Development Discussion Paper No. 29, Geneva: 1-17.

Gillis, Malcolm
1988   Public Policies, Resource Management and the Tropical Forest. In: R. Repetto and M. Gillis (eds.) *Public Policies and the Misuse of Forest Resources.* Cambridge University Press: 43-113.

Godoy, Juan Carlos
1991   *Políticas y programas de protección y conservación en America Central.* UNRISD. Ms.

Goldsmith, Edward and Nicholas Hildyard
1985   *The Social and Environmental Effects of Large Dams* (Vol. 2). Wadebridge Ecological Centre.

Good, Kenneth
1986   *Papua New Guinea: a false economy.* Anti-Slavery Society, London.

Goodell, Grace
1990   The Philippines. In: John P. Powelson and Richard Stock (eds.) *The Peasant Betrayed.* Cato Institute, Washington, DC: 15-34.

Goodland, R., E. Asibey, J. Post and M. Dyson
1990   *Tropical Moist Forest Management: the urgent transition to sustainability.* World Bank, Washington, DC.

Government of Indonesia/FAO
1990   Indonesia: national forestry action plan (Country Brief). Jakarta.

Gram Vikas and Pradan
1990   Communal Rights vs Private Profit: tribal peoples and tea
plantations in Northeast India. *The Ecologist* 20(3): 105-107.

Grantham, R.
1990   *Report on Preliminary Efforts to Form an NGO Rainforest
Network in Africa*. African NGOs Environment Network, Nairobi.

Griffin, Keith
1979   *The Political Economy of Agrarian Change*. Macmillan, London.

Grindle, Merilee S.
1990   Agrarian Reform in Mexico: a cautionary tale. In: Roy L.
Prosterman, Mary N. Temple and Timothy M. Hanstad (eds.)
*Agrarian Reform and Grassroots Development: ten case stud-
ies*. Lynne Riener Publishers, Boulder and London: 179-204.

Hafner, James A.
1990   Forces and Policy Issues Affecting Forest Use in Northeastern
Thailand 1900-1985. In: Mark Poffenberger (ed.) *Keepers of
the Forest: land management alternatives in Southeast Asia*.
Kumarian Press, West Hartford: 69-94.

Hafner, James A. and Yaowalak Apichatvullop
1990   Migrant Farmers and the Shrinking Forests of Northeast Thailand. In: Mark Poffenberger (ed.) *Keepers of the Forest: land
management alternatives in Southeast Asia*. Kumarian Press,
West Hartford: 187-219.

Hall, Anthony L.
1990   Land Tenure and Land Reform in Brazil. In: Roy L. Prosterman,
Mary N. Temple and Timothy M. Hanstad (eds.) *Agrarian
Reform and Grassroots Development: ten case studies*. Lynne
Riener Publishers, Boulder and London: 205-232.

Hancock, Graham
1989   *Lords of Poverty*. Mandarin Press, London.

Hardin, G. et al.

1988   *Development Policy and Deforestation: report to the World Resources Institute.* World Resources Institute, Washington, DC.

Harms, R.

1974   *Land Tenure and Agricultural Development in Zaire, 1895-1961.* University of Wisconsin Press.

Hayami, Yujiro et al.

1990   *Towards an Alternative Land Reform Paradigm: a Philippine perspective.* Ateneo de Manila University Press, Manila.

Hecht, Susanna

1985   Environment, Development and Politics: the livestock sector in Eastern Amazonia. *World Development* 13(6): 663-684.

Hecht, Susanna and Alexander Cockburn

1990   *The Fate of the Forests: developers, destroyers and defenders of the Amazon.* Harper.

Hecht, Susanna, R. Norgaard and G. Possio

1988   The Economics of Cattle Ranching in the Eastern Amazon. *Interciencia* 13(5): 233-241.

Hegde, Pandurang

1988   *Chipko and Appiko: how the people save the trees.* Quaker Peace and Service, London.

Hemming, John

1978   *Red Gold: the conquest of the Brazilian Indians.* Macmillan, London.

Herring, Ronald J.

1990   Explaining Anomalies in Agrarian Reform: lessons from South India. In: Roy L. Prosterman, Mary N. Temple and Timothy M. Hanstad (eds.) *Agrarian Reform and Grassroots Development: ten case studies.* Lynne Riener Publishers, Boulder and London: 49-75.

Hicks, James F., H. E. Daly, S. Davis and Maria de Lourdes de Freitas

1990   *Ecuador's Amazon Region.* World Bank, Washington, DC.

Hicks, R.
1991   Forest Land Use, Forest Use Zonation and Deforestation in Indonesia: a summary and interpretation of existing information. Background paper to UNCED prepared for State Ministry of Population and Environment and Environmental Impact Management Agency, June 1991.

Hirsch, Philip
1987   Deforestation and Development in Thailand. *Singapore Journal of Tropical Geography* 8(2): 130-38.

1990a   Forests, Forest Reserve and Forest Land in Thailand. *Geographical Journal* 156(2): 166-174.

1990b   *Development Dilemmas in Rural Thailand*. Oxford University Press, London.

Holland, Luke
1984   From Conquest to Counter-insurgency: four centuries of oppression and resistance in Guatemala. *Survival International Review* 43: 101-109.

Hughes, Philip J. and Charming Thirlwall (eds.)
1988   *The Ethics of Development: choices in development planning*. University of Papua New Guinea Press, Waigani.

Hurst, Philip
1991   *Rainforest Politics*. Zed Books, London.

IBON Databank
1988   *Land Reform in the Philippines*. IBON, Manila.

ICATA
1984   *Perfil ambiental de la republica de Guatemala*. Universidad Rafael Landivar, Instituto de Ciencias Ambientales y Tecnologia Agricola. Two volumes.

ICIHI
1987   *Indigenous Peoples. A Global Quest for Justice*. Zed Books, London.

Indonesia
1986   *Indonesia: news and views* VI(21). Indonesian Embassy, Washington, DC.

Ingold, Tim, David Riches and James Woodburn (eds.)
1988 *Hunters and Gatherers.* 2 vols. Berg, Oxford.

Instituto Mixto Nocturno Humanidades
1988 *La Deforestación en Guatemala.* Ms.

Interamerican Development Bank
1989 *Guatemala: Rural Water Supply Program.* Fifth Stage (GU-0102). Project report. PR-1697-A.

ITTO
1990 *ITTO Guidelines for the Sustainable Management of Natural Tropical Forests.* International Tropical Timber Organization, Technical Series 5, Yokohama.

IUCN
1989 *Guidelines for the Management of Tropical Forests.* Gland, Switzerland.

Ivor, Chris
1992 Land Reform a Pressing Issue in Zimbabwe. *Third World Network Features.*

IWGIA
1986 *The Naga Nation and Its Struggle against Genocide.* International Work Group for Indigenous Affairs, Copenhagen.

James, R.W.
1985 *Land Law and Policy in Papua New Guinea.* Law Reform Commission Monograph No. 5. Port Moresby.

Jewsiewicki, Bogumil
1983 Zaire Enters the World System: its colonial incorporation as the Belgian Congo, 1885-1960. In: G. Gran (ed.) *Zaire, the Political Economy of Underdevelopment.* Praeger, New York.

Jira Jintanugool and Round, Philip
1989 Thailand. Ms., Bangkok.

Johnson, Nela
1989 *Variedad biologica y bosques tropicales en Guatemala: recommendaciones para su preservación y futuro aprovechamiento.* World Resources Institute, Washington, DC.

Jones, Jeffrey R.
1990 *Colonization and Environment: land settlement projects in Central America.* United Nations University Press, Tokyo.

Kalala, K.

1988 *Actual Situation of Agriculture in Sub-Saharan Africa: the case of Zaire*. African Study Monographs 10(1).

Kamon Pragtong and David E. Thomas

1990 Evolving Management Systems in Thailand. In: Mark Poffenberger (ed.) *Keepers of the Forest: land management alternatives in Southeast Asia*, Kumarian Press, West Hartford: 167-186.

Kanogo, Tabitha

1987 *Squatters and the Roots of Mau Mau: 1905-63*. Heinemann Kenya, Nairobi.

Kanvalli, Sadanand

1990 *Quest for Justice*. Samaj Parivartana Samudaya, Dharwad.

Karliner, Joshua

1989 Central America's Other War. *World Policy Journal* 6(4): 787-810.

Kenrick, Justin

1990 *Deforestation and the Forest Peoples of Central Africa*. Report produced for the Institute for Ecology and Action Anthropology (Infoe), Monchengladbach, Germany, and for Rainforest Action Network.

Kilusang Magbubukid ng Pilipinas (KMP)

1988 *Sowing the Seed*. Proceedings of the International Solidarity Conference for the Filipino Peasantry, 11-21 October 1986. KMP, Manila.

Lamprecht, Hans

1989 *Silviculture in the Tropics*. GTZ, Eschborn.

Langub, Jayl

1988a Some Aspects of Life of the Penan. Paper presented to the Orang Ulu Cultural Heritage Seminar, Miri, 21-23 June 1988.

1988b The Penan Strategy. In: Julie Sloane Denslow and Christine Padoch (eds.) *People of the Rain Forest*. University of California Press, Berkeley.

Lanly, J. and P. Gillis

1981 *Provisional Results of the FAO/UNEP Tropical Forests Assessment Project: tropical America*. FAO, Rome.

Leonard, H. Jeffrey
   1987   *Natural Resources and Economic Development in Central America.* Transaction Books, New Brunswick.

Lim Teck Ghee and Alberto G. Gomes (eds.)
   1990   *Tribal Peoples and Development in Southeast Asia.* University of Malaya, Selangor.

Lintner, Bertil
   1990a   *Land of Jade: a journey through insurgent Burma.* Kiscadale, Edinburgh.

   1990b   *Outrage: Burma's struggle for democracy.* Kiscadale, Edinburgh.

Little, Peter D., Michael M. Horowitz and A. Endre Nyerges (eds.)
   1987   *Lands at Risk in the Third World: local level perspectives.* Westview Press, Boulder.

Lohmann, Larry
   1990   Commercial Tree Plantations in Thailand: deforestation by any other name. *The Ecologist* 20(1): 9-17.

   1991a   Who Defends Biological Diversity? Conservation Strategies and the Case of Thailand. *The Ecologist* 21(1): 5-13.

   1991b   Peasants, Plantations and Pulp: the politics of eucalyptus in Thailand. *Bulletin of Concerned Asian Scholars* 23(4): 3-17.

Lopez, Maria Elena
   1987   The Politics of Land at Risk in a Philippine Frontier. In: Peter Little et al. (eds.) *Lands at Risk in the Third World: local level perspectives.* Westview Press, Boulder: 230-248.

Lumad Mindanaw
   1991   *Land Reoccupation: a significant step towards self-determination.* Suwara, Davao City.

Lynch, Owen
   1990   *Whither the People? Demographic, Tenurial and Agricultural Aspects of the Tropical Forestry Action Plan.* World Resources Institute, Washington, DC.

Lynch, Owen and Janis Alcorn
   1991   *Empowering Local Forest Managers: towards more effective recognition of tenurial claims and management capacities among people occupying "public" forest reserves* (pah sa-nguan) *in the Kingdom of Thailand.* World Resources Institute. Ms.

MacGaffey, J.
1986   Fending for Yourself: the organization of the second economy in Zaire. In: Nzongola-Ntalaja (ed.) *The Crisis in Zaire: myths and realities*. Africa World Press, New Jersey.

McKinnon, John and Wanat Bhruksasri (eds.)
1986   *Highlanders of Thailand*. Oxford University Press, Singapore.

McKinnon, John and Bernard Vienne (eds.)
1990   *Hill Tribes Today*. White Lotus/ORSTOM, Bangkok.

Mahar, Dennis J.
1979   *Frontier Policy in Brazil*. Methuen, New York.
1989   *Government Policies and Deforestation in Brazil's Amazon Region*. World Bank, Washington, DC.

Maher, Alexander S.
1990   *Global Forest Resources*. Belhaven Press, London.

Mair, Lucy
1984   *Anthropology and Development*. Macmillan, London.

Manz, Beatriz
1988a   *Refugees of a Hidden War: the aftermath of counter-insurgency in Guatemala*. State University of New York Press.
1988b   *Repatriation and Return: an arduous process in Guatemala*. Center for Immigration Policy and Refugee Assistance, Washington, DC.

Marglin, Stephen A.
in press Agriculture as a System of Knowledge. In: Frederique Apffel-Marglin and Stephen A. Marglin (eds.) *Decolonizing Knowledge: from development to dialogue*.

Marshall, George
1990   The Political Economy of Logging: the Barnett Enquiry into corruption in the Papua New Guinea timber industry. *The Ecologist* 20(5): 174-181.

Martin, Claude
1991   *The Rainforests of West Africa: ecology, threats, conservation*. Birkhauser Verlag, Basel.

May, R.J. (ed.)
1987   *Micronationalist Movements in Papua New Guinea.* Australian National University, Political and Social Change Monograph No.1, Canberra.

Meillassoux, Claude
1981   *Maidens, Meal and Money.* Academic Press, New York.

Mey, Wolfgang
1984   *Genocide in the Chittagong Hill Tracts, Bangladesh.* International Work Group for Indigenous Affairs, Copenhagen.

Mifsud, Frank M.
1967   *Customary Land Law in Africa with Reference to Legislation Aimed at Adjusting Customary Tenures to the Needs of Developing Countries.* FAO, Rome.

Migot-Adholla, Shem, Peter Hazell, Benoit Blarel and Frank Place
1991   Indigenous Land Rights Systems in Sub-Saharan Africa: a constraint on productivity? *World Bank Economic Review* 5 (1): 155-175.

Mikesell, Raymond and Laurence Williams
1992   *International Banks and the Environment.* Sierra Club Books, San Francisco.

Miranda, Mariano Jr
1988   The Economics of Poverty and the Poverty of Economics: the Philippine experience. In: *Land, Poverty and Politics in the Philippines.* Catholic Institute for International Relations, London.

Mitschein, T.A. et al.
1989   *Urbanizacão, selvagem e proletarizacão passiva na Amazônia.* CEJUP, Belem.

Monbiot, George
1991   *Amazon Watershed: the new environmental investigation.* Michael Joseph, London.

Monteroso, Tulio and Oscar Murga
1989   *Efectos sobre el ambiente de proyectos financiados en Guatemala por bancos multilaterales de desarrollo.* Ms.

Montgomery, John D.
1984   *International Dimensions of Land Reform.* Westview, Boulder, Colorado.

Moody, Roger
1991   *Plunder!* Partizans, London.

Moore Lappe, Frances and Joseph Collins
1986   *World Hunger: twelve myths*. Grove Press, New York.

Moore Lappe, Frances and Rachel Schurman
1989   *Taking Population Seriously*. Earthscan, London.
1990   Taking Population Seriously. In: Suzanne Head and Robert Heinzman (eds.) *Lessons From the Rainforest*. Sierra Club Books, San Francisco: 131-144.

Morales, Cesar Eduardo Ordonez
1978   Estructura agraria del altiplano. *Serie separado anuario* (Vol. 2). Universidad de San Carlos de Guatemala.

Morales, Julio
1990   *Cobertura forestal de Guatemala*. Trabajo Inedito, IIQB-USAC.

Moran, Emilio (ed.)
1983   *The Dilemma of Amazonian Development*. Westview Press, Boulder.

Morris, Brian
1982   *Forest Traders: a socio-economic study of the Hill Pandaram*. Athlone Press, London.
1983   Forest Tribes and Deforestation in India. Paper presented to the Fauna and Flora Preservation Society, 1 October 1983.

Movimento dos Trabalhadores Rurais Sem Terra
1990   *Denuncia*. São Paulo. Ms.

Murdock, George Peter
1959   *Africa: its peoples and their cultural history*. McGraw Hill, New York.

Myers, Norman
1989   *Deforestation Rates in Tropical Forests and their Climatic Implications*. Friends of the Earth, London.

Napat Sirisambhand
1988   Types of Spontaneous Pioneer Settlement in Thailand. In: Walther Manshard and William B. Morgan (eds.) *Agricultural Expansion and Pioneer Settlements in the Humid Tropics*. United Nations University, Tokyo.

363

Nations, James et al.
1988   *Biodiversity in Guatemala*. World Resources Institute, Washington, DC.

Ndagala, D. K.
1988   Free or Doomed? Images of the Hadzabe Hunters and Gatherers of Tanzania. In: Tim Ingold, David Riches and James Woodburn (eds.) *Hunters and Gatherers*. 2 volumes. Berg, Oxford.

Nectoux, Francois and Yoichi Kuroda
1989   *Timber from the South Seas: an analysis of Japan's tropical timber trade and its environmental impact*. World Wide Fund for Nature, Gland, Switzerland.

Nelson, Craig and Kenneth Taylor
1983   *Witness to Genocide: the present situation of Indians in Guatemala*. Survival International, London.

Nepal
1988   *Master Plan for the Forestry Sector, Nepal*. Executive Summary, Katmandu, April 1988.

Ngo, Mering
1991   Ambiguity in Property Rights: lessons from the Kayan of Kalimantan. Paper presented at the Interdisciplinary Conference on Kalimantan, New York, 21-23 June.

Nicholas, Colin
1990   In the Name of the Semai? The State and Semai Society in Peninsular Malaysia. In: Lim Teck Ghee and Alberto G. Gomes (eds.) *Tribal Peoples and Development in Southeast Asia*. University of Malaya, Selangor: 68-85.

Nicholas, Colin (ed.)
1989   *Towards Self-Determination: indigenous peoples in Asia*. Asia Indigenous Peoples Pact, Bombay.

Niedergang, Marcel
1971   *The Twenty Latin Americas* (Vol. 1). Penguin, Harmondsworth.

Norgaard, Richard
1990   The Development of Tropical Rainforest Economics. In: Suzanne Head and Robert Heinzman (eds.) *Lessons of the Rainforest*. Sierra Club Books, San Francisco: 171-183.

Northrup, D.
1988   *Beyond the Bend in the River: African labor in Eastern Zaire, 1865-1940*. Ohio University Press, Ohio.

Okoth-Ogendo, H.W.O.
1991   *Tenants of the Crown: evolution of agrarian law and institutions in Kenya*. African Centre for Technology Studies, Nairobi.

Oliver, R.
1991   Survival in the Rainforest. *Times Literary Supplement*, 22 February.

PAFG
1990a   *Acción forestal* (Boletin del Plan de Acción Forestal para Guatemala), Año 1, No. 2.

1990b   *Documentos distribuidos para la segunda mesa redonda*. ms.

Pakenham, Thomas
1991   *The Scramble for Africa*. Weidenfeld & Nicholson, London.

Painter, James
1989   *Guatemala: false hope, false freedom*. Latin America Bureau, London. 2nd edition.

Panini, Carmela
1990   *Reforma agraria: dentro e fora da lei. 500 años de historia inacabada*. Edicoes Paulinas, São Paulo.

Pantoja, Alvaro
1992   Paper presented to the Conferencia Internacional sobre Impactos de Variações Climaticas e Desenvolvimento Sustentavelem Regiones Semi-Aridas, Fortaleza, 27-31 January.

Pearce, David, Anil Markandya and Edward Barbier
1989   *Blueprint for a Green Economy*. Earthscan, London.

Pearce, Jenny
1989   *Promised Land: peasant rebellion in Chalatenango, El Salvador*. Latin America Bureau, London.

Peluso, Nancy Lee
1990   A History of State Forest Management in Java. In: Mark Poffenberger (ed.) *Keepers of the Forest: land management alternatives in Southeast Asia*. Kumarian Press, West Hartwood: 27-55.

PER
1990   *The Muang Faai Irrigation System of Northern Thailand*. Project for Ecological Recovery, Bangkok.

1991   *People and the Future of Thailand's Forests: an evaluation of the state of Thailand's forests two years after the logging ban*, edited by Pinkaew Luangaramsri, PER, Bangkok.

1992   *Northeastern Villagers Win First Round in Fight Against Khor Jor Kor*. Press release, 5 July.

Pereira, Winin and Jeremy Seabrook
1990   *Asking the Earth: farms, forestry and survival in India*. Earthscan, London.

Persoon, Gerard
1985   From Affluence to Poverty: the "development" of tribal and isolated peoples. In: Leen Boer, Dieke Bujis and Benno Gljart (eds.) *Poverty and Interventions: cases from developing countries*. Leiden Development Studies No. 6, Institute of Cultural and Social Studies, University of Leiden: 89-110.

Peterson, Richard
1989   Spontaneous Immigration and Colonization in the Ituri Forest. New York Zoological Society, New York.

Philippines
1989   *Master Plan for Forestry Development: towards sustainable development in the Philippines*. 3 volumes. Manila, 12 August 1989.

Place, Frank and Peter Hazell
1992   *Productivity Effects of Indigenous Land Tenure Systems in Sub-Saharan Africa*. World Bank, Washington, DC.

Plant, Roger
1978   *Unnatural Disaster*. Latin America Bureau, London.

Ploenpoch Varapien
1992   Land Resettlement Compromise Reached. *Bangkok Post*, 5 July.

Poffenberger, Mark (ed.)
1990   *Keepers of the Forest: land management alternatives in Southeast Asia*. Kumarian Press, West Hartwood.

Pompermeyer, M.
1979   *The State and Frontier in the Amazon*. Ph.D. thesis, Stanford University.

Ponciano Gomez, Ismael
1989   *Comentarios al proyecto de ley forestal*. 17 May 1989. Ms.

Population Institute
n.d.   *No Matter What Your Cause, It's a Lost Cause if We Don't Come to Grips with Overpopulation*. Pamphlet.

Pornjai Termwarii
1991 Wikritkaan thii din kasetakam nai yuk thii din mii raakhaa. In: Vitoon Panyakul (ed.) *Weethii Chaaw Baan 34*. Non-Governmental Organization Coordinating Committee on Rural Development, Bangkok: 365-492.

Porter, Gareth and Delfin J. Ganapin Jnr.
1988 *Resources, Population and the Philippines' Future*. World Resources Institute, Washington, DC.

Powelson, John P. and Richard Stock
1990 *The Peasant Betrayed*. Cato Institute, Washington, DC.

Putzel, James
1992a Agrarian Reform, the State and Environmental Crisis in the Philippines. In: *Agrarian Reform and the Environment in the Philippines and Southeast Asia*. Catholic Institute for International Relations, London.

1992b *A Captive Land: the politics of agrarian reform in the Philippines*. Catholic Institute for International Relations and Monthly Review Press, London and New York.

Putzel, James and Cunnington, John
1989 *Gaining Ground: agrarian reform in the Philippines*. War on Want Campaigns, London.

Regpala, Maria Elena
1990 Resistance in the Cordillera: a Philippines tribal people's historical response to invasion and change imposed from outside. In: Lim Teck Ghee and Alberto G. Gomes (eds.) *Tribal Peoples and Development in Southeast Asia*. University of Malaya, Selangor: 112-140.

Renner, Daniela
1990 *People in Between*. International Work Group for Indigenous Affairs, Copenhagen.

Repetto, Robert
1988 *The Forest for the Trees? Government Policies and the Misuse of Forest Resources*. World Resources Institute, Washington, DC.

Repetto, Robert and M. Gillis
1988 *Public Policies and the Misuse of Forest Resources*. Cambridge University Press.

Rich, Bruce
1985   Multilateral Development Banks: their role in destroying the global environment. *The Ecologist* 15(1/2): 56-68.

Rietbergen, Simon
1989   Africa. In: Duncan Poore (ed.) *No Timber Without Trees: sustainability in the tropical forests.* Earthscan, London: 40-73.

RIC
1990a   *The World Bank Tropical Forestry Action Plan for Papua New Guinea: a critique.* Rainforest Information Centre, Lismore, Australia.

1990b   *Pacific Eco-Forestry Project, Papua New Guinea and Solomon Islands. Year One.* Report for AIDAB, Rainforest Information Centre, Lismore, Australia.

Rice, Delbert and Nonoy Bugtong
1989   Democratization of Resources: the Kalahan experience. In: Chip Fay (ed.) *Our Threatened Heritage.* Solidarity Foundation, Manila: 107-113.

Richards, John H. and Richard P. Tucker (eds.)
1988   *World Deforestation in the Twentieth Century.* Duke University Press, Durham.

Rocamora, Joel
1979   The Political Uses of PANAMIN. *Southeast Asia Chronicle* 67 (October): 11-21.

Rosada-Granados, Hector
1988   La realidad agraria y sus clamores. *Revista Universidad de San Carlos de Guatemala* 4: 35-43.

Royal Forest Department (RFD)
1987   *Forestry Statistics of Thailand.* RFD, Bangkok

Sandoval Villeda, Leopoldo
1988   Reforma agraria en Guatemala: condiciones y posibilidades. *Revista de la Universidad de San Carlos de Guatemala* 4: 50-77.

Sanitsuda Ekachai
1992   Man and the Forest. *Bangkok Post*, 24 January.

Santos, R.
1984   Law and Social Change. In: Marianne Schmink and Charles
        Wood (eds.) *Frontier Expansion in Amazonia.* University of
        Florida Press.

Saphaa Phuu Thaen Rassadorn
1990   Khrongkaan sammanaa rueng nayobaay thii din kap kaan
        phattanaa chonabot khrangthii nueng rueng thaang lueak nay
        kaan kae khay panhaa thii tham kin nai kheet paa. Bangkok, 12-
        13 December 1991.

Sargent, Caroline and Peter Burgess
1988   *The Wokabaut Somil: some issues in small-scale sawmilling in
        Papua New Guinea.* International Institute for Environment and
        Development, London. Ms.

Schmink, Marianne and Charles H. Wood
1984   *Frontier Expansion in Amazonia.* University of Florida Press.

Scholz, Ulrich
1988a   Types of Spontaneous Pioneer Settlement in Thailand. In:
        Walther Manshard and William B. Morgan (eds.) *Agricultural
        Expansion and Pioneer Settlements in the Humid Tropics.*
        United Nations University, Tokyo: 44-61.
1988b   Resource Use of Frontiers and Pioneer Settlement in Southern
        Sumatra. In: Walther Manshard and William B. Morgan (eds.)
        *Agricultural Expansion and Pioneer Settlements in the Humid
        Tropics.* United Nations University, Tokyo: 141-159.

Scofield, Rupert W.
1990   Land Reform in Central America. In: Roy L. Prosterman, Mary
        N. Temple and Timothy M. Hanstad (eds.) *Agrarian Reform and
        Grassroots Development: ten case studies.* Lynne Riener Pub-
        lishers, Boulder and London: 139-177.

Serrao, E.A. and J. M. Toledo
1988   Sustaining Pasture-based Production Systems in the Humid
        Tropics. Paper presented at the MAB Conference on Conver-
        sion of Tropical Forests to Pasture in Latin America, Oaxaca,
        Mexico, October 4-7.

Shalardchai Ramitanondh
1989   Forests and Deforestation. In: Siam Society (ed.) *Culture and
        Environment in Thailand.* Siam Society, Bangkok.

Shiva, Vandana
  1987   *Forestry Crisis and Forestry Myths.* World Rainforest Move-
         ment, Penang.
  1989   *The Violence of the Green Revolution: ecological degradation
         and political violence in the Punjab.* Third World Network,
         Penang.

Singh, K.S. (ed.)
  1982   *Tribal Movements in India.* 2 vols, Manohar, Delhi.

SKEPHI
  1990   *Selling Our Common Heritage: the commercialization of Indo-
         nesia's forests.* SKEPHI, the Indonesian Network on Forest
         Conservation, Jakarta.
  1991a Moving Problems: transmigration in Irian Jaya. SKEPHI, Ja-
         karta.
  1991b Siberut: Where will the Tuddukat play again? Joint report with
         SOS Siberut (England) of field investigation. July 1990 to
         September 1991.
  1991c *Kedung Ombo Dam Disaster: myth and marginal reality.*
         SKEPHI, Jakarta.

Smith, Martin
  1991   *Burma: insurgency and the politics of ethnicity.* Zed Books,
         London.

Spears, John and Edward S. Ayensu
  1985   Resources, Development, and the New Century: forestry. In:
         Robert Repetto (ed.) *The Global Possible: resources, develop-
         ment, and the new century.* World Resources Institute, Wash-
         ington, DC.

Special PIR Team
  1976   Report on Repelita II Plans for the Indonesia Government.
         Jakarta.

Stearman, Allyn Maclean
  1983   Forest to Pasture: frontier settlement in the Bolivian lowlands.
         In: Emilio Moran (ed.) *The Dilemma of Amazonian Develop-
         ment.* Westview Press, Boulder: 51-64.

Stewart, Stephen O., Pietro Diaz and Hugo Castaneda
  1988   *Evaluation of the CARE-administered Cardamom Cultivation
         and Commercialization Project, Playo Grande, Ixcan, 1984-
         1987.* USAID. Ms.

Survival International
  1984   *Genocide in Bangladesh*. Survival International, London.

  1987   Les Pygmées. *Ethnies* 6-7: 20-32.

  1987   *Akha Villages Torched*. Survival International, London.

  1991   *Ethiopia: more light on resettlement*. Survival International, London.

SWDC
  1990a   *Micro Watershed Sangha: a model for people's participation*. State Watershed Development Cell, Bangalore, India.

  1990b   *Common Property Resource Management in District Watershed Areas*. State Watershed Development Cell, Bangalore.

  1990c   *Watershed Management as a Tool for Increasing Production and Employment in Rural Karnataka*. State Watershed Development Cell, Bangalore.

TABAK
  1990   *Struggle Against Development Aggression: tribal Filipinos and ancestral domain*. TABAK, Manila.

Tapol
  1988   *West Papua: the obliteration of a people*. 3rd edition. Tapol, London.

Tapp, Nicholas
  1986   *The Hmong of Thailand: opium people of the Golden Triangle*. Anti-Slavery Society, London.

Tenaza, Richard
  1990   Can Siberut be Saved? *Cultural Survival Quarterly* 14(1): 74-76.

TFAP
  1990   *Plan d'Action Forestier Tropical: Republic du Zaire* (Vol. 2).

Thai Development Research Institute
  1987   *Thailand Natural Resources Profile*. TDRI, Bangkok.

Thai Development Support Committee (TDSC)
  1992   Information Sheet No. 5, August 1992, Bangkok.

Thiesenhusen, William C. (ed.)
  1989   *Searching for Agrarian Reform in Latin America*. Unwin Hyman, Boston.

Throup, David W.
  1988   *Economic and Social Origins of Mau Mau: 1945-53.* Heinemann Kenya, Nairobi.

Timberlake, Lloyd
  1985   *Africa in Crisis.* Earthscan, London.
  1988   *Africa in Crisis.* 2nd edition, Earthscan, London.

Tomasevski, Katarina
  1989   *Development Aid and Human Rights.* Pinter Publishers, London.

Tomasson Januzzi, F. and James T. Peach
  1990   Bangladesh: a strategy for land reform. In: Roy L. Prosterman, Mary N. Temple and Timothy M. Hanstad (eds.) *Agrarian Reform and Grassroots Development: ten case studies.* Lynne Riener Publishers, Boulder and London: 77-101.

Treace, Howard Van
  1987   *The Politics of Land in Vanuatu: from colony to independence.* Institute of Pacific Studies, University of South Pacific, Suva.

Tucker, Richard P.
  1988   The British Empire and India's Forest Resources: the timberlands of Assam and Kumaon, 1914-1950. In: John H. Richards and Richard P. Tucker (eds.) *World Deforestation in the Twentieth Century.* Duke University Press, Durham.

Turton, Andrew
  1987   *Production, Power and Participation in Rural Thailand: experiences of poor farmers' groups.* UNRISD, Geneva.

Uhl, C. and G. Parker
  1986   Is a Quarter-pound of Hamburger Worth Half a Ton of Rainforest? *Interciencia* 11(5).

Uhlig, Harald
  1984   *Spontaneous and Planned Settlement in Southeast Asia.* Institute of Asian Affairs, Hamburg.
  1988   Spontaneous and Planned Settlement in South-East Asia. In: Walther Manshard and William B. Morgan (eds.) *Agricultural Expansion and Pioneer Settlements in the Humid Tropics.* United Nations University, Tokyo: 7-43.

UNDP
1990 *Human Development Report*. UNDP, Geneva.

1992 *Human Development Report*. UNDP, Geneva.

UNEP
1989 *United Nations Environment Programme Statement on Sustainable Development*. Governing Council, Fifteenth Session, 23 May 1989.

UNICEF
1992 *The State of the World's Children*. UNICEF, Geneva.

UNRISD
1990 *La modernización forzada del trópico: el caso de Tabasco*. El Colegio de Mexico, Mexico.

USAID
1982 *Land and Work in Guatemala: an evaluation*. USAID, Washington.

Valladares, Alfonso Batres
1979 Estructura agraria — conceptos. *Serie Separatos Anuario*, Vol.14. Universidad de San Carlos de Guatemala.

Vansina, Jan
1990 *Paths in the Rainforest: towards a history of political tradition in Equatorial Africa*. James Currey, London.

Von Geusau, Leo Alting
1986 Dialectics of Akhazang: the interiorization of a perennial minority group. In: John McKinnon and Wanat Bhruksasri (eds.) *Highlanders of Thailand*. Oxford University Press, Singapore.

Walinsky, Louis J. (ed.)
1977 *Agrarian Reform as Unfinished Business: the selected papers of Wolf Ladejinsky*. Oxford University Press, New York.

Wanjala, Smokin
1990 *Land Law and Disputes in Kenya*. Oxford University Press, Nairobi.

Wanjiku Mwagiru, E.
1991 Social Dynamics of Deforestation in Kenya: a brief overview. Paper presented to the Workshop on the Social Dynamics of Deforestation in Developing Countries, Nanyuki, Kenya, 15-18 July 1991, UNRISD.

373

Warford, Jeremy
  1987   *Environment, Growth and Development.* World Bank Development Committee Reports No. 14.

Warry, Wayne
  1987   Chuave Politics: changing patterns of leadership in the Papua New Guinea highlands. *Political and Social Change Monograph 4*, Australian National University, Canberra.

WCED
  1987   *Our Common Future.* Oxford University Press, Oxford.

Westoby, Jack
  1987   *The Purpose of Forests.* Basil Blackwell, Oxford.
  1989   *Introduction to World Forestry.* Basil Blackwell, Oxford.

Whittemore, Claire
  1981   *Land for People: land tenure and the very poor.* Oxfam, Oxford.

Wichterich, Christa
  1988   From the Struggle against "Overpopulation" to the Industrialization of Human Production. *Issues in Reproductive and Genetic Engineering* 1(1): 21-30.

Witoon Permpongsacharoen
  1990   *Tropical Forest Movements: some lessons from Thailand.* Project for Ecological Recovery. Ms.

WOLA
  1986   *Uncertain Return: refugees and reconciliation in Guatemala.* Washington Office on Latin America, Washington, DC.

Woodburn, James
  1988   African Hunter-Gatherer Social Organization: is it best understood as a product of encapsulation? In: Tim Ingold, David Riches and James Woodburn (eds.) *Hunters and Gatherers.* 2 vols. Berg, Oxford: 31-64.

Woodwell G., T.A. Stone and R. Houghton
  1988   *Deforestation in Para, Brazilian Amazon Basin. Report to ORNL.* Woods Hole Research Centre.

World Bank
  1975   *Land Reform Policy Paper.* Washington, DC.
  1978   *Forestry Sector Policy Paper.* Washington, DC.

1982a *Involuntary Resettlement in Bank-financed Projects.* Operational Manual Statement 2.33. Washington, DC.

1982b *Tribal Peoples in Bank-financed Projects.* Operational Manual Statement 2.34. Washington, DC.

1982c *Tribal Peoples and Economic Development: human ecologic considerations.* Washington, DC.

1987 *Agricultural Mechanization: issues and options.* Washington, DC.

1988 *Rural Development: World Bank experience 1965-1986.* Washington, DC.

1989a *Nepal Hill Community Forestry Project.* Staff Appraisal Report No. 7631b-NEP, Washington, DC.

1989b *Guatemala: public sector expenditure review.* Report No 7478-GU.

1989c *Philippines Forestry, Fisheries and Agricultural Resource Management Study.* Report No. 7388-PH, 17 January. World Bank, Washington, DC.

1990a *Indigenous Peoples in Bank-financed Projects.* Operational Directive 4.40. Washington, DC.

1990b *The World Bank and the Environment.* First Annual Report. Washington, DC.

1990c *Poverty: world development report 1990.* Oxford University Press, Oxford.

1991a *The World Bank and the Environment: a progress report.* Washington, DC.

1991b *The Forest Sector.* Agriculture and Rural Development Department. Washington, DC.

1991c *Annual Sector Review: agriculture and rural development FY91.* Washington, DC.

1991d *Poverty Reduction.* Operational Directive 4.15. Washington, DC.

1991e *The Forest Sector: a World Bank policy paper.* Washington, DC.

1992a *Agricultural Strategy Paper.* Washington, DC. Draft 1 May 1992.

1992b *World Development Report. Environment and Development.* Washington, DC.

World Wide Fund for Nature
1991 *Deforestation: banning logging imports.* WWF, Gland, Switzerland.

REFERENCES

Worsley, Peter
  1957   *The Trumpet Shall Sound: a study of "cargo cults" in Melanesia.* MacGibbon and Kee, London.

WRI
  1990   *World Resources 1990-1991.* Oxford University Press, Oxford.
  1991   *World Resources 1991-1992.* Oxford University Press, Oxford.
  1992   *World Resources 1992-1993.* Oxford University Press, Oxford.

WRM/SAM
  1990   *The Battle for Sarawak's Forests.* World Rainforest Movement/ Sahabat Alam Malaysia, Penang.

ABOUT THE AUTHORS

Marcus Colchester is an anthropologist who spent several years researching land use among the northern Yanomami Indians of Amazonia. In the 1980s he worked as Projects Director for Survival International focusing on the land struggles of indigenous peoples in South and Southeast Asia. He has authored and co-authored a number of books and published extensively in academic, environmental and popular journals. He is presently Director of the Forest Peoples Programme of the World Rainforest Movement.

Susanna Hecht is a social scientist who has pioneered a political ecology approach to deforestation in Amazonia. Her studies have focused on the environmental effects of cattle ranching, the agronomy of native peoples and the politics of land. She is presently Associate Professor at the Graduate School of Planning at the University of California, Los Angeles, and is author of a large number of academic papers. She is co-author with Alexander Cockburn of the bestselling book *The Fate of the Forest: Developers, Destroyers and Defenders of the Amazon* (Verso, 1989).

Rachel Kiddell-Monroe is a lawyer who has worked with the Asia Wetlands Bureau, the Indonesian Environmental NGO Network, WALHI, and the Indonesia Forest Conservation Network, SKEPHI. In 1990 she established SOS Siberut, an international campaign to protect the people and environment of the island of Siberut in western Indonesia. She is presently researching the social and environmental impact of softwood plantations and timber estates in the tropics and works for Tapol, the Indonesia human rights campaign.

Marvic Leonen is a professor and attorney working for the Legal Rights and Natural Resources Centre, Friends of the Earth (Philippines), in Manila. His research and advocacy has focused on the human rights and the ancestral domain rights of the indigenous peoples of the Philippines. The Centre carries out legal assistance programmes among indigenous communities all over the Philippines and includes field offices in Mindanao and the Cordillera.

Larry Lohmann is an Associate Editor of *The Ecologist* magazine. He spent much of the 1980s working with voluntary organizations in Thailand on environmental and social issues. He has published in academic and environmental journals.

George Monbiot is a journalist and investigative travel writer focusing on the politics of land in the tropics. His first book *Poisoned Arrows* (1989) won international acclaim and was followed by *Amazon Watershed: The New Environmental Investigation* (1991), which won the 1992 Sir Peter Kent Prize for Conservation Writing. His recent TV documentary "Your Furniture, Their Lives" illustrates the connections between the timber trade, forest destruction and the annihilation of Brazilian Indians.

Roger Plant is an independent specialist in plantation labour, land tenure and human rights. He has worked as a consultant for a number of international, human rights and labour organizations, including the Anti-Slavery Society, Oxfam (UK), Amnesty International, the International Commission of Jurists, the Overseas Development Institute, the Ford Foundation, the UN Human Rights Centre and the International Labour Office. His books include *Guatemala: Unnatural Disaster* (1978) and *Sugar and Modern Slavery* (1987). He is presently completing a global survey entitled *Land Rights in Rural Development Policy*.

John Witte is a pseudonym.

Index